LITERARY CRITICISM AND CULTURAL THEORY

OUTSTANDING DISSERTATIONS

Edited by

William E. Cain
Professor of English
Wellesley College

A ROUTLEDGE SERIES

LITERARY CRITICISM AND CULTURAL THEORY
WILLIAM E. CAIN, *General Editor*

THE SELF IN THE CELL
Narrating the Victorian Prisoner

Sean Grass

Routledge
New York & London

Published in 2003 by
Routledge
29 West 35th Street
New York, NY 10001
www.routledge-ny.com

Published in Great Britain by
Routledge
11 New Fetter Lane
London EC4P 4EE
www.routledge.co.uk

Routledge is an imprint of the Taylor & Francis Group
Printed in the United States of America on acid-free paper

Portions of chapter 2 appear as "Narrating the Cell: Dickens on the American
Prisons," in *JEGP: Journal of English and Germanic Philology* 99.1 (2000): 50–70, and
as "Pickwick, the Past, and the Prison," in *Dickens Studies Annual* 29 (2000): 17–39.
Reprinted by permission.

10 9 8 7 6 5 4 3 2 1

Library of Congress Cataloging-in-Publication Data
Grass, Sean.
    The self in the cell : narrating the Victorian prisoner / by Sean Grass.
      p. cm. — (Literary criticism and cultural theory)
    Includes bibliographical references and index.
    ISBN 0-415-94355-8
    1. English fiction—19th century—History and criticism. 2. Prisons—Great
Britain—History—19th century. 3. Prisoners in literature. 4. Prisons in litera-
ture. 5. Narration (Rhetoric) 6. Self in literature. I. Title. II. Series.
PR878.P7 G73 2003
823'.809355—dc21
                                                2002153815

For Alfred DePolis

Contents

Acknowledgments

A FIRST BOOK, I HAVE LEARNED, IS AN ADVENTURE, AND NO ADVENTURE ENDS happily unless one has excellent companions from the beginning and receives unexpected help along the way. I cannot express warmly enough my gratitude to the dozens of people who journeyed with me and became my benefactors during the four years it took to complete this project, a period that began when I was a graduate student at the Pennsylvania State University. Chief among those who deserve thanks is Christopher Clausen, whose tireless reading and advice during the last several years have made this work—indeed, all of my work—more thoughtful, sophisticated, and precise. This project and the Department of English at Penn State are infinitely richer for his guidance. I also want to thank Philip Jenkins, Michael Anesko, Robert Lougy, Katherine Hume, and Elizabeth Jenkins at Penn State; Marjean Purinton and Donald Rude at my new department at Texas Tech University; and Greg Colón-Semenza at the University of Connecticut. All of these excellent people gave advice where it was most wanted and support when it was most needed, and Greg in particular has been an irreplaceable friend and academic co-conspirator. My thanks to all of them for making such shrewd, lively, and delightful companions. When they read the pages that follow, I trust they will conclude that their energy and affection were not lavished upon me in vain.

Thanks are also due to the College of Liberal Arts at Penn State, for fellowship support that allowed me to complete much of the research for this project in just twelve months of study; to the English departments at Penn State and Texas Tech University, for grants that allowed me to travel and present parts of this work to colleagues and peers; and to the

ix

astonishing and indefatigable librarians at Penn State's Pattee Library, the Georgetown University Law Library, and the Texas Tech University Library, all of whom proved incredibly adept at securing materials—often obscure and rare—that allowed me to complete my researches into the history of Victorian imprisonment. I also appreciate the generosity of AMS Press and the University of Illinois Press, who granted me permission to publish the work on Charles Dickens's *Pickwick Papers* and *American Notes* that appears in Chapter Two. Those arguments first appeared—in rawer form, to be sure—in 2000 as essays in *Dickens Studies Annual* and the *Journal of English and Germanic Philology*. Finally, my thanks go to Damian Treffs, Paul Johnson, John Shea, and the other editors at Routledge who reviewed the manuscript, marshaled it through its editorial stages, and steered this novice author gently but unfailingly through the complexities of publishing a book.

Before ending these expressions of gratitude, I want also to thank those people whose interest in my work is always personal rather than professional, and who take joy in my joy rather than in my success. My infinite thanks are due to my parents, Robert and Deborah, my brother Eric, and all of the grandmothers, aunts, uncles, cousins, and friends who offer so much personal support at all times and in all seasons. I also thank my lover, companion, and best friend, Iris Rivero, whom I met even as I was conceiving of this project in 1997. As important as this book has been to me since, she has come to mean much, much more. The project could not have become what it is without her loving presence. I share this success with her and look forward to other successes—personal and professional—we will share through the years. We shared one triumph even as I finished this manuscript during the summer of 2002.

Reader, I married her.

List of Abbreviations

A	*Armadale*, Wilkie Collins
AN	*American Notes and Pictures from Italy*, Charles Dickens
AT	*The Autobiography of a Thief, and Other Stories*, Charles Reade
HNL	*His Natural Life*, Marcus Clarke
LD	*Little Dorrit*, Charles Dickens
Letters	*The Letters of Charles Dickens*, eds. Madeline House, Graham Storey, and Kathleen Tillotson
Life	*The Life of Charlotte Brontë*, Elizabeth Gaskell
ED	*The Mystery of Edwin Drood*, Charles Dickens
NTL	*It Is Never Too Late to Mend*, Charles Reade
PP	*Pickwick Papers*, Charles Dickens
Times	The *Times* of London
Truth	*"Truth is Stranger Than Fiction": True Account of the Proceedings Leading to, and a Full and Authentic Report of, the Searching Inquiry, by Her Majesty's Commissioners, into the Horrible System of Discipline Practised at the Borough Gaol of Birmingham*, ed. Joseph Allday
TTC	*A Tale of Two Cities*, Charles Dickens
V	*Villette*, Charlotte Brontë

THE SELF IN THE CELL

Introduction

Solitude, Surveillance, and the Art of the Novel

Side by side with the major technology of the telescope, the lens and the light beam . . . there were the minor techniques of multiple and intersecting observations, of eyes that must see without being seen; using techniques of subjection and methods of exploitation, an obscure art of light and the visible was secretly preparing a new knowledge of man.

—Michel Foucault, *Discipline and Punish*

Because the Panopticon was a vision of Big Brotherism, which mercifully came to nothing, Bentham is apt to be remembered as a sort of malevolent clown of penal history.

—Giles Playfair, *The Punitive Obsession*

I N LATE DECEMBER 1786, JEREMY BENTHAM AUTHORED A NOVEL PROPOSAL FOR the discipline, punishment, and reformation of England's growing number of criminal offenders: a surveillant penitentiary and workhouse, contrived ingeniously so that a single observer positioned at a central vantage could watch every inmate there confined. The plans called for an enormous, enclosed circular penitentiary with a guard tower at its center and individual cells arranged along the height and circumference of the interior wall. In each cell, a window through the outside wall would admit light, while the inner wall would be entirely "formed by an iron grating, so light as not to screen away any part of the cell."[1] The guard tower, on the other hand, would always remain dark so that, although the line of sight between guard and cells would be unimpeded, no individual prisoner could ever tell when he was being observed.

Unable to place each prisoner under perfect surveillance, Bentham reasoned, "the next thing to be wished for is, that, at every instant, seeing reason to believe as much, and not being able to satisfy himself to the contrary, he should conceive himself to be so."[2] Bentham conducted experiments in acoustics and optics, and he designed productive labor for prisoners to perform so that they would learn trades, grow used to earning their bread, and make the prison self-sufficient, or perhaps profitable. He also planned to open his prison to the public, so that public scrutiny would prevent abuse. Ideologically and economically Bentham's prison was a fabulous innovation, "a simple idea of architecture" intended to produce model convicts and make them productive.[3] He called his simple idea "Panopticon."

In England the time seemed right for prison reform. A decade earlier, in 1776, England had suddenly lost her primary outlet for social malefactors when the upstart American colonials unexpectedly declared independence and halted the flow of convicts to the New World. Confident the rebellion would soon be put down, English authorities employed temporary stopgaps to cope with the growing convict population. Some were pressed into military service and sent to America as soldiers rather than transportees; others were thrust into old ships called "prison hulks" until space could be cleared in Newgate or transportation could resume. But the surprising result of the war eliminated this first expedient and, worse, cast hundreds of these same soldiers adrift in an English society already suffering economically from a failed war and diminished empire. Newgate was full, and the prison hulks and local jails quickly filled and overflowed. Saddled with a "Bloody Code" that designated some 200 crimes as capital offenses, the Crown began to rely more heavily upon the gallows. Executions from 1783 to 1787 were carried out at a rate 82 percent higher than in the previous five years, with 97 in 1785 alone.[4] This ferocious display of state power soon exhausted the public's tolerance for brutality, so much so that juries became loath to convict any but the most serious offenders and the public gallows at Tyburn had to be removed to the safer confines of Newgate. Government officials were growing convinced that England required new methods of dealing with criminals, of doing so at home, and of doing so in a way that would prepare convicts to return to the very society they had offended.

Bentham's Panopticon would have served these aims, which explains perhaps why Michel Foucault regards the proposal for the Panopticon as the first movement toward the modern penitentiary. Had Bentham struck while the iron was hot, England may well have built his prison and ushered in a new era in convict administration. But twenty-five years later England still had no Panopticon, and Bentham had been summarily dismissed from England's discussions about discipline and punishment. Though his proposal for the Panopticon was ready in 1786, more than four years passed before he presented it to Sir William Pitt.[5] By that time, the Pitt cabinet had happily "rediscovered" Australia and concluded that convicts could be stored much less troublesomely at the antipodes than at home. During the next eighty years, England transported 160,000 convicts to Australia, continuing across the globe the very system of colonization and criminal punishment they had been obliged to abandon in America. Still, Bentham persisted, and in 1794 he finally won a contract to build his Panopticon. Parliament advanced him £2000 to conduct experiments in acoustics and optics and spent £12,000 more to purchase a marshy plot of land near Vauxhall Bridge.[6] But the experiments failed so miserably that they devoured not only the advance but much of Bentham's private fortune besides.[7] In 1800, citing the "number of years which [had] elapsed since the first steps were taken," the secretary of state called for the project to be abandoned.[8] When England did finally open its first reformative prison, Millbank Penitentiary, in 1816 on the site meant for the Panopticon, the new jail bore only passing architectural and disciplinary resemblances to its more famous precursor. Its six pentagonal buildings had hallways radiating outward from a central guard tower, like a wagon wheel, and inmates were locked in separate cells closed off from the tower's view.[9] Even two decades later, when Parliament created England's first national Prison Inspectorate, the inspectors endorsed a program of separate confinement rather than surveillance. The "Model Prison" at Pentonville, which opened in 1843 as England's first full-scale experiment in reformative imprisonment, used solitude to inspire prisoners to self-reflection, moral regeneration, and self-narration undertaken from the cell.

What ought to interest literature scholars in all this is the extent to which even this cursory account of English imprisonment places Bentham, Panopticism, and Foucault upon tenuous ground. Those who study the nineteenth-century novel, especially, have used Foucault's work to help explain the recurrence of policing, detection, public scrutiny, and even omniscient narration in the works of authors from Dickens to Henry James, since these themes indicate a particular Victorian anxiety about individual privacy and the invasive social pressures that shape—and misshape—private identity and secret desire. As D. A. Miller charged in *The Novel and the Police* (1988), "no openly fictional form has ever sought to 'make a difference' in the world more than the Victorian novel," and no author more than Dickens developed in the English novel such a "massive thematization of [the] social discipline" that the Panopticon implies.[10] This argument is persuasive because it is correct, at least in the sense that Victorian novels by Dickens and others bristle with social critiques that pit individual protagonists against social forces that threaten to buffet them into physical and psychological submission. We need only look at Jane Eyre, or Pip, or Maggie Tulliver, or innumerable other Victorian characters besides to know it. He is also correct, along with critics like Mark Seltzer and Audrey Jaffe, when he suggests that the Victorian novel tried to "make a difference" mostly by embracing a realism so exhaustive that even omniscient narration occasionally buckles under its weight.[11] Omniscient narration in Victorian fiction is thus Foucaultian not only because it watches and sees, but also because it becomes a vehicle for including and even producing knowledge about those things most alien to respectable middle-class readers: poverty, madness, criminality, prostitution, and imprisonment. By serving this function, Foucaultian critics suggest, the novel replicates the Panopticon's determination to watch over, account for, and discipline social aberration.

This really is the crucial point, not only for Foucault but also for the critics who draw from him in assessing the Victorian novel. The Panopticon's inmate is watched, or believes that he is, and he adjusts his behavior as a result. The lesson, Foucault tells us, is that individuals are never more than the sum of the disciplinary forces brought to bear upon them—that they have no genuine selfhood or identity that is free from the power of society's many prisons. Miller suggests that Victorian novels offer this same lesson when omniscient narrators exert their surveillant powers upon individual fictional subjects, so that we are permitted to "enjoy our privacy in the act of watching privacy being violated."[12] These are persuasive arguments about Victorian society and fiction, especially since so many Victorian novelists seem, at least, to reach Foucault's pessimistic conclusions about the possibility of unfettered selfhood. Indeed, if we wished to extend this principle to its most general form, we might be hard-pressed to find a Victorian novel in which detection and social oppression exert no pressures upon the individual self. Because literature always emerges from within social contexts governed by these kinds of power relations, and because the author always exercises a certain discursive power over the materials he represents, it may really be true that the Foucaultian model is as universally applicable as it is apparently inescapable. As Seltzer wrote of Henry James, perhaps the most deliberately apolitical nineteenth-century novelist, "James's art of representation always also involves a politics of representation," at least insofar as his ideological stance always inheres in the form and content of his texts.[13] Every novel, in other words, is almost equally subject to suspicions that its ideological agenda parallels the Panopticon's.

But where in these discussions is the Victorian prison? No prisoner ever spent a day in the Panopticon, nor probably in a prison much like it. Instead, someone convicted of a crime in nineteenth-century England

could expect to be transported to Australia to work under nearly unendurable privations; held for weeks or months in an overcrowded and
filthy local jail while awaiting quarterly assizes; committed for debt and
thrust into the Marshalsea or the Fleet, where a greedy jailer demanded
exorbitant fees for a squalid cell and cursory amenities; or driven, as happened all too often, utterly mad by solitary confinement, the very tool
that Victorian authorities hoped would produce moral reform. Between
1750 and 1850, English authorities employed everything from hangings
to hulks in order to deal with criminal offenders, acting more frequently
according to expediency than ideology. Victorian novel after Victorian
novel shows us these various prisoners, from Dickens's Fagin, Amy
Dorrit, and Alexandre Manette to Charles Reade's Thomas Robinson,
Marcus Clarke's Richard Devine, and Samuel Butler's Ernest Pontifex.
Only rarely do Foucaultian critics turn to these representations of literal
Victorian prisoners, likely because the prisons in which these prisoners
are confined have, rather inconveniently, very little to do with
Panopticism. Under the circumstances, it is worth wondering whether
recent scholarship focused upon surveillance has forged provocative
links between the novel and the prison or only between the novel and
Foucault.

Certain critiques of literature and the prison have departed from this
orthodoxy in useful ways. Jeremy Tambling, for instance, offers a largely
Foucaultian reading in *Dickens, Violence and the Modern State* (1995), but
he does include several novels, *Little Dorrit* (1857) and *A Tale of Two Cities*
(1859) among them, in which prisons play a large role.[14] Forty years ago,
in *Dickens and Crime* (1962), Philip Collins pushed the historical mode
near to its limits by contextualizing exhaustively Dickens's experiences of
and writings about a variety of English prisons, from Newgate and
Coldbath-fields to the Marshalsea. Indeed, Collins's work has been indis-
pensable to my own, though he does not examine the narrative strategies
implicit in Victorian punishment or analyze the relation between the
prison and narrative production. John Bender provides a more current
and intriguing analysis in *Imagining the Penitentiary* (1987) by arguing
that the key to the emergence of the penitentiary during the eighteenth
century was the "penitentiary idea" implicit in novels like *Robinson
Crusoe* (1719) and *Moll Flanders* (1722) and narrative sequences like *A
Harlot's Progress* (1731-32) and *A Rake's Progress* (1734-35). Together,
Bender argues, these texts "restructured the chaotic (though once cultur-
ally functional) experience inside the old prisons, [and] implied a new
kind of confinement—the penitentiary—conceived narratively on the
lines of the realistic, consciousness-centered novel."[15] This suggestion
that the novel inspired the prison may appeal to the sentimentality of
those of us who, like Auden, wish to resist the notion that "poetry makes

nothing happen."[16] But Bender either ignores or disregards the practical and ideological pressures that combined to produce the penitentiary early in the nineteenth century. The development of the reformative penitentiary depended much more heavily upon social dislocations, increasing poverty, and the work of early penologists like Cesare Beccaria and John Howard than upon the influence exerted by eighteenth-century narrative. By the Victorian period, the prison was much more a place for narrative construction than a place constructed through narrative.

Given this state of scholarly affairs, my purpose in this study is to show how the prison—by evolving during the nineteenth century as a private space explicitly designed to wield psychological and narrative power over those it confined—provided both the impetus and the model for increasingly interior fictions of the psychological self. In 1775, before England turned to reformative imprisonment as a penal option, criminal punishment was deliberately punitive and visible: executions, stocks, pillories, and even brandings served to identify and injure those who had broken the law, and to dissuade others from doing the same. Imprisonment, whether at Newgate or in local jails, likewise permitted and even encouraged commerce between inmates and the public. But by 1850, with the penitentiary firmly ensconced as England's primary sentencing option, punishment had become a much more private endeavor, expressly intended to remake convicts somewhere beyond the reach of the public stare. Most convicts endured some form of the national disciplinary program established by the Prison Inspectorate in 1835, which called for separate confinement intended to inspire self-reflection, moral regeneration, and (often) self-narratives that prison chaplains read, edited, and interpreted in order to ensure that they told the "truth" about the prisoner's guilt and the beneficent effects of the cell. This prescribed role for autobiography under separate confinement gives us a clue to the relation between narration and imprisonment, for it shows that narrative authority and subjectivity were both at stake for those confined in England's new penitentiaries. Much the same was true in Australia where convicts and free settlers mingled in the streets. In that vast carceral society, the power to give a proper account of one's self constituted a crucial part of the distinction between the guilty and innocent. Farther away than the American colonies had been, this new theater for convict transportation also made it far less likely that convicts or their self-accounts would ever return to England. As imprisonment became more private and psychological during the first half of the nineteenth century, it also raised increasingly complex questions about how to account, fully and honestly, for the Victorian prisoner.

These questions placed Victorian novelists, uncomfortably, at the intersection of opposing propositions. On the one hand, realist and

reformist authors like Dickens, Reade, and Clarke needed facts and physical details about the prison in order for their novels to "make a difference," since such objective materials would provide their accounts with
social and cultural legitimacy in the eyes of Victorian readers. On the
other, these same authors came to understand—precisely because of their
careful scrutiny of the prison—that facts about confinement, now that it
was stubbornly private, were hard to come by, and that in any case facts
were no longer adequate to narrate a prison that operated upon the mind
rather than the body of the confined. Throughout the 1830s and 1840s,
defenders of the prison offered "proofs" that prison discipline was having its desired psychological and reformative effects. At the same time,
growing numbers of critics in the press and in literary circles argued that
separate confinement, transportation, and even debtors' prisons were
inflicting disastrous physical and psychological consequences. Both sides
were in some measure correct. By mid-century the Victorian prison in
each of its forms clearly demanded fictional treatment as a place of powerful psychological—rather than just physical—moment. Victorian novelists accordingly needed to justify their inclusion of psychological narration and invention within novels they hoped would be taken as objective, irrefutable portrayals of the self in the cell.

They found grounds for that justification in the prison. Treating prisoner bodies and self-accounts as texts to be read, interpreted, and narrated by agents of the prison, separate-confinement penitentiaries had
already authorized and even institutionalized the practice of inventing—
from an external perspective—the psychological "truth" about the
imprisoned self, its motives, and its sufferings in the cell. Treating transportees as objects of discipline and suspicion, Australia authorities had
already erected a vast carceral society in which prisoners were not to be
believed, even in accounting for themselves, if a free settler could be
found to tell their stories. Both major forms of imprisonment had therefore accomplished by mid-century what Victorian novelists required: the
narrative subjugation of the Victorian prisoner. By embracing and even
mimicking the explicit and implicit narrative aims of the prison,
Victorian novelists recognized that they could engage in deliberate psychological invention without compromising the apparent legitimacy or
integrity of their realist fictions. Reading and narrating prisoner bodies
and texts, insisting thematically upon the prisoner's solitude, adopting
the form of self-narration undertaken from the cell—these modes all
became part of Victorian novelists' repertoires in accounting for the
prison. Perhaps this explains why the figure of the self in the cell that
endures in nineteenth-century figures like William Dorrit and Alexandre
Manette is not that of the Panopticon's incessantly watched prisoner. It
is, rather, that of the hopelessly isolated inmate, broken by confinement,

struggling through solitude to narrate a private and idiosyncratic experience of the cell.

This distance between the Panoptical inmate and the prisoner of Victorian fiction is crucial: partly for what it shows us about prison novels, but mostly for what it reveals generally about nineteenth-century fiction. Isolation and psychological trial recur in any number of Victorian novels, and particularly those that—like *Jane Eyre* (1847), *Villette* (1853), and *Armadale* (1866)—hinge upon the self-narration of psychological identity, motive, and desire. Even in novels like these which contain no literal prison, solitude and confinement are necessary preconditions to the self-ordering, self-exposition, and narrative self-invention that occupy the heart of the text. This reliance upon images of solitary confinement suggests that the narration of the private self that the prison enabled had broad implications for nineteenth-century fiction, and even that Victorian novelists may have culled from the prison the lesson that any private self can be invented and narrated if only it is offered as guilty—as the sort of self, that is, that polite society deems least capable of self-accounting in a reliable, complete, and coherent way. Insofar as this is true, prison novels bear more striking resemblances to Freudian case histories than to Foucault's writings about the Panopticon. By treating prisoner bodies and self-accounts as texts for interpretation, Victorian prison novels both imitate the prison's narrative logic and presage Freud's desire to account fully for maimed selves incapable of speaking the truth about their own identities and desires. More, they do so even as they insist—in opposition to Foucault—that the prisoner contains an essential subjectivity, which must be silenced and circumvented narratively by both the prison and the novel. We see in the prison novel (as in the prison) less a negation of subjectivity than an obliteration of the self's power to account for its subjectivity. In this sense, the representation of the prisoner in the Victorian novel is not a display of authorial omniscience but a display of narrative creativity, in which authors call deliberate attention to the "inventedness" of their psychological portrayals, and in which they critique the strategies—implicit in the prison—from which they derive their authorial power over the private self.

Critics preoccupied with Panopticism have done precious little to explore this relation between the prison and private narration, but Foucault was not himself insensible either to separate confinement or its ramifications. In *Discipline and Punish* (1975) he observed that "solitude assures a sort of self-regularization of the penalty and makes possible a spontaneous individualization of the punishment"—an individualization, he might have continued, that requires an equally individualized and self-centered narrative form.[17] Indeed, Foucault's writing on the penitentiary has much less to do with the particular innovation of disciplinary surveillance than with the way in which "[d]iscipline 'makes' individuals" by trying to account for the private self of the prisoner, turning human subjectivity into the object and product of the penitentiary's power.[18] Victorian prison novels participate in this same project, but less through omniscient narration than through the innumerable letters, diaries, autobiographies, and confessions of Victorian fiction's imprisoned selves. Partly, the relation between narrative and imprisonment is historical, born of the struggle between agents and inmates of the prison for narrative control over autobiography from the cell. Partly, it is imaginative and creative, the result of Victorian novelists' determination to narrate psychic aberration, to do so realistically, and to find social and institutional justifications for their intrusions upon private identity and desire. Laying aside the Panopticon, the chapters that follow take up an unfamiliar history of English imprisonment rife with implications for psychological invention and narrative production. By examining how authors from Dickens to Wilkie Collins and Charlotte Brontë use the figure of the Victorian self in the cell, they also show that nineteenth-century prison fictions anticipated Freud's psychoanalytic techniques and helped to shape the inward migration of the modern novel.

Chapter 1

Narrating the Victorian Prisoner

Providence has ordained that the change from evil to good is not to be wrought but at the price of suffering often recurring and long endured. And if the selection were left to criminals themselves, experience justifies the assertion, that, whatever might be the choice of the young offender, few punishments, indeed, would not be preferred by the veteran in crime to passing through a full course of reformatory discipline.
—Matthew Davenport Hill, *A Charge Delivered to the Grand Jury of the Borough of Birmingham*, 1848

CONVICTED IN 1723 OF DELIVERING FALSE TESTIMONY IN AN ATTEMPT TO EARN rewards, John Middleton was sentenced to stand for one hour upon the pillory at Charing Cross. Things could have been worse. He could have been whipped, or transported, or even hung. Instead, hands and head fixed to a wooden frame, he would simply stand for sixty minutes exposed to the scrutiny and derision of a London crowd. In the days leading up to Middleton's appearance on the pillory, the authorities probably advertised the event, and they likely scheduled it—as was the custom—for the middle of a market day, when passers-by would be most numerous. Though Middleton probably knew these things, he could not have been prepared for what happened that day. An exceptionally ill-tempered crowd gathered even before Middleton arrived, and the moment he appeared, he was attacked. One eyewitness reported, "The mob was so numerous and violent . . . and pelted the said Middleton so barbarously that tho' this Deponent hath seen several persons before stand upon the pillory he never saw any so much abused."[1] Both the judge and the Crown had likely counted on eliciting just this public

13

response. Few figures were more despised during the eighteenth century
than informers, and false informers—like Middleton—were the most
detestable variety.[2] Worse yet, Middleton had testified against London's
printers, ballad-singers, and pamphleteers, who were collectively expressing and fueling popular disaffection in the city. His lies constituted a sin
against public opinion, and the very sight of him at Charing Cross incit-
ed the crowd. Within minutes of mounting the pillory, battered and
choked by the rocks, mud, and other refuse heaped upon him, John
Middleton breathed his last.

Very few convicts suffered quite this horribly on the pillory during
the eighteenth century, but in many ways Middleton's case is unexcep-
tional. As J. M. Beattie writes in *Crime and the Courts in England
1660–1800*, "[t]he offenses that judges and magistrates were anxious to
punish by the pillory were acts that aroused deep public anger and hostility," like crimes against children, sexual predation and deviancy, and
various kinds of fraud.[3] Sentences to the pillory allowed judges to identify and expose these offenders and allowed the public—if it wished—to
participate directly in the administration of justice. Occasionally, the
strategy backfired, and a prisoner pilloried for breaking an unpopular law
or speaking out against an unpopular figure was treated indulgently or
even freed by the crowd. More frequently, criminals from homosexuals
to keepers of bawdy-houses were viciously abused. Less than a decade
after Middleton's death, John Waller died on the pillory at the Seven
Dials, his ribs and skull fractured when he was trampled by an angry
mob. Another man was stoned to death at Smithfield Market in 1756.[4]
Despite their savagery, incidents like these accorded perfectly with the
Crown's more comprehensive strategy for dealing with criminals during
the eighteenth century: to punish publicly and severely, so that particular offenders would be disabled and others would be terrified into obey-
ing the law. In pursuit of this aim, the authorities employed the pillory,
stocks, public whippings, and public executions to deal with England's
criminals, since all of these punishments tended to display the operation
of government power. They rarely sent convicted criminals to prison.

It may be impossible now to imagine a system of criminal punishment that does not have the penitentiary at its center—that does not
depend, that is, upon the prison's power to control offenders and perhaps even reform them in a separate space hidden from the public eye.
We rely on penitentiaries to inculcate discipline and order, or at least to
prevent disorder from seeping into the comfortable nooks of our contemporary world. We insist upon mandatory minimum prison terms for
drug offenders, and life sentences without parole for the violent criminals we most fear. But it was not always so. Early in the 1700s, England's
prisons had to do with neither punishment nor discipline, for criminals

typically stopped there only on the way to trial, sentencing, or execution. Almost all long-term inmates were debtors. As temporary depots for criminal transients but more permanent homes for the insolvent poor, prisons in 1750 were disorganized, unregulated, and uproarious—far cries from anything we would now recognize as institutions for punishing and disciplining criminality. A century later, this was no longer true. England's penitentiaries became orderly, private institutions dedicated to the moral and psychological reformation of the criminal offender. The transformation of imprisonment during these hundred years emerged from evolving notions of criminality, the aims of punishment, and how those aims could best be achieved. As England remade its system of convict management between 1750 and 1850, it created modes of punishment with enormous social and psychological consequences, to be sure. It also created punishments with momentous narrative consequences for the Victorian prisoner.

II

Literature scholars have devoted a great deal of attention to the importance of spectacle in the whippings, tortures, and executions that characterized eighteenth-century punishment but have done far less to consider how England's prisons, too, played a deliberately public role. Just a year before John Middleton died at Charing Cross, Daniel Defoe caused the title heroine of *Moll Flanders* (1722) to observe of Newgate:

> . . . 'tis impossible to describe the terror of my mind, when I was first brought in, and when I look'd round upon all the horrors of that dismal place . . . . the hellish noise, the roaring, swearing and clamour, the stench and nastiness, and all the dreadful afflicting things that I saw there, joyn'd to make the place seem an emblem of hell itself, and a kind of an entrance into it.[5]

It is undoubtedly difficult for an astute reader to imagine Moll much "terrified" by anything, let alone by such mundane occurrences as roaring, swearing, and clamour. Even so, and despite her deliberate personal evasiveness, Moll's description of Newgate captures the genuine state of most eighteenth-century jails. They were squalid, licentious, poorly built, and poorly managed. As temporary way-stations for criminals destined for other punishments, they needed to be little else. No government agents oversaw the old jails or ensured that they met particular standards, nor did money for their operation come from the Crown. Instead, jails were owned or at least operated by private entrepreneurs who hoped to turn a profit from managing their wards. The goal was to govern the most convicts at the least expense, and most old prisons were filthy, pestilent, and overcrowded as a result. More important, as Moll's testimony hints, they differed from the penitentiaries of the following century in one especially crucial respect: the degree of contact they permitted inmates to have with the world beyond their cells.

Bender observes correctly in *Imagining the Penitentiary* that "most eighteenth-century prisons were not built purposely for confinement but were domestically organized," which means that prisons—even including Newgate—were more like boarding-houses than places of punishment and detention.[6] During the day, prisoners associated with one another quite freely in airing yards and common rooms, with the result (as Moll's testimony shows) that most jails were deplorably awash in smoke, alcohol, and the oaths and blasphemies of the confined. Authorities cared little for how criminals whiled away the hours, so long as they attempted no violence or escape. For debtors, as the familiar experience of Charles Dickens shows, the comparison between prisons and boarding-houses was especially apt, since debtors could and frequently did bring their families to live with them in the squalor and misery of the cell. After all, debtors were obliged to pay rent for their cells, and they could hardly afford a second rent for family members who wished to live outside the prison. In many instances, though certain prisons were reserved for debtors, jails that held both kinds of inmates did not segregate debtors and criminals, so that civil prisoners and minor offenders were exposed to the rowdiest and most incorrigible of the lot.[7] This easy contact between offenders of all kinds made prisons perfect places for criminals to meet, form associations, and plan future crimes. Not surprisingly, most Englishmen during the 1700s assumed that prisons played a greater role in countenancing crimes than in preventing or punishing them.

This easy familiarity characterized, too, the commerce that prisoners had with those outside of the prison walls. Lawyers, magistrates, constables, judges, and the families of inmates had obvious reasons for entering prisons, but jails teemed as well with other visitors, from provenders to prostitutes. As Paul Rock observes of debtors' prisons, particularly, "[a]ny goods or services available outside the prison could be bought inside it and, as a result, the more prosperous institutions resembled market places" complete with butchers, chandlers, surgeons, and tap-houses.[8] Criminal prisons, too, were commercial enterprises, and jailers were astonishingly creative at finding ways to make prisons into profitable places. Until the practice was outlawed in 1815, fee-taking was a natural feature of most jails and required prisoners to pay for their accommodations, meals, clothing, and other essentials. The prisoner who could pay handsomely could secure the best conditions, even including more comfortable chains. For the right price, he could also procure access to more tantalizing commodities: conjugal visits with spouses, lovers, or whores. In 1757, *Gentlemen's Magazine* described Clerkenwell bridewell as a "great brothel," but Clerkenwell was no special case.[9] As late as 1814, during a Parliamentary inquiry into the administration of the Fleet and King's Bench prisons, the warden of the Fleet called his jail "the largest brothel in London."[10] The keeper of Newgate confessed that he permitted conjugality, too, but only in order to prevent the outbreak of "more atrocious vice" like homosexuality and masturbation.[11] Meantime, under certain circumstances prisons afforded even more spectacular opportunities for commerce between inmates and the English public. Far from being the closed disciplinary institutions we now imagine, eighteenth-century jails, as Bender observes, "were treated as holiday curiosities."[12] According to popular legend 3000 people turned out to visit the notorious highwayman James Maclean on the day before his execution in 1750, and the keeper of Newgate made £200 by "exhibiting" Jack Sheppard.[13] All of these circumstances suggest that the old prisons, unlike modern penitentiaries, remained curiously liminal spaces, distinct from but nonetheless intimately connected with the world beyond the cell.

Prisons were permitted to persist in this remarkable—and remarkably public—fashion for several reasons. Simply put, allowing private jailers to manage convicts in *any* way was simpler for England's authorities than regulating, staffing, funding, and policing the hundreds of local prisons that received English inmates during the eighteenth century. Indeed, the Crown seems to have been quite aware that its ability to staff prisons at all depended upon maintaining the profitability of the enterprise. In 1701 a bill that would have halted overcrowding at the Fleet and Queen's Bench debtors' prisons was rejected on the grounds that, with fewer prisoners, profits from the prisons would decline.[14] Besides, prisons were not explicitly meant to punish or reform, and implicitly the old jails were far more punitive than their laxity suggests. The filth and stench of the prisons were unbearable and polluted entire neighborhoods. Through most of the century, prisons also posed a very real threat of deadly disease. During John Howard's famous tour of England's prisons in the early 1770s, he was obliged to travel on horseback, since the smell of his clothing after just a few hours in one of the prisons rendered him unfit for coach travel.[15] He also disinfected his notes before he used them by laying them before the fire. As Seán McConville observes, "[o]utbreaks of gaol diseases were often fatal to witnesses, counsel and judges, besides prisoners and staff," and such outbreaks contributed to the public perception that prisons really were dangerous places.[16] In this objectionable way, the stench and pestilence of the prisons may even have reminded observers of just how far the prisons' reach extended into the public sphere.

Beyond making prisons unpleasant and even hazardous for inmates,

England's authorities faced genuine ethical limitations to what they could impose upon the confined. Howard's tour of the prisons revealed that 2,437 of England's 4,084 inmates—or 60 percent—were in prison for debt, even though rates of incarceration for criminals, specifically, had risen since early in the century.[17] The remainder were mostly accused or convicted criminals awaiting trial, sentencing, or execution. Through the eighteenth century, the preponderance of debtors in England's prisons complicated the question of whether punitive or even disciplinary aims could fairly be introduced. It would have been improper, some reasoned, to subject debtors to mandatory labor and discipline, or to punish those prisoners who had not yet been found guilty but might be obliged to wait months for the next quarter sessions or assizes. While those awaiting execution clearly merited punishment, their sentences had already been handed down, and the ultimate exaction of justice for them would anyway come before God, not at the gallows. If they chose, therefore, to spend their last days drinking, carousing, or playing to the crowds gathered outside the prison, they would soon be justly served. This is all to say that, despite what we might now regard as dreadful physical conditions and deplorable disciplinary laxity in these eighteenth-century prisons, the Crown had few incentives to curtail the eminently public nature of the cell.

The English prison's predominantly public character during this period mirrors, in most important respects, the Crown's more comprehensive strategy for dealing severely and publicly with criminal offense. At least 160 crimes had been classified as capital felonies by the end of George II's reign, and that number swelled to more than 200 under George III.[18] While less than fifty percent of those sentenced to die actually went to the gallows, the severity of the criminal code and public nature of eighteenth-century executions suggest the emphasis that legislators placed upon deterrence. Until 1783, when the gallows was finally removed from Tyburn to Newgate, executions were preceded by a procession through London, during which the assembled witnesses could view and even participate in punishments by throwing rocks or other convenient missiles at the condemned. Public confession, written or oral, was usually part of this ritual, a condition of the condemned person's shriving before facing the noose. Particularly brazen offenders might play to the crowd by jesting, drinking, and generally making light of the occasion on their way to the gallows.[19] At the other extreme, especially detested criminals arrived at Tyburn already bloodied and battered, then were hung while tens of thousands of spectators looked on. After death, the most despicable felons could be gibbeted near the place of their offense or delivered to the medical college for dissection. These post mortem practices—designed to "display" the fruits of criminality—were codified under the 1752 Murder

Act, which aimed "to impress a just horror in the mind of the offender, and on the minds of such as shall be present, of the heinous crime of murder."[20] Lesser sanctions, including pillorying and whipping, also aimed to make punishment a public matter. In 1699, a new law governing claims to benefit of clergy changed the punishment from branding on the hand to branding on "the most visible part of the left cheek nearest the nose," since authorities feared that a mark on the hand was too easy to conceal.[21] Seven years later, the law was repealed: the more obvious mark had made offenders so subject to public scorn and mistrust that they became unemployable and were driven to poverty and, inexorably, back to crime. Like Middleton, Waller, and other criminals murdered on the pillory, offenders branded on the face during the eighteenth century fell victim to a system of public punishments that occasionally worked too well.

Among the sentencing options available to eighteenth-century judges and magistrates, only transportation seems at first glance to have served no explicitly public role. Really, though, transportation performed exactly the "public service" that England's national program of convict management required. Sentences to transportation accounted for some 60 percent of all criminal offenders between 1700 and 1775, which means that most of England's convicts were removed from rather than exposed to the public view.[22] Even so, the Crown embraced transportation for many of the same reasons it embraced punishments like pillories, whippings, and executions: the punitive nature of the sentence, and the public reputation—if not quite the spectacle—of the penalty. Early in the century, the voyage was exceedingly miserable and dangerous, and those who survived the trip could expect to arrive in colonies that were still, by English standards, scarcely habitable. By the 1770s this perception had changed, and many of the social dregs whom England transported to America had better opportunities in the new world than in the old. Conventional wisdom tells us that the American Revolution suddenly and dramatically halted the flow of convicts to the New World on July 4, 1776, but it is worth noting that between 1772 and 1775 sentences to transportation declined by more than 40 percent in Surrey.[23] Partly, England had begun to fear delivering more human capital to colonies who seemed poised for rebellion. But the decline also reflects concerns that faster, safer ships and more civilized colonial sites were blunting transportation's punitive and deterrent edge. As stories of newly settled and newly prosperous transportees—and, occasionally, the transportees themselves—made it back to England, the publicity afforded to transportation undermined its utility, and authorities began searching for punishments better able to discourage future crimes. Though transportation shipped convicts across the Atlantic to suffer their punishments at a distance, its popularity as a sentencing option always depended partly upon its public reputation at home.

Foucault argues in *Discipline and Punish* that the shift from punitive to disciplinary modes of punishment stemmed, in the main, from the pervasiveness of a new capitalist ideology determined to make prisoner bodies economically efficient and productive. To the extent that some English observers regarded issues of crime as issues of class, he is correct. In the main, English crime during the mid-1700s resulted from the social ills—dislocation, urbanization, unemployment, and poverty—produced by early industrialization and the emergence of the world's first modern capitalist economy. The old poor laws were inadequate to the new society, and so were the old methods of dealing with criminal offense. The poor laws and criminal laws alike were subject at mid-century to critiques that meant to attack crime at its perceived root: the ignorance and moral depravity of the lower class. Henry Fielding argued in 1753 for a program of convict management including "periods of solitude, a fully structured work regime, and religious instruction that would act as a 'correction of the mind' as much as 'of the body.'"[24] Observers like William Hay and Joseph Massie argued for similar innovations, citing the model of the English bridewell or "house of correction" that had been used since Elizabethan times to teach the value of industry to the vagrant poor.[25] Such measures would have constituted a significant departure from the traditional philosophy that emphasized punishment rather than prevention and reform, and they seem as well to suggest a proto-Benthamite determination to turn England's convicted criminals into efficient cogs in the new capitalist machine. In 1753, though, real penitentiary reform was still some decades off, and even ideas like Fielding's, Hay's, and Massie's would not necessarily have produced a penitentiary that served capitalist aims more effectively or completely than the old system of public punishments and local prisons.

For one thing, private ownership of prisons had been profitable throughout the eighteenth century for entrepreneurial jailers, and permitting private ownership had freed the Crown from most of the financial responsibility of handling criminal offenders. For another, England had gained substantially and almost effortlessly from transportation, since transportees were largely thrown upon their own resources and forced for their survival to participate in empire-building once they reached the New World. Capitalism and imperialism had both been served well under the old system of punishments. That system might have continued unchanged into the nineteenth century had certain practical and philosophical pressures not intervened. In 1763, the end of the Seven Years' War sent hundreds of jobless and penniless soldiers into the mix of an English society already groaning under new industrial and urban pressures. Prosecutions, convictions, and executions between 1763–1770 all increased compared with the seven years before, but the proportion of capital offenders actually executed continued to decline, all the way to 15 percent in Surrey during the same period.[26] Normally, the overflow of executable criminals would have been transported, but judges and magistrates were increasingly reluctant to ship convicts to America. With no other major outlet for criminals during the early 1770s, the proportion of sentences to imprisonment quadrupled in Surrey between 1772 and 1775 as transportation fell out of favor.[27] Well before the American colonies put a formal end to transportation in 1776, Newgate was overcrowded, the Crown had begun renting spaces in local jails, and prison hulks were being anchored in the Thames.

At this opportune time, two men gave England serious pause to reconsider the purpose and function of its prisons. One of these was Cesare Beccaria, an Italian philosopher whose treatise *Dei Delitti e delle Pene* (1764) provided the first serious challenge to conventional notions of criminal administration. Like most who had come before, Beccaria urged the common argument that punishment ought to deter potential offenders from committing crimes.[28] But Beccaria argued that certainty rather than severity of punishment would best achieve this aim, since potential offenders would then perceive that punishment inevitably followed the commission of crime. Under the system of gibbet-justice in place in England and other parts of Europe during the eighteenth century, only a tiny proportion of all offenders were actually caught, prosecuted, convicted, and put to death. While those executions could be quite spectacular, most capital offenders never reached the gallows. The "Bloody Code" even made many victims of minor crimes loath to prosecute, since they hardly wished to see the poor robber of sixpence hung for his offense.[29] Less severe secondary punishments must be developed, Beccaria reasoned, so that no offenders escaped scot-free. Translated into English in 1767, Beccaria's essay reached England at the very moment when lawmakers were questioning the wisdom of continuing wholesale transportation of England's convicts—and questioning, more generally, the shape of penal practice. Beccaria never argued for penitentiaries. But by arguing convincingly that milder punishments could deter crime, he influenced not only Bentham but also William Eden, William Blackstone, and Samuel Romilly, all of whom later helped to mitigate England's criminal statutes.[30]

A decade after Beccaria's essay reached England, John Howard showed a wider body of English readers the deplorable condition of their jails. Howard's *The State of the Prisons* (1777), based upon his personal visits to every English jail, exposed the frightful conditions under which most English convicts lived during the 1770s. The breadth of his research made the book a formidable weapon for proponents of penological reform. He remarked the prisons' inadequate provisions for ventilation, sanitation, and diet, and he also called the English public to recognize that the association of criminals in common areas contributed to the spread of not only physical but also moral contagions, since inmates hardened in vice frequently corrupted novice criminals who might still mend their ways. A deeply religious conservative Protestant, Howard argued that moral reclamation should be the principle aim of imprisonment, a sentiment that to some extent echoed Fielding and that Howard had cultivated during a tour of the prisons, *lazarettos*, and monasteries of Italy. Howard learned that *lazarettos* employed solitude to arrest the spread of physical disease, and that monasteries used it to inspire introspection, spiritual cleansing, and moral awakening. Physical and spiritual cleansing were aims that Howard could advocate in English prison discipline as well, and he argued consequently for a new prison system in which solitary confinement would produce guilty feelings as prisoners were forced to the lonely contemplation of their past wickedness. Based upon these physically and spiritually salutary precepts, Howard's book "impressed the public as much by . . . its moral fervor" as by the thoroughness of its research.[31]

It also signaled the end of the sort of riotous old prison that so "terrified" Moll Flanders. Howard's book made clear, above all, that no disciplinary or reformative program could possibly be implemented in England's existing prisons. They were too old, too poorly constructed, and too badly managed. Worse, they already held in 1777 more inmates than they could reasonably accommodate, and only the government's failure to regulate local jails had allowed jail-owners to cram so many prisoners into such appalling cells. By that year the Crown was rather exacerbating the overcrowding of local jails by renting space in them, and sending to them those criminals who could not be crammed into Newgate and the hulks. The genuine dangers and miseries of *squalor carceris* made these prisons implicitly punitive, it is true. But if incarceration were punitive *only*, inmates would never become suitable for release, and more jails would always have to be built in order to accommodate the endless supply of criminals left perpetually unfit to be loosed from the cell. In Parliament and in public opinion, this argument carried the day, likely because of Howard's moral persuasiveness and the pressures exerted upon England's jails by the war. Growing less and less hopeful about events in America in 1779, Parliament approved a Penitentiary Act and made Howard a supervisor to the construction of England's first two national penitentiaries.

III

For the next three decades, England moved perceptibly but falteringly toward a new prison system based upon privacy, reformative discipline, and the psychological transformation of the self in the cell. The Penitentiary Act should, perhaps, have been the first pivotal step, but Parliament's action really reveals more about what lawmakers embraced in spirit than about what they were prepared to do in practice. For more than two years, Howard and the other two supervisors failed even to agree upon a site for the new prisons. When three new supervisors finally approved both a site and an architectural plan in 1782, Treasury refused to release the funds, saying, "new measures were about to be taken with respect to felons which made the hastening of the Penitentiary Houses less necessary."[32] Really the government was caught between its pressing need to manage convicts immediately and its desire to resume transportation—as soon as possible—to America or elsewhere. In the meantime, the authorities hedged. In 1779, the same year as the Act, the House of Commons established a committee to consider where convicts could be sent now that America was closed to England. During the next seven years, the Crown considered locales like Gibraltar and the island of Lemane in West Africa before finally settling, in 1786, on Australia's Botany Bay.[33] In 1788 Parliament established a committee to decide upon the best plan for a new penitentiary, but the gesture meant little. The First Fleet had already sailed for Australia and ushered in a new era in English convict administration. As for Bentham, McConville concludes that much of his decade-long exchange with Parliament "seems to have been delaying tactics and a camouflage for the scuttling of the scheme: government was committed to the expensive colony in New South Wales, and judged it could not have that and the Panopticon."[34] No longer facing after 1788 the prospect of coping domestically with its convicts, the English authorities predictably lost the urge to reform them. As the Molesworth Committee lamented a half-century later in its grim review of Australian transportation, "[w]ith the war of independence, transportation to America ceased. Instead of taking that opportunity for framing a good system of secondary punishments . . . the Government of the day unfortunately determined to adhere to transportation."[35]

The desire for a reformative penitentiary reemerged only when the supply of convicts in England began again to outstrip the new transportation system's ability to absorb them. Between 1790 and 1820, as Parliament whittled the "Bloody Code" from more than 200 capital offenses to fewer than ten, victims became more inclined to prosecute for lesser crimes. Also, like the end of the Seven Years' War a half-century earlier, the end of the Napoleonic Wars created social dislocation and unrest by leaving thousands of military personnel unemployed. Committals for trial rose nearly 300 percent between 1806 and 1820, from fewer than 5000 per year to almost 14,000.[36] The enormous increase in convicted offenders overwhelmed England's national and local jails, with the result that by 1810 many of the prisons Howard had vilified in 1777 had actually grown worse. By the second decade of the nineteenth century, it was increasingly clear that—even if used only as a depot for convicts awaiting transportation—an enormous national penitentiary must be built. In 1810, Parliament established one more group, this time the Holford Committee, to consider the possibility of a new penitentiary.

Sixteen years after contracting with Parliament to build his Panopticon, Bentham was on the outside looking in. He remained interested in putting his plan to practice and even testified before the Committee, but experiments in the new Gloucester Penitentiary charmed those considering a new prison. Drawing its most important features from Howard's rather than Bentham's philosophy, Gloucester Penitentiary functioned primarily through solitary confinement, in which isolation was mitigated by the moral influence of a prison chaplain. Its planner and director, George Onesiphorus Paul, testified before the Committee in 1811 that the jail had, under his superintendence, "succeeded beyond the theory imagined by the original projectors of the system; far, indeed, beyond [his] most sanguine expectations."[37] He lauded the tendency of solitude "to create a sense of guilt and awareness of folly," as Howard had done years before, and he criticized Bentham's plan by charging that, in an industrial prison, moral reform and spiritual salvation would always be subsidiary to utility and profit.[38] Bentham conversely claimed to have realized that "perfect solitude" had only one use—"the breaking of the [convict's] spirit"—and he had accordingly amended his plan so that prisoners would be watched within a system of silent association rather than solitary confinement.[39] In the end, the Committee devoted itself to solitude and spiritual reform rather than Bentham's more secular program, and they opted for a scheme like that at Gloucester. The decision was an explicit rejection of the Panopticon and the economic principles it espoused. England's new penitentiaries would pursue spiritual and psychological convict reform, and they would do so by rejecting the old prison's eminently public role.

Or at least they would do so eventually. In 1816, following the advice of the Holford Committee, England opened Millbank Penitentiary near Vauxhall Bridge on the marshy plot originally purchased for the Panopticon. Though meant as England's first genuine attempt to implement reformative prison discipline on a large scale, Millbank was at best an equivocal effort. Its unsalutary location made the new penitentiary damp and cold and created problems as well for sewage and ventilation. Meantime, critics angered by the enormous expense of building the new prison—it cost some £500,000—fueled a public outcry over the improved conditions under which the convicts were kept, arguing that these convicts were less eligible to live well than were the thousands of free, honest, but wretchedly poor citizens in London and other urban centers. This principle of "less eligibility" became a refrain throughout the early nineteenth century for those who wished to keep the prisons squalid, miserable, and explicitly punitive. At Millbank, as at other prisons and workhouses early in the century, the results of less eligibility complaints were severe dietary restrictions and crises in convict health. In the case of Millbank, especially, the poor diet compounded the effects of the dismal location and caused repeated bouts of disease. Scurvy reached such epidemic proportions at Millbank in 1823 that the inmates had to be removed, and prison officials asked Parliament for £23,000 to clean up the buildings.[40] Sir Robert Peel grumbled that "it must be after very full inquiry and investigation, if ever he was induced to send prisoners there again" (*Times* 3/2/24, 3e). But prisoners did eventually return, and throughout the first decade and more of Millbank's operation, bouts with scurvy and other diseases remained common. When prisoners finally acted out against the physical privations in 1827, Millbank officials restricted privileges and canceled disciplinary incentives, provoking a full-scale riot the following year.

Giles Playfair reads these events at Millbank as evidence that, despite Parliament's expressed desire to build a reformative penitentiary, the "punitive obsession" was still very much with those who set England's penal policy.[41] The authorities and the public wished to reform inmates, at least in theory, but they were reluctant to abandon wholly the practices that made incarceration punitive. Accordingly, Millbank failed for two decades to reform or punish consistently, and deplorable deficiencies in diet and ventilation existed alongside the best laid reformative plans of the Holford Committee and Millbank's administrators. In arranging to construct Millbank, the Committee had been convinced of the importance of "zealous and fruitful inculcation of religious instruction" in "promoting the reformation of the criminal," and the chaplain accordingly became the "principal instrument of penal therapy" there.[42] What is more, inmates subject to the disciplinary regimen instituted upon Millbank's opening in 1816 lived in the separate cells Howard had advocated, though they took exercise in groups of three and participated in vocational (and hence reformative) associated labor. Female prisoners, who were thought to be less able to withstand long periods of silence or solitude without suffering psychological injury, occupied one of Millbank's seven buildings and got more opportunities for contact with each other, though the demand for order still prevailed. If not for the dismal physical and dietary conditions, Millbank's first disciplinary plan might have been reformative, indeed. As it was, however, the 1828 riot prompted prison officials to eliminate incentives for good behavior and to abolish, too, both associated and vocational labor—measures that, predictably, availed little. Frustrated and tired by 1837, Captain Benjamin Chapman, who had presided over the troubled penitentiary for more than a decade, tendered his resignation.

Millbank had not become a strictly reformative penitentiary under Chapman, it is true, but it did nonetheless establish the new English prison as a closed space very unlike the jails of the century before. Solitary cells, orderly and closely guarded common rooms and airing yards, attempts to prevent "contamination"—all of these measures tended to isolate prisoners from their fellows. More important, the disciplinary regimen at Millbank also isolated prisoners from the English public. When prisoner unrest first troubled Millbank in 1827, a reporter for the *Times* failed even to discover whether a disturbance had occurred, or why officials had scheduled for that very night an inquest into the death of a prisoner. Chapman curtly denied that anything had happened, and, despite leaks by magistrates and multiple visits to the penitentiary, the reporter reluctantly confessed, "From the secrecy observed we could not ascertain the cause [of the inquest]" (3/23/27, 4b). By the end of the following decade, an outraged correspondent to the *Times* complained—in excellent English fashion—that Millbank had become "a secret tribunal, ay, it was even worse than the Bastile [sic] in France. . . . The prison was a secret prison, as ought not to have existence in this country." (6/6/40, 6a). A prison into which neither the public nor local magistrates could see was, after such failures as Millbank experienced during the 1820s, ample cause for suspicion and complaint.

This is not to suggest that by 1830 either Millbank Penitentiary or reformative imprisonment had become the panacea of English criminal administration. Thousands of convicts each year were transported to Australia throughout the 1810s and 1820s, and despite Millbank's disciplinary endeavors most local jails attempted to reform under other guises. Not all advocates of reformative discipline believed that separate confinement was the best method, and many locally administered jails lacked the money and the space to give each inmate a cell of his own. These typically embraced silent-associated prison discipline, which "compelled prisoners to maintain a profound silence" of both voice and gesture as they toiled together at some form of labor. "Productive" labor in such prisons usually consisted of picking oakum, while "unproductive" labor demanded that prisoners walk upon an enormous tread-wheel or perhaps turn a hand-crank for a predetermined number of hours or revolutions.[43] While prisoners picked oakum or worked at "the wheel," guards watched continuously to prevent communication. By demanding labor in silence as a condition of imprisonment, prison governors hoped to fend off complaints about less eligibility and prevent contamination between prisoners. Without solitude to work on prisoners' minds and morals, warders relied upon other methods for encouraging prisoner reform. At Coldbath-fields, for instance, G. L. Chesterton implemented a "successive stages" system in which prisoners could graduate to progressively less punitive levels of discipline through good behavior, careful observance of silence, and diligent work. U. Henriques argues that Chesterton really believed "the London thieves [to be] incorrigible.[44] Whether or not this is true, the disciplinary regimen Chesterton devised had a genuine reformative germ, and it served as a prototype for successive stages systems implemented later by Alexander Maconochie in Australia and Sir Walter Crofton in Ireland.

While convicts in England during the 1820s and 1830s endured increasingly complex disciplinary technologies in the new penitentiaries, most transportees to Australia faced very different prospects: service to the Crown as a laborer, or assignment to work for a private citizen, for a given span of years. At the end of that span, a convict could receive a pardon or a ticket-of-leave, either of which permitted him to sell his labor freely and choose his place of work.[45] Early on, most convicts worked for the government on public works projects designed to create infrastructures for the new colonies at Botany Bay, Parramatta, and Sydney in New South Wales, as well as Hobart Town and Launceston in Van Diemen's Land (modern Tasmania). By the middle of the 1820s, only one in ten worked for the Crown, while the rest were distributed through the "assignment system" to free immigrants or former convicts whose sentences had expired.[46] From the perspective of the Crown, assigning convicts had several merits. First, it shifted the costs of feeding and housing transportees to private settlers—expenses that private settlers were happy to incur in exchange for cheap and reliable labor on their ranches and farms. Assignment also tended to scatter convicts all over New South Wales and Van Diemen's Land rather than allow them to form large and potentially dangerous associations. With more convicts than free settlers in Australia, dispersal was a crucial aspect of social control. By 1821, 53 percent of Van Diemen's Land's population were convicts under sentence, and probably at least half of the remainder were convicts whose sentences had expired.[47] There and in New South Wales, convicts outnumbered settlers so overwhelmingly in the 1810s that scarcely one convict in eight could be assigned.[48] England's new penal colony was less a prison than a vast carceral society in which class distinctions were drawn between convict and free. For the former, who received a fresh start and a chance to live freely, honestly, and decently in their new home, reformation was an opportunity rather than an enforced demand, and especially convicts who had been driven to crime by economic necessity became law-abiding citizens. Those who did not embrace their opportunity to start fresh soon learned that Australia had worse terrors.

The most dangerous and most incorrigible transportees—about 5 percent of those who went to Australia—faced the prospect of a new imprisonment at the antipodes, but not in reformative penitentiaries like those in England.[49] They were sent to convict outposts that functioned as Australia's most secure jails. In 1819, colonial secretary Lord Bathurst demanded that Australia be "rendered an Object of real Terror" to those transported there.[50] The military men who governed convict outposts like Norfolk Island, Macquarie Harbor, and Port Arthur happily obliged by making their prisons into unbearably brutal places. During the 1820s and 1830s, convicts at these prisons endured body-breaking labor, unthinkable physical privations, and frequent recourse to the cat-o'-nine-tails. 245 prisoners received a total of 33,723 lashes during a five-year span at Macquarie Harbor according to the meticulous records left by the scourgers.[51] At Norfolk Island, a prisoner named William Riley received 1000 lashes, eleven months' solitary confinement, and three months' jail time in just two years, for such offenses as "Singing a Song" and "Asking Gaoler for a Chew of Tobacco."[52] In these terrible places, as Norfolk Island prisoner Robert Douglas remarked, "Let a man's heart be what it will when he comes here, his Man's heart is taken from him, and he is given the heart of a Beast."[53] Only with the arrival of Alexander Maconochie in 1839 did the character of Norfolk Island change, for Maconochie hoped to reclaim these brutalized prisoners through a "marks system" that resembled Chesterton's successive stages. Despite promising early results, Maconochie lasted only a year before he was replaced by a more severe disciplinarian.[54] In Australia, at least, England's punitive obsession was alive and well.

The enormous differences between Millbank, Coldbath-fields, and Australia during the early decades of prison reform conceal the fact that, in two crucial respects, English convict administration was becoming more rather than less consistent. First, despite a lingering impulse to punish, English authorities by the 1830s had nearly reached consensus in support of the idea that reclaiming and reforming criminals ought to be the first aim of incarceration. Experts disagreed over methods, of course, and have continued to do so until the present day. But by 1839 the impulse to reform prisoners had even reached—however fleetingly— Norfolk Island, notorious for brutalizing further those murderers and violent offenders who had already been deemed too dangerous to be at liberty once they reached Australia. At bottom, this impulse reflects not only early Victorian humanism but also an essentially positivist faith that the individual is malleable, and that he will react predictably if acted upon by carefully measured forces. Second, even English prisons other than Millbank had become by the 1830s almost uniformly withdrawn from the view of the English public. Despite the vigilance of authorities inside the prison, Coldbath-fields had become—like Millbank—a closed system very unlike the jails of the century before. Prisoners no longer communicated freely with one another, and the easy commerce of old Newgate had been replaced by sterner rules and regulations governing who could visit, and how often. Visitors like Dickens, who befriended Chesterton and admired his successive stages system, had to write to prison governors in advance and receive written permission to enter the grounds, a step that would have been entirely unnecessary fifty years before. In Australia, meantime, transportees were separated from England far more effectively and irrevocably than they had ever been in America. The voyage was again a genuine peril, and neither transportees nor their stories returned very often from half a globe away. Like Millbank, Coldbath-fields, and England's other prisons during the 1830s, Australia tended to make convict punishment and reformation very much a private matter.

IV

Chapman's resignation from Millbank in April of 1837 signaled just how far authorities now meant to go to make reformation in private the new standard for convict discipline. Throughout the 1830s, Chapman had responded to prisoner outbursts at Millbank by tightening the punitive screws. But Parliament's Select Committee on Secondary Punishments, considering Millbank's troubles early in 1837, concluded that Chapman himself was to blame for prisoner misconduct because he had discontinued "those indulgences which had a natural tendency to produce . . . temporizing conformity."[55] Weary and frustrated, Chapman departed, and home secretary Lord John Russell was persuaded to promote Millbank's chaplain, Daniel Nihill, to the dual-role of administrative and spiritual head of the penitentiary.[56] Nihill had been instrumental even under Chapman in creating changes consonant with separate discipline, supporting especially Chapman's decision to abolish associated labor. Now in complete control of Millbank, he moved it even more precipitously toward unbroken solitary confinement. The change in policy epitomized in almost every way the more general tone of English prison reform after 1835. In that year Parliament's Select Committee on Gaols produced "An Act for effecting Great Uniformity of Practice in the Government of the Several Prisons in England and Wales; and for appointing Inspectors of Prisons in Great Britain."[57] The act did not endorse a particular reformatory scheme, but it did announce the appointment of five inspectors who would oversee the gradual unification and regulation of England's myriad national and local prisons. All five inspectors were ordered to oversee the prisons and assist them to overcome any obstacles that might inhibit "the establishment of uniformity, silence, and separation, or prevent the good effects of religious and moral instruction" (*Times* 10/21/35, 6c). In practice, however, the two inspectors for the Home District—the Reverend Whitworth Russell and William Crawford—were separate-system zealots and assumed de facto control of the Inspectorate. They used their new positions to force, as much as they could, adoption of an across-the-board policy of separation in England's prisons.

Russell had preceded Nihill as the chaplain at Millbank, and his experiences with refractory prisoners there had convinced him that separation was the only adequate means of achieving the moral and spiritual reform that authorities and the public desired. In the Inspectors Report for 1837–1838, Russell exulted over the workings of solitude, where "in his separate cell all the moral machinery of the system is brought to bear . . . as if the prison contained no other but the culprit himself."[58] Crawford, on the other hand, had become an advocate of separation after the Whig government sent him to observe the Eastern Penitentiary at Philadelphia—the first prison to adopt separation on a wide scale and the object, a decade later, of Dickens's withering scorn in *American Notes* (1842). In America, Crawford saw the order and submissiveness of the Eastern Penitentiary's inmates, and he considered that England might even be able to improve upon the original by shortening and otherwise mitigating the period of solitude. Later advocates of the separate system, like the Reverend John Field, hoped to distinguish England's system from the Eastern Penitentiary's and denied that prisons on the western side of the Atlantic had influenced English prison reform. But looking back it is clear that the Eastern Penitentiary, at least, influenced Crawford considerably. Russell and Crawford's enthusiasm for separation likely prompted the promotion of Nihill at Millbank, and it decided Parliament, as well. On June 22, 1839 Parliament passed a new Prisons Bill that established separation as the new disciplinary standard for England's penitentiaries.

Russell, Crawford, and their allies based their arguments before Parliament upon separation's deterrent effects, ability to prevent contamination, and power to reform, but clearly this final point was the crowning one. The Marquis of Normanby later observed that he endorsed separation because it was "calculated to promote [the prisoner's] repentance and reformation" and thus was "a punishment more consonant with the spirit of our religion" (*Times* 4/14/40, 6b). Advocates assured Parliament that separate confinement could be milder in England than at the Eastern Penitentiary, where rumors of prisoner insanity already abounded. Periods of separation would be limited to eighteen months and always include the intermittent care of the prison chaplain, who would guide the prisoner through self-contemplation and encourage him to understand the wickedness of his past actions. Such guidance was necessary, the argument ran, because a criminal lacked the capacity for self-contemplation and moral understanding; otherwise, he would not have transgressed. Moral reformation thus depended upon going over the inmate's past life, and teaching him to recognize, interpret, and overcome his old failings. The prisoner's admittance to a separate cell was to signify the end of one portion of his life and the start of a new one founded upon conscience, self-reflection, and moral principles. Field, the chaplain at Reading Gaol, put it this way: "Deprived of most of the resources of educated men; constantly reminded of the cause which brought him to this situation; undisturbed by any distracting objects; enveloped in silence—he needs must *think*."[59]

These arguments suggest that the prisoner was supposed to "think," mostly, in a confessional, autobiographical, and even self-psychoanalytical way. The aim was complete narrative coherence, a self-understanding that would include the origins of criminality, the commission of crime, and—as a final chapter—an awareness of guilt inspired by the beneficent effects of the cell. The governor of one separate penitentiary argued that reformation was impossible without investigating the criminal's "past life, the nature and frequency of his convictions, the quality of his crimes, the circumstances which originated and influenced his criminal course, [and] the restraints which family ties and social relations are likely . . . to impose."[60] By learning of their charges, prison chaplains could really make the punishment fit the crime. The drunk could be discovered and warned against the evils of ale and spirits; the thief could be drilled in the importance of the Eighth Commandment. Effective treatment required individualization of the reformative endeavor, as much as possible, so prisoners were called upon to identify themselves through narrative. With literate inmates, chaplains often turned separate discipline into an explicitly autobiographical process by compelling prisoners to write their lives during their hours of isolation. In other cases chaplains simply wrote down the stories themselves, either verbatim or in notes meant to capture the spirit of the prisoner's story. All of these self-accounts were to end with the prisoner's return to moral right-thinking. As chaplain John Burt put it, each prisoner must be impressed "with the conviction that there is over him an irresistible power" so that "the will is . . . subdued . . . bent or broken, and the moral character is . . . made plastic by the discipline."[61] Really it was the self-account that was to become malleable stuff. In this way, separate confinement functioned less like Bentham's invisible surveillance than like a prototype of psychoanalysis, complete with divulgences, interpretations, and case histories constructed through the exchanges between analyst and analysand.

By the time Parliament approved separate discipline as the national standard in 1839, Russell and Crawford had already concluded that no such system could be made to work at Millbank. For a time, Millbank did return to a promising semblance of order and discipline under Nihill, and the penitentiary's new tendency toward separation pleased the Inspectors. But within a few years, reconviction rates for Millbank "graduates" soared to more than 50 percent, and rumors spread that prisoners were suffering shocking mental derangements under separate confinement.[62] Advocates of separation did not take this failure as an indictment of the discipline; rather, they argued that now as always Millbank's location and physical conditions simply made genuine reformative efforts impossible. By 1840, Preston Gaol and Brixton House of Correction had also adopted separate confinement, and dozens more prisons did so during the decade. That this is true indicates not only that separation was increasingly the disciplinary arrangement of choice but also that, since Millbank's opening in 1816, politicians and the public had warmed to the idea that England's prisons should—above all—aim to reform. Compared with the old jails and even silent-associated prisons, separate-system penitentiaries were costly since each prisoner required a cell, and many communities had to abandon their old prison buildings altogether in order to implement separate confinement. But they did so willingly, for by 1840 England wanted desperately to reform the wayward criminal, and in a cell of his own.

Opened at the start of 1843, the Model Prison at Pentonville was the grand institutional fulfillment of that desire. The Prison Inspectors meant for Pentonville to replace Millbank as the center of national prison administration and provide local authorities with a "model" of separate confinement rightly managed. Surrounded by a perimeter wall eighteen feet high, England's new prison was spectacularly isolated and dauntingly adequate to the task at hand.[63] It adopted a radial-wing design like the one at the Eastern Penitentiary, with four arms thrusting outward from the central building so that a guard situated at the hub could see down each main corridor.[64] Along Pentonville's high-ceilinged hallways, three levels of solitary cells were ranged, the door to each ingeniously contrived so that visitors, including guards delivering meals, could be seen only if they wished. Henry Mayhew and John Binny called Pentonville's "distinctive feature" the "airy quality of the building; so that, with its long, light corridors, it strikes the mind, on first entering it, as a bit of the Crystal Palace"; but even the prison's airiness did not prevent them wondering about solitude's "danger to the intellects of the prisoners."[65] Inmates spent eighteen months in separate confinement and were allowed just one fifteen-minute visit every six months; they could write and receive two letters each year.[66] Closed to outside contact, the Pentonville inmate was nearly as isolated as if he had quit the earth altogether—which he did, in a way, by being transported to Australia at the end of his term. In a letter to Pentonville's first commissioners, Sir James Graham wrote: "no prisoner shall be admitted to Pentonville without the knowledge that it is the portal to the penal colony: and without the certainty that he bids adieu to his connections in England."[67] But for the few, fleeting visitors inmates received, only the chaplain, the governor, and warders saw the prisoner in his cell. Only they knew what he endured. The *Times* gave its readers a portrait of the new prison late in 1842 with a flurry of articles divulging every particular of the cells, from furnishings and fixtures to dimensions and diet.[68] Then the gates of the Model Prison snapped shut.

During the first several years of separate discipline's preeminence in England's prisons, proponents of the system reassured the English public that, within these forbiddingly private penitentiaries, separate discipline was working as planned. John Silby, governor of the Brixton House of Correction, declared even before Pentonville was built that he had found "separate confinement . . . alone competent to effect the great purposes for which criminal laws were enacted, and prison discipline instituted," and the Reverend John Clay's 1840 report from Preston Gaol attested that "the prisoners, in many cases, have shown that softening of the heart which is evinced by tears."[69] During the 1840s Clay interviewed and reported upon thousands of separate inmates, and he remained a consistent advocate of the system. He observed in his 1841 report that "[i]t is seldom that under other circumstances I find a prisoner melting into tears when I converse with him; but with regard to the solitary—for him to remain unmoved when 'the things which belong to his peace' are offered to his acceptance is the very rare exception."[70] Seven years later, he celebrated separation's ability to reform even those inmates of whom he had entertained little hope:

> But the change has been effected. The dogged or turbulent glance disappears; the countenance undergoes a change beyond all feigning; it bespeaks a disposition subdued, peaceful, cheerful; except, indeed, when words of kindness or sympathy from the governor or chaplain touch the springs of good feeling, and the full heart finds relief in tears.[71]

Clay's experiences apparently were not unique. Pentonville's officials claimed to receive numerous letters from former convicts praising the effects of the discipline there, and Field had, according to him, "thousands of letters" from Reading Gaol inmates expressing the same.[72] He felt confident enough of separation's positive effects to declare, in 1848, that "[w]herever it has been pursued the anticipations of good have been realised . . . Those best acquainted with its effects speak most loudly in its praise."[73]

Field takes little trouble to consider that former inmates who had gone mad or relapsed into criminality were unlikely to send thanks to the tormenters who oversaw their old jails. His words also hint at a graver objection to this account of the separate system's excellence: that "those best acquainted" with the effects of separation—the prisoners them-selves—spoke only rarely, though they were spoken for a great deal. In prisons like Pentonville and Preston, England's great experiment in penal reform had become a struggle for narrative power. Since chaplains had the greatest degree of contact with individual inmates, chaplains natu-rally had the most credibility in accounting for them and describing the progress of their psychological reform. As a result, other authorities from prison governors to local magistrates often based their "official" findings largely upon chaplains' reports about the efficacy of separation. Piously certain that separation was the most effective disciplinary program, most chaplains planned their reports as defenses of separation, complete with prisoners' testimonials written "in their own words." In 1853, Chester Castle Gaol chaplain H. S. Joseph published *Memoirs of Convicted Prisoners*, which consisted of fifteen convict autobiographies and twenty-six letters from former prisoners. All of these praised the reformative effi-cacy of separate confinement. In the volume's "Preface," Joseph wrote, "To check evil is the chief aim the writer has in view. . . . and even the discharged prisoner himself, into whose hands this little volume may come, will find many hints, in the following pages, which will not fail to have a tendency . . . to diminish the number of inmates in our gaols."[74] By disseminating these edifying stories, Joseph hoped to counteract the "wide circulation of immoral and infidel works."[75] Two years later, after his father's death, Walter Clay published the biography *The Prison Chaplain: A Memoir of the Reverend John Clay* (1855), which excerpts hun-dreds of pages of the chaplain's notes from his conversations with indi-vidual inmates. The picture that emerges from these notes is of John Clay the amanuensis, adopting the self-narrative "I" on behalf of prisoners who wish to self-narrate but cannot write for themselves.

These examples only begin to suggest the extent to which prison authorities—especially chaplains—controlled the discursive framework by which the stories of separate prisoners could be known, and the extent to which prisoner self-narratives were expected to play more than a therapeutic role. Like slave autobiographies from the American eigh-teenth and nineteenth centuries, prisoner accounts cannot be judged according to traditional ideas of narrative control or autobiographical truth, since some editor or amanuensis finally "controlled the manuscript and thus decided how a 'statement of facts' became a 'fiction of factual representation'."[76] Written or at least enabled by white abolitionists, slave autobiographies were expected to play a particular ideological or even propagandistic role in the struggle against slavery. Prisoner autobiographies were expected to do the same in defense of separation. Accordingly, men like Joseph, Field, and the Clays made these self-narratives into stories-within-the-story of separate discipline's power to reform. Joseph's preface and concluding remarks ensure that we cannot misconstrue the prisoner autobiographies that come between. Field brandishes his letters from convicts, not as expressions of criminality and private identity, but as evidence in support of his "point." In the case of the Clays, prisoner narratives are twice-distilled, since they filter through the dual lens of the father's notes and the son's biographical work. By wielding such control over inmates' attempts to account for themselves, these defenders of separation ensured that prison narratives would say the right thing to prison governors, magistrates, inspectors, and the public. More telling, when prisoners' tongues fell mute, their bodies were made to speak. Tears, John Clay's notes tell us, stem from "softening of the heart" or "relief" or a release of "the springs of good feeling"; the "countenance" reveals whether a prisoner is turbulent or serene, and whether serenity is real or feigned. Under separate discipline, reading the body became for chaplains a legitimate mode of "exposing" psychological truth, interpreting it, and finally narrating it in any way they wished. When Clay's prisoners say nothing at all, they are made to speak most reassuringly of the conditions of their confinement.

Because our records of separate inmates come—even in prison records—primarily from these separate-system officials, we must conjecture that prisoner narratives were finally shaped, at least partly, by "official" political demands. Certainly illiterate prisoners who dictated rather than penned their stories fell under the narrative control of chaplains who recorded, reworked, and even interpreted their stories and their bodies. But questions of narrative control and autobiographical truth are at stake in prison narratives even when prisoners really do speak for themselves. Prison authorities all wished—usually for the most benevolent reasons—to hear convict self-accounts that began in depravity and ended in the glorious religious awakening engendered by separate discipline. After all, confessing the fullness of one's guilt was the essential first step in reform, and prison authorities devoutly wished for reform to happen. Since criminality was thought to stem from a kind of self-narrative failure—a failure, that is, to reach back into and make correct moral sense of past experience—one wonders how frequently chaplains pressed prisoners to "complete" their stories by admitting to more guilt than they owned. To curry favor with prison authorities, many prisoners would gladly have bent their stories to these purposes. More often, perhaps, inmates exaggerated the heights of their religious feeling after a term of separate discipline, like Dickens's humbugging (and tellingly nick-named) "Model Prisoner," Uriah Heep. Subject to the narrative demands of the penitentiary, the very prisoner accounts that were meant to permit individualization of discipline tended instead to impose a chilling uni-formity upon convict narratives. Joseph's fifteen convict autobiographies all tell essentially the same story of childhood neglect, adolescent ruffi-anism and recklessness, and adult dissipation ending in crime. They all end in moral reform. Demanding autobiographies from inmates as part of the price of moral and psychological reform, serving as the most reli-able witnesses to the lives these autobiographies meant to reflect, chap-lains wielded over prisoners' self-accounts the narrative power reposed in them by the prison.

Though transportees to Australia faced very different conditions than convicts in England, they faced similar challenges to their self-narrative power. Especially at the brutal penal stations, imprisonment intended to impress upon convicts their depravity and debasement and etched these upon prisoner bodies with every lash of the cat. Prisoners who were not brutal and incorrigible when they arrived at Norfolk Island or Macquarie Harbor rapidly became so. Even in their own private imaginings, where once they had owned a sympathetic human identity, they invariably became the guilty, vicious wretches that the law had declared them. For assignees the narrative risks were subtler, but no less cruel. Assignees earned their freedom either through a pardon or a ticket-of leave, neither of which would be granted unless the assignee received a positive char-acter from his master. Eager to keep their assigned servants, many mas-ters were less than honest. In 1838 New South Wales' governor, George Gipps, reported to the Home Office:

> . . . it is a matter of very frequent complaint that Masters prevent their Servants from getting Tickets of Leave from an unwilling-ness to lose their labour; and that they even cause (in some cases) their men to be punished, for the sake of retaining their services. . . I am willing to hope that the cases are few.[77]

Robert Hughes believes, as I do, that Gipps hoped in vain. In Australia's vast carceral society, any free citizen could denounce an assignee, or even a convict who had already earned a ticket-of-leave. Both groups lived in constant uncertainty lest their hopes of freedom be dashed.[78] Though the governments of New South Wales and Van Diemen's Land included courts in which convicts could complain against their masters, often it was the word of one against the word of the other. Understandably, convicts were most likely to succeed in their suits when they complained about corporal punishments, since then "the physical evidence, the wounds and weals, spoke clearly in court."[79] Like dispersal, narrative power was a formidable mechanism of social control in colonies where convicts under sentence outnumbered emancipists and free settlers combined. Convicts' narratives like their bodies were irremediably scarred by their time in Australia, for they were forced, time and again, to attest to the old guilt of their criminal past.

Like separate-system discipline in England, then, Australia's social structures and peculiarities transformed prisoner self-narratives into discursive exercises meant to construct human identity in particular ways, for particular aims. Separate-system authorities wished to bring their wards to narrative completion in order to demonstrate the prison's power to reform. Australian authorities, from prison overseers to the free settlers who commanded convict labor, wished to heap guilt upon guilt for the opposite reason: to show that the convict had *not* reformed, and to prevent his being set at liberty. In both cases, the prisoner was presumed to have no trustworthy or honest voice capable of accounting for the fullness of his private identity. In both cases, he became a narrative construct of his prison, which was concerned for its own interests to invent a particular account of his "true" psychological origins and guilty desire. Hidden from public view and obviously incapable—because of his criminality—of narrating himself, the Victorian prisoner became the particular narrative domain of the prison and its agents, who constructed him as they saw fit. By reading his body, insisting upon his narrative participation, then wrenching away his power to fix the meaning of his life story, English authorities institutionalized the practice of inventing the Victorian prisoner from a vantage outside of the narrative subject. They also made careful narrative invention the official vehicle for conveying "true" information about prisoners to the English public.

By 1851 the enthusiastic reports of men like Clay and Field had convinced local authorities all over England to join Preston and Brixton in owning locally administered separate prisons.[80] On an average day at mid-century, England's new separate penitentiaries held more than one-fourth of all prisoners in England and Wales, and a much higher proportion of those who had already been convicted and sentenced.[81] In contrast, only about 7 percent of the 150,000 prisoners who annually "passed through" England's prisons at mid-century were debtors.[82] The Marshalsea and Fleet were closed, a separate-system juvenile penitentiary had been operating at Parkhurst for fifteen years, and within three years more Brixton would become solely a women's penitentiary. By the early 1860s, according to Playfair, England could claim 79 local jails with nearly 15,000 cells designed for the separate confinement of criminal inmates.[83] Gone were the common rooms, open airing yards, and public commerce that had characterized England's prisons only a half-century before. Victorian convicts were sent to endure new technologies of physical, moral, and psychological discipline, and they were sent to endure them alone. As Michael Ignatieff observes, "Discipline . . . was a new rite, one from which the public was locked out. Unlike the condemned man, the prisoner was bound to silence. Even if he or she did cry out, there was no one to listen."[84] It was the very closing off of imprisonment that Bentham had designed his Panopticon to avoid—that he had feared would lead to abuse, atrocity, and the psychological destruction of the confined. But some Victorians did listen, and by 1851, despite the enthusiastic reports to the contrary, even Victorians who had never heard of the Panopticon were coming to share Bentham's old fears. All around them, mounting evidence was beginning to suggest that England's new penitentiaries maimed and misshaped the prisoners under their care.

V

Even during the 1820s the difficulties at Millbank Penitentiary had done little to inspire public confidence in the plans for nationally managed prisons intended to reform England's criminal inmates. Magistrates pointed out—quite correctly—that scurvy epidemics and prisoner riots did not happen at the houses of correction they oversaw, and they blamed above all Millbank's inaccessibility to themselves and the English public. Though magistrates clamored for increased access to Millbank, they got instead the Prison Inspectorate, which promised to solidify national control of England's jails and pressed even upon local officials the demand for prison discipline that was more rather than less private. The subsequent developments under Nihill's separate-discipline regimen at Millbank made this demand all the more alarming. In 1838, even as Russell and Crawford attempted to sell Parliament on a national program of separate confinement, the rate of recidivism at Millbank reached 50 percent and Lord Lyndhurst complained to the House of Lords that two healthy young men had been reduced to "idiots" by separate discipline.[85] Armed with the official report of the Prison Inspectors, home secretary Russell denied the charge, pointing to the report's conclusion that these "were persons of disorderly behaviour, and were spoken of as not conforming to the rules of the prison, rather than in any other character" (*Times* 2/27/38, 3c). For the next fifteen years, disputes like these characterized discussions of the new Victorian prisons and their effects upon inmates. Though Victorians likely found themselves at a loss to know which side to believe, the underlying message was clear: whether inmates were being helped or harmed by reformative discipline, the new prisons were powerfully able to inflict profound psychological transformations upon the prisoners they confined.

Some of the strongest proof of this emerged in September 1838 when the Whig government, already under fire because of developments at Millbank, issued its own crushing review of penal conditions in Australia. Home secretary Russell and the Whigs had been responsible for creating the Prison Inspectorate, and they generally supported the idea of keeping convicts at home and reforming them in penitentiaries designed for the task. In 1836 Russell and his cabinet had even initiated plans to liberalize criminal laws in order to reduce the number of capital and transportable offenses, a measure that would have kept half of England's annual number of transportees in prisons at home.[86] But Millbank's persistent failures forced Russell to buttress public support for an expansion of reformative discipline. To accomplish that aim, he organized an official public relations attack against Australia, the one penal station that even the Whigs could happily deplore. No reformative program had ever been tried in Australia, so no amount of grim information about convicts there would reflect poorly upon the Whigs' plans to expand the penitentiary system at home. Quite the opposite, Russell calculated that a shocking exposé of Australia's most appalling features might turn the public against transportation altogether. In April 1837, Parliament convened the Molesworth Committee and charged it with inquiring into transportation, its efficacy, and the moral state of the society it had created in Australia. As Hughes observes, the Committee was less an objective inquiry than a "heavily biased show trial designed to present a catalog of antipodean horrors."[87] For sixteen months the Molesworth Committee heard testimony from colonial administrators, clergymen, and others who knew the colony and its prisoners at first hand. Then, in September 1838, it issued its scathing report.

Few Englishmen could have read the Molesworth Report without believing, at least partly, that transportees and free settlers were being scarred indelibly by conditions in Australia. The Report's major charges against Australia were clear: society there was debauched, the assignment system had failed, and penal stations countenanced horrors that no proper Victorian could imagine. Sydney was so sunken in "drunkenness and shameless profligacy" that it was worse than "the lowest purlieus of St. Giles's"—though no worse, according to the Report, than other places in Australia.[88] Much of the problem stemmed from convict assignment, which inflicted such uneven conditions upon convict laborers that it could be relied upon neither to punish nor to reform. Colonial administrators screened applicants for convict labor, but they could not always know good masters from bad, nor were there always enough masters of any kind to go around. Though many masters used their convicts honestly and well, the unlucky assignee could face years of injustice and brutality. Citing these inconsistencies, the Report concluded that assignment's main characteristics were "inefficiency in deterring from crime, and remarkable efficiency . . . in still further corrupting those who undergo the punishment."[89] It also alleged that Australia's social licentiousness was caused by the pernicious effects of transportation. A colony made up primarily of transported convicts was bad enough. But the Report worried that the hearts and minds of even the best free settlers must invariably be deadened "by the perpetual spectacle of punishment and misery—by the frequent infliction of the lash—by the gangs of slaves in irons—[and] by the horrid details of the penal settlements."[90]

These last places, and Norfolk Island most of all, provoked the Committee and its witnesses to eloquent disgust. Sir Francis Forbes, Chief Justice of Australia, testified that Norfolk Island's convicts routinely committed capital offenses, since they considered death better than life under the brutal discipline. Asked if the discipline there did any good, Forbes answered "no," then added, "if it were to be put to himself, he should not hesitate to prefer death, under any form that it could be represented to him, rather than such a state of endurance as that of the convict at Norfolk Island" (*Times* 9/12/38, 6a). Father William Ullathorne had been sent to Norfolk Island in 1834 to minister to prisoners who had participated in an uprising against their brutal governor and were awaiting word on their sentences. He told the Committee:

> I said a few words to induce them to resignation, and then I stated the names of those who were to die; and it is a remarkable fact, that as I mentioned the names of those men who were to die, they one after the other, as their names were pronounced, dropped on their knees and thanked God that they were to be delivered from the horrible place, whilst the others remained standing mute; it was the most horrible scene I ever witnessed. (*Times* 9/14/38, 6e)

Horrible, too, were the Report's charges that Macquarie Harbor and Moreton Bay—like Norfolk Island—were dens of brutality, homosexuality, and atheism. As Parliament heard the Report's findings during September 1838, the English public found the dismal details spread before them day after day in the pages of the *Times*.[91]

Fifty years earlier, no Englishman would have doubted that prisons injured their inmates, nor would many even have cared. In 1838, however, these accounts of convicts in Australia inspired enough disgust to hasten the end of transportation, just as Russell and the Whigs had wished. Transportation to New South Wales stopped in 1840 amid minor political opposition, and it continued to Van Diemen's Land only at the rate necessary to accommodate those convicts whom the growing penitentiary system could not yet absorb. In the meantime, the number of prisoners at Millbank doubled, from 715 in 1839 to more than 1400 the following year (*Times* 5/1/41, 12d). In matters of penal policy, the Whigs' clever stratagem had given them exactly what they wanted. It also gave them something they did not: increased scrutiny for Millbank, and for England's other domestic prisons. Separated from England by half the globe and rendered invisible by the distance, Australia had required a full Parliamentary investigation to drag to light the lurid truths about what convicts were being forced to endure. Who could say for certain that England's new hidden penitentiaries at home were inflicting no atrocities of their own? Inspired by this concern, and perhaps also by the impending construction of the new Model Prison and a grotesque fascination with the grisly facts about Australia, the public and the papers fixed their attention more steadily upon England's prisons during the 1840s.[92] The Prison Inspectorate had promised new penitentiaries that would reform inmates through solitude, self-reflection, and self-narration undertaken in the cell. But Victorians saw only forbiddingly private penitentiaries, and bits of evidence that the psychological transformations being inflicted inside were not all of the beneficent kind.

This was certainly the case at Millbank where, by 1841, even the Inspectors could no longer deny that inmates were being injured by conditions at the prison. A year earlier, Sir Peter Laurie complained to the Middlesex magistrates that seven prisoners had just been removed from Millbank to the Middlesex House of Correction "in a state of mental derangement," and that in 1838 "no fewer than 66 prisoners [had been] discharged [from Millbank] prior to the termination of their respective sentences, in consequence of ruined health by solitary confinement" (*Times* 6/6/40, 6a). In 1841 the Sixth Report of the Inspectors of Prisons corroborated Laurie's complaint, though it disputed the number and cause of the removals. According to the Inspectors, only five prisoners had become insane during 1840, and these had been sent to Bedlam rather than to Middlesex. Refusing to blame prisoners' mental afflictions on separate discipline, the Inspectors claimed in their Report that the problem had already been corrected by improvements in diet and extended periods of outdoor—though still solitary—exercise. Laurie was incensed. In a long attack printed by the *Times*, he wrote of the Inspectors:

> . . . it is clear that their attention has been drawn to this appalling state of things, that they are cognizant of the reckless derangement of mind and body which is being perpetrated, and how do

they express their contrition! Why, when the body or mind of one of these wretched prisoners is broken down to the extreme verge either of insanity or death, they order the surgeon to report it to the governor! (1/15/42, 5b)

In another letter Laurie pointed out that, while England remained intent upon building Pentonville, America was already abandoning the separate system because of its insidious effects. After a quarter-century of failures at Millbank, Laurie probably voiced a popular sentiment when he wrote, "If there was ever anything in this country more disgraceful than another, it was the existence of such a prison as the Penitentiary" (*Times* 6/6/40, 6a).

Laurie's complaints did not alter plans for Pentonville, but they did make Crawford and Whitworth Russell more anxious to ensure the Model Prison's success. To safeguard against problems and failures, the Inspectors decided to hand-select Pentonville's first inmates from among the healthiest, sanest convicts that Millbank had to offer—a practice they continued until 1847. Despite this precaution, separate discipline rapidly took its toll. In November 1843, just ten months after Pentonville opened, two hand-selected inmates were removed to Bedlam, and another left in January of the following year. Officially, Pentonville's administrators recorded fifteen cases of insanity between 1843 and 1850, a rate nearly five times higher than in England's other prisons.[93] Unofficially, things were worse. Though only three prisoners left Pentonville for Bedlam during the first year, nineteen others were removed in consequence of mysterious "illness and infirmities" (*Times* 3/12/44, 3f). One medical officer at Pentonville estimated that the rate of "mental disease" during the 1840s was five times greater than the recorded rate of insanity.[94] Another, Benjamin Brodie, made that number even higher, as he told a Select Committee of the House of Lords in 1847:

> There are a certain number of persons who suffer to a certain extent mentally in our prison besides those who are reputed to be insane. . . . some who have partial delusions, such as a man thinking that he is sure to be pardoned when he is not, or thinking that he hears somebody calling him at night when he is alone in his cell.[95]

At the time, Brodie guessed that "twelve or thirteen" prisoners were so disturbed—seven times the number removed to Bedlam.[96] Perhaps these were the prisoners later spotted by observers in Australia, who reported that Pentonville graduates there often "suffered from bouts of hysteria and crying" or begged for wool to stop up their ears since they found the noises of every-day life "deafening."[97] As Mayhew and Binny mused years later, "had the prisoners throughout England and Wales been treated according to the same system, there would have been, instead of an average of 85 lunatics per year in the entire prison population of the country, upwards of 850 madmen produced."[98]

This is not to suggest that separate discipline never produced any good among England's convicts, for most Pentonville graduates probably never committed another crime. But Victorians were at least as alarmed by Pentonville's insanity rate—even under "model" conditions—as impressed by its power to reform. They were also horrified to learn that the privacy afforded by England's new prisons had, as Bentham feared, opened the door for neglect and abuse. In 1842 Joseph Rowley and four other former prisoners of the Northleach House of Correction testified that severe dietary restrictions and unreasonable labor requirements at the prison had permanently ruined their health (*Times* 10/10/42, 3c). Two years later, the *Times* announced that it had discovered "A Black Hole in Birmingham" made "out of the cellar of an old house" and adapted to confine more than twenty-five debtors who had been "subjected to the greatest degree of bodily torture" (*Times* 1/12/44, 6a). Chesterton's Coldbath-fields came under investigation, too, when the father of a prisoner who died there brought a complaint before the magistrates. The aggrieved parent alleged that his son had "gone into the prison in the most perfect health, that he had been put upon the wheel, that he had complained of being ill, that he had been deprived of a portion of his meat, that he had been again put on the wheel, and had eventually died" (*Times* 12/28/44, 6f). The ensuing investigation found that food deprivation was common at Coldbath-fields and England's other prisons when prison doctors believed an inmate might be "shamming" illness. Other abuses were equally widespread. The Ninth Report of the Inspectors of Prisons confirmed that some prisons had been using fetters and dark solitary confinement—neither of which was an authorized punishment—to deal with refractory inmates.

Revelations like these confirmed many Victorians' worst fears about their hidden prisons. Even in 1843, when the first of Pentonville's inmates were removed to Bedlam, a *Times* correspondent wondered what the public should do and how it would know if a "convict were to die under . . . [such] maltreatment" (*Times* 12/29/43, 5c). The Inspectors' Ninth Report intensified these worries, and criticisms grew more shrill. One reporter called dark confinement and fetters "new aggravation[s] of the horrors of the solitary system" and "a monstrous outrage of authority" (*Times* 1/27/45, 5f). A former Millbank warder, Edward Baker, came forward to the House of Commons with new charges of abuses, beatings, deaths, and suicides at the Penitentiary. The proliferation of such charges prompted Sir Eardley Wilmot and Charles Pearson to demand Parliamentary inquiries. Even so, the disciplinary strategy pursued at Pentonville and in England's other prisons began to change only after 1847, when the unexpected deaths of both Whitworth Russell and William Crawford made possible a fundamental shift in penal administration.[99] Rather than continue to hand-select prisoners for Pentonville, the new inspectors decided to open the jail to the general population of English criminals, with disastrous results. The rate of insanity spiked in 1848, and Pentonville's commissioners were obliged to issue both an apology and an explanation.[100] The following year the commissioners shortened the period of solitude at the Model Prison from eighteen months to twelve, then finally to nine in 1851. Through the rest of the decade local officials continued to build separate prisons, and prison chaplains like Field and Joseph continued to sing the separate system's praises. At Pentonville, however, the great national experiment in separate discipline was over.

The horrors spawned by the separate system were not, as Victorians learned in 1853 from England's first full-scale prison scandal at separate-system Birmingham Gaol. The trouble began in May when fifteen-year-old prisoner Edward Andrews hung himself from the window-bars of his solitary cell. He was sent to Birmingham for stealing a piece of beef and had been jailed twice before on charges of garden-robbing and throwing stones (*Times* 9/12/53, 9f). According to one warder, the boy was "quiet and respectful," and Birmingham Gaol's chaplain Sherwin Ambrose said he was a "mild, quiet, docile boy" (*Times* 9/12/53, 9f). As part of his sentence, Andrews was set to hard labor upon a hand-crank that nominally offered five pounds of resistance, though the prison's governor, William Austin, knew it weighed nearly four times as much.[101] Predictably, the boy routinely failed to complete his daily requirement of 10,000 revolutions. Each time he failed, he suffered dietary restrictions and other punishments that tended to sap further his ability to finish his work. With each new failure, he was punished afresh. Perhaps like the convicts at Norfolk Island, the boy finally concluded that death was a welcome alternative to the life he was obliged to lead in the prison. Shortly after Andrews's death, the local magistrates investigated the suicide and—fans, one and all, of Austin's punitive tendencies—announced that they could find nothing amiss. A second, more thorough investigation by a Royal Commission produced very different results. The privacy of the separate discipline practiced at Birmingham Gaol had merely given cover to Austin and his warders during several years of miserable neglect and abuse. The results of the Commission's investigation underscored the difficulty of discovering the truth about the transformations of mind and body inflicted by England's separate-system prisons.

Like other prison governors at mid-century, Austin had routinely used dietary restrictions and dark solitary confinement in order to punish prisoners he considered to be refractory. But the Royal Commission learned that he also employed water-dousings and a vicious device called the "punishment jacket" to inflict varying degrees of physical and psychological torments upon the inmates under his care.[102] Edward Andrews's age made his sufferings and suicide especially appalling, but other prisoners, too, suffered abuse. Thomas Brown, whom Austin called a "filthy Irishman," was subjected to reputedly "hygienic" water-dousings, and Thomas Hodgetts was left ill and unvisited in his cell for nearly a week, then found almost dead surrounded by twenty-one uneaten loaves of bread (*Times* 9/8/53, 7f). Among these stories of abuse and neglect, perhaps the saddest was that of a mentally retarded convict named Samuel Hunt, who was hung in the punishment jacket until he screamed in pain and terror, then tortured by having handsful of salt crammed into his open mouth (*Truth* 80). Austin had gotten away with these abuses because he had falsified, in almost every conceivable way, the prison's official records of discipline and punishment. Under oath, Austin testified that he did not consider dietary restrictions or water-dousings "punishments" and had therefore seen no reason to include them in his punishment logs (*Truth* 37). He also kept inaccurate records of prisoner suicides and suicide attempts, probably to conceal the dismal results of his vicious habits (*Truth* 40). His warders were complicit in this systematic neglect and deceit. Chief warder Thomas Freer conjectured unhelpfully that many records must have been "lost" or "destroyed," and Birmingham medical officer John Blount confessed grudgingly that he had falsified his records, and that he had not examined prisoners as frequently as the law required (*Truth* 34; 37). In Austin's grossest attempt at deception, he had even returned to and altered the records kept by his predecessor—none other than Alexander Maconochie, the kindly reformer of Norfolk Island—so they would show that a cruel punishment of Austin's devising had been practiced by the previous administration. As it had done with the Molesworth Report exactly fifteen years before, the *Times* printed during several days grim excerpts from the report on Birmingham Gaol.[103] This time, it did so for Victorians already worn out by the horrors of their prisons.

The Royal Commission eventually untangled enough of these "official" frauds to incriminate William Austin, who spent six months in prison for the cruelties he had inflicted upon prisoners at Birmingham. Had he been pilloried and set upon by the mob, it would have been no more than he deserved. He had presided over horrors at Birmingham—horrors that culminated, in many ways, the fears and failures of nearly a century of change in England's prisons. Events at Birmingham demonstrated the dreadful dangers of making prisons into private institutions, and the extraordinary difficulty of *knowing*, under those circumstances, the truth about what went on in the prison, no matter how many official files and reports purported to contain the truth about the cell. More important, Edward Andrews's suicide and the terrible consequences suffered by other prisoners demonstrated once and for all the separate prison's power to transform inmates, body and mind, through the power of discipline and solitude. The lesson was not lost on the Victorian public. In 1857 W. Bayne Ranken remarked sadly that former inmates of England's prisons seemed always "at a loss whither to go, or how to obtain a livelihood" after their long separation from human fellowship, and Mary Carpenter later observed that prisoners all seemed to share a certain "indescribable expression of countenance and peculiarity of demeanor."[104] Matthew Davenport Hill expressed this same point more strongly when he remarked that the trials of imprisonment made the English convict into an "alien to his race."[105] Victorians had spent decades making their prisons into private places capable of inflicting profound transformations upon the inmates under their care. For their pains they got Pentonville and Birmingham, which corrected some inmates even as they drove others to illness, misery, and despair. Edward Andrews's despair belonged also to the convicts at Norfolk Island; the madness engendered by Pentonville was the same produced by Millbank, and at Reading. Like the nineteenth-century prisons that preceded it, Birmingham Gaol succeeded above all at transforming Victorian prisoners in private cells beyond the reach of the public stare. It also, as Edward Andrews's suicide suggests, turned incarceration into an event of singular psychological crisis, narratable only as the private sufferings of the Victorian self in the cell.

VI

This was the particular challenge for Victorian novelists who wished to write of the prison: to narrate this psychological crisis, and to do so within fictions that were identifiably truthful and "real." It is true that throughout the Victorian period, novelists wrote of prisons for the same reasons that they wrote of crime more generally, and of madhouses, mysteries, and scandals. Hidden prisons with dire secrets were excellent fodder for sensation fiction and too profitable to ignore, as even Defoe had discovered with *Moll Flanders* early in the eighteenth century. By the 1830s a new generation of authors—Edward Bulwer-Lytton, W. Harrison Ainsworth, and even Dickens—were turning such "Newgate novels" to good financial account.[106] This same sensational impulse underlies Dickens's mid-century prison novels, too, not to mention Reade's *It Is Never Too Late to Mend* and Clarke's *His Natural Life*. But it is not the case that these novelists aimed *only* at sensation in writing of Victorian confinement. They aimed also to educate their readers about the prison—to introduce them to a hidden world that most of them would never see. In 1837 Dickens used *Pickwick Papers* to teach the public about the miseries of the Fleet, and three years later in a letter to the home secretary he offered to write "a vivid description of the terrors of Norfolk Island and such-like places" to help convince the English public of the severe punishment inflicted by transportation to Australia.[107] While Dickens had private reasons for writing didactically about England's prisons, in this as in so many other things other authors soon followed his lead. Reade designed his sensational account of the Birmingham Gaol scandal in *It Is Never Too Late to Mend* for commercial success and political utility as an exposé of separate confinement. Clarke's *His Natural Life* is often sensational as well, but it is also a rigorously researched history of Australia's collective convict past. Both men defended vigorously the veracity of their novels amid intense criticism from the press.

This determination to achieve realism, even documentary truth, shaped the language and content of many Victorian prison novels, but it is not that surprising if we consider the peculiar narrative status of the prison during the first half of the nineteenth century. As the new prisons became more private, Victorians increasingly experienced their jails only discursively, as the narrative sums of what was written in official reports and newspaper accounts and upon the bodies of the confined. Victorians could know what prisoners saw and what they ate, how many were confined in Pentonville and the precise size of the cells there. When we see, however, observers like Ranken, Carpenter, and Hill attempt to "read" the scars etched by confinement, we find evidence of a much greater desire to penetrate the mysteries of confinement and account for a truth from which most Victorians were isolated. By the time the reformative experiment at Pentonville ended, these mysteries had come to constitute the most significant "truth" about what Victorian prisoners experienced in the cell, and attempting to read, interpret, and narrate them had become common cultural practice. In this fashion, even those who deplored separate confinement came to replicate its strategies for narrating the confined. Even more so than newspapers and government reports, novels were perfect vehicles for that narration, since even explicitly realist novels had greater license to speculate about the private meanings that most Victorians understood imprisonment to entail. In Victorian prison novels, we see repeatedly this particular blend of fact and narrative invention, as authors insist upon objective accounts of confinement even as they imply, over and over, that facts alone are insufficient to penetrate the real story of confinement.

Only by adopting explicitly interior modes of narration could authors hope to represent the psychological crises engendered by the cell. Only by moving from facts to deliberate invention could they pretend to account for the prisoner's intensely private world of solitude, madness, and despair. Since the 1830s England's prisons had provided explicit models for this deliberate invention in the form of inspectors, officers, and chaplains who claimed to speak for the prisoner, and sometimes to speak as him. By studying these prisons, Victorian novelists learned and came to employ the prisons' own strategies for narrating the private self. Prison novels treat prisoners' bodies as legible texts of confinement, to be read and interpreted for what they reveal of the permanent psychological transformations inflicted by the cell. They adopt the first-person narrative perspective—even within otherwise omniscient texts—so that prisoners seem always to tell their own stories, though all the while it is the omniscient narrators who fix the place of these private utterances within the greater text. They also insist, above all, that the prisoner cannot narrate himself to completion, and that finishing his story requires deliberate narrative invention from a perspective outside the narrating self. Drawing from Foucault's theories about surveillance, Jaffe has argued that Victorian novels mimic the Panopticon by engaging in "fantas[ies] of omniscience" and "emphatic display[s] of knowledge."[108] In Victorian prison novels, where we might most expect to find such mimicry, this is not the case. Prisoners are hidden and own psychological pains that cannot finally be "known" in any objective way. Instead, prison novels engage a different fantasy: of unlimited narrative power over the private story of the imprisoned self. To the extent that prison novels exercise this fantasy—to the extent that they force narrative constructions upon prisoners who are abnormal, dangerous, and psychically maimed—they engage the same narrative processes and power relations as Freud's attempts to write case histories from the fragmentary utterings of the human unconscious. During the middle decades of the nineteenth century, this fantasy of narrative power pushed the novel ever inward upon the private world of the self in the cell.

Chapter 2

Prisoners by Boz: *Pickwick Papers* and *American Notes*

The hidden life is, by definition, hidden. The hidden life that appears in external signs is hidden no longer, has entered the realm of action. And it is the function of the novelist to reveal the hidden life at its source . . .

—E. M. Forster, *Aspects of the Novel*

WHEN CHARLES DICKENS WAS A BOY AT CHATHAM, HE SOMETIMES wandered by an old convict hulk anchored in the Medway "'like a wicked Noah's ark,' all cribbed and barred and moored by rusty chains . . . 'ironed like the prisoners' themselves.'"[1] Back in the dockyard along the river, the boy stared mesmerized by long files of convicts engaged in heavy labor, hauling long wooden planks. He could hardly have foreseen then his father's imprisonment for debt and his own miserable trials at Warren's Blacking warehouse, but it is fitting that an author whose work turned so often to the prison should have been so captivated by it is a child. He wrote of "A Visit to Newgate" in 1835 in one of his best-known *Sketches by Boz* and put that piece to fictional use in his account of "Fagin's Last Night Alive" in *Oliver Twist*. His first novel, *Pickwick Papers* (1837), contains Dickens's reflections upon the Fleet Prison, a genuinely tragic episode despite the playfulness and exuberance that characterize the rest of the text. Indeed, Dickens's career as a novelist might be said to have begun in the Fleet with Samuel Pickwick, just as it seems to have been destined to end in the condemned cell with John Jasper—yet another fictional return to his earliest work on the prison—had Dickens's own life not ended first. For more than three decades Dickens attempted to educate his readers about debtors' prisons, the old rowdy jails, and the new penitentiaries. In novels from *Pickwick Papers* to *The Mystery of Edwin Drood* (1870) he aimed at least partly to show his readers the psychological transformations and torments inflicted by the cell.

Dickens's accounts of these prisons are not like any fictions that came before, nor even do they much resemble the "Newgate novel" of England's 1820s and 1830s. Instead they are emotional and psychological explorations that treat imprisonment itself as a fundamental movement of the plot. In *Moll Flanders*, for instance, Defoe uses the riotous backdrop of old Newgate primarily to complement and explain the licentiousness of Moll's character, but he never finally treats the prison in any comprehensive way. He wishes rather to show us his wily heroine and the complicated social and psychological factors that encourage her to pursue a life of crime. In this sense, Defoe's novel is very much the forerunner of nineteenth-century Newgate novels like Edward Bulwer-Lytton's *Pelham* (1828), *Paul Clifford* (1830) and *Eugene Aram* (1832) and also W. Harrison Ainsworth's *Jack Sheppard* (1839), all of which take greater pains to show us the origins, motivations, and allures of criminality than to portray the miseries of Victorian confinement. Of the novelists who preceded Dickens in writing of the prison, William Godwin in *Caleb Williams* (1794) came nearest to investigating the prison for its own sake, and for the sake of exposing the physical and psychological calamities it inflicts upon its inmates. But even here Godwin's aim is different than Dickens's. *Caleb Williams* is partly a detective story and partly about social injustice, and—finally—Caleb spends much less time in prison than he spends combating the insidious evils of a legal system predicated upon the ability of the complainant to pay for "justice." Dickens's prison novels are also often about social injustices. They, too, are sometimes sensational accounts of criminality rather than confinement. At their best, however, Dickens's accounts of confinement reveal a desire to narrate, as Peter Brooks puts it, "the narratable . . . which deviates most markedly from the normal, in the criminal, the outside-the-law, the unsocialized, and ungoverned."[2] Considering Dickens's acute awareness of the traumas inflicted by confinement, it should come as no surprise that this "determination to give voice to the voiceless" leads him, again and again, to narrate the psychological disruptions of the self in the cell.[3]

Perhaps no author was better qualified than Dickens to accomplish this task. His knowledge of Victorian and pre-Victorian prisons was prodigious, acquired in part during his stints as a journalist with a number of London papers. At sixteen Dickens learned shorthand, and he began reporting on Parliamentary matters for the *True Sun* and the *Mirror of Parliament* in 1828. Edgar Johnson observes quite correctly in his biography of Dickens that, during seven years as a Parliamentary reporter, the young writer saw debates over critical issues like the 1832 Reform Bill, the 1833 Factory Act, and the new Poor Law of 1834.[4] Johnson omits, however, the penology debates Dickens would also have seen during these years: over the 1828 riot and consequent disciplinary adjustments at Millbank, for instance, and over the creation of the Prison Inspectorate in 1835.[5] Dickens frequently conducted his own visits, too, to the prisons in and around London during the 1830s and investigated several American prisons during this 1842 tour of the United States. While preparing materials for his *Sketches by Boz* during 1835 and 1836, Dickens visited both Newgate and G. L. Chesterton's Coldbath-fields, and he returned to both prisons several times after, at least once with John Forster and other friends in tow.[6] Forster recalls that Dickens was fond of discussing "the improvement during the last few years of the London prisons," and remembers a tour of nearly all of these in 1838 and 1839.[7] He struck up a friendship with Chesterton as a result of his trips to Coldbath-fields and befriended Alexander Maconochie when the latter returned from Norfolk Island. Philip Collins tells us that Dickens even introduced Maconochie to Chesterton and Lieutenant Augustus Tracey, the governor of Westminster Bridewell at Tothill-fields, and that Dickens admired Maconochie's "marks system" so much that he eventually persuaded Angelina Burdett Coutts to implement it at Urania Cottage.[8] Curiously, Dickens never seems to have visited Pentonville, though he nonetheless lampooned it to great effect in *David Copperfield* (1851) by making Uriah Heap a humbugging "model prisoner." On his 1842 American tour, though, Dickens missed no opportunities to see the prisons in New York, Boston, Philadelphia, Pittsburgh, and Kingston, Ontario.

He also, much to his shame, knew the Marshalsea. Forster and the biographers who have followed him have never failed to underscore the psychic consequences to the young Dickens of his father's imprisonment for debt and his own brief service labeling bottles at Warren's Blacking.[9] We know from them that John Dickens was imprisoned in the Marshalsea because of "the Deed" on February 20, 1824, only two weeks before Charles's twelfth birthday, and we know also that the father was subsequently released on May 28 when his mother's death left him a legacy sufficient to settle his debts.[10] As was typical in debtors' prisons, John Dickens took his wife and the smaller children into the prison with him, where they lived together in a tiny cell he leased from the warden. The two elder children, Fanny and Charles, lived elsewhere, but in nothing like equivalent circumstances. While Fanny went away to study music at the Royal Academy, Charles simply went to work so that he could pay his own way and cease to drain the meager family income. During the day he earned a tiny income labeling bottles, a job he had received through the "charity" of a cousin. He spent the rest of his time mostly in a dingy room his father found for him, near Warren's but across London from the Marshalsea. In this tiny apartment Dickens endured a miserable succession of lonely evenings.

Forced into shabby company at work and isolation at home, Dickens took to ferreting about London in search of cheap bread and occupations that could take his mind off his dismal situation. Years later he recalled: "I know that I have lounged about the streets, insufficiently and unsatisfactorily fed. I know that, but for the mercy of God, I might easily have been, for any care that was taken of me, a little robber or a little vagabond."[11] After two months John Dickens took notice of his son's miserable solitude and found him an apartment nearer the Marshalsea, which allowed Charles to begin taking his supper with the family. On Sundays the whole family, Fanny included, gathered at the prison. During these visits, according to Johnson, Charles was "endlessly curious about all the prisoners and their histories, and untiringly observant of their characters and behavior."[12] He told Forster that he even "made out [his] own little character and story for every man" he watched, inscribing their "different peculiarities of dress, of face, of gait, of manner . . . indelibly upon [his] memory."[13] Understandably, Dickens was most observant of his father, who initially despaired at his hardship and developed the nervous play of the fingers about the mouth that Dickens later attributed to William Dorrit.[14] From Dickens's earliest acquaintance with the Marshalsea, he witnessed the outward signs that betrayed inward turmoil, and he treated the prison as a site of narrative invention by fashioning pasts and identities from these visible marks of confinement.

That he did so suggests that Dickens knew intimately the prison's power to wound and maim. Though John Dickens had been imprisoned for only three months, Charles was left to labor at bottle-labeling for more than a year.[15] The boy's deep shame at having been so reduced—at having been denied companionship, education, and respectability— marked his character profoundly and indelibly. His experiences in the debtors' prison left him permanently isolated, as he thought, from the wider world. By Dickens's own admission, he never fully disburdened his mind on the matter until he presented Forster with the start of an autobiography more than fifteen years later:

> From that hour until this at which I write, no word of that part of my childhood which I have now gladly brought to a close has passed my lips to any human being. I have no idea how long it lasted; whether for a year, or much more, or less. From that hour until this my father and my mother have been stricken dumb

upon it. I have never heard the least allusion to it, however far off
and remote, from either of them. I have never, until I now impart
it to this paper, in any burst of confidence with any one, my own
wife not excepted, raised the curtain I then dropped, thank God.[16]

After his liberation from Warren's, Dickens felt the difference between
himself and his schoolfellows that these days of misery had created, so
much so that he continually found "at extreme points in his life, the
explanation of himself in those early trials."[17] In other words, Dickens
came to recognize that suppressing these childhood experiences could
not expunge them, and that any coherent self-account would have to
include and cope with the psychological traumas inflicted by the prison.
    Natalie McKnight suggests that Dickens's muteness on his childhood
trials explains his determination to voice "experiences with poverty,
alienation, and marginalization" in his novels, but in making this argument she misses a fundamental part of the point.[18] Dickens *did* finally
explain this deeply felt and shameful period of his life, and in doing so
he recovered crucial reasons and strategies for narrating the prison. First,
he came to understand that imprisonment, whether or not it entails disciplinary aims, inflicts psychological transformations that cannot be
measured through the body alone. In Dickens's prison novels the marks
left upon the body always indicate a deeper story that must be read and
interpreted from what is visible to the eye. He relies upon the sense and
logic created by his own experience of the prison—which he later discovered had scarred his behavior and his sense of self—to narrate prisoners whose ticks and idiosyncrasies always bear the psychological meanings of their confinement. Second, Dickens came to understand that
imprisonment could itself be a fictional plot, since the transformation of
identity that constitutes the crux of imprisonment could supply the fundamental movement of the novel. Though Dickens's accounts of the
prison combine Defoe's physical realism with Godwin's study of social
injustice, they also, even in early works like *Pickwick Papers* and *American
Notes*, deliver a portrait of imprisonment that these earlier authors do
not: of the imprisoned psychological subject, struggling through his
incarceration to a new identity shaped by the cell.
    As a beginning novelist, Dickens was most proud of his prodigious
ability to render the people and events and scenes of London so vividly
that his readers recognized his fictions "as bits of actual life."[19] To be sure,
his earliest novels accomplish this much, and his determination to write
realistically of the world around him characterizes as well his early writing on the prison. *Pickwick Papers* and *American Notes* detail the Fleet
Prison, New York's Tombs prison, and Philadelphia's Eastern Penitentiary
as tirelessly as they show us any other scenes from London and American

life. They measure and describe; they insist time and again that they are
honest and objective, even historical and documentary. Indeed, as a travel book *American Notes* is explicitly and designedly so, and both works
reflect the young Dickens's penchant for physical caricature and journal-
istic assessment. Even the young Dickens knew, though, that imprisonment constituted a genuine psychological peril. That knowledge drove
him, when he wrote of the prison, to push beyond physical realism so
that he could provide a more complete and genuine account of the self
in the cell. *Pickwick Papers* and *American Notes* do not contain the sustained investigations of imprisonment that Dickens delivered later in
Little Dorrit and *A Tale of Two Cities*. But they do prepare the way for these
works and even hint at the methods that Dickens—and eventually a
much wider group of Victorian novelists—would use later to penetrate
the psychological story of Victorian confinement.

II

No critic has ever argued that *Pickwick Papers* is fundamentally "about"
the Victorian prison, and very probably it is not. It is Dickens's greatest
comic achievement, set in an exuberant present-tense filled with picturesque characters who engage in a series of remarkable and often farcical
adventures. Even the most egregious acts carry no serious consequences,
and characters drift in and out of the novel without disturbing the good
humor of its action. Much of the novel's comedy arises from this wandering menagerie of characters, whose various social classes, dialects, and
figures of speech create an engaging linguistic playfulness.[20] As part of
this backdrop, the Fleet chapters serve primarily to resolve the novel by
reuniting the main characters—Pickwick, Sam, Mrs. Bardell, Alfred Jingle,
Job Trotter, and even Perker, Stiggins, and Tony and Susan Weller—so
that the conflict between Pickwick and Mrs. Bardell can be resolved, and
so that Pickwick can complete his education regarding the wide world
the Pickwickians have sent him to explore.[21]

Beyond these observations, most critics have dismissed the prison
from more detailed consideration. Collins's *Dickens and Crime*, concerned
with punishment for crime rather than for financial insolvency, understandably ignores *Pickwick Papers'* portrayal of the Fleet.[22] Angus Easson
has paid it somewhat more attention by analyzing the historical accuracy of Dickens's portrayal, and by discussing the extent to which the
unflattering portrait of England's debtors' prisons indicates his social
reformist aims.[23] This suggestion that the Fleet chapters are designed to
illustrate and indict contemporary debtor law and prison conditions is by
no means incorrect, but Dickens means to provide Pickwick and the
novel's audience with an education regarding the Fleet that reaches
beyond the power of history and physical detail to render. Though he

had not yet, perhaps, come to grips with the Marshalsea's impact upon his own life, Dickens was astute enough even in 1837 to recognize that confinement creates deep mental wounds only dimly etched upon the body. Pickwick's education thus includes not only an initiation into the physical hardships of the Fleet but also an insistence on Dickens's part that Pickwick must learn to read the psychological story of confinement in order to understand fully the prison's effects. Each physical mark upon Dickens's Fleet prisoners attests to a psychological meaning of imprisonment that rests beneath the story's surface. In part, the novel thus returns to Dickens's boyhood, and to the prisoners he had seen and considered at the Marshalsea. First among Dickens's innumerable narrative returns to the prison, however, *Pickwick Papers* marks also the earliest stirrings of his impulse to narrate the cell as a place of psychological as well as physical concern. In this sense, at least, *Pickwick Papers'* account of the Fleet transcends its obvious concern with facts.

The account does not begin that way. When Dickens first turns to write of the Fleet in *Pickwick Papers*, he deliberately goes to great lengths—presumably to ensure that readers will not miss the truth of his social critique—to saturate his descriptions with details that affirm the hard realism of his portrayal. Upon Pickwick's initial entry into the Fleet, he views through the open doors of the cells "four or five great hulking fellows, just visible through a cloud of tobacco-smoke . . . engaged in noisy and riotous conversation over half-emptied pots of beer, or playing at all-fours with a very greasy pack of cards. . . . [or] some solitary tenant . . . poring, by the light of a feeble tallow candle, over a bundle of soiled and tattered papers, yellow with dust and dropping to pieces from age."[24] "Chummed" to his room, he immediately notices the "still remnants of loaves, and pieces of cheese, and damp towels, and scraps of meat, and articles of wearing apparel, and mutilated crockery, and bellows without nozzles, and toasting-forks without prongs" (*PP* 650). Such vivid descriptions of Pickwick's squalid surroundings leave us little room to doubt their accuracy. Indeed, Dickens even takes an opportunity to render the fetid interior of the Insolvency Court—a significant but obscure feature of imprisonment for debt in pre-Victorian years—by gratuitously introducing old Tony Weller's friend George, who otherwise plays little role in the novel.[25]

Steven Marcus has argued that *Pickwick Papers* begins in a "cluster of negations, othernesses and circumstances" because of the conflicting prefaces Dickens wrote for the novel, and because the book's origins in both Robert Seymour's drawings and Dickens's imagination confuse the creative ownership of the project.[26] This may be true of the prefaces, but the novel itself rather favors the documentary style that pervades Dickens's account of the Fleet. *Pickwick Papers* announces itself from the first as authorized and indisputable, not an invention at all but rather a "true" account of the:

> . . . Transactions of the Pickwick Club, which the editor of these papers feels the highest pleasure in laying before his readers, as a proof of the careful attention, indefatigable assiduity, and nice discrimination, with which his search among the multifarious documents confided to him has been conducted. (*PP* 1)

Admittedly, in many ways, this narrative ploy is just a return to convention, designed like many eighteenth-century novels to argue for the authenticity of a text that writer and reader alike know to be a fiction. Convention or not, however, the claim to authority tends from the beginning to ground even the novel's most farcical events—to say nothing of its more sober prison scenes—in the real (if whimsical) world of human experience. All in a moment, Dickens begins his first novel by negating his role as a writer of fiction, instead telling us that *Pickwick Papers* consists of true events carefully sifted by an editor in order to establish its meaning. This avowal of narrative authority persists throughout Chapter One as we read that the facts of the narrative, while not an "official statement," have been "carefully collated from letters and other MS. authorities, so unquestionably genuine, as to justify their narration in a connected form" (*PP* 7). The comment is crucial, for it implies that only *orderly* authenticity produces coherent narrative, and that the narrator's editorial undertaking has merely provided an otherwise chaotic story with the meaning it requires. Certain later chapters of the novel are attributed to "the notebook of Mr. Snodgrass," and the interpolated tales that so many critics have lamented as flaws in the novel are validated by their having been "recorded on the Transactions of the club" (*PP* 53; 41). After the first several chapters, our narrator drops the pretense that the novel is an editorial chore—stops insisting so loudly, that is, that the novel is "true." But occasionally, and especially at the end of the novel, Dickens resumes his posture as an editor and brings *Pickwick Papers* to an orderly close.

Dickens's explicitly documentary approach to the Fleet thus reinforces and is reinforced by the tone of the rest of the novel. But his minor touches in detailing the interior of the prison only anticipate the much longer narrative intrusion that announces the indisputability of his portrait. Eschewing the playful tone that typically characterizes the storytelling, the narrator begins his account of the Fleet's "poor side" by invoking the reader's contemporary knowledge of the prison:

Most of our readers will remember, that, until within a very few
years past, there was a kind of iron cage in the wall of the Fleet
Prison, within which was posted some man of hungry looks . . .

Although this custom has been abolished, and the cage is now
boarded up, the miserable and destitute condition of these
unhappy persons remains the same. We no longer suffer them to
appeal at the prison gates to the charity and compassion of the
passers by; but we still leave unblotted in the leaves of our statute
book . . . the just and wholesome law which declares that the stur-
dy felon shall be fed and clothed, and that the penniless debtor
shall be left to die of starvation and nakedness. This is no fiction.
(*PP* 654)

The curious tag that concludes this quote captures the equivocal status of
the novel that would portray the prison. In part, we see here Dickens the
reformer at work: denouncing the injustice of the poor laws, invoking
the principle of less eligibility for felons, and noting anxiously the
increasing separation of prisoners from the society beyond the prison's
walls. Immersed in the "facts" of the case, however, this narrative intrusion suggests how hard those facts are to come by, for the prisoner is no
longer on display to the outside world. Though the novel is "fiction,"
Dickens suggests, it can also be a tool for presenting the truth: for pene-
trating the cell, discovering its secrets, and producing knowledge about
the experience of the prisoner.

Sam Weller's Fleet roommate, the cobbler, also professes to tell the
truth about the prison, and his story, too, is a curious blend of fact and
fiction. The cobbler tells Sam that he is in the Fleet because he has acted
as trustee for a will later contested by one of the deceased's nephews. The
disgruntled nephew has entered a caveat—what Sam calls the "brother-
in-law o' the have-his-carcase" (*PP* 680)—against the cobbler, and as a
result the poor trustee has been taken in *Bleak House* fashion to the Fleet,
where he must remain until the case is resolved in Chancery. At the end
of his account of his unmerited sufferings, the cobbler proclaims, "And
this is God's truth, without one word of suppression or exaggeration, as
fifty people, both in this place and out of it, very well know" (*PP* 681).
When he does so, we are certain that we have just witnessed more of
text's rhetorical posturing. But a letter from Dickens to George Beadnell
in July 1837 shows that this story really *is* true, having been related by a
Mr. Clarke to Beadnell earlier that year. Mr. Clarke's story, Dickens tells
Beadnell in the letter, has been "put into a Cobbler's mouth who tells it
in the next number," though Dickens asks Beadnell to suppress the fact
that the author has ever heard the tale (*Letters* I 289). The letter goes on
to express Dickens's desire to be free from any inundation of actual
accounts of imprisonment in composing his novel, and insists that his

inclusion of Clarke's tale has been "the only reality in the whole business of and concerning the Fleet" (*Letters* I 289).

This statement is naturally troublesome, for it muddies the question of what Dickens meant by composing a "realistic" account of the Fleet. The novel's prison portrayal both is and is not documentary, an ambiguity that underscores Dickens's struggle to find an adequate means of narrating the cell. Explaining to Beadnell his desire to avoid real accounts, Dickens wrote in the letter: "Fictitious narratives place the enormities of the system in a much stronger point of view, and they enable one to escape the personalities and endless absurdities into which there is a certainty of rushing if you take any man's account of his own grievances" (*Letters* I 289). In other words, Dickens wanted to produce a qualitative rather than quantitative truth about imprisonment, and he felt that doing so required that he divorce his novel from strict facts just enough that the real force of the prison narrative could emerge. It is also possible that Dickens decided to use this one real story simply because he found the idea of a hopelessly entangled will—which reemerges in *Jarndyce v. Jarndyce* fifteen years later—too rich to ignore. Placing Clarke's story in the mouth of the cobbler, Dickens assumes the real editorial role that his narrator has already claimed. The result is a novel that combines fact with fiction to enable a more complete story of imprisonment than either alone would permit.

Just as important, Dickens's hesitancy to use the real experience of any one individual illustrates that the aim of *Pickwick Papers* is to educate Pickwick and the reader regarding the prison as an institution rather than to unearth any particular story of confinement. The cobbler's story contains much of caveats, councils, lawyers, and Chancery but virtually nothing of his time in the Fleet, and even such as it is the story falls, apparently unheard, upon the ears of the blissfully dozing Sam. Other prisoners, too, lack their essential stories. We receive no further information about the "young woman, with a child in her arms, who seem[s] scarcely able to crawl" (*PP* 636). The worn and hollow Alfred Jingle, whom we have met frequently earlier in the novel, relates his entire prison experience with the words, "Live on a pair of boots—whole fortnight. Silk umbrella—ivory handle—week—fact—honour—ask Job—knows it" (*PP* 658). This is *Pickwick Papers'* apparent strategy: to reveal the physical marks left by long confinement, but to veil the psychological effects and hidden meanings of those marks, leaving the reader to rely wholly upon observable evidence for understanding. Within the narrative, we see no explicit evidence of Dickens's private debates over whether to make use of fact or fiction in assembling his novel. On the contrary, we are left with what seem to be the factual, physical miseries of the cell. Educating Pickwick regarding these appears to be the entire thrust of the novel.

Having worked this hard in the narration to establish his novel as documentary, factual, and credible, Dickens moves Pickwick through the corridors and cells of the Fleet, acquainting him with the new world of cruelty and altered meaning that exists within the prison. Early in the novel Pickwick demonstrates his ignorance of the horrors of confinement by reveling in the misfortunes of a "mere boy of nineteen or twenty" confined at Namby's who exhibits what Pickwick considers a deplorable brazenness in the face of adversity (*PP* 618). At first, the boy receives visitors who he believes will "make it all right," but he despairs minutes later when he learns it is impossible to remove his present difficulties (*PP* 620). Uncharacteristically cold, our good-natured hero is "[v]ery much satisfied with this sudden bringing down of the youth's valour" (*PP* 620). First admitted to the Fleet, Pickwick notes as well the "vagabondish" air of the more swaggering of the confined, and he soon concludes that "imprisonment for debt is scarcely any punishment at all" (*PP* 633). Hardly the compassionate man we have seen throughout the first forty chapters of the novel, Pickwick exhibits an unconscionable satisfaction at the misfortunes of the "mere boy," and his reaction to the devil-may-care self-assurance of many of those suffering confinement is no more generous. Pickwick's education will teach him just how wrong he is about what he sees. Like Pickwick, we will learn that this underworld—or at least other-world—of the debtors' prison is neither as kind nor as simple as it seems.

In part, Pickwick's education as a Fleet prisoner is linguistic, as we see from the moment of his arrest when Namby arrives at the George and Vulture just in time to hear Pickwick ask Sam for shaving water. "Shave you directly, Mr. Pickwick," Namby interjects (*PP* 616). The implicit meaning of his words is intelligible to Sam but not to Pickwick himself. During his ensuing trip to the Fleet, Pickwick encounters other phrases that have come detached from their familiar meanings. "Sitting for your portrait" means undergoing scrutiny by the warders so that they may know the prisoners from the visitors; the "paper" that has been Smangle's ruin is "bills," not a job as a stationer; "chummage" is a cell assignment; and a "bail" is one who accepts money to commit perjury—only a "legal fiction," we are told (*PP* 626; 642; 647; 623). To Sam the bird-cage in the lobby is a woeful reminder of the Fleet itself, "Veels within veels, a prison in a prison. Ain't it, Sir," but this "philosophical remark" is lost on Pickwick, who does not yet recognize the way meaning changes in the prison—the way that its physical space always indicates a darker world of hidden and terrible truths (*PP* 626). Coming upon a row of "stone vaults beneath the ground," Pickwick learns how terrible when he mistakes them for coal-cellars for the "convenient" use of the prisoners (*PP* 631). Mr. Roker quickly corrects him:

"Yes, I shouldn't wonder if they was convenient," replied the gentleman, "seeing that a few people live there pretty snug. That's the Fair, that is."

"My friend," said Mr. Pickwick, "you don't really mean to say that human beings live down in those wretched dungeons?"

"Don't I?" replied Mr. Roker, with indignant astonishment; "why shouldn't I?"

"Live!—live down there!" exclaimed Mr. Pickwick.

"Live down there! yes, and die down there, too, wery often!" replied Mr. Roker; "and what of that?" (*PP* 630)

Here the Fleet yields up its darkest horror—its makeshift dungeon—to the unsuspecting Pickwick, and the disclosure is surely meant to shock the reader as well.

These realizations, these horrors to which Pickwick is exposed, constitute his prison education and ours. Only after witnessing the world within the prison's walls can Pickwick comprehend the full meaning of confinement: that the prison is capable of inflicting in secret a slow, hidden, inexorable destruction upon those it holds. This realization fully emerges in the pathetic figure of the Chancery prisoner, who has "been slowly murdered by the law for six months" (*PP* 686). When Pickwick holds a bedside vigil during the man's final hours, he realizes that the Chancery prisoner "had grown so like death in life, that they knew not when he died" (*PP* 688). His lessons regarding the horrors of the prison are complete, and the end of the next chapter finds him proclaiming that he has "seen enough" and locking himself away from the rest of the Fleet, something that Sam advised him to do—"Don't witness nothin', Sir . . . Shut your eyes up tight, Sir"—the moment Namby came to arrest him (*PP* 707; 617). But it is too late to blot from memory the evils he has witnessed. The measure of his education is evident if we weigh his charity to Jingle and his determination not to let Mrs. Bardell continue to suffer the Fleet's ills against his earlier satisfaction at the brazen youngster's fate and his initial belief that debtors' prison is hardly a punishment at all. Really the Fleet chapters of *Pickwick Papers* insist everywhere that the 1820s debtors' prison is a punishment out of all proportion to the social offense of being poor, and that the physical hardships imposed by imprisonment are such, as Perker reminds Pickwick, "to which no man should ever be consigned if I had my will, but the infliction of which, on any female, is frightful and barbarous" (*PP* 726). The Fleet chapters work throughout to illustrate this charge, and the novel's central concern in addressing the debtors' prison has been, as one would expect from a young reform-minded author, to show the physical horrors of confinement.

Yet for all *Pickwick Papers'* explicit concern with physical depriva-
tions, social injustices, and contemporary facts about the prison, the past
is not wholly absent from this novel, either in the Fleet chapters or in the
novel's larger fictional world. The *Bardell v. Pickwick* lawsuit may, as Anny
Sadrin suggests, disappear during the chapters between the court decision and Pickwick's arrest, but the suit's effects do finally interrupt the
novel's celebration of the "passing moment."[27] The remarkable fat boy,
Joe, who apparently requires constant stimulation in order to keep
awake, proves sentient indeed when he witnesses an event that will make
the spinster aunt's "flesh creep," or when food is involved (*PP* 119). Even
Mr. Blotton's simple solution to the mystery of "BIL STUMPS HIS MARK,"
which would deny implicitly any significant meaning to the past world
of the novel, is decried by the other Pickwickians who want to turn the
giant stone into an antiquarian riddle (*PP* 157). As Stan Rubin suggests of
the novel's political content, *Pickwick Papers* is not devoid of history, and
looking closely at Dickens's exploration of the prison, we find ways in
which the past—and particularly the past of the prisoner—comprises one
of the novel's primary preoccupations.[28] The interpolated tales insist as
much, as do the indelibly marked bodies that inhabit the Fleet. In both
we find repeated acknowledgments that a crucial psychological narrative
rests beneath the obvious scars of confinement. Like Pickwick's giant
stone, the prisoner bodies of the Fleet bear old marks that must be read
and interpreted to discover their hidden meanings. These are Dickens's
reminders that reading the prison—and narrating it—requires recourse to
a concealed psychological world that facts alone cannot penetrate.

III

The fundamental lesson that Pickwick must learn during the Fleet chapters is that understanding the prisoner's story requires reading the psychological past through the physical marks displayed in the present.
Confined within the Fleet, the other debtors display in every haunted
glance and wasted form the legible marks of their imprisonment. Some
prisoners show signs of the Fleet's physical hardships, like the woman of
"emaciation and misery" and the Chancery prisoner with his "tall, gaunt,
cadaverous" assortment of "sunken cheeks," "bloodless" lips, and "bones
[worn] sharp and thin" by "the iron teeth of confinement" (*PP* 636; 652).
We must also recall the gauntness and pallor of both Alfred Jingle and Job
Trotter when Pickwick reencounters them in the Fleet, walking evidence
of the prison's hardships who had chapters earlier been hale enough to
dupe Pickwick and Sam at Miss Tomkins's boarding-school. Other physical details carry more disturbing implications. The "strong-built country-
man" absently strikes his riding boot with "a worn-out hunting whip"
while he mutters a horseman's commands to an imagined mount (*PP*

657). A grandfather—foreshadowing *The Old Curiosity Shop* (1840)— ignores the "thousand childish devices" by which his granddaughter tries to rouse him, his face having "settled into an expression of the deepest and most hopeless despair" (*PP* 657). And the Chancery prisoner's pitiful death ends mercifully an existence so grotesque that it scarcely resembled life. Even the indomitable and lovable Pickwick, we are told, will be the worse for wear after his confinement. "'He goes in rayther raw, Sammy,' said Mr. Weller metaphorically, 'and he'll come out done so ex-ceedin' brown, that his most formiliar friends won't know him. Roast pigeon's nothin' to it, Sammy'" (*PP* 668).

Though the Fleet chapters thus insist upon the presence of a sub-merged psychological text, they consistently deny us present-tense access to this hidden world of misery and transformation. Instead, the psycho-logical traumas of imprisonment are laid bare in certain of the novel's interpolated tales, which together provide the windows by which past sorrows creep into the Pickwickian world. The nine separately titled interpolations all allow the past to intrude fantastically and even grotesquely upon the novel's present tense, and "The Old Man's Tale about the Queer Client" and "The Story of the Convict's Return" dwell explicitly upon the past of the Victorian prisoner. The former offers a prison more obviously insidious than the Fleet in which Pickwick later finds himself, perhaps because it unfolds in the prison that had blighted Dickens's youth. More important, George Heyling's story indicates Dickens's awareness that the body is a legible register of psychological pains. "Hunger and thirst, and cold and want" shatter Heyling's son, but the boy fades also because "[h]is recollections . . .were all of one kind— all connected with the poverty and misery of his parents" (*PP* 312). The prison represents external restraint and profoundly internal transforma-tion, and here Dickens makes his greatest early departure from earlier novels of the prison. Injustice and criminality are certainly concerns of Heyling's story, but the center of that story is the prison itself, for the psy-chological transformation it engenders constitutes the climax of the plot. Dickens gives Heyling a narrative being that contains the most fascinat-ing psychological exploration of *Pickwick Papers*. We witness his violent dreams, we comprehend his desire for revenge against his father-in-law, and we witness and comprehend these things through the lens of his indelible past experience of the prison. He allows his wife's brother to drown and sues his father-in-law for debt. The actions become something besides cruelty only because we are able to measure them against the anguish inflicted by his confinement.

"The Story of the Convict's Return" is different, but like Heyling's story it suggests the importance of the past in accounting for the prison-er's present. The convict of this tale returns from transportation and resumes a normal life—stops, in essence, being a convict—only when he sheds the self-narrative of his imprisonment and transportation. Changed in appearance by years of hardship in Australia, and silent about his identity and past, "No one," the clergyman telling the story relates, "knew in that man's life-time who he was, or whence he came" (*PP* 93). The prison has eradicated his physical identity, and he has suppressed his narrative one. Shedding the mark of the convict means abandoning the story of imprisonment as well, and entering the world as an individual with no past and no identity except in a remade physical being. It means undergoing, in fact, rebirth into a world of present and future only. Like the other eight, this interpolated tale infuses the novel with hints of a dark past that constantly threatens the pleasantness of the present. Like Sam's "Wellerisms," it makes present meaning depend upon the experiences and proper interpretation of the past. As the recipient of these bits of wisdom, and as the reader and auditor of the official interpolations, Pickwick encounters repeatedly this demand that he read present signs for hints of their past or hidden significance. Indeed, his whole reason for being sentenced to the Fleet approximates this interpretive process, as the court mines "Chops and Tomata sauce" for latent meanings. The marks that Pickwick views in the countenances of the emaciated Chancery prisoner, Jingle, and Trotter bear witness in the present to the psychological transformation wrought by the prison.

It is, Dickens suggests, a leveling transformation and implies the presence and even production of sameness among those confined within the prison walls. The prison replicates the "great hulking fellows" that smoke and play cards in one room, for "in a fourth, and a fifth, and a sixth, and a seventh, the noise, and the beer, and the tobacco-smoke, and the cards, all [come] over again in greater force than before" (*PP* 632). Pickwick's other observations, too, underscore this sameness even beneath a veneer of apparent individualization. He observes in the galleries of the prison:

> . . . many classes of people . . . from the labouring man in his fustian jacket, to the broken down spendthrift in his shawl dressing-gown, most appropriately out at elbows; but there was the same air about them all—a kind of listless, jail-bird, careless swagger; a vagabondish who's-afraid sort of bearing, which is wholly indescribable in words . . . (*PP* 632–633)

But Dickens *has* just described it in words, and he suggests that even in the debtors' prison—devoid of disciplinary schemes that attempt to normalize and reform the confined—incarceration creates inhabitants curiously different from those outside. Moreover, he has shown us in many other places the pitiable transformations that the Fleet has inflicted upon its individual prisoners, all of whom eventually arrive at the same end in misery, frailty, and despair. These demonstrations show that Dickens recognized the prison's power not only to confine but also to produce the self. He consequently made accounting for that production of the self— its identity, its motives, and its desires—irrevocably part of the Victorian prison novel.

IV

Despite the novel's insistence that the prison story inheres in this psychological account, *Pickwick Papers* stubbornly denies us more than oblique and momentary access to the private world of the self in the cell. Each time the novel approaches psychological disclosure it recoils and omits. Early in Pickwick's imprisonment he feels "the depression of spirit and sinking of heart, naturally consequent upon the reflection that he was cooped and caged up," but the novel reveals none of his gloomy thoughts, nor his private reflections or fears, even though it has meant all along to educate us about a Fleet we do not understand (*PP* 636). After the lengthy narrative intrusion on debtors' prisons, the narrator asserts that Pickwick is "[t]urning these things in his mind" (*PP* 654). But the preceding reflections have decidedly been in tone and address the narrator's rather than Pickwick's, and the latter's mind remains unavailable to the text. While Pickwick "ruminate[s]" on Mr. Winkle's strange behavior when his friend visits the prison, the outcome of those ruminations serves nonetheless to reinforce the narrator's evasions (*PP* 686). As Pickwick says, "I have no right to make any further enquiry into the private affairs of a friend, however intimate a one . . . . There—we have had quite enough of the subject" (*PP* 684). Nor can we be surprised when Pickwick's attempt to comprehend the prison becomes a three-month retreat into his own private cell. Repeatedly shrinking in this manner from intrusions upon psychological privacy and the missing narrative that underlies the prison experience, the novel becomes at best a partial account of the prison, productive of only the most basic truths about the cell. In this sense, Sam's attempt to stare Mr. Smangle out of countenance parallels the novel's treatment of the prison, for like Smangle the prison and its prisoners are examined "steadily . . . with every demonstration of lively satisfaction, but with no more regard to . . . personal sentiments on the subject, than . . . had he been inspecting a wooden statue, or a straw-embowelled Guy Faux" (*PP* 645). The story of imprisonment that *Pickwick Papers* offers is a story of the observable physical body, a story that can be defeated in its telling when Pickwick vanishes for three months within his cell's concealing walls.

It is tempting to suggest that Pickwick—and perhaps his novice author—simply lacks the imaginative capacity to apprehend the psychological experience of incarceration. At first Pickwick sees himself as "without prospect of liberation" from the Fleet though he has entered voluntarily, and Sam rather than Pickwick notes the symbolic significance of the Fleet's birdcage, the "prison within a prison" (*PP* 636). Nor can Pickwick recognize the analogy of Sam's arrest and refusal to pay his creditor on "principle," or the irony of his own observation that the lazy fly crawling over his pantaloons must be crazy since it stays in the Fleet "when he [has] the choice of so many airy situations" (*PP* 639). Garrett Stewart sees Pickwick's educative journey as one toward not only awareness but also the expansion and liberation of his imagination, so that it may handle the "imaginative intensity" of what he sees in the prison.[29] This may well be true, for Pickwick is imaginatively ill-equipped to investigate the concealed narrative that the novel insists is everywhere present in the bodies, habits, and language of those confined within the Fleet. Indeed, even Pickwick's confinement must be voluntary, subject to end at any time, almost as if both protagonist and author require the certainty of swift release from too deep a delving into the psychological truths of the cell. But Dickens was not, even this early in his career, incapable of psychological portraiture, as both "A Visit to Newgate" and *Oliver Twist* suggest. Instead, he may have eluded psychological accounting in *Pickwick Papers* for the same reason that he avoided the Marshalsea—the prison he knew best—in favor of the Fleet: his fear of delving deeply into his own recollections of the cell.

Five years later Dickens did delve into the psychological story of confinement, when he wrote of the Eastern Penitentiary at Philadelphia in *American Notes*. Tony Weller's advice to write "a book about the 'Merrikins'" seems to have been in Dickens's mind at least as early as 1837, but he did not visit the United States until 1842 (*PP* 700). When he did so with the intention of writing a travel book, he was largely following the example set by older contemporaries—Harriet Martineau, Frederick Marryat, James Silk Buckingham, and Frances Trollope—who had preceded him to America and whose fuller, often multi-volume accounts of life in the New World dwarfed Dickens's own.[30] According to Sidney Moss, contemporary critics on both sides of the Atlantic found the book "shallow, slipshod, and spiteful."[31] Though that perception has changed somewhat, most critics have considered the book only insofar as they have attempted to explain Dickens's hostility to what he witnessed in America. Several factors have been held more or less responsible, among them Dickens's quarrel with the American press over international copyright, disgust with the distinctly American habit of expectorating and the impropriety of American intrusiveness, disappointment with American social institutions—most notably slavery—and irritation that his American experiences revealed not America's biases and short-comings but his own.[32]

Missing from these discussions are Dickens's observations on the American prisons. Perhaps the most interesting passages in the book—and certainly the most crucial for students of Dickens's novels—describe the Tombs prison in New York City and the Eastern Penitentiary in Philadelphia, though critics have paid these scenes very little attention. Discussing what he feels is a neglected section of the travel book, William Sharpe, for example, details Dickens's complex reactions to New York City with no more than a mention of his visit to the Tombs. Edgar Johnson simply laments that Dickens's "repeated accounts of prisons, workhouses, hospitals, and orphanages, grow tiresome after the first two or three."[33] These observations hardly give the prisons their due, considering that the prisons reappear in at least five different geographic locations (Boston, New York, Philadelphia, Baltimore, and Kingston, Ontario) and occupy far more total space than the chapters on slavery or the American press.[34] Indeed, in Philadelphia the Eastern Penitentiary seems to have been the only item Dickens found worthy of lengthy mention, for he titled Chapter VII of *American Notes* "Philadelphia, and Its Solitary Prison." As Dickens composed the book during September 1842, he wrote to Forster, "The Philadelphia chapter I think very good, but I am sorry to say it has not made as much in print as I hoped" (*Letters* III 311). His concern over the chapter's brevity did not, however, lead him to expand upon other facets of the city—an indication that Dickens found the Eastern Penitentiary, much more than Philadelphia's significance as the cradle of American democracy, crucial to his book. His instincts were correct, for his portrayal of the Eastern Penitentiary prisoner constitutes his first genuine attempt to penetrate the psychological experience of imprisonment.

Critical neglect of Dickens's writing on the American prisons is to some extent understandable. After all, *American Notes* is largely an attack on solitary confinement, and his attitudes toward such prisons are explicit in any number of his essays, editorials, and letters. His portrayal of the solitary confinement practiced at the Eastern Penitentiary makes his attitudes likewise clear, pointing us emphatically to the cruelty such confinement inflicts. What may surprise, though, is that Dickens finds· this solitude so much more transformative and debilitating than the surveillance that Foucaultian critics analyze so frequently in other Victorian works. It is not that Dickens failed to recognize the psychological and physical effects of surveillance; as a constantly hounded spectacle during his American tour, Dickens became all too familiar with the horrors of incessant scrutiny. But for Dickens the greater horror was the specter of the Eastern Penitentiary's solitary prisoner, locked away for years upon years and destroyed psychologically by the terrors of the cell. The solitary prisoner really becomes *American Notes'* refrain, materializing as well in Laura Bridgman and the young boy sequestered at the Tombs. For Dickens, these solitary figures provided crucial imaginative space that permitted him to justify explicit narrative invention—even in an ostensibly objective travel book—in accounting for the hidden world of the cell.

This explicit determination to invent narratively the Victorian prisoner's psychological experience constitutes *American Notes'* real significance to the development of nineteenth-century prison fiction. Dickens found in the Eastern Penitentiary not the dismal squalor of the debtors' prison but a new kind of confinement: private, concealed, and comprised of a mind turned inward upon itself. Narrating this disciplinary arrangement drove Dickens to narrative invention, since he had to extrapolate from a single visit to the Eastern Penitentiary entire psychological histories that would explain the outward scars inflicted by confinement. His fiction of a hypothetical Eastern Penitentiary inmate is the centerpiece of the book, and the account is so powerful that even a half-century later it was being challenged by the Howard Association for the study of prison reform.[35] Collins observed nearly forty years ago that Dickens's writing in the Eastern Penitentiary passages is "essentially the work of a journalist and creative writer."[36] Indeed, it is explicitly so: a mixture of fact and fiction that calls attention deliberately to both the inventedness and the "truth" of its account of the cell. Beginning with details about the disciplinary regimen, Dickens guesses at the effects; noting the marks confinement leaves upon the body, he reads them for their psychological meaning. By 1842 Dickens like Pickwick had learned his lesson about the prison. Faced with the impossibility of *knowing* the minds of the prisoners he observed, Dickens tacitly affirms in *American Notes* his right to *invent* them. The result is an account of imprisonment that established the solitary figure of the self in the cell as the literary archetype of the Victorian prisoner.

V

As a travel book *American Notes* should have required none of *Pickwick Papers'* explicit claims to authenticity in accounting for American life or the miseries inflicted by America's prisons. Travel books were, after all, meant to be factual, and *American Notes'* readers would likely have assumed it was so unless they were given grave reasons for suspicion. It is telling, then, that Dickens originally intended to attach to *American Notes* a preface called "Introductory, and Necessary to be Read," pointed-

ly designed to justify his account of the United States and explain the
"design and purpose" of the book:

> It is not statistical. Figures of arithmetic have already been heaped
> upon America's devoted head, almost as lavishly as figures of
> speech have been piled above Shakespeare's grave.
>
>   This book is simply what it claims to be—a record of the
> impressions I received from day to day, during my hasty travels in
> America, and sometimes (but not always) of the conclusions to
> which they, and after-reflection on them, have led me . . . [37]

Patrick McCarthy points out that Dickens also originally dedicated his
travel book "to those friends of mine in America" who "can bear the
truth," and that the preface elsewhere challenges dissatisfied readers to
find the "'fact' that will prove him right or wrong."[38] Such defensiveness
seems unnecessary for a travel book. But the truth of the matter is that
Dickens had reached very unpleasant conclusions about America during
his "after-reflections," and that he came to suspect from "certain warn-
ings" that his book would be received coolly because of its criticisms of
America (*AN* 252). Even so, Dickens might have worried less had his
observations in *American Notes* been uniformly factual and objective.
They were not, especially when Dickens wrote of America's prisons.
    This is not to say that Dickens was deliberately dishonest in account-
ing for the Tombs or the Eastern Penitentiary. On the contrary, his determination to tell the whole "truth" about American confinement is in
part what drove him to narrative invention. Six years earlier, in "A Visit
to Newgate," the young Dickens had laid out for his readers the particular program for his writing about the prison:

> . . . we do not intend to fatigue the reader with any statistical
> accounts of the prison; they will be found at length in numerous
> reports of numerous committees, and a variety of authorities of
> equal weight. We took no notes, made no memoranda, measured
> none of the yards, ascertained the exact number of inches in no
> particular room: are unable even to report of how many apart-
> ments the gaol is composed.
>
>   We saw the prison, and saw the prisoners; and what we did see,
> and what we thought, we will tell at once in our own way.[39]

This passage makes clear that even as a young author Dickens found simple facts about confinement insufficient, perhaps even ancillary, to the
process of telling the truth about confinement. As he observes, the facts
had been rehearsed again and again by the middle of the nineteenth century. What was wanted was a qualitative account of the cell, so that read-

ers could understand how the inmate suffered and what he endured. This was especially true in writing about Philadelphia's Eastern Penitentiary, where Dickens saw during his visit the physical signs that irreparable psychological harms were being inflicted upon prisoners subjected to unbroken solitary confinement. Though Dickens ultimately decided to omit his original preface to *American Notes*, that preface might have served not only as a defense against criticism but also as an admonition to readers: to understand that the most important kind of "truth" is not always strictly factual, especially in accounting for the prison.

Thus *American Notes* is strictly factual in accounting for prisons only when Dickens believes that the mode of imprisonment has inflicted no psychological injuries upon the confined. During his trip to America, Dickens felt this way mostly about the silent-system prisons he saw at Boston and Kingston, both of which he describes in scrupulous detail. At the Boston House of Correction, we are told, the cells are arranged such that "an officer stationed on the ground, with his back to the wall, has half their number under his eye at once; the remaining half being equally under the observation of another officer on the opposite side; and all in one great apartment" (*AN* 53). Certain inmates are watched even more closely, being "overlooked by the person contracting for their labour, or by some agent of his appointment. In addition to this, they are every moment liable to be visited by the prison officers appointed for that purpose" (*AN* 52). The surveillant disciplinary regimens at these prisons hint of Bentham's influence, as does the demand that inmates be economically productive. At Boston, "those who are sentenced to hard labour, work at nail-making, or stone-cutting," some of which is intended to contribute to a "new custom-house in course of erection at Boston"; meantime, the "women, all in one large room, were employed in making light clothing, for New Orleans and the Southern States" (*AN* 52). The other silent-system prison at Kingston houses men "employed as shoemakers, ropemakers, blacksmiths, tailors, carpenters, and stonecutters; and in building a new prison, which was pretty far advanced towards completion. The female prisoners were occupied in needlework" (*AN* 207).

Though Foucault has made modern critics especially sensitive to the surveillant modes of discipline inside these prisons, Dickens never expresses concern regarding their possible psychological effects. On the contrary, he begins his remarks on the prison at Boston by expressing doubts about the apparent leniency of the discipline:

> In an American state prison or house of correction, I found it difficult at first to persuade myself that I was really in a jail: a place of ignominious punishment and endurance. And to this hour I

> very much question whether the humane boast that it is not like
> one, has its root in the true wisdom or philosophy of the matter.
> (*AN* 51)

Even at home in England Dickens disapproved of productive labor for
convicts, for he believed that such "economical" discipline took work
opportunities away from honest unskilled laborers. He also believed firmly—despite his social liberalism—that the principle of less eligibility
ought to be applied to inmates in all prisons. These factors, rather than
any particular anxiety about the psychological effects of silent-system
discipline, made him skeptical of the prisons he saw at Boston and
Kingston.

   This inattention to the likely psychological effects of surveillance is
nonetheless puzzling, especially in light of Dickens's experiences as a
public spectacle during his tour of the United States. In the first days after
his arrival, Dickens repeatedly alluded in his personal letters to the wild-
ly enthusiastic receptions he received at the hands of the adoring
American public, but his wonder soon turned to frustration and fatigue.
Just four days after reaching Boston, Dickens was already complaining to
Charles Sumner that he had "been beset and torn to pieces all day long"
(*Letters* III 20).[40] Less than a week later, Dickens lamented to Thomas
Mitton: "I am so exhausted with the life I am obliged to lead here . . . If
I go out in a carriage, the crowd surround it and escort me home. If I go
to the Theatre, the whole house (crowded to the roof) rises as one man,
and the timbers ring again. You cannot imagine what it is" (*Letters* III
42–43). Nor had Dickens yet recognized fully what "it" was likely to
become: surveillance stretched over the course of weeks and months
without respite even in his sleep. Jerome Meckier suggests that "gaping
Americans taught him the meaning of dehumanization" by requesting
locks of his hair, intruding upon his rooms, and gawking at him whenever he ventured out in public.[41] Perhaps the most outrageous event
occurred four months into Dickens's visit, at Cleveland on April 26,
when "a party of 'gentlemen' actually planted themselves before our little cabin, and stared in at the door and windows *while I was washing,* and
Kate lay in bed" (*Letters* III 209). Dickens was understandably "incensed,"
having already spent four months under the impertinent scrutiny of the
American public (*Letters* III 209).

   By late February, he had had enough. He confided to Forster that he
and Kate "were inexpressibly worn out," and he complained elsewhere:

> I can do nothing that I want to do, go nowhere where I want to
> go, and see nothing that I want to see. . . . I go to church for quiet,
> and there is a violent rush to the neighbourhood of the pew I sit

in, and the clergyman preaches *at* me. I take my seat in a railroad car, and the very conductor won't leave me alone. I get out at a station, and can't drink a glass of water, without having a hundred people looking down my throat when I open my mouth to swallow. Conceive what all this is! . . . I have no rest or peace, and am in a perpetual worry. (*Letters* III 68; 87)

This tirade is one of Dickens's longest in his letters from America and indicates his growing exasperation with his role as a spectacle. By the time he had completed his visit to New York City, he had even determined to rely upon deceit to escape the continuous vigilance of the American public. Before leaving New York he wrote to George Putnam:

Do not talk about our movements, except so far as Philadelphia is concerned, to anybody. I have so much enjoyed the quiet I have had here for the last two or three days (owing to its having been generally supposed that I left New York on Monday), that I am more anxious than ever, to travel peaceably. (*Letters* III 98–99)

Meckier is correct, I believe, to argue that such episodes help to explain Dickens's increasingly negative reactions to what he saw in America and his scathing portrayal of Americans in *Martin Chuzzlewit* (1844).[42] For six miserable months Dickens must always have anticipated the next knock at the door, the next interruption of his night's sleep, and the next intrusion upon his person and his privacy.

Dickens writes not one word of this misery in *American Notes*, though he did not want for the opportunity. After all, most of the travel book was reconstructed from the letters he had written to Forster from America, many of which expressed his growing irritation. If Dickens omitted such material from the account of his travels, he can only have done so deliberately, perhaps because he wanted to avoid seeming boastful of his popularity, or because he hoped to allow the typical English reader to encounter America as he or she—rather than as Dickens—might find it. But this does not explain why he would have ignored the debilitating effects surveillance had on the inmates at Boston and Kingston, had he believed them really to be suffering. Indeed, throughout his career Dickens was prone to include his miserable experiences as part of the history of one character or another, especially when those trials involve the prison. Nor did he ever shrink from criticizing—melodramatically, at times—social practices and institutions he found illogical, unjust, or destructive. We find none of these things in Dickens's portrayals of the prisons at Boston or Kingston, however, and the absence of such ruminations in *American Notes* suggests that Dickens found the effects of surveillance to be normative, or perhaps simply non-existent. In either case, they did not constitute the sort of crushing, transformative imprisonment we see in *Pickwick Papers'* portrayal of the Fleet. As a result, his descriptions of the houses of correction at Boston and Kingston remain safely objective and observational, seeming to require none of the reading, interpretation, and psychological portraiture at which *Pickwick Papers* constantly hints. For Dickens, narrating the surveillant penitentiaries we know so well from Foucault required no particular innovation or imagination. The plain facts of the case were all.

The same cannot be said for his treatment of the solitary confinement prisons he visited in Pennsylvania. The separate discipline utilized at Philadelphia and Pittsburgh was actually stricter than that established at Pentonville in 1842, for the Pennsylvania prisons were modeled after the Quaker principle of uninterrupted solitary confinement, sometimes stretched across decades rather than the eighteen months required initially at Pentonville. Indeed, the shorter period of confinement at Pentonville and the kinder and more frequent ministrations of the prison chaplain resulted at least partly from rumors that the longer periods imposed in Pennsylvania engendered insanity. The first goal of solitude at the Eastern Penitentiary was to punish hardened criminals in a way that might also tend to "soften" them. In numbered cells, hooded any time they moved beyond the cell walls, prevented from seeing even those who delivered their meals, the Eastern Penitentiary's prisoners were indescribably alone.[43] Cases of insanity abounded. But only the prisoner himself finally knew what half-imagined horrors haunted him during the innumerable days and nights of his solitary confinement. Even he, engaged in the perpetual self-surveillance and self-reflection demanded by the prison, perhaps hardly understood the nature of his transformation. Divided even from prison authorities by the walls of the prison, the walls of his cell, and the unfathomable workings of his own troubled mind, the solitary prisoner stood trebly removed from any external attempt to "know" or "understand" his experience.

Dickens was fascinated and troubled by the hidden psychological transformation inflicted upon the solitary prisoners in America's prisons, and in their unknown and ultimately unknowable plights he found fertile ground for the exercise of his imaginative powers. His anxiety about these prisoners creeps into his letters to a greater extent, even, than into *American Notes*. In a letter to Forster that contains Dickens's account of the Tombs, Dickens asserts that while "[t]he institutions at Boston, and at Hartford, are most admirable . . . this is not so at New York; where there is an ill-managed lunatic asylum, a bad jail, a dismal workhouse, and a perfectly intolerable place of police-imprisonment" (*Letters* III 101). If the Tombs were not bad enough, he was also horrified by the Eastern Penitentiary, solitary imprisonment at which he called "an awful punishment," and the prisoners of which looked to him as "men who had been buried alive, and dug up again"—a phrase to which he returned in *American Notes* (*Letters* III 124).[44] Whatever Dickens's concerns regarding solitary confinement at the Eastern Penitentiary, they clearly centered around its concealed psychological effects. His March 22 letter to David Colden called it "dreadful to believe that it is ever necessary to impose such a torture of the mind upon our fellow creatures," and to Forster he worried "whether [the administrators of the penitentiary] are sufficiently acquainted with the human mind to know what it is they are doing. Indeed, I am sure they do not know" (*Letters* III 110; 124). Dickens could not "know" either, but here as in *Pickwick Papers* he acknowledges that knowing the facts about the prison is not really the point when that prison operates upon the mind, somewhere beyond the power of facts to explain. Accordingly, hoping to illustrate the horrors of isolation for those who lacked the imagination to understand, Dickens chose consciously to make his travel book a vehicle for the truth that rests beyond facts: the private truth of the Eastern Penitentiary prisoner, driven mad by the operation of the cell.

VI

Dickens first shows his concern with the psychological trials of the Eastern Penitentiary's prisoners—and with the proper strategy for their narration—in his portrayal of the Tombs in New York City. This prison operates according to neither the silent nor the separate system, instead receiving serious offenders who are awaiting trial and sentencing. What distinguishes the passage introducing the Tombs from Dickens's earlier descriptions of Boston and Kingston is that, as in the later writing on the Eastern Penitentiary, Dickens's tone is not objective but imaginative. His account of the Tombs begins, "What is this dismal-fronted pile of bastard Egyptian, like an enchanter's palace in a melodrama!—a famous prison, called The Tombs. Shall we go in?" (*AN* 83). Pictures of the Tombs suggest that Dickens's fantastic description of it is appropriate; nevertheless, the tone of that description implies that the account to follow will be fairy tale rather than report, a primarily fictive passage. The encounter with the guard (the "man with keys" [*AN* 83]) is provided with full narrative detail, including a dialogue between the guard and the author. We discover that a small boy is being held here as a witness against his father in the murder of his mother. Immediately after this awful revelation, we discover the link between the practical arrangement of the prison and the psychologies of those it contains. Our narrator asks, "Pray, why do they call this place The Tombs?" and is told that it is because some suicides happened there long ago (*AN* 85). And why are there no hooks upon which prisoners can hang their clothes? "When they had hooks they *would* hang themselves, so they're taken out of every cell" (*AN* 85).

Bending the rules of the informational travel book, Dickens thus transforms his observations about the Tombs into a pseudo-fiction, complete with a narrator, characters, dialogue, and a mystery to be solved. He "controls the discursive framework" of the account, offering his portrayal of the Tombs as unreal, as if the horror cannot be conveyed factually.[45] The strategy is appropriate, for the horror of the Tombs cannot be known or articulated fully, and the psychological process that leads prisoners to suicide remains secret and interior. It also reminds us of Dickens's letter to George Beadnell regarding the Chancery prisoner, in which Dickens asserted that the "enormities of the system" could be brought forward more completely in a fictional than in a factual account. Transforming his account of the Tombs into a pseudo-fiction permits Dickens narrative access to a psychological world absent from earlier parts of the book, and absent as well from *Pickwick Papers*. In the case of the Tombs and the Eastern Penitentiary, the "enormities of the system" are misery, madness and despair. Dickens's willingness to manipulate the narrative stance of his travel book indicates his sense that the solitary prisoner's experience requires a departure from the strict facts of the case.

When Dickens first turns to the Eastern Penitentiary, he begins objectively as he did in describing the prison at Boston. Here, however, he condemns outright the workings of the separate system. We find no equivocation in Dickens's pronouncement that "[t]he system here is rigid, strict, and hopeless solitary confinement. I believe it, in its effects, to be cruel and wrong" (*AN* 99). These effects are related, Dickens tells us, to the "slow and daily tampering with the mysteries of the brain . . . immeasurably worse than any torture of the body" (*AN* 99), though the body, too, is marked indelibly by these psychological trials. Showing his readers these marks becomes Dickens's chore for the next several pages. We meet a German prisoner, who initially seems content in the manufacture of his Dutch clock—a contrivance of "[v]eels within veels," like the birdcage of *Pickwick Papers*—but when Dickens turns from the clock's contrivances to view the prisoner, he sees that the man's "lip trembled, and [he] could have counted the beating of his heart" (*AN* 102). Dickens asks about the man's wife, but the prisoner merely "[shakes] his head at the word, turn[s] aside, and cover[s] his face with his hands" (*AN* 102). The man claims he is resigned now, but after deploring the slow passage of time within his cell he "gaze[s] about him . . . and in the act of doing so, [falls] into a strange stare as if he ha[s] forgotten something" (*AN* 102).

Other prisoners carry similar hints of weirdness. One cries during Dickens's visit, and another who raises rabbits is "haggard . . . wan and unearthly as if he ha[s] been summoned from the grave" (*AN* 103). A sailor, a prisoner of eleven years, will not speak at all:

> Why does he stare at his hands, and pick the flesh upon his fingers, and raise his eyes for an instant, every now and then, to those bare walls which have seen his head turn gray? It is a way he has sometimes. . . .
>
> It is his humour too, to say that he does not look forward to going out; that he is not glad the time is drawing near . . . that he has lost all care for everything. It is his humour to be a helpless, crushed, and broken man. (*AN* 104)

In 1861 the *Journal of Prison Discipline and Philanthropy*, the official publication of the Philadelphia Prison Society, attacked these portrayals, identifying these prisoners by name and citing official records as evidence that Dickens grossly exaggerated the psychological imbalances from which they suffered.[46] According to those records, this "helpless, crushed, and broken man," Samuel Davis, visited the former warden after his release and was found mentally "as sound as on the day he entered the prison" (perhaps not a positive reflection, after all); the poor German, meantime, begged for readmission to the prison long after his release so that he could die where he had so long lived.[47] Such evaluations and debates demonstrate the uncertainty of Dickens's project in interpreting the meaning of the physical marks and indicate the desire of prison officials to defend the humaneness and efficacy of the system. They also implicitly sanction the validity of Dickens's portrayal, despite its implicit inventedness, by finding the conclusions of *American Notes* worth disputing at all. As Dickens charged in *American Notes*, "very few men are capable of estimating the immense amount of torture and agony which this dreadful punishment, prolonged for years, inflicts upon the sufferers" (*AN* 99). Thus Philip Collins concludes that Dickens criticized the Philadelphia authorities "for a failure in imagination" rather than deliberate cruelty.[48] Perhaps only Dickens, with his incredible imaginative faculties and enormous readership, could have earned such a detailed reaction from the prison's defenders. Not that their arguments would have satisfied him, for, as Collins points out, Dickens would hardly have viewed the wretched German's return to the prison as a vindication of its psychologically brutal regime.[49] The exchange between Dickens and the authorities shows, though, how completely Dickens succeeded at placing interpretation and conjecture—narrative invention—on a level with facts as part of the account of the solitary Victorian prisoner, especially for a Victorian public accustomed to encountering the prison as a discursive rather than physical institution. The consequence is that confinement within the walls of a solitary cell does not present here, as it had in *Pickwick Papers*, an insurmountable obstacle to narration.

The extent to which Dickens demolishes that obstacle is clear from his fictional account of a hypothetical Eastern Penitentiary prisoner. Unlike the rest of *American Notes*, this account is from the beginning an explicit fiction, for Dickens says outright that the scene is what he can "picture" or has "imagined" (*AN* 106). Perhaps the most striking feature of his rendering is that it remakes the prisoner's solitude into an existence haunted perpetually by imagined surveillance. The prisoner's descent into madness begins when he can no longer stand "the insupportable solitude and barrenness of the place," and he "humbly begs and prays for work. 'Give me some work to do, or I shall go raving mad!'" (*AN* 106). He creates faceless, spectral neighbors who occupy the cells on either side of his own, and he envisions them "until he is almost distracted" (*AN* 107). Soon, however, his desire for work, contact, and companionship becomes an engrossing paranoia that he is being watched. He grows edgier about his confinement and "begins to feel that the white walls of the cell have something dreadful in them . . . [and] that there is one hateful corner which torments him" (*AN* 107). Waking in the morning, he hides "beneath the coverlet" to escape the watchfulness of "the ghastly ceiling looking down upon him" and the "ugly phantom face" of the sun (*AN* 107).[50] His apprehension about the "hateful corner" intensifies with time, until he feels it give "birth in his brain to something of corresponding shape, which ought not to be there, and rack[s] his head with pains" (*AN* 107). The corner finally becomes "the lurking-place of a ghost: a shadow:—a silent something, horrible to see," and, as the prisoner's waking life becomes a fearful, watched endurance, at night he remains unable to escape his waking nightmare, for "there stands the phantom in the corner" (*AN* 107). Even the loom for which he earlier begged, "even that, his comfort, is a hideous figure, watching him till daybreak" (*AN* 107).

Dickens's unexpected transformation of the Eastern Penitentiary's solitude to a maddening surveillance gives this passage a Foucaultian flavor. But to say that Dickens engages in a "fantasy of omniscience" or invents the prisoner because he rejects the prisoner's subjectivity is to misread the scene. He pretends to no knowledge about the operation of solitude. He makes clear from the start that his depiction of the hypothetical prisoner depends upon what he can picture or has imagined. Far from attempting to construct the prisoner in order to deny him subjectivity, Dickens attempts to imbue him with subjectivity. He insists throughout *American Notes* that each prisoner carries with him a private, idiosyncratic, psychological apprehension of the cell and its effects. Indeed, Dickens shows us a kind of surveillance in this scene that stems directly from that subjectivity rather than from guards, wardens, or even the watching narrator and author. The solitary prisoner becomes the subject and the object of an uninterrupted self-narrative gaze. Eight years after *American Notes*, in his essay "Pet Prisoners," Dickens wrote:

> It is most remarkable to observe, in the cases of murderers . . . that the murdered person disappears from the stage of their thoughts, except as part of their own important story; and how they occupy the whole scene. *I* did this, *I* feel that, *I* confide in the mercy of Heaven being extended to *me*; this is the autograph of *me*, the unfortunate and unhappy . . . [51]

What solitary prisoners suffer from, in Dickens's estimation, is an overabundance of subjectivity rather than an absence of it. His rendering of the Eastern Penitentiary prisoner reveals that overabundance, showing us what Dickens imagines as the prisoner's self-absorption, self-scrutiny, and self-loathing—the very dimensions of punishment, oddly enough, that penologists hoped would lead to self-narrative and reformation in separate-system prisons. But the surveillance and the omniscience of the scene are not real, nor are they meant to masquerade as such. If Dickens engages in a fantasy here, it is a fantasy of narrative authority only, in which he exercises his prerogative to place narrative inventions alongside the facts of the prison.

The individual in Dickens's hypothetical narrative emerges finally as a man intent upon "Heavenly companionship . . . easily moved to tears . . . gentle, submissive, and broken-spirited," divided forever from the typical individual outside the prison walls (*AN* 108). "Better to have hanged him in the beginning," Dickens writes, "than bring him to this pass, and send him forth to mingle with his kind, who are his kind no more" (*AN* 108). Myron Magnet suggests that for Dickens "it is in the nature of society to transform the inner nature of man, conferring on him in the process the full measure of his humanity," and that by imposing isolation the Eastern Penitentiary demonstrated this proposition "from a negative point of view."[52] But these poor creatures *are* still human. They are only—as prison observers like Ranken and Carpenter would point out a decade later—a race apart. As in *Pickwick Papers*, Dickens finally returns to the idea of transformation, production, and sameness in the prison, finding that "[o]n the haggard face of every man among these prisoners, the same expression sat. . . . In every little chamber . . . I seemed to see the same appalling countenance" (*AN* 108). Though women apparently fare better under the system, for their faces "it humanises and refines," they too are transformed, and Dickens declares solitude "fully as cruel and as wrong in their case, as in that of the men" (*AN* 109). *American Notes* is more Foucaultian in these observations than in its account of the surveillant solitude of the Eastern Penitentiary prisoner. Dickens, like Foucault, insists that the prison is able to produce delinquency (or at least difference) among the entire population of inmates it confines.[53]

VII

Dickens's significance as a prison novelist inheres especially in his recognition of this productive power, and in his determination to place psychological transformation at the center of his accounts of Victorian confinement. At the start of the Victorian period, he rejuvenated and redefined the genre, changing the prison novel from the inquiry into social justice it had been during the eighteenth century into the eminently internal, psychological narrative that we recognize even today as a modern understanding of the effects of the cell. Indeed, by the time he wrote *American Notes* in 1842, Dickens had already discarded the predominantly factual, observational, documentary approach to the prison that had characterized his portrayal of the Fleet five years earlier—not because he meant to circumvent or distort the truth of imprisonment, but rather because he meant to capture that truth more effectively and more completely than he could through facts alone. The Eastern Penitentiary had baffled his power to *know* just what went on in the prison cell, and even the Marshalsea that Dickens had known years before suggested that a psychological story of imprisonment always lurked beneath the surface. That story was ultimately unknowable, and unobservable, too, except in the marks it left upon the body. In *American Notes* he reads and interprets those marks and constructs from them a coherent account of their creation, implying all the while that his invented psychological story of imprisonment ought to supplant the factual one as the "truth" about the cell. Taking us where even *Pickwick Papers* denies us entry, *American Notes* marks the start of the prison novel's inward migration toward the first-person account of confinement.

More, it marks that inward migration even while retaining its status—socially and publicly—as an apparently legitimate record of the operation of the cell. The exhaustive attempts to discredit *American Notes* show this much, for the Society's members took the time to refute factually what Dickens had offered as explicit fiction. Perhaps only an author as gifted and as popular as Dickens could have persuaded so many that his inventions were truths, and certainly at the start of the Victorian age only Dickens did so in writing of the prison. In the process he supplied us with the archetypal figure of the prison novel: the solitary self, tormented and broken by the miseries of the cell. Pickwick's retreat into his cell and the hypothetical Eastern Penitentiary prisoner's lonely descent into madness are the images of imprisonment to which Victorian novels return, and which they recreate in novels from *Jane Eyre* to *The Way of All Flesh* (1903). Indeed, the lasting image of Victorian imprisonment is not of a mind hounded by surveillant pursuers but rather of a mind turned inward upon itself, pursuing itself, caught in the act of a dreadful self-surveillance. Making the prison novel into an eminently private text, Dickens delivered to an entire generation of Victorian novelists strategies for inventing the prisoner's psychological truth: narrative claims to authenticity, meticulously detailed representations of the cell, and marks upon the body that always indicate a deeper, psychological story of confinement. Using these strategies, and relying upon his own popularity and inventive powers, Dickens was the first Victorian author to legitimize the prison novel's inward migration toward the first-person account of the cell.

Chapter 3

Charles Reade, the Facts, and Deliberate Fictions

> I have taken a few undeniable truths, out of many, and have laboured
> to make my readers realise those appalling facts of the day, which most
> men know, but not one in a hundred comprehends, and not one in a
> hundred thousand realises, until fiction . . . comes to his aid, studies,
> penetrates, digests, the hard facts of chronicles and blue-books, and
> makes their dry bones live.
>
> —Charles Reade, *Put Yourself in His Place*

O F THE VICTORIAN NOVELISTS WHO FOLLOWED DICKENS IN WRITING OF THE prison, none was as determined as Charles Reade to stick to the facts in accounting for the cell. Very few people bother with Reade's books these days, though less than a century ago Walter Clarke Phillips ranked Reade with Dickens and Wilkie Collins as a sensation novelist of the first rank.[1] Occasionally a critic still produces an essay on his best-known book, the medieval romance *The Cloister and the Hearth* (1861), but for the most part George Orwell's 1943 observation about Reade still holds true: "it is unusual to meet anyone who has voluntarily read him."[2] This is so partly because Reade's novels are, like many Victorian works, narrowly topical, rooted in contemporary news items and the scandals of the day. It is also true because his fiction is labored and meticulous, with none of Dickens's vivid characters or lively action. A Baconian thinker who was well aware of the limits of his creative skills, Reade devised at the start of his career a "great system" for writing what he considered a new kind of novel:

> The plan I propose to myself in writing stories will, I see, cost me
> undeniable labor. I propose never to guess where I can know. . . .
> I must read books and letters, and do the best I can. Such is the
> mechanism of a novel by Charles Reade. . . . If I can work the
> above great system, there is enough of me to make one of the
> writers of the day; without it, NO, NO.[3]

Reade called his new sort of novel a "matter-of-fact romance—that is, fiction built on truths" and proclaimed in the "Preface" to *Hard Cash* (1863)
that his main aim in writing fiction was "to get at the heart of [the] main
topic I have striven to handle."[4] At his death Reade left behind thirty-six
volumes of notebooks that attest to his dogged pursuit of this documentary method of composition, a circumstance that caused E. G. Sutcliffe to
call Reade "the earliest deliberately and thoroughly documentary novelist" in English.[5] The first novel he produced through his great system was
also the novel that made him famous: *It Is Never Too Late to Mend* (1856),
a persuasive, powerful, and deceptively complex account of the Victorian
prison.

   When Reade's novel appeared in 1856, defenders of the separate system of prison discipline recognized it immediately as a transparent and
sensational reworking of the scandal at Birmingham Gaol. Reade's novel
takes place in "——— Gaol," where a vicious prison governor named
Hawes torments an adolescent convict by subjecting him to hard labor,
food deprivation, and a torture device called the "punishment jacket"
until the boy finally hangs himself from the window-bars of his cell. As
the names alone indicate, Reade took little trouble to disguise the factual source of his novel; he made "Hawes" a phonetic echo of "Austin" and,
perhaps inspired by Henry Fielding, turned the real-life "Andrews" into
"Josephs." According to the sanguine claims of the god-son and nephew
who compiled Reade's literary *Memoirs*, the English public devoured the
novel as enthusiastically as they did Harriet Beecher Stowe's *Uncle Tom's
Cabin* (1852) and Reade ascended to a legitimate station as a man of letters.[6] Those closest to the prison liked the novel much less, for they
believed Reade had introduced sensational embellishments that blackened Birmingham and its officials far more than they deserved.

   Their irritation was, of course, inevitable. Reade had used the scandal
to make his literary reputation and a tidy sum of money besides; his critics were not far wrong when they accused him of making wholly merce-
nary distortions of the literal truth. James Fitzjames Stephen made the
novel the focus of an article that appeared in the *Edinburgh Review*, in
which he vilified Reade (as well as Dickens and Elizabeth Gaskell) for taking immoral liberties with real events.[7] Recorder of Birmingham Matthew
Davenport Hill, though he never even looked into the government blue-

books on the scandal, reassured Lord Brougham by letter that Reade had "cruelly distorted and exaggerated the facts."[8] Likewise Walter Clay, in editing and introducing his father's memoirs, called the novel "a great literary screech" and a "grotesquely absurd caricature of the actual facts."[9] These censures have persisted even in more modern criticism. Forty years ago, in the only article to appear on the novel in the last half-century, Sheila Smith accused Reade of having concocted a mixture of "propaganda and hard facts" that fails to address "soberly" the truth about Birmingham Gaol.[10]

These vehement complaints about the dishonesty of Reade's novel would be provoking under any circumstances, but they are made especially so in this case by a singular fact about this particular book: that Reade did not originally plan it as an account of the scandal at Birmingham. In 1871, looking back on his first important novel, Reade claimed in a letter to the *Times* that "a noble passage [on the Birmingham scandal] . . . of September 7 or 8, 1853" in that very newspaper had "touched [his] heart, inflamed [his] mind, and was the germ of [his] first important work."[11] Regrettably, even twentieth-century critics like Smith have taken this statement at face value, though the "germ" of Reade's novel lay not in the *Times* in 1853 but rather in a series of investigations he made a year earlier, designed to permit Reade to learn about discipline inside England's separate-system prisons. In Reade's original conception, the novel was supposed to focus on fictional inmate Thomas Robinson, who would be reformed by separate discipline and whose story would thus demonstrate the novel's titular thesis. The center of the novel was to be Robinson's self-account, his "Autobiography of a Thief," which would appear in the novel exactly as if it had been written as part of the ordinary course of separate discipline. As Reade completed this first version of the novel, news of the Birmingham scandal hit the pages of the *Times*, and the possibility the scandal presented for popular success caused Reade to rethink the design of the story. Even so, the novel's final version shows everywhere the signs of Reade's original research. Of the critics who have commented on *It Is Never Too Late to Mend*, only Walter Frewen Lord in 1906 credited Reade with having a "knowledge of prison life [which] makes one marvel how it could have been acquired except as a warder or an amateur convict."[12] Reade came by that knowledge painstakingly and it suffuses his account of ——— Gaol, though very few critics who have written on the novel have regarded it as a documentary success.

By studying both the separate-system prison generally and the specific case of Birmingham Gaol, Reade learned lessons about Victorian imprisonment that make *It Is Never Too Late to Mend*—along with *Little Dorrit* and *A Tale of Two Cities*—part of a crucial triumvirate of prison fictions published during the last half of the 1850s. He learned, like Dickens before him, that imprisonment produced psychological transformations for which facts alone could not account, and which left legible scars upon the bodies and behaviors of Victorian inmates. He also learned from studying the Birmingham scandal that facts about England's secret prisons were anyway incredibly difficult to come by, since the prisoners themselves were hidden and the "official" records could not be trusted to tell the truth about confinement. Most important, Reade learned that the separate prison's own narrative logic demanded the production of prisoner autobiography and authorized an external narrator—the prison chaplain—to seize narrative power over that autobiography, so that the "truth" about the Victorian prisoner became a matter of invention rather than fact. Ironically, only an author who studied the facts this closely would have discovered, as Reade did, that the prison itself authorized him to depart from facts in composing a realistic and honest account of the prison. The result is a novel that expands upon the theses of *Pickwick Papers* and *American Notes* by showing us what Dickens does not: that the power to narrate the psychological transformations and traumas inflicted by Victorian confinement derives, at bottom, from the prison's own power over the story of the self in the cell.

II

When Reade began researching for *It Is Never Too Late to Mend* in 1852, he was forty years old and already a failure as a man of letters. He had for years fancied himself a playwright, but his dramatic accomplishments included mostly unacted plays adapted from the French stage and from English novels and a handful of moderately successful collaborations with Tom Taylor.[13] The collaborations had begun to earn the pair modest accolades by 1852, and Elton Smith suggests that some contemporary critics regarded Reade and Taylor as the most able playwrights of the age. But Reade had not yet composed on his own a successful original work, and he craved the recognition that such a success would bring. His single-volume novels *Peg Woffington* (1851) and *Christie Johnstone* (1852)—both of which were adaptations of French plays—flopped miserably in a reading culture that favored Dickens and triple-deckers. The failures hardly satisfied Reade's desire for critical and popular acclaim. In September 1852 Reade wrote in his diary, "I want to show people that, though I adapt French pieces, I can *invent* too, if I choose to take the trouble. And it *is* a trouble to me I confess."[14] Eventually Reade's desire to succeed led him to conceive of his "great system," but in 1852 that was still a year away. For the time being he simply sketched—despite his deeply felt creative limitations—the plot of a new and original drama called *Gold*, with which he intended to capitalize on contemporary interest in the

1851 gold rush in Australia. He placed at the center of this play his earliest version of Thomas Robinson, the convicted thief whose fortunes are the main interest of *It Is Never Too Late to Mend.*

This first version of Robinson's story had nothing to do with the prison, though the play and the novel share basic features of plot: both find Robinson convicted, imprisoned, reformed, transported, and finally made rich by Australian gold. For the play, however, Reade intended to learn only as much of the prison as he needed to create a plausible sketch of his imprisoned thief. He "gained the *entrée* of Durham Gaol" in August of 1852 and began "studying thieves" there by looking at letters and autobiographies supplied to him by Durham's chaplain.[15] He took little interest, though, in the physical and theoretical workings of prison discipline, and he conducted his researches haphazardly as a consequence. He meant only to write the story of a character who happened to be a thief, so thievery rather than imprisonment occupied his interest. In what was for Reade a dizzying creative burst, he completed *Gold* in less than five months, staging it at the Theatre Royal, Drury Lane on January 10, 1853.[16] Perhaps because it was his first individually written drama to be acted, Reade believed the play was his finest work yet, and buoyed by public interest in its topic *Gold* enjoyed several weeks of popular success. As his play's audiences dwindled, however, Reade came to recognize that a fictional adaptation of *Gold* would require a subject of more lasting interest. Impressed by the international success Stowe had achieved with *Uncle Tom's Cabin,* Reade considered whether his play could become a political and social exploration of comparable importance. In the end, he decided to transform his rags-to-riches drama into a documentary account of discipline inside England's separate-system penitentiaries.

Beyond the character sketch he had made of Thomas Robinson for *Gold,* Reade knew at the outset very little about England's separate-system prisons. He spent several months conducting more rigorous research. Preparing to write late in the spring of 1853, he articulated the tenets of his "great system" and went on in the same diary entry to report that he had already "been to Oxford Gaol and visited every inch," and that he intended to "do the same at Reading."[17] He must have followed through, for among Reade's notebooks Sutcliffe found a copy of the "Rules relating to the conduct and treatment of prisoners in the County Gaol and House of Correction, at Reading," complete with Reade's annotations indicating that he had used these rules in writing his novel.[18] They are probably the same rules to which Eden refers when he complains to Mr. Lacy of Hawes's mistreatment of ——— Gaol's inmates; if so, they comprise a fundamental portion of Reade's understanding of separate discipline.[19] According to Wayne Burns, Reade also acquainted himself with contemporary books on prison discipline by separate-system zealots like

Field and Pentonville's chaplain, Joseph Kingsmill.[20] Influenced partly by his mother's Evangelicalism, Reade was greatly impressed by claims that "the permanent moral benefit of the prisoner" was the great "object of separate confinement."[21] From these texts, he would have learned of the roles supposedly played by self-reflection and self-narration under separate discipline, and he may well have decided upon the thesis of his novel. Convinced of the efficacy of separation and thoroughly acquainted with the details of its operation, Reade composed during 1853 his earliest version of *It Is Never Too Late to Mend*.

This version of the novel affirmed implicitly the ideals of separate discipline. Unlike *Gold*, *It Is Never Too Late to Mend* focuses upon the time Robinson spends in the prison under the guidance of ———— Gaol's chaplain, Francis Eden, the novel's aptly named good angel. In a letter to his American publisher James T. Fields, Reade called this reformative story "in which a bad man is . . . not despaired of by a wise and good man but encouraged, softened, converted" the "immortal part of the work."[22] Indeed, he felt so strongly on this point that he changed the title of his novel-in-progress from *Susan Merton* to *It Is Never Too Late to Mend*, thus breaking his early pattern of naming his novels after their heroines. Drawing from the prisoner autobiographies he had read at Durham Gaol, Reade even planned to let his prison chapters culminate with Thomas Robinson's self-account, in which the thief would record his past criminality and express his "hope" that in God's mercy he might yet fully recognize and repent of the "enormity of [his] crimes."[23] The narrative device would have resembled any number of prisoner autobiographies from the period, even down to its use of an "appendix" filled with the guiding comments and editorial suggestions supplied to Robinson by his prison chaplain. With this "central gem of his little coronet" in place, Reade probably completed the first draft of his novel about separate-system discipline in August of 1853 (*AT* 1).

When the Birmingham scandal reached the pages of the *Times* only a few weeks later, Reade reconceived radically the shape of the novel. He had set out to emulate Stowe by writing a novel about a troubling social institution; now Birmingham Gaol had given him, in William Austin, a real-life Simon Legree. On September 8, 1853 the first article appeared on Birmingham and described the torments endured by four of the Gaol's prisoners. Within a few days, the *Times* reported on Edward Andrews's pathetic death, as well. These deplorable events became the melodramatic focus of Reade's novel and the key to its commercial success. He spent two years excavating the newspaper accounts and government blue-books on the scandal, learning the particulars of the abuses and the prisoners and warders involved. With the instincts of a tabloid journalist, he selected the most lurid facts about Birmingham and placed them alongside Robinson's story of hopeful reform. The novel that resulted filled nearly five volumes rather than the standard three, and Reade's publishers chafed. When they demanded substantial cuts if the novel was to go forward, Reade sacrificed his "central gem" at the altar of popular success. Pleading lamely that "a story-within-a-story is a frightful flaw in art," he excised the 9000 words of Robinson's autobiography and with it the portion of the novel that he had previously considered his crowning success (*AT* 1). The decision has tended to obscure *It Is Never Too Late to Mend*'s extensive documentary basis and Reade's painstaking efforts to portray the principles and mechanisms of separate confinement.

The documentary basis of the novel is still there, however, for like Dickens in *Pickwick Papers* Reade clearly meant to use his novel to educate readers about England's hidden penitentiaries. Dickens proposed to do so by giving his readers Samuel Pickwick, whose inexperience provided Dickens with a pretext for rendering the prison in vivid detail. Reade, conversely, provides us with veteran inmate Thomas Robinson, who is able, upon his admittance to ——— Gaol, to compare England's new model of discipline with the old. Robinson, the narrator tells us, has not been in prison "this four years, and, since his last visit, great changes had begun to take place" (*NTL* 88). Robinson's capacity for analyzing his surroundings at ——— Gaol permits Reade to deliver a series of factual revelations about the inside of the prison. The narrator catalogs the furnishings of Robinson's "exquisitely clean" cell, lingering over the "mattress (made of cocoa bark . . . [and the] waterspout so ingeniously contrived, that, turned to the right, it sends a small stream into a copper basin, and to the left, into a bottomless close stool at some distance" (*NTL* 87). Addressing the reader directly, he also delivers a history lesson, explaining the operation of the hand-crank that will play such a role in Josephs's sufferings and that has replaced the tread-wheel as the primary mode of hard labor:

> . . . if I am so fortunate as to have a reader aged ten, he is wondering why the fool [at the hand-crank] did not confine his exertions to *saying* he had made the turns. My dear, it would not do. Though no mortal oversaw the thief at his task, the eye of science was in that cell and watched every stroke, and her inexorable finger marked it down. (*NTL* 98–99)

As Robinson moves through ——— Gaol during the first days of his sentence, the narrator shows us also the prison's chapel, its airing yards, and even the concealing hoods its inmates are forced to wear whenever they leave the cell.

The meticulous details of the early part of Reade's account of ——— Gaol are, to be sure, meant to convince us that his novel has its basis in facts. Even the facts hint at the prison's power to inflict psychological transformations upon the confined. The description of the "eye of science" that watches over the prisoner laboring at the hand-crank recalls the solitary prisoner of *American Notes*, who always imagines himself watched despite his absolute isolation from the rest of the world. As Robinson learns more about the new prison discipline, he grows increasingly uneasy about the implications of his separation from human fellowship. He feels "dismay" when he realizes that the prison chapel consists of sentry-boxes "open only on the side facing the clergyman," and again after the service when the airing yards turn out to be nothing more than long hallways separated from one another by "thick walls" (*NTL* 91; 92). He is haunted, too, by the terrible sight of the convicts assembled to walk to the chapel:

> To his dismay, the warder who opened his cell bade him at the same time to put on the prison cap, with the peak down; and when he and the other male prisoners were mustered in the corridor, he found them all like himself, vizor down, eyes glittering like basilisks' or cats' through two holes, features undistinguishable. (*NTL* 91)

Here, on the first day of his sentence, Robinson has already been transformed into a nameless, faceless, even monstrous being, the image of which is thrown back to him by every other inhabitant of his prison. The moment reflects Reade's acute consciousness that the prison's primary aim was to destroy the criminal's old identity, and to fashion him a new one from the physical and moral clothing supplied by the prison.

This awareness, too, comes from Reade's study of the facts, for he learned about the theoretical as well as the physical details of separate confinement. Indeed, the narrator tells readers in introducing ——— Gaol that the prison is, during the 1850s, in a "transition state" between competing systems of discipline (*NTL* 88). "Under the old [system]," he remarks, "gaol was a finishing school of felony and petty larceny. Under the new it is intended to be a penal hospital for diseased and contagious souls" (*NTL* 88). Deliberately, more than likely, Reade makes his narrator echo Matthew Davenport Hill's speech at the opening of Birmingham Gaol in 1848, when he lauded the new separate penitentiary as a "moral hospital" for the reform of the convicts there confined.[24] Reade also shows off his great familiarity with a number of mid-century proposals for improving upon reformative discipline. Just over halfway through the novel's prison chapters, Reade causes Eden to dream of "a prison in the air—a prison with a farm, a school, and a manufactory attached" (*NTL* 202). This ideal prison, the narrator observes, combines "the good points of every system" by providing "separation and silence for those whose moral case it suits" and "[o]ccupation . . . outside the prison gates" for prisoners who deserve it (*NTL* 202). The manufactory attached to Eden's prison is distinctly Benthamite, while the measures to provide employment beyond the prison walls were already part of the Irish system administered by Sir Walter Crofton and the marks system devised by Maconochie.[25] As for the school, mid-Victorian writers like Mary Carpenter, Frederic Hill, and Dickens had argued for years that education provided the surest means of preventing future crimes.[26] Reade seems to have been aware of all these arguments before he sat to write *It Is Never Too Late to Mend*.

He also knew the Birmingham blue-books and—whatever the complaints of the separate system's defenders—used them extensively and mostly faithfully in fashioning his account of the prison. Just as Josephs and Mr. Hawes are the fictional versions of Andrews and Austin, other real Birmingham prisoners appear in Reade's reworking of the scandal. The novel's Hatchett is Birmingham's Thomas Hodgetts, and Carter is the fictional Samuel Hunt. Robinson, who was originally conceived before the scandal, is nevertheless based partly upon John Dodson, who heard Andrews's anguished screams as the boy suffered the agonies of the punishment-jacket.[27] Dodson never saw Andrews as Robinson sees Josephs, but even here Reade sticks partly to the facts. Robinson comes upon Josephs in the punishment jacket looking "white, his lips livid, his eyes . . . nearly glazed, and his teeth chatter[ing] with cold and pain"—a description that matches the testimony of a surgeon during the Birmingham investigation, who testified that severe constriction in the jacket would produce "ecchymosis" (*NTL* 100; *Truth* 13). In fact, Birmingham chaplain Sherwin Ambrose had once found Andrews strapped into the jacket so tightly that he could not even force a finger between the straps and the boy's body (*Truth* 61-62). Other prisoners testified that they had been similarly treated, and that they had been left, like Josephs and Robinson, in dark cells without bedding or food (*Truth* 39; 13). Even Hawes's rise to power at ——— Gaol recreates faithfully the real dismissal of Maconochie from Birmingham in favor of Austin, the sterner disciplinarian.[28] In the real case, as Joseph Allday writes, "Up to the time of the noble declaration of Her Majesty's Commissioners, that the Visiting Justices would be 'examined upon oath the same as other witnesses,' their favourite Governor, Lieutenant Austin, received the daily incense of their adulation" (*Truth* 3-4). The same is true at ——— Gaol, where the visiting justices are grossly reluctant to acknowledge Hawes's abuses. The justices in both instances abjure the brutal discipline only when they are called formally to account and face the prospect of looking foolish and cruel before the public.

This is not to suggest that Reade never departs from the facts in fashioning his account of the prison. He does so, sometimes unfairly, to attack those who presided over the horrors at Birmingham. There is no proof to suggest that Austin ever read *Uncle Tom's Cabin*, or that—if he did—he reacted so coarsely to its message about slavery and abuse. By the same token, though the visiting justices behaved abominably at Birmingham, they likely did not display the particular hypocrisy of Reade's Mr. Wright and Mr. Williams, who discuss Josephs's "damnable" crimes one minute and recall the next that they had great fun engaging in the same pranks when they were boys (*NTL* 108). He also neglects to have Josephs smash the glass plate on his hand-crank's index of revolutions, as Andrews did four times in his frustration over the impossible demands for labor that Austin placed upon him. Reade's aim, of course, is to make the authorities especially brutal and wicked and Josephs an unequivocal object of pity, so that we will cheer all the more when Eden consigns Hawes "to the flames of hell for ever—and for ever—and for ever" (*NTL* 285).

These distortions are deliberate and melodramatic, to be sure, but before dismissing them as mere "sensation" and "propaganda," we ought to consider what Reade's researches taught him about the Victorian prison. He learned that the prison inflicted psychological transformations—for good and for ill—wholly beyond the power of facts alone to explain. He also learned from the Birmingham scandal that "facts" could be manipulated, hidden, and misrecorded in ways that made strict factual accounting impossible. As Reade wrote in "A Terrible Temptation":

> I . . . discovered terrible things: a cap of torture and infection in one northern gaol: in a southern gaol the prisoners were wakened several times at night, and their reason shaken thereby. In another gaol I found an old man sinking visibly to his grave under the system; nobody doubted it, nobody cared. In another, the chaplain, though a great enthusiast, let out that a woman had been put into the "black hole" by the gaoler, against his advice, and taken out a lunatic, and was still a lunatic, and the visiting justices had treated the case with levity.[29]

Beneath the explicit disciplinary methods of the separate system, Reade discovered, there lurked horrors of all kinds—horrors for which the factual records of imprisonment did not account. When Eden describes Hawes's day-book to the Home Office as a "tissue of frauds, equivocations, exaggerations, diminutions, and direct falsehoods," he voices

Reade's anxieties about the insufficiency of facts in accounting for the Victorian prison (*NTL* 187).

This explains why, despite his determination to write a documentary novel, Reade obsessively points to the ways in which prisoners are read, interpreted, and invented by agents of the prison. Touring ——— Gaol for the first time, Eden takes notes on the prisoners' appearances and mannerisms and asks Mr. Lepel to do the same, though separately from himself. Reade juxtaposes the two sets of notes in order to show the different versions of "truth" they produce. Lepel's notes reflect the credulous separate-system zeal that Reade encountered in the writings of Field and Kingsmill. Of convict no. 37 Lepel remarks, "[a] very promising subject, penitent and resigned. . . . Has learned 250 texts, and is learning fifteen a day" (*NTL* 128). Eden, on the other hand, sees through this religious humbug, making a note to "[p]ray for this self-deceiver as I would for a murderer" (*NTL* 128). Lepel calls old Strutt "[s]ullen, impenitent, and brutal," while Eden reads these qualities as signs of "deep depression" and goes on to muse, "I much fear the want of light, and air, and society is crushing him" (*NTL* 128). In Robinson, Lepel sees a "bad subject, rebellious and savage," and he reflects with satisfaction that "the discipline" will eventually crush and soften him, but Eden reads Robinson's behavior as evidence that he is "surely . . . a great sufferer" and prays for enlightenment so that he can guide this object of sympathy (*NTL* 129). These competing accounts of the prisoners at ——— Gaol underscore Reade's awareness that the real "truth" about these prisoners is hidden and internal, subject to construction and interpretation. They show also the power that the prison's agents wield over that truth as they attempt to account for each inmate's idiosyncratic reaction to confinement.

The narrator remarks, tellingly, during the prison chapters of *It Is Never Too Late to Mend* that "every cell [is] a volume" in the prison's vast tale (*NTL* 194). To the extent that this is true, Reade's departures from fact in this novel are less distortions and exaggerations than attempts to penetrate to the very heart of Victorian imprisonment. Reade's researches into imprisonment and its effects had taught him that the real story of confinement is private and psychological—is fundamentally about, that is, how a prisoner is either mentally broken or morally reformed by the rigors of solitary confinement. If Reade wished to narrate every "volume" of the prison novel, therefore, he needed to account for each inmate's idiosyncratic response to the cell. Indeed, it is clear that after the fact, at least, Reade acknowledged that he had overstepped strict factual bounds in order to provide a prison novel that penetrated nearer to the truth than any documentary could have. As he wrote to a reader in 1857:

> Those black facts have been before the public before ever I han-
> dled them; they have been told, and tolerably well told, by many
> chroniclers. But it is my business, and my art, and my duty, to
> make you ladies and gentlemen *realize* things, which the chroni-
> cler presents to you in his dim, and cold, and shadowy way . . .[30]

To draw the true horrors of the Birmingham scandal out from the shadows—and, for that matter, to tell adequately the story of Thomas
Robinson's reformation—Reade needed to press beyond the facts, to
interpret and invent the private stories of confinement that, together, tell
the story of the prison. He did so by appropriating the separate prison's
own methods of accounting for the self in the cell.

III

Reade did not embrace such opportunities for psychological exposition.
Phillips suggests that Reade, like other sensation novelists, "rejected psychological analysis and exposition" and relied instead upon dramatiza-
tion of intense emotional and psychological states.[31] Sutcliffe, though he
characterizes Reade more kindly as a "transitional" author in psychological narrative, still argues that Reade's approach to psychological exposition is characterized by narrative evasion rather than intrusion.[32] Perhaps
the best example of Reade's evasiveness is the rather unsatisfactory
account the narrator gives of Susan Merton's grief when George departs
for Australia. Like Pickwick when he cannot handle the emotional intensity of the Fleet, Susan locks herself in her bedroom, leaving the narrator
to remark:

> What she suffered . . . the first month after George's departure I
> could detail perhaps as well as any man living; but I will not;
> there is a degree of anguish one shrinks from intruding upon too
> familiarly in person: and even on paper the microscope should
> spare sometimes these beatings of the bared heart. (*NTL* 43)

The comment is, of course, narrative posturing: Reade did not excel at
psychological exposition and knew that he did not. He banishes Susan,
as a consequence, to a cell of her own so that he may excuse himself from
the responsibility of narrating her private thoughts. Ironically, this was
precisely the path that Reade could not take later in the novel if he
wished to penetrate the truth about separate confinement. Robinson and
Josephs *must* be narrated in their separate cells. More to the point, they
must be narrated in ways that expose the psychological trials their confinement engenders, so that readers can come to "realise" the prison's
power both to maim and to reform the private self. In the prison chap-

ters of *It Is Never Too Late to Mend*, we find Reade experimenting with methods of psychological exposition that will allow him to invent prisoner psychology without violating the apparent honesty of his documentary fiction. In the main, these methods are the prison's own.

As in Dickens's early prison accounts—and in the writings of men like Clay and Field besides—the scars upon prisoner bodies in Reade's novel provide a legible register of the effects of confinement. Josephs, having long suffered from Hawes's malice, has been physically shattered. "The result was that his flesh withered on his bones; his eyes were dim, and seemed to lie at the bottom of two caverns; he crawled stiffly and slowly instead of walking" (*NTL* 214). Hawes has "extinguished his youth," we are told, and perhaps more effectively than he realizes: as his eventual suicide proves, the boy is much nearer to death at the age of fifteen than are many men thrice his age (*NTL* 214). When Robinson nearly dies in the punishment jacket, his body also becomes a text of his suffering. He is "black in the face, his lips livid, insensible, throttled, and dying," and when the warders scrub him roughly in an effort to revive him, his flesh turns "red as blood" (*NTL* 105). As the prison chapters progress, prisoners' bodies become much more reliable texts of imprisonment than even the spoken words of the convicts who bear the marks. When Eden shows Mr. Lacy around the prison in an effort to prove that Hawes abuses the inmates, bodies rather than words become the surest access to truth. In one cell, Eden orders a prisoner to strip and show his back, "striped livid and red by the cutting straps" of the punishment jacket (*NTL* 258). Two prisoners tell Lacy they have been treated "like Mr. Hawes's own children" but are made liars by scars their bodies cannot conceal (*NTL* 259). Eden tells Lacy, "[U]se your eyes," and forces him to take notice of one prisoner's "hollow eye and faded cheek . . . trembling frame, and . . . halting pulse"; Eden forces the other prisoner to strip so that Lacy can see his "emaciated person and several large livid stripes on his back" (*NTL* 259). At times Reade's account of prisoner bodies even seems to borrow directly from Dickens's work, as with the aged and distracted Strutt who bears a remarkable resemblance to the German prisoner of *American Notes*, and Robinson's thought that his separate confinement is like being "buried alive" (*NTL* 95).

By elevating these marks upon prisoners' bodies to the status of "evidence" during Lacy's investigation, Reade replicates the very methods of reading and interpretation validated by real prison chaplains inside England's separate-system prisons. He suggests, as they did, that learning to "read" these marks is necessary to any coherent account of the cell. Isaac Levi is able to serve as the novel's benevolent *deus ex machina* precisely because he owns this skill. He comprehends in a "lightning flash" that John Meadows and Will Fielding both love Merton, for he reads both men "to the bottom line of their hearts. For two hours he had followed the text, word by word, deed by deed, letter by letter, and now a comment on that text was written in these faces" (*NTL* 30). Eden shares this ability to read others from the moment he enters the novel. The first time he meets Susan, he reads her hidden sorrow over George's emigration:

> Shall I tell you how I know? You often yawn and often sigh; when these two things come together at your age they are signs of a heavy grief; then it comes out that you have lost your relish for things that once pleased you. . . . You are in grief, and no common grief. (*NTL* 69)

Eden begins his acquaintance with the characters in this novel, then, as an amateur psychoanalyst, "reading" the behaviors and countenances of those around him for hidden meanings. On what authority he does so is quite another matter.

The narrator intimates that Levi's ability to read others comes from his vast experience of the world and the people in it. The mind is to Levi "a little human chart spread out flat before him, and not a region in it he had not travelled and surveyed before to-day" (*NTL* 29). Because he can treat the mind of Meadows as a "text" and "chart," he proves eminently able to frustrate Meadows's machinations against George and Susan. We have no basis for knowing, though, whether Eden's wisdom about Susan's grief also comes from old experience—whether Eden, too, has suffered loss and pain. We know only that experience *does* seem to serve Eden when he begins to interpret the marks etched by the prison. Upon his arrival at ———— Gaol, Eden asks Lepel and Evans to lock him in the dark cell for the evening so that he may learn what prisoners suffer when they are sent there. When Eden is released from dark solitude and Hawes asks him to describe the experience, Eden refuses, saying only, "I shall have the honour of telling you that in private, Mr. Hawes" (*NTL* 127). The chaplain also submits to be bound in the punishment jacket for one half-hour so he can learn what prisoners endure under the torment, and he encourages Evans to do the same. For Eden, reading the meaning of imprisonment seems to depend upon experiencing for himself the individual and idiosyncratic trials of the self in the cell. Having fashioned himself into a perfect tool for the discovery of this individual account of confinement, Eden becomes the novel's primary guide to the prison's truth. He uncovers the fraud of Hawes's day-book and bares prisoner bodies to the scrutiny of Mr. Lacy. It is also significant that he refuses to tell Evans about his time in the punishment-jacket, much as he has refused to discuss dark solitude publicly with Hawes. He tells Evans instead, "such knowledge can never be imparted by description; you shall take your turn in the jacket" (*NTL* 134).

If Eden is correct in asserting that knowledge about the prison "can never be imparted by description," then Reade's project in *It Is Never Too Late to Mend* is on tenuous ground. Reade wished to write a documentary novel and get at the "truth" about confinement, but here he suggests that no novel can convey adequately the story of imprisonment no matter how it sets about attempting the task. Representation cannot replace experience; making the torment imposed by the punishment jacket into an object of narration is no substitute for subjective knowledge. The novel's ensuing scene, however, implicitly revises Eden's thesis as we watch Evans suffer his turn in the jacket. While Evans is tormented and constricted, Eden begins to narrate the peculiar physical and psychological sensations he felt during his own experiment: first, a "terrible sense of utter impotence, then . . . racking cramps . . . The jagged collar gave me much pain too; it rasped my poor throat like a file" (*NTL* 135). Evans berates the chaplain for not having told him these things before, but Eden slyly responds, "I had my reasons for not telling you," and departs (*NTL* 135). On the surface, Eden's decision to withhold information about the particular pains inflicted by the jacket seems designed simply to convince Evans that the jacket is not so bad, and that the guard should try it himself. But the moment is also powerfully suggestive, in two primary ways. First, it is so because it shows that Eden acquires the power to narrate on Evans's behalf the moment that Evans submits to the jacket—the moment, that is, that Evans becomes a prisoner. Second, it suggests that Eden's new power to narrate manifests itself primarily as an imposition of his subjectivity upon Evans, so that the story that masquerades as an account of Evans's torments in the jacket really recalls Eden's own. Persuading Evans to become a prisoner himself, Eden suddenly becomes an "authority" on imprisonment, capable of delivering a socially legitimate—if invented and displaced—account of the self in the cell.

It Is Never Too Late to Mend recreates the prisoner's narrative subjugation, too, by replicating the disciplinary logic of the separate-system Victorian prison. Like his real-life counterparts, Eden sets his inmates to compose autobiographies that he intends to read, interpret, and edit to ensure that they tell the truth about confinement. He instructs them "to review their past lives candidly, and to relate them simply, with reflections" so that the self-narratives can serve as beacons to others and reformative tools to themselves (*NTL* 176). He tells Robinson particularly to write "[t]he only kind of story that is worth a button—a true story" and advises him not to "dress or cook [his] facts" (*NTL* 238). In words that recall Levi's ability to study human motivations and desire, Eden even tells Robinson, "When your own life lies thus spread out before you like a map, you will find you regret many things you have done, and view others with calmer and wiser eyes; for self-review is a healthy process" (*NTL* 238). What Eden means, of course, is that self-review is "healthy" because he himself intends to supervise the inmates' autobiographical productions and judge whether these speak the factual and moral truth. When a female prisoner calls herself "unfortunate" in her title, Eden criticizes her choice of words:

> "Unfortunate means one whom we are bound to respect as
> well as pity. Has that been your character?"
> "No," was the mournful reply.
> "Then why print a falsehood?" (*NTL* 177)

In this swift exchange Eden banishes the young woman's narrative construction of her identity in favor of his own telling. Under Eden's orders, she changes "unfortunate" to "penitent" and reconceives the entire meaning of her self and self-account (*NTL* 177).

Had Reade not finally excised Robinson's autobiography from *It Is Never Too Late to Mend*, the novel would have made this point about imprisonment and narrative power even more clear. The success of his prison novel convinced Reade to publish *The Autobiography of a Thief* separately in 1858. In the "Introductory" note to the piece, Reade proclaimed tellingly that this companion would supplement the novel's "water colour" portrait of Robinson with the thief's painting "in oils by himself, and retouched by Mr. Eden" (*AT* 1). Though Robinson self-narrates his criminal past, imprisonment, and remorse, Eden rather than Robinson has the final word. *The Autobiography of a Thief* seems at first as if it will consist of Robinson's straightforward self-narration of his adventures as a thief, a coiner, a sham-druggist, and perhaps even a rapist. But before long Eden's notations begin to punctuate and interrupt Robinson's words. At one point, Eden simply corrects the wording: "'Collected' and 'took with me.' No such thing. 'Stole' is the word that represents the transactions" (*AT* 20). At another, when Robinson recounts a robbery he committed one Sunday while the owners of the house were at church, Eden derides Robinson for egotism and accuses him of trying to disguise self-congratulation as remorse. Robinson recalls having left the family the cruelly mocking note, "Watch as well as pray!" an action of which the thief says he now feels ashamed (*AT* 17). "Ashamed?" Eden chides. "The little humbug could not resist showing me his wit, of which he says he is ashamed" (*AT* 21). When Robinson expresses deep sorrow for having violated the only woman he ever loved, Eden remarks coolly that Robinson "never really loved" this "poor girl" and demands that he not flatter himself otherwise (*AT* 21). We must assume that Eden does not share with Robinson any such experiences of dissolution and wickedness. Even so, Eden presumes repeatedly to know Robinson's innermost thoughts and to understand the thief's narrative far more thoroughly than its author. Though the final version of the novel does not contain Robinson's autobiography, it does reflect Eden's confidence that he—not the narrating prisoner—holds power over the thief's private narrative truth.

The novel's determination to penetrate individual and idiosyncratic truths about Victorian confinement thus shapes up as a struggle for narrative power, in which the novel and Eden alike adopt the prison's power to narrate the self in the cell. Though Robinson and the "penitent" young woman try to author their own lives, it is always Eden, the editing and interpreting other, who invents and fixes the meanings their self-accounts will convey. Robinson's near-relapse into thievery and dissipation once he reaches Australia may indicate that Eden was right to criticize the thief's pretensions to moral awakening and reform. The "penitent" woman's easy acquiescence to Eden's criticism may suggest that he has divined her secret motives shrewdly and correctly. But the novel shows after all that the relative merit of Eden's editorial comments matters far less than his power to impose those comments upon prisoners who have lost control over their own stories. That power derives from the prison, which presumes *prima facie* that the inmate is guilty, and that he cannot narrate his story honestly or fully. Only when prisoner autobiographies become stories-within-the-story told by Eden do they take their proper place as the truth about the prison. Only when a credible narrator assumes control over the story of the inmate can that story penetrate to the heart of Victorian confinement. In the prison's narrative logic, *It Is Never Too Late to Mend* finds that authority by which it, too, can move beyond the plain facts to invent an account of the psychological transformations inflicted by the cell.

Perhaps this is why our narrator shows none of his old reticence about interior exposition when prisoners—rather than Susan—are the objects of narrative intrusion and invention. Critics have treated the scene of Josephs's last hours alive as the greatest example of Reade's attempt to create melodrama in handling the materials he borrowed from Birmingham. This is undoubtedly true. But ignoring the other part of Reade's extensive investigations into separate discipline, they have neglected to notice that the prison's own narrative logic authorizes the liberties Reade takes with the facts of the case. The scene begins in Josephs's separate cell after Hodges has taken away the boy's bedding and light, and at first the narrator seems only mildly inclined to intrude upon private thoughts. As the novel nears the moment at which Josephs decides to enact his self-destruction, however, the narrator goes on to conduct a much more powerful rendering, beginning—almost like Dickens's account of the Eastern Penitentiary's solitary prisoner—with the explicit tag, "Thus ran his thoughts" (*NTL* 222). What follows is hardly Joycean stream-of-consciousness, but it is interior monologue—a deliberate attempt to capture the progress of the boy's thoughts as he moves psychologically toward despair and suicide. "I wonder what Hawes was going to do with me to-morrow," his thoughts run, "[s]omething worse than all I have gone through, he said. That seems hard to believe" (*NTL* 222). His mind turns next to Robinson, then to the fate of his soul if he kills himself. He wonders, too, whether hanging himself will much hurt. Once, his resolution wavers fleetingly when he thinks, "My mother will fret," but he reminds himself that he "should be dead any way before the fourteen days [without bedding or light] were out" (*NTL* 223). At the end, he asks silently for his mother's and God's forgiveness then hangs himself before his "hands [are] crippled with cold" (*NTL* 222).

Sutcliffe argues, perhaps naively, that it is ridiculous that a young man "should ponder suicide in an orderly, rational way," but in the process he ignores a much more important point.[33] In the end, it matters less that Reade does an unspectacular job of providing interior narration than that he should attempt to provide it at all. Reade tested the facts of the prison during three years of research, and—though Josephs is based upon flesh-and-blood prisoner Edward Andrews—he found those facts wanting. Unlike Reade's other melodramatic exaggerations and distortions, those we find in Josephs's last hours alive do not merely invent what characters said or what abuses prisoners were forced to endure. Instead, Reade's narrator adopts the self-narrative "I" and "me," speaking for and as Josephs and, in a way, as the real Andrews as well. More important, he does these things in order to help his readers "realise" those truths that chroniclers of facts cannot convey. Neither Reade (in accounting for Andrews) nor his narrator (in accounting for Josephs) employs a narrative strategy that has not already been tested and legitimized by the prison. The portrait of imprisonment Reade creates in *It Is Never Too Late to Mend* is thus as true a portrait as can possibly be conceived, or at least as true a portrait as prisons, their official records, and their chaplains ever provide. He turns Josephs into a narrative object by masquerading as the narrating subject, after the very fashion of the penitentiary's narrative agents.

The same thing happens in the case of Robinson, whose time in solitude becomes the most complete psychological study of the novel. Reade treats Robinson's solitary confinement differently at various points in the novel. During the thief's first days in jail, the narrative of his imprisonment remains distant from his private thoughts. He is "dull and lonely" during his first day in the prison and eats his gruel slowly "to eke out a few minutes in the heavy day" (*NTL* 92). We also learn twice in three paragraphs—rather artlessly—that Robinson feels "dismay" at the various disciplinary practices of the prison, almost as if Reade is incapable of inventing a more idiosyncratic reaction to confinement or even of producing a new adjective (*NTL* 91). This inability to render Robinson's private self seems, at least, to stem from the thief's psychological stasis during the early days of his confinement. Like Susan's self-imposed isolation earlier in the novel, Robinson's period of solitude carries no particular psychological implications. It marks no moment of passage from one mental condition to another. With no psychological transformation at the heart of Robinson's early confinement, Reade leaves the thief's thoughts comfortably unexplored. On day five of his imprisonment, Robinson feels the "heavy hours, like leaden waves . . . roll over his head and suffocate him, and weigh him down, down, down to bottomless despair," and five days later Robinson emerges from the "black-hole" trembling and sobbing, "white as a sheet" and eyes dazzled by the light (*NTL* 93; 94). But he is no nearer to reform, nor has he spent time engaged in the self-reflection at which the separate system aims. Instead, he has turned every thought to the possibility of human contact, work to perform, and other means of lightening the burden of his solitude. The stasis of his character, at least this early in his sentence, precludes any need to account for his psychological trials.

This changes when Robinson returns to dark solitude, for his second term in isolation drives him to revise his self-understanding according to the aims of the prison. The scene begins as an explicit attempt to transform and destroy Robinson—to enact Hawes's determination to "break" the thief's mind and will (*NTL* 144). Hour by hour the novel tracks the course of the thief's descent into mental trauma, and with each hour the narrator undertakes more detailed psychological exposition. Robinson enters the dark cell at six o'clock in the evening filled with "rage and wild desire for vengeance," and he spends his first hour—like his first days of separate confinement—doing rather than thinking (*NTL* 147). But finally the lack of light and sound drives him to the very self-contemplation to which the prison has tried to force him since he entered. The rest of the passage mixes Robinson's voice and the narrator's in a riveting portrait of growing self-awareness and despair. First, Robinson contemplates his wretchedness, but soon he directs another volley of anger at Hawes for trying to drive him "to Bedlam" (*NTL* 148). "Patience," Robinson reminds himself, "or I shall go mad," but soon he falls again to cursing and weeping (*NTL* 148). By the third hour he feels the anguish of his "past . . . coming with all its weight upon him," and, all at once, he feels his guilt and a sharp fear for his unclean soul if Hawes should leave him in the cell to die (*NTL* 148). "Thus passed more than two hours; and now remorse and memory concentrated themselves on one dark spot in this man's history": the sexual violation of the woman he has loved (*NTL* 149). By hour six, Robinson's psychological torment is so acute that the narrator confirms the thief is "going mad," a fate from which Eden saves him by arriving at the door of his cell and speaking the word "BROTHER!" loudly enough for Robinson to hear (*NTL* 149). The word interrupts Robinson's moment of inner turmoil and trial, ends his transformation, and—in so doing—erases the need for further psychological exposition.

IV

Though Eden brings to a premature end Reade's psychological exploration of the solitary Victorian prisoner, the scenes of Josephs's and Robinson's periods of solitude and psychological trial still illustrate several critical points about the relationship between the prison and the novel at the middle of the nineteenth century. These scenes are important partly because Reade delivers them at all, considering his reticence to undertake psychological exposition in Susan's case earlier in the novel. The question, of course, is why Reade provides interior narrative in two cases but not in the third. In part, that decision seems to stem from a qualitative difference between Josephs's and Robinson's solitary confinements, on one hand, and Susan's on the other, for of the three only Susan undergoes no discernible psychological transformation as a result of her solitude. Of course, this may seem so simply because Reade shows us so little of her—so little of her, in fact, that it is hard to see why he might ever have considered giving her name to the novel. Conversely, Josephs's and Robinson's moments of solitude *must* be narrated precisely because their solitude engenders fundamental transformations of self and self-understanding, and because these transformations constitute the truth Reade wishes us to realize about the Victorian prison. Whether the result of discipline was Josephs's despair or Robinson's reform, Reade needed to narrate these psychological implications if he wanted his novel to tell the truth about Victorian confinement. In this sense Reade implies in *It Is Never Too Late to Mend* that his documentary novel presents a truer account of the prison by becoming implicitly inventive rather than factual.

   It Is Never Too Late to Mend is also crucial because it shows us that Reade drew quite deliberately and directly from the prison's own narrative models as he considered justifications and strategies for narrating the private self. He takes great pains to show us the "true" and fabricated versions of official prison records and the different conclusions at which

Eden and Lepel arrive when they take notes on —— Gaol's prisoners. He is careful in *The Autobiography of a Thief* to imitate and reveal the prison's explicit power to control private narrative, and to shape discursively the "truth" about prisoner identity and desire. Indeed, like the Victorian separate prison Reade's novel suggests that criminality and psychological disruption must be narrated from outside, since the criminal or disrupted subject cannot be trusted to tell its own story honestly or completely. This suggests, too, that Susan goes unnarrated because her "normality" precludes the need for any interference from a narrator located outside the private self. Within the confines of Robinson's autobiography, Eden assumes this narrative power over the criminal self. Within the novel as a whole, the narrator assumes it, and he undertakes to narrate Josephs and Robinson to their psychological cores. At bottom, as Reade's novel repeatedly suggests, the ability to narrate the Victorian prisoner does not depend upon facts or experience. It depends only upon power—power that is reflected and refracted from the narrative authority reposed in the prison.

The prison seems simultaneously to have driven Reade to the necessity of psychological exposition and to have provided the strategies he required to undertake it. To the extent that this is so, his novel begins to indicate the ways in which the penitentiary both demanded and helped to shape increasingly interior narratives of the self. Curiously, though Reade vilified Birmingham Gaol and its abominable scandal, he retained enough faith in separate discipline to stand by his novel's titular thesis in drawing Robinson's story and to remain apparently unconcerned by the implicit dangers of the prison's narrative power over the confined. Indeed, had the champions of Victorian separate discipline only been wise enough to see it, they would have recognized that Reade's novel attacks only those who, like Hawes and Austin, *abused* the principles of separate discipline. Eden does little more in this novel than return the prison to its correct and lawful operation as a tool of psychological transformation and an institution designed to wrest self-narrative power away from the self in the cell. Though the authors who followed him in writing of the prison were terrified by the prison's power to do these things, neither the psychological nor the narrative implications of Victorian separate confinement seem to have troubled Reade. Of Reade's prison novel, it is enough to note that the great interest of the book has very little to do with whether he did or did not make certain facts about Birmingham melodramatic when he incorporated them into his fiction. The great interest is rather that *It Is Never Too Late to Mend*, the most factual and documentary of Victorian prison novels, reaches its greatest truths about confinement in bursts of proto-Freudian narration authorized by the prison's own power to invent the self in the cell.

Chapter 4

"How Not to Do It": Dickens, the Prison, and the Failure of Omniscience

The house of fiction has in short not one window, but a million—a number of possible windows . . . They are but windows at the best, mere holes in a dead wall, disconnected, perched aloft; they are not hinged doors opening straight upon life. But they have this mark of their own that at each of them stands a figure with a pair of eyes, or at least with a field-glass, which forms, again and again, for observation, a unique instrument, insuring to the person making use of it an impression distinct from every other.

—Henry James, *The Art of the Novel*

W HILE CHARLES READE COULD WRITE HOPEFULLY ABOUT REFORMATIVE discipline as late as 1856, by then Dickens had abandoned such great expectations of the prison. Dickens's early novels had deplored debtors' prisons and the squalid misery of Newgate. After his 1842 visit to America he opposed separate confinement bitterly as well, so much so that in 1850 he lampooned Pentonville's "Model Prisoners" in *David Copperfield* with the new but unimproved Uriah Heep, and he recorded his "grave objections" to separation that same year in a piece he wrote for *Household Words*.[1] As Dickens settled into middle age, he seems to have grown increasingly cynical about the notion that *any* disciplinary program could reform England's criminals. Reviewing Frederic Hill's *Crime: Its Amount, Causes and Remedies* in 1853 for *Household Words*, Dickens chastised Hill for "[c]onsidering prisons as hospitals for cure . . . [but] forget[ting] how often they would be hospitals for incurables."[2] He went on to ask:

103

> Does he think it possible that the twelve professional thieves of
> East Lothian; the fifty or sixty thieves of Inverness; or the woman
> of eighteen years' law and window-breaking experience who was
> committed to jail seventeen times in twenty-eight days; could
> ever be made to serve in the ranks of honest folk by any sort of
> such hospital treatment as he recommends?[3]

Apparently Hill did think so, and a decade earlier Dickens had thought so, too. By 1860, though, a surlier Dickens demanded "to have the Ruffian kept out of my way, and out of the way of all decent people," even if that required "perpetual imprisonment."[4] He also—despite unwavering opposition to capital punishment during the 1840s—bristled angrily in 1859 over the trial of a surgeon found guilty of poisoning his wife, writing to Forster that he wished to "hang any Home Secretary . . . who should step in between that black scoundrel and the gallows."[5] Dickens may have been expressing privately a ferocity that he did not really feel, or at least that he would not have owned to publicly. Even so, these comments sound unlike the Dickens who had earlier advocated the "total abolition of the Punishment of Death, as a general principle," befriended Maconochie and Chesterton, and proposed a version of the "marks system" to Angelina Burdett Coutts.[6] Arrived at economic and artistic maturity, Dickens took up the new penal motto, "Always a Ruffian, always a Thief. Always a Thief, always a Ruffian."[7] It is no wonder that Philip Collins concludes in *Dickens and Crime* that the young social reformer became in middle age a conservative social thinker whose opinions on penal matters were "running level with, or even behind, public opinion."[8] In some ways, Dickens scarcely resembled by the 1850s the man who had written *Pickwick Papers* and *American Notes*.

It is tempting to assume on these grounds that Dickens's mature prison novels, *Little Dorrit* and *A Tale of Two Cities*, reflect deepening cynicism regarding Victorian confinement. This is true at least to the extent that these novels—unlike *Pickwick Papers*—surround their prisons with grim, confining worlds. *Little Dorrit's* Marshalsea is only one of that novel's prisons, all of which tend to waste bodies, shatter minds, and destroy individual identity. *A Tale of Two Cities'* Bastille does the same within the brutal context of revolutionary France. But the fact of the matter is that Dickens could hardly have reached bleaker conclusions about prisons and their effects than he had reached in *Pickwick Papers* and *American Notes*. Whether part of his early or late fiction, Dickens's accounts of the prison all testify to the prison's power to wound and maim. William Dorrit is destroyed no more completely by the debtors' prison than is the Chancery prisoner of *Pickwick Papers*, nor does solitary confinement take a greater psychological toll upon Alexandre Manette than upon the hypothetical solitary inmate of *American Notes*. In the end, the difference between Dickens's mature accounts of confinement and his early ones has far less to do with his conclusions about the effects of imprisonment than with his sense of how these effects ought to be expressed. In *Little Dorrit* and *A Tale of Two Cities*, Dickens suggests that the experience of the Victorian prisoner can only be expressed adequately in the form of a first-person account narrated by the self in the cell.

Dickens did not, like Reade, require an explicit model to compose such an account, or to justify its inclusion within a realistic portrayal of the cell. He had instead imagination and reputation, not to mention his own private struggles with the psychological consequences of confinement. Scenes in *Pickwick Papers* had been drawn from his memories of the Marshalsea, and his fascination with prisons generally had emerged in various novels since. But not until 1847, when he told Forster his history, did Dickens begin in earnest to work out narratively his complex apprehension of the prison. He first attempted the autobiography that Forster saw in January of 1849, and that Dickens intended would "be found among [his] papers when its subject should be concluded" (*Letters* VII 544). Approaching the painful episode of his failed romance with Maria Beadnell, though, he claimed to have "lost courage and burned the rest" (*Letters* VII 544). Whether or not he really destroyed the manuscript, Dickens likely did stop writing the autobiography when he reached the period of his young manhood. We know for certain that he abandoned it early in 1849 so that he could begin *David Copperfield*. This novel, too, returned to Dickens's memories of the Marshalsea by making the Micawbers David's surrogate family and thrusting them into the King's Bench Prison. Peter Ackroyd believes that many of Dickens's memories find their way "practically unchanged" into *David Copperfield*'s account of the Micawbers, and Edgar Johnson argues that there is something "almost compulsive in [Dickens's] hovering return to the Marshalsea" that "reveals how deep had been the wound of his childhood humiliation and grief."[9] For Dickens, these compulsive narrative returns to the debtors' prison were intensely personal, touching as they did upon questions of his own psychological wounds and private identity. This may explain why, late in the 1840s, he turned for the first time to first-person narration in his attempts to account for the Marshalsea and its enduring effects upon his character. As Dickens's last sustained narrative return to the debtors' prison, *Little Dorrit* is one culmination of his compulsion to narrate the cell, and it records his struggle to find an adequate means of expressing confinement.

That struggle also took its shape from Dickens's memories of the Eastern Penitentiary, and the ways he planned to use those memories in his mature fiction. In *American Notes*, Dickens concluded his account of the Eastern Penitentiary by writing:

> In every little chamber that I entered, and at every grate through which I looked, I seemed to see the same appalling countenance. It lives in my memory, with the fascination of a remarkable picture. Parade before my eyes, a hundred men, with one among them newly released from this solitary suffering, and I would point him out. (*AN* 108–109)

From that day the image of the Eastern Penitentiary inmate, "buried alive; to be dug out in the slow round of years," became grist for Dickens's imaginative mill (*AN* 101). Toying with ideas for a new fiction in 1846, Dickens considered the "idea of a man imprisoned for ten or fifteen years," the time of imprisonment constituting a narrative gap between the two parts of the story.[10] Nine years later, as he wrote the early chapters of *Little Dorrit*, he recorded a similar idea, scribbling in his notebook the possibility of writing next "a story in two periods—with a lapse of time between, like a French Drama."[11] In part, Dickens's mention of French drama reflects his collaborative dramatic work with Wilkie Collins during this period, which led Dickens onto the stage in 1857 as an actor in Collins's *The Frozen Deep* (1858). The combination of imprisonment, narrative gap, and French subject matter points as well toward *A Tale of Two Cities*. But perhaps the most important aspect of Dickens's ruminations over his future novel is this hint that, even as he wrote *Little Dorrit*, he came to envision imprisonment not only as a means of psychological transformation but also as an absence rather than presence of the story.

These two conceptions of the prison—as intensely psychological in its operation and as a narrative absence from the novel—shape Dickens's mature accounts of the cell. On one hand, in what they say of the prison's power to transform prisoners, *Little Dorrit* and *A Tale of Two Cities* do little more than extend Dickens's conclusions in *Pickwick Papers* and *American Notes* about the effects of confinement. On the other, Dickens's mature novels take up the question of narrative form, experimenting with methods for acknowledging and narrating the gap constituted by the Victorian prison. In *Pickwick Papers*, Dickens had acknowledged the gap simply by replicating it—by thrusting Pickwick and his psychological transformation behind the closed door of his solitary cell. *American Notes* had narrated the gap only by underscoring the narrative's inventedness rather than its truth. Dickens's mature prison fictions neither evade nor apologize for the necessity of narrating the cell; instead, they take up the challenge of that narration, attempting to acknowledge the prison's inviolable privacy and to narrate anyway the psychological traumas the cell engenders. In *Little Dorrit* and *A Tale of Two Cities*, Dickens figures the prison as a narrative gap that cannot be accounted for by omniscience but instead must be rendered as the first-person narrative of the self in the cell.

II

Dickens's private letters show that he began *Little Dorrit* with a narrative experiment in mind. In March of 1855 he wrote to Elisha Morgan that he was "in the first stage of a new book, which consists in going round and round the idea, as you see a bird in his cage go about and about his sugar before he touches it" (*Letters* VII 571–572). In this image of the birdcage that recalls *Pickwick Papers'* "prison within a prison," Dickens envisioned his new novel. This letter suggests the germ of *Little Dorrit's* Circumlocution Office, of course, but it also shows that Dickens meant his novel as a narrative performance of circumlocution, not just a dissertation upon it. He meant the novel, in other words, to show "how not to do it" at the level of narrative exposition. He also wished to approximate this technique in narrating private identity and desire. Explaining to Forster his aim with Miss Wade's "History of a Self-Tormentor," Dickens wrote of having "had an idea, which [he] thought a new one, of making the introduced story so fit into surroundings impossible of separation from the main story, as to make the blood of the book circulate through both" (*Letters* VIII 280). He hoped to avoid direct psychological exposition with Miss Wade, wanting instead to make her psychological meanings emerge into the visible world of the novel's action. In the end, Dickens and Forster both believed the experiment failed, and the final version of *Little Dorrit* reflects the rather unsatisfactory resolution to the problem: Miss Wade's "History" is formally separated from the novel's omniscient narrative, so that it stands out as starkly as *Pickwick Papers'* interpolated tales. Though Dickens did not realize it, no other conclusion to his experiment could have reinforced so completely his critique of circumlocution. *Little Dorrit's* omniscient narration, circumlocutory as it is, performs in Miss Wade's case the very narrative failure that Dickens wished to express: the failure of omniscience to narrate adequately the private self.

In a novel that centers upon prisons and prisoners, this failure is a crucial narrative concern. By 1855 Dickens recognized fully the privacy of the traumas inflicted by the prison. To the extent that narrating the prison requires accounting for the private self, *Little Dorrit's* several prisoners remain fundamentally unavailable to the story omniscience tells. On one hand, of course, omniscience accounts for each of the novel's prisons: the criminal jail and the quarantine barracks at Marseilles; the sepulchral Clennam house; the joyless homes of London's working poor;

the dismal Marshalsea; and even London itself. On the other, though we see these prisons, the novel insists that we do not see them entirely, for something of the prison always baffles the omniscient stare. Partly the obscurity of *Little Dorrit*'s prisons is physical, characterized by shadows that constantly shroud the novel's cells. But by taking considerable pains at the start of the novel to show that the visible world is the omniscient narrator's domain, Dickens makes this physical obscurity signify a larger failure to see into the whole story of confinement. The novel suggests that no omniscient narrator can account adequately for the psychological transformation of William Dorrit in the Marshalsea, or for the indescribable taint that falls upon his children. Just as important, *Little Dorrit* insists that the privacy of the prison has been constructed deliberately by the social demand that uglinesses like criminals, debtors, and their taints be removed from the public eye. The novel's prisons are institutional manifestations of this desire to conceal misery, contain guilt, and confine difference. At the same time, the solutions to the novel's mysteries depend upon discovering these illicit secrets, so that Dickens—by insisting that the prison cannot be accounted for by omniscience—places the essential story of *Little Dorrit* beyond the power of his omniscient narrator. Thus *Little Dorrit* is enormously complex in its narrative form, for its omniscience must finally fragment into a multitude of private accounts, each of which attests to the psychological wounds inflicted by the prison.

In a recent book-length study of *Little Dorrit*, Brian Rosenberg argues that the novel is, "in most ways that matter, of a piece with Dickens's other work. He devises no new techniques here, develops no new stylistic habits, and manifests no major new concerns."[12] It is hard to know how he can reach this conclusion. Stagnation has rather been characteristic of criticism on *Little Dorrit*'s prisons than it is of the novel itself. Just after *Little Dorrit*'s first number appeared in November 1855, Hepworth Dixon pointed out in a review for the *Athenaeum* that the novel's early chapters are thematically bound by the prison, in the parallel they draw between the criminal jail and the quarantine barracks at Marseilles. In the years since, and especially during the 1940s and 1950s, critics turned often to *Little Dorrit*'s images of confinement in order to discuss the psychological consequences of the cell.[13] Edmund Wilson wrote of the novel's prisoners in *The Wound and the Bow* in 1946, and a decade later J. Hillis Miller drew from Wilson in suggesting that imprisonment in *Little Dorrit* is largely a "state of mind."[14] For Lionel Trilling, the novel is about more than prisons and prisoners, for it portrays the greater problem of "society in relation to the individual human will."[15] So thorough and convincing are these analyses that more recent critics have avoided *Little Dorrit*'s prisons, except to consider Dickens's accuracy in portraying the historical Marshalsea, or to examine the Foucaultian dimensions of the novel's omniscient stare.[16] Ultimately psychological trauma, the real physical space of the prison, and considerations of form *all* help to shape Dickens's last narrative return to the Marshalsea. The result is a novel that illustrates the failure of omniscience in accounting for the prison, and the need to narrate the prison in the first-person account of the self in the cell.

III

The first chapter of *Little Dorrit* establishes staring as the central activity of the novel. As the narrator reports on the very first page:

> Everything in Marseilles, and about Marseilles, had stared at the fervid sky, and been stared at in return, until a staring habit had become universal there. Strangers were stared out of countenance by staring white houses, staring white walls, staring white streets, staring tracts of arid road, staring hills from which verdure was burnt away.[17]

Things in Marseilles are eminently *visible*: brightly lit and dazzlingly colored, with no escape from the glare of the sun. Invited into the novel by this staring narrator who is capable of retreating to 1825, crossing the channel to the continent, and showing us Marseilles' brilliant details, we stare along with him. We stare at the curiosity of a sea demarcated into "black and blue," the line indicating the point beyond which "the pure sea would not pass" (*LD* 1). We stare also at boats without awnings that are "too hot to touch" and ships that "blister[ed] at their moorings" (*LD* 1). Thronging amid the docks and quays is a bewildering assortment of "Hindoos, Russians, Chinese, Spaniards, Portuguese, Englishmen, Frenchmen, Genoese, Neapolitans, Venetians, Greeks, Turks, descendants from all the builders of Babel" (*LD* 1). The scene is a remarkable record of difference, recorded by a narrator who can take it all in and bring it carefully into focus. While the narrator and the sun look down upon this scene, the people of Marseilles turn for protection to their "[b]linds, shutters, curtains, awnings . . . all closed and drawn to keep out the stare" (*LD* 2). From the start, that is, the novel implies that there are obstacles and limits even to what omniscience can see.

As the narrator gets on with his glaring and staring, he invites us to look especially at the novel's many prisons. The first of these is the criminal jail at Marseilles, notable chiefly for squalor that echoes *Pickwick Papers'* Fleet. The cell is "repulsive," the narrator tells us, with a "notched and disfigured bench" and a set of draughts "made of old buttons and soup bones" (*LD* 2). A "prison taint was on everything there," coating the stone with slime, the iron with rust, and even Blandois and Cavalletto with a haggardness that makes them "faded" and indistinct (*LD* 2). Elsewhere in Marseilles, the fellow travelers enjoy the more wholesome prison of the quarantine barracks, though it threatens to afflict them with "the plague" (*LD* 15). As the novel's early chapters continue, the omniscient narrator spies ever more variations of the prison. "[G]loomy, close and stale" London is a Sabbath-day jail to its "million or so of human beings," who have been sentenced to "daily labour, six days in the week . . . the sweet sameness of which they had no escape between the cradle and the grave" (*LD* 26; 29). "Clearly," the narrator observes, the poor "could want nothing but a stringent policeman" to complete their Sabbath rest and ease (*LD* 29).[18] The Clennam house is but one of these London prisons, and the narrator takes great pains to show that it looks every bit the part.[19] It has a courtyard surrounded by "rusty" railings and has been arrested, so to speak, in the course of its collapse by "some half dozen gigantic crutches" that brace against its sideways slide (*LD* 32). Inside are a cellaret like a coffin and an old dark closet, plus the garret bedroom that is "the place of banishment" for old furniture, threadbare carpet, and Arthur's dreary memories of his childhood (*LD* 38). Flintwinch even haunts the house like an executed prisoner, looking as if he had "hanged himself at one time or other, and [had] gone about ever since halter and all, exactly as some timely hand had cut him down" (*LD* 37). In this prison Mrs. Clennam bides her time, and Affery lives under the dominion of the two "clever ones" (*LD* 39).

Though the narrator takes considerable pains to render these lesser prisons in detail, he is most concerned to show us the Marshalsea, as Dickens must have recalled it from his youth. In his study of the "real Marshalsea," Trey Philpotts marvels at the factual accuracy of *Little Dorrit*'s account of this prison, pointing out that William Kent cited the novel in 1927 as the most detailed extant description of the old structure.[20] The account seems to have been drawn wholly from memory, for Dickens visited the old prison grounds just days before *Little Dorrit* was to be published in book form to see "whether or no any portions of the Marshalsea Prison [were] yet standing" (*LD* "Preface").[21] Though Dickens found the prison's front courtyard "metamorphosed into a butter-shop" and the barrack renamed "Marshalsea Place," the transformations did not change what he could recall (*LD* "Preface"). As the narrator moves us through the prison, we see its "oblong pile of barrack building, partitioned into squalid houses," its "narrow paved yard, hemmed in by high walls," and the "cooped-up apartment" that serves as the Snuggery (*LD* 58; 84). We also see, in vivid detail, the shabby room in which William Dorrit has spent a quarter century as the prison's Father.[22] Most important, we see William himself, and the other miserable inhabitants of the prison. Dickens wrote in his "Preface" to the book edition of the novel that the new inhabitants of Marshalsea Place must "stand among the crowding ghosts of many miserable years" (*LD* "Preface). As the narrator takes in the debtors' prison, we stare at some of these dismal shades. The doctor who delivers Amy Dorrit plays at all fours when we first see him, altogether "hoarser, puffier, more red-faced, more all-fourey, tobaccoer, dirtier, and brandier" than his opponent (*LD* 61). Frederick Dorrit is "an old man" with a "greasy hat," "long and loose" trousers, and "shoes so clumsy and large, that he shuffle[s] like an elephant" (*LD* 76). The inmates and their visitors wear "the cast-off clothes of other men and women; [are] made up of patches and pieces of other people's individuality, and [have] no sartorial existence of their own . . . Their walk [is] the walk of a race apart" (*LD* 87). Transformed, stripped of individuality, and made into a separate race, the Marshalsea's prisoners recall Dickens's descriptions of his earlier fictional prisoners, all of whom bear an unmistakable prison taint. Though William especially tries to maintain a fiction of pitiful gentility, his tell-tale throat-clearing punctuates his speech. It is a characteristic we see no hint of fifteen pages and a quarter-century before.

Remarking the thematic parallel between the narrator's perpetual staring and the Marseillaise sun's obtrusiveness at the start of the novel, McKnight argues, predictably, that the sun's staring and the narrator's imply the Panoptical dimensions of *Little Dorrit*'s imprisoning world.[23] This argument seems unlikely, since sun and narrator alike consistently fail to see into the prison. As the narrator remarks, the squalid criminal cell at Marseilles is so awful that "even the obtrusive stare blinked at it, and left it to such refuse of reflected light as it could find for itself. . . . Like a well, like a vault, like a tomb, the prison had no knowledge of the brightness outside" (*LD* 2). The Clennam house is also "so dingy as to be all but black," and its dark compartments and layers of dust are scarcely illuminated by the candles Affery and Flintwinch carry about its rooms (*LD* 31). It is also worth noting that Arthur's first approach to the Marshalsea is made in the evening, under the cover of darkness, as he follows Amy from his mother's house to learn more about her private story. When he finally meets Frederick at the Marshalsea's gate and persuades the old man to lead him to Amy, Arthur finds it so dark that he is unsure whether Frederick turns in "at the third or fourth doorway" of the prison's oblong pile (*LD* 78). Pointing Arthur up the stairs to William's room, Frederick reassures the younger man, "They are rather dark, sir, but you will not find anything in the way" (*LD* 78). In reading of the novel's prisons, we are never quite sure ourselves what is "in the way." But some obscurity, to be sure, seems always to conceal them from the eye.

Little Dorrit's prisoners likewise lurk always in the shadows. Blandois, as he tells Cavalletto of his wife's mysterious death, stands near the window of the cell "with his back to the light"—an indication that he may hide more of the truth than he reveals (*LD* 12). When he feels he has been accused by Cavalletto's statement that the story is "ugly," Blandois paces the cell silently, stopping occasionally "as if he were going to put his case in a new light" (*LD* 12; 13). Tattycoram and Miss Wade, who are prisoners to rage and psychological self-suppression, also dwell out of the light. We first see Tattycoram at the quarantine barracks shrouded by the lustrous veil of "her rich black hair," and Miss Wade has equivocally "withdrawn herself from . . . or been avoided by the rest" (*LD* 25; 22). After breakfast on the day the fellow travelers leave quarantine, we are told, Miss Wade retires to a "remote corner of the great room," the shadow in which she sits "falling like a gloomy veil across her forehead" so that "[O]ne could hardly see the face" (*LD* 23). Partly the darkness of these women suits the fictional type of passionate, violent, and dangerous women like *Bleak House*'s Hortense and *Jane Eyre*'s Bertha Mason. It also aligns them with the novel's other prisoners: Mrs. Clennam, enthroned upon her "black bier-like sofa" and wearing widows' weeds; and Affery, who emerges from the "dimness" behind Mrs. Clennam's bed to greet Arthur (*LD* 33; 34). More so even than these prisoners, Amy Dorrit, the Marshalsea's child, seems always tucked away among the gloom. At first, in his mother's dimly lit room, Arthur cannot even tell whether a person really stands beside Affery in the corner, but the next day reveals Amy's "diminutive figure, small features, and slight spare dress" (*LD* 52). Even so, the narrator muses, it "was not easy to make out Little Dorrit's face; she was so retiring, plied her needle in such removed corners, and started away so scared if encountered on the stairs" (*LD* 52). Deceptively small, surprisingly old, and hidden always in the shadows, Amy defeats the novel's gaze repeatedly after the very fashion of the prison.

As these physical descriptions imply, the gloom that seems always to obscure *Little Dorrit*'s prisons are part of the novel's thematic mode: they distinguish imprisonment from freedom and give visual meaning to the idea of a prison "taint". But in a story that invites us to stare, and that makes staring the basis of its narrative authority, shadows are also obstacles to narration. Standing in the cell's shadows, Blandois keeps himself and his story quite literally in the dark, and despite our narrator's omniscience we do not know if he is guilty. We do not know, either, whether the elusive Miss Wade has withdrawn from or is avoided by the others. And though we know the history of their lives in the Marshalsea, the Dorrits suffer an imprisonment that the narrator admits he is unable to explain. He confesses, "as nobody on the face of the earth could be more incapable of explaining any single item in the heap of confusion than the debtor himself, nothing comprehensible could be made of his case" (*LD* 60). The narrator can describe Marseilles, London, Italy, and Calais. He can retreat thirty years to the time of the novel's action, and twenty-five more to narrate the "making" of the Father of the Marshalsea. He can also show us *Little Dorrit*'s myriad prisons, linking them together with imagery that juxtaposes the darkness of the cell and the brilliance of the world beyond its walls. But showing us the shadows is not the same as showing us what they conceal, so that *Little Dorrit*'s gloom indicates a deeper resistance: to the power of the omniscient stare that narrates the novel's world. As Rosenberg argues, the gloom that obscures the novel reflects a deeper failure of narrative and perception, a "profound . . . anxiety about the potential for even the most perceptive observer to see reliably . . . [and] to arrive at the truth."[24] None of *Little Dorrit*'s characters are more constantly in shadow than its invisible, unnarratable prisoners.

They are so partly because "Society" would rather not see what the prison conceals. Far from caring what evils lurk in the prison, in fact, *Little Dorrit*'s "Society" prefers to create surfaces that satisfy the needs of the world's (and the narrator's) incessant stare. "Society is," Mrs. Merdle explains to Fanny and Amy, "so arbitrary . . . so exacting. . . . But . . . we must take it as we find it. We know it is hollow and conventional and worldly and very shocking, but unless we are Savages in the Tropical seas . . . we must consult it. It is the common lot" (*LD* 234). To be part of Society, the novel suggests, is to be hypocrite, participating in its arbitrariness while acknowledging the shallowness of participation. This is the Society that attends Merdle's dinner parties and declares him the most capital of men, that hounds and stares at Merdle's carriage as it carries Merdle and William to the bank, and that cares more for displays of wealth than for knowing how wealth has been acquired. As for Merdle himself, he has even married a surface: a "broad unfeeling handsome bosom" that is "a capital bosom to hang jewels upon" (*LD* 233; 241). The form of a bosom without the content, Mrs. Merdle is a miniature of society's much greater superficial expanse. The houses of Harley Street, Cavendish Square, are "expressionless [and] uniform . . . all to be knocked at and rung at in the same form, all approachable by the same dull steps, all fended off by the same pattern of railing" (*LD* 240). Even the narrator, despite his implicit criticisms, participates in this shocking Society, remarking carelessly that Merdle is "Chairman of this, Trustee of that, President of the other" but not bothering himself with the details (*LD* 241). Form, surface, uniformity—a neurotic over-concern with what is seen—comprise the novel's social ideology, and the Merdles' staring Chief Butler is that ideology's shining emblem.

So, too, is the Circumlocution Office, which functions thematically as the site for rejecting meaning in favor of form—which makes wanting "to know, you know" the worst possible offense (*LD* 108). The office's vast surface is clung to by a "shoal of Barnacles" and provides "the express image and presentment of How not to do it" (*LD* 390; 106). For this scathing government satire alone, Edwin Pugh remarks, the novel "would have been well worth writing."[25] Mrs. General also epitomizes *Little Dorrit*'s social ideology by demonstrating that Society wishes to impose circumlocution, surface, and sameness even upon the private self. Hired by William Dorrit because her "name" rather than her character has become "more honorable than ever," Mrs. General undertakes to "form the mind[s]" of the Dorrit women (*LD* 436). Her notion of that work is that she must "prevent [the mind] from forming opinions" and spread her soothing veneer of "prunes and prism"—words that give proper form to a young lady's mouth—over the world (*LD* 438; 462). The aim is to cover whatever Society would rather not see:

> Mrs. General was not to be told of anything shocking. Accidents, miseries, and offences, were never to be mentioned before her. Passion was to go to sleep in the presence of Mrs. General, and blood was to change to milk and water. The little that was left in the world, when all these deductions were made, it was Mrs. General's province to varnish. (*LD* 438)

Wandering the novel as Society's quintessence, Mrs. General totes her varnish everywhere, covering over and sealing away whatever ugliness intrudes upon her notice. As she tells Amy and Fanny, "Nothing disagreeable should ever be looked at" (*LD* 463). To "form the mind" in Mrs. General's estimation is to do precisely that: to *form* it, to give it shape without content, and to make Amy and Fanny into absences rather than presences of self. Living in willed blindness and continual self-negation, the self who would participate in *Little Dorrit*'s Society must eradicate outward ugliness and the dark desires that rest within.

To the extent that this is true, society in *Little Dorrit* is a Foucaultian nightmare dominated by the constant vigilance of prunes and prism, and imprisonment is the "state of mind" that Edmund Wilson and J. Hillis Miller have called it. Characters suppress their deepest desires; they become, necessarily, self-policing. Meagles struggles to hide the "passing cloud" that crosses his face whenever he spies Pet with Henry Gowan, and Tattycoram's litany of "five-and-twenty" is meant to give her self-control (*LD* 198; 311). Mrs. Clennam, too, conceals not only the missing codicil and the secret of Arthur's birth but also her long rage against Arthur's father. Indeed, Mrs. Clennam is both gaoler and inmate, exiling

Arthur and his father to China and locking herself away in solitude. Even Arthur, when he finds he has become fond of Pet, buries that part of himself rather than reveal his desire or suffer the pangs of unrequited love. As Trilling suggests, imprisonment in *Little Dorrit* is, at least partly, a proto-Freudian psychological condition in which the social demands upon the individual create a divided self, one part of which must always police, censor, and thwart the other in order to satisfy the social will.[26] It is no wonder, then, as the narrator observes, that the Merdle house falls under the "the shadow of no more common wall than the fronts of other establishments of state on the opposite side of the street" (*LD* 240). Society is the novel's greatest prison, and its most curious and complex. In *Little Dorrit's* society, psychological imprisonment is the cost of participation, a means of eradicating differences between social selves rather than of differentiating them one from the next. Seeking this illusion of sameness, society forces the self to arrest thought before it becomes action, creating in the process a sort of imprisonment that is essentially hidden from the narrator's incessant stare.

The novel's physical prisons are, ostensibly, products of this desire to hide the aberrant self. The criminal cell at Marseilles confines two men suspected of crimes, and quarantine guards Society from foreign bodies and the threat of contamination. William's imprisonment is exemplary in this regard, for it results, quite literally, from his failure to satisfy social obligations: his failure, that is, to pay his debt to the Circumlocution Office. These prisons help preserve the social fiction of pleasantness and propriety by removing from view what might mar the smooth regularity of the social veneer. But along with this act of concealment, the prisons also serve the implicit purpose of discovering, declaring, and rendering visible the aberrance of those they confine. Indeed, the novel suggests that the purpose of physical prisons like the Marshalsea is to impose difference by misshaping the private self. As Meagles complains of the quarantine and the suspicion that he has the "plague," "I have had the plague continually, ever since I have been here. . . . I came here as well as ever I was in my life; but to suspect me of the plague is to give me the plague. And I have had it—and I have got it" (*LD* 15). While Meagles escapes quarantine no worse for psychological wear, many of the novel's other characters—Miss Wade, Mrs. Clennam, and the Dorrits—never shed the taint of the cell. Miss Wade says of confinement, "If I had been shut up in any place to pine and suffer, I should always hate that place and wish to burn it down, or raze it to the ground" (*LD* 22). Self-imprisoned and self-despising, she is true to her words. To imprison the self is to charge it with difference, and to inscribe difference upon it within view of the public eye. The inevitable result is the creation of a new public and private identity inseparable from the prison's taint. Overcoming that taint requires remarkable personal concealments that create a new surface that Society approves. The alternative is to fall, like Miss Wade, beyond the margins of Society and the novel.

The product of a social ideology that banishes from view what is disagreeable to see, imprisonment in *Little Dorrit* always implies the presence of a private meaning that is concealed from the visible world. In the criminal cell at Marseilles, Blandois denies his difference from those outside the cell by calling himself a "gentleman" and "citizen of the world," but after his acquittal he discovers that his taint is not easily shed (*LD* 10). He must lie "in prison for security, with the place of [his] confinement kept a secret," and he escapes Marseilles only "in the dead of night . . . carried leagues away from it packed in straw" (*LD* 125). He even changes his name—twice—to escape the taint upon it. Gentleman or not, convict or not, Blandois like Meagles finds that to be imprisoned is to be guilty, and to be forced to hide the plague of his confinement throughout the novel. The Clennam house, too, is filled with surfaces that conceal its prisons. The missing codicil is contained within the inscrutable surfaces of an iron box, which is itself hidden from view. The acronym "D. N. F.," worked in beads upon the watch-paper of old Clennam's watch, is a complex surface of another kind. The phrase for which the acronym stands, "Do Not Forget," is at once a message from Arthur's true mother to old Clennam, a reminder of Mrs. Clennam's anger at her husband's infidelity, and a continuous reproach to Mrs. Clennam for having concealed the missing codicil. The acronym must be read for its meaning, just like the surface constituted by Affery's "dreams." On one hand, as the end of the novel reveals, Affery's "dreams" are not dreams at all; rather, they are a series of clues to the novel's mysteries. On the other, disturbing in their psychological implications—and, because of Flintwinch's threats, in their physical implications, too—the dreams are part of a greater surface that Affery fears to look through, and that comes to constitute her prison. William Wall implies that it is insignificant that Affery accepts her realities as "dreams," arguing that she "seems to have decided that anything confusing is a dream . . . because there is an unreal quality to confusing events."[27] But Affery's "dreams" imply secrets and violence and crime. Because they do, her decision to conceal them mimics the function of the novel's prisons.

So does Amy Dorrit, whose concealments belie her identity as the child of the prison. The Dorrits all bear the taint that the Marshalsea has stamped upon them. Tip is always "foredoomed" to fail and "take[s] the prison walls with him" wherever he goes; though he loves Amy, he does so "with that Marshalsea taint upon his love" (*LD* 74; 225). William, the narrator remarks, is "a captive with the jail-rot upon him, and the impurity of his prison worn into the grain of his soul" (*LD* 222). Both Dorrit men are visibly blighted by the prison—indeed, they are the only Dorrits who technically are prisoners—but both are also deliberately concealed by the Marshalsea's child.[28] Amy's "theory" is that William must never know that Tip has also become a prisoner, and she provides her father with the "elaborate form" that hides Fanny's shabby stage career (*LD* 83; 72). As the narrator says, "over and above her other daily cares, the Child of the Marshalsea had always upon her, the care of preserving the genteel fiction that they were all idle beggars together" (*LD* 72). Like the prison, she both reveals her father's taint to Arthur and, at other times, creates fictions to conceal that taint from view. The strategy that she adopts in creating her fictions is telling, for finding it impossible to deny the Marshalsea's real physical presence, she erases her father's pitiful decline by including the whole family in a fiction of "idle beggary" that eradicates his difference from the selves who are his nearest relations. William's own airs achieve something similar, for he recasts the Marshalsea as a Society in which he is not different but the same, and indeed better than the same: he is the patron and Father of the Marshalsea's race apart. Revising his difference in this way, William—with Amy's help—tries to eradicate the visible traces of the prison's taint. By doing so he hides his true self from the view of the novel and becomes a perfect embodiment of the narrative problem posed by the prison.

For in *Little Dorrit*, amid the stare of a narrative omniscience that shares Society's over-concern with surfaces, to hide people away in the prison is to defeat the narrator's power to disclose. It is one thing that Affery, harried by Flintwinch and her own fear, should be driven to construe her visions as "dreams." It is quite another that the narrator, despite his omniscience, seems to share her confusion. He first tells us that Affery has "a curiously vivid dream" on the night of Arthur's return, but in the very next sentence he seems less sure: after all, the dream "was not at all like a dream, it was so very real in every respect" (*LD* 40). Confused by this scene of indeterminate reality, the narrator stumbles and simply says, "It happened in this wise" (*LD* 40). Arthur's suppressed feelings for Pet create another curious narrative hiccough. Arthur owns the original impulse to conceal his interest in Pet, but the narrator—not Arthur—decides to call these feelings the province of "Nobody" at all. Arthur's love for Pet becomes "Nobody's Weakness" and Gowan becomes "Nobody's Rival" (*LD* 183; 197). When "Nobody's State of Mind" melts away on the eve of Pet's wedding, we read also of "Nobody's Disappearance" (*LD* 298; 324). Buried and removed from view according to the social ban upon what is unpleasant, Arthur's sorrow, regret, and desire have lost their proper entry into the novel. Repeatedly in *Little Dorrit* narrative omniscience misses what cannot be seen, from the meanings of "D. N. F." to Blandois's guilt to the shame that attaches to the

Clennam name. When Pancks's secret efforts finally win the Dorrits their release from the Marshalsea, the narrator is powerless to explain their release, just as he had been unable earlier to explain how they had gotten into the Marshalsea. These mysteries are partly the machinery of Victorian sensation fiction: they establish, in Book One, the intrigues that the plot will unravel. But in a novel that establishes the stare as the basis for its narration and that insists upon the failure of surfaces to produce meaning, these narrative failures suggest a deeper message about privacy and its disclosure.

Citing the mysteries in the novel that never reach resolution—Arthur's continued ignorance regarding his own birth, for instance, and Blandois's role in his wife's death—Sylvia Manning argues that "the Circumlocution Office becomes . . . [a] figure of the novel itself. At the Circumlocution Office, as at the novel, you can ask and ask, but you cannot know."[29] But *Little Dorrit* is more complicated than this, for it sets out to solve the problem of circumlocution—to discover, that is, where and how to account for the truth when it is locked away behind surfaces and forms in the dark recesses of the cell. After all, the meanings that the narrator seeks are contained within the margins of the text. Blandois certainly knows whether he is innocent or guilty, just as Mrs. Clennam knows the secrets of Arthur's birth and the missing codicil. And if neither the Dorrits nor the narrator can explain the family's financial entanglements, Pancks proves eminently able to steam his way to the bottom of the matter. Pushing past the surfaces that conceal the Dorrits' story, Pancks demonstrates that the meanings the novel misses are nonetheless there, awaiting discovery, hidden among the secrets of the prison. *Little Dorrit* thus raises the question of, not *whether* one may know the prison, but *how* one may know. The narrative failure it records is of a particular kind: the failure of omniscience to account for the fundamental meanings of the cell.

Quarantined in Marseilles at the novel's start in quarters more comfortable than the criminal cell, the fellow travelers feel more confined than Blandois, with his wine and cigarettes and grand claims to gentility. Meagles declares that he has "the plague," and Miss Wade remarks bleakly that she feels the world is a place where "we shall meet the people who are coming to meet *us* . . . and what it is set to them to do to us, will all be done" (*LD* 24). Indeed, Miss Wade seems finally to embody Tattycoram's imprisoned passions, for the younger woman tells Miss Wade, "You seem to come like my own anger, my own malice" (*LD* 25). Arthur also feels himself a prisoner, telling Meagles, "I have no will . . . Trained by main force; broken, not bent; heavily ironed . . . shipped away to the other end of the world before I was of age" (*LD* 20). A boyhood transportee who has been altered irrevocably by the experience, Arthur like the narrator sees London as a vast jail and the houses opposite Ludgate Hill as "places of imprisonment" for their inhabitants (*LD* 31). He also reinforces the idea that the Clennam house is a prison by remembering his mother's severity and his hours locked up alone in an old, dark closet like another boyish inmate, David Copperfield.[30] Each quarantined traveler possesses his or her own idiosyncratic sense of confinement. Filling his novel with such inmates, Dickens fashions *Little Dorrit* into a novel that the staring narrator can never adequately complete. But there is a possible solution to this problem, as the novel repeatedly implies: to abandon omniscience and turn instead to the first-person account of the self in the cell. Each of Tattycoram's outbursts reveals a little of her psychological self-thwarting; each of William Dorrit's throat-clearings permits the prison's hidden psychological meaning to percolate to the novel's surface. Having attempted to get at the truth by staring, the novel reaches completion in Book Two only because it fragments, turning finally to the first-person narratives that can reveal the secrets of its prisons.

IV

Book Two begins, however, still mired in the stares, surfaces, and confusions that characterize Book One. As "Riches" opens, we find ourselves again on the continent, again among a party of fellow travelers, and again invited to stare at the fantastic scenery of a foreign land, this time amid the Swiss Alps at the Pass of the Great Saint Bernard. We have circumlocuted back into a novel of sights—"[s]hining metal spires and church-roofs" and "[m]ountain-peaks of great celebrity" that stand against "the red dye of the sunset" (*LD* 419). Here as before, surfaces deceive. The mountains are so impressive and the roof-tops so scintillating that to "unaccustomed eyes" they look to be "within . . . easy reach," their charms "cancelling the intervening country" (*LD* 419). The largest party of fellow travelers is adorned by "a courier, two footmen, and two waiting-maids," all of whom are necessary parts of proper social form (*LD* 422). The young gentleman of the party is especially well varnished, outfitted "in the very fullest and completest travelling trim. The world seemed hardly large enough to yield him an amount of travel proportionate to his equipment" (*LD* 425). So well-concealed are these travelers, in fact, that the narrator does not identify them for us, calling them instead—as he called Merdle's guests—by generic titles: "the Chief," "the insinuating traveller," and "the young lady" (*LD* 422). Though we may identify the travelers ourselves by observing William Dorrit's idiosyncratic throat-clearing, for instance, or Blandois's "nose coming down over his moustache," we do not know their identities for certain until they sign the guest register, almost as if they are signing the novel (*LD* 435). It is the first of many self-declarations of identity in the novel's second half. Each reveals a truth, solves a mystery, or discloses a meaning of imprisonment that is hidden from the narrative stare.

If the Dorrits seem particularly heavily concealed beneath a proper social veneer, they are so because they wish to conceal the truth of their Marshalsea past. Their aim is to expunge from knowledge and remembrance the miseries of their long confinement. Mrs. General is crucial to this aim though she is not aware of the family's past, for it falls to her to varnish Amy's and Fanny's prison taints. But all of the Dorrits—excepting Amy—participate in this family fiction. Tip chides Amy for using his familiar name "because," he tells her, "that's an old habit and one you may as well lay aside" (*LD* 440). Fanny complains of her sister's continued correspondence with Arthur and accuses Amy of "perseveringly and systematically" reviving the past in these letters in an "absolutely infamous" fashion (*LD* 441). Even William encourages Amy to follow his example and "sweep [memories of the Marshalsea] off the face of the earth and begin afresh":

> If *I* can put that aside, if *I* can eradicate the marks of what I have endured, and can emerge before the world a—ha—gentleman unspoiled, unspotted—is it a great deal to expect—I say again, is it a great deal to expect—that my children should—hum—do the same . . . (*LD* 464)

But the degree to which William has *not* placed the prison aside—to which his self-division persists as a psychological wound—is evident in each halting line of his speech and in his obsessive invocation of the Marshalsea as a subject that must not be invoked. He is radically split, constantly feeling and veiling over his difference from the Society in which he moves. At the convent of the Great Saint Bernard, he notes the "confinement" of the isolated place and remarks to his host that the convent is "[s]o small. So—ha—very limited" (*LD* 430). When his host remarks that "Monsieur does not realise . . . how the mind accommodated itself in such things to the force of necessity," William suddenly says that they should "not pursue the subject" (*LD* 430). At Martigny, too, learning that the innkeeper has permitted Mrs. Merdle and Edmund Sparkler to use the Dorrits' rooms, William accuses the proprietor of making "distinctions" between him and "other gentlemen of fortune and station" (*LD* 446). The distinction is all William's, of course: it is his lingering sense of the Marshalsea's shame. But he projects his awareness of his difference onto others, constantly fearing that the social stare will discover his taint. Struggling mightily to conceal his self-division, William widens the gap between his true and social selves, always varnishing over the former and its legacy of the prison.

The Dorrits' determined attempts to eradicate the Marshalsea from memory suggest that the narrative quandary the prison poses in Book One is still present in Book Two. In this second book, however, the narrator begins immediately to peer beneath surfaces to narrate the hidden truths of the cell. He does so partly by offering to narrate the prison's taint through Amy's eyes—an apt choice, since she has always escaped the narrative stare because she has, quite literally, too little surface rather than too much. Fixing his gaze upon her, the narrator proposes to show us the "unreality of her own inner life," maimed by the psychological wounds of long confinement (*LD* 451). We learn that, traveling among the sights of Switzerland and Italy, Amy finds everything "new and wonderful . . . [but] not real"; she rather always expects as they travel that they will, "turning some abrupt corner, bring up with a jolt at the old Marshalsea gate" (*LD* 451). For Amy, the narrator says:

> The gorges of the Simplon, its enormous depths and thundering waterfalls, the wonderful road . . . the descent into Italy, the opening of that beautiful land, as the rugged mountain-chasm widened and let them out from a gloomy and dark imprisonment—[was] all a dream—only the old Marshalsea a reality. (*LD* 451)

Here the narrator seems to know that what Amy sees are not "dreams"; he offers no story of "Nobody" traveling in Europe. Rather, here for the first time the narrative stare turns confidently inward and tells an unequivocal story of imprisonment that has been concealed throughout the novel. The narrator concludes his account of Amy's travel by showing us Amy, staring into Venice's Grand Canal, "as if," he says, "in the general vision, it might run dry, and show her the prison again, and herself, and the old room, and the old inmates, and the old visitors: all lasting realities that had never changed" (*LD* 454). In part, the passage bears witness to the ineradicability of the prison's taint. More important, the narrator's simile betrays his desire for a prison suddenly laid bare to the omniscient stare.

In the very next chapter, after offering this hope, the novel rejects the possibility that this stare can narrate adequately the secrets of the prison. During her travels Amy writes to Arthur describing all that she has seen, and in nearly the same words that the narrator has used. She tells Arthur that as they travel she fears that "the Marshalsea must be behind that great rock," and that the new, grand visions she sees invariably blend with the ineradicable ones she "knew before" (*LD* 456). But her letter also goes further, speaking to a deeper sense of her taint and providing a fuller expression of it than the narrator provided. Marveling at Fanny's ability to adapt to their situation, Amy writes, "This reminds me that I have not been able to do so, and that I sometimes despair of ever being able to do so. I find that I cannot learn. . . . As soon as I begin to plan, and think, and try, all my planning, thinking, and trying go in old directions" (*LD* 456). Child of the prison, Amy finds herself fundamentally divided from the Society outside the cell. Not only can she not, as the narrator tells us, free her visions of Italy from the shadow cast by the prison, but she cannot acquire the habits of the world. Considering what the novel shows us of that world, her failure is to her credit; nevertheless, she has no choice. She is one of the Marshalsea's race apart, and much more literally than the others, for she is its Child. Her pain at missing the Marshalsea is a longing for "home" (*LD* 538).[31] Though her letter reinscribes the narrator's words, Amy's disclosures go farther, attesting more completely to the psychological wounds inflicted by the Marshalsea. By divulging truths that the narrator does not, Amy demonstrates the inadequacy of the narrator's account of the private trauma inflicted by the prison.

Thus William Dorrit must finally narrate his own taint if he is to enter fully the world of the novel. Free of the Marshalsea but prey constantly to his fear of discovery, William has traded the debtors' prison for a social one defined by its perpetual stare. He fears discovery and undertakes concealment all the while he is on the Continent, and returning to London he threatens to "take the poker" to John Chivery for daring to show himself a former friend (*LD* 610). He also fears that the valet on his coach to Rome has "suspicions" about his passenger (*LD* 617). The most fearsome watcher of all is the Chief Butler, under whose stare William falls at one of Merdle's dinners:

> That stupendous character looked at him, in the course of his official looking at the dinners, in a manner that Mr. Dorrit considered questionable. He looked at him, as he passed through the hall and up the staircase, going to dinner, with a glazed fixedness that Mr. Dorrit did not like. (*LD* 597)

Feeling himself regarded "with a cold and ghostly eye," he wonders if the Chief Butler knew a Collegian or "had been presented to him" as a visitor to the prison (*LD* 597). Though he does not recognize the Chief Butler, of course, William fears nevertheless that the man recognizes *him*, and he considers telling the Chief Butler that this "confinement in his eye was disagreeable" (*LD* 597). Tainted by the prison, and seeking to conceal that taint, William's new psychological confinement is comprised chiefly by the fear that signs of his old identity remain visible in the world of the novel.

As the novel shows us repeatedly, however, William has nothing to fear from the Chief Butler; rather, only he can bring to light an account of his confinement. Determined to varnish over the story of his prison past, William spends the ride to Rome building a "Castle in the Air" that will help him to become a newer, better self. But by the time he reaches Rome, his power to conceal his taint is gone. He finds Amy's stare uncomfortably "particular" and falls into a "heavy doze" as he stands with his daughter (*LD* 620). More important, he can no longer prevent his private self from emerging into narrative. At first, William displaces his self-narrative, attributing his own decline to Frederick and calling his brother "very feeble" (*LD* 620). When Frederick retires to bed, William mentions to Amy that her uncle "is less—ha—coherent, and his conversation is more—hum—broken, than I have—ha hum—ever known" (*LD* 620). As before, William's halting words perform the taint he will not admit. They also recreate Frederick as the darker self that William has tried throughout the novel to conceal—a recreation that is reinforced thematically when Frederick, by the bedside of his dead brother, expires as well. At the Merdles' dinner party and in his own words, William finally self-narrates the identity he has so long suppressed:

> Those who are habituated to the—ha—Marshalsea, are pleased to call me its Father. I am accustomed to be complimented by strangers as the—ha—Father of the Marshalsea. Certainly, if years of residence may establish a claim to so—ha—honorable a title, I may accept the—hum—conferred distinction. My child, ladies and gentlemen. My daughter. Born here! (*LD* 626)

William's sad confession finally illustrates a dimension of the prison taint for which the narrator has been unable to account: that, psychologically maimed by the Marshalsea, William is more than stained or self-divided. He is rather doomed to remain always the inmate that the prison has made him. Though Philip Collins calls William's disclosure "sudden," the collapse only culminates a long process that has given him a self-account that begins and ends in the cell.[32]

Of the prisoners who narrate their cells in *Little Dorrit*, Miss Wade best exemplifies the novel's narrative engagement with the prison. Miss Wade's imprisonment epitomizes, in part, the novel's insistence upon an invisible, psychological confinement that escapes the omniscient stare. She is the most elusive of *Little Dorrit*'s prisoners, always haunting the novel's fringes and shadows: the corner of the breakfast room at Marseilles; a "dingy house, apparently empty" in one of the "dull bye-streets of the Grosvenor region"; the "deserted scene" of the Adelphi at dusk where she speaks with Blandois; and the "dead sort of house, with a dead wall over the way and a dead gateway at the side" in Calais (*LD* 317; 316; 514; 635). Indeed, for Arthur to find her, he must find the "dead house" and enter its "cool, dull, and dark" rooms, where Miss Wade produces her private narrative, suggestively, from the deeper confines of an "inner drawer" (*LD* 635; 636; 641). The scene bespeaks intrusion and penetration, and when she speaks to Arthur about her "History," she does so "as if she were speaking to her own looking-glass" (*LD* 641). Self-narrated, self-heard, and self-referential, the narrative she gives to Arthur offers him entry into her private world. And, as we discover in the reading, Miss Wade is absent from the novel because she represents the things that Society most wishes to banish from view: misanthropy, passion, violence, social and perhaps even sexual deviance, the psychological underworld that must never be seen.[33] She also represents the narrative dilemmas and failures that characterize the novel.

Before offering Arthur her "History," Miss Wade explains her reasons for doing so by insisting, "You don't know what I mean by hating . . . you can't know," and claiming that her narrative will help him to comprehend (*LD* 640). The failure to understand subjectivity that she describes is precisely the narrative logic that underlies the failure of omniscience. Yet the very first paragraph of Miss Wade's "History" records the faulty bias that shapes her prison:

> I have the misfortune of not being a fool. From a very early age I have detected what those about me thought they hid from me. If I could have been habitually imposed upon, instead of habitually discerning the truth, I might have lived as smoothly as most fools do. (*LD* 644)

Born into a condition of difference because she is an orphan, Miss Wade has constantly felt her own taint—a sense of separation from the Society around her. But Miss Wade's self-narrated account of her private identity ultimately reveals something that is narratively crucial: for all her claims to see and know what those around her think, Miss Wade draws no credible psychological portrait but her own. Originally seeking one sort of narrative significance for Miss Wade's character—the seamless entry of the private self into the active, public world of the novel—Dickens invested this "History" with quite another. Miss Wade shows us the impossibility of looking into another private self, and the failure of the fantasy of omniscience. By making this fantasy the key fault of the novel's most misguided character, Dickens reveals the misery inflicted by a delusive belief in one's power to *know* the other. Thematically *Little Dorrit*'s most hidden prisoner, Miss Wade becomes as well a narrative figure of the novel, erroneously denying to others the very indecipherable subjectivity that she claims for herself. In so doing, she demonstrates a condition in which faith in omniscience itself becomes dangerous—itself becomes a prison that is accounted for by the first-person narrative of the self in the cell.

Working toward the resolution of its mysteries, *Little Dorrit* becomes a mosaic of self-accounts that reveal the truths contained by the cell. We learn the nature of "Mr. Merdle's complaint" when he authors his suicide and leaves behind a letter that reveals his secret: that he "was simply the greatest Forger and the greatest Thief that ever cheated the gallows" (*LD* 691). Tattycoram returns to the Meagleses, bearing not only the iron box that contains the novel's most pivotal secrets but also an explanation of her self-imposed exile into Miss Wade's hands. Like Miss Wade's, Tattycoram's prison has hinged upon the apprehension that "people were all against [her] because of . . . [her] beginning" (*LD* 787). In the Clennam house many prisons are suddenly broken and their mysteries explained, as Blandois, Flintwinch, Mrs. Clennam, and even Affery narrate the secrets associated with the Clennam name. When Blandois threatens that he will tell her story, Mrs. Clennam finally confesses her secrets over Flintwinch's protestations:

> I tell you, Flintwinch, I will speak. . . . I will tell it with my own lips, and will express myself throughout it. What! Have I suffered nothing in this room, no deprivation, no imprisonment, that I should condescend at last to contemplate myself in such a glass as *that!* (*LD* 753)

And indeed it *is* a story that Mrs. Clennam must tell, for her long imprisonment is laden with hidden desires and motives, ancient psychological ruminations, and implications that arise from her private idiosyncrasies. As Mrs. Clennam guesses, permitting Blandois to narrate the story, though he knows the "facts," would transform her concealment of the codicil into an act "impelled" by "the money" (*LD* 756). Her motivations are actually broader and more complex, reaching into a childhood of "repression, punishment, and fear," the disappointment of her dismal marriage, and her compulsion to discover the meaning of "Do not forget" (*LD* 753). The meaning of her confinement is individual and complex, known only to herself, and like the novel's other prisoners she must self-narrate her cell if it is to enter *Little Dorrit'*s fictive world. When she remarks to Flintwinch that "it is closing in," she implies something as well about the novel's narrative perspective, which shrinks inexorably in Book Two to the size of the individual self (*LD* 746).

Though the novel's prisoners finally narrate the meanings of their own prisons and reveal the truths that solve the novel's mysteries, *Little*

Dorrit denies us hope that such self-narration will—as it had in *It Is Never Too Late to Mend*—free the self from the cell. At the end of the novel, the Circumlocution Office is still quite well, attended no doubt by its shoal of Barnacles; the Chief Butler has resigned his post with the Merdles but will certainly light upon another; and, though Mrs. General has not married William Dorrit, she lives to varnish another day. Subjected still to the demands of the Society that permits such things to be, no character in *Little Dorrit* can be free of the prison. Miss Wade will never, we are reasonably certain, recover an identity not subject to the torments of her self-apprehended difference. While Tattycoram escapes a similar fate, she does so by returning to a prison of another kind and accepting the continuous psychological self-division that it requires. She tells Meagles: "I won't stop at five-and-twenty, sir. I'll count five-and-twenty hundred, five-and-twenty thousand" (*LD* 787). Even Pancks, the champion of Bleeding Heart Yard, humiliates the Patriarch before the crowd only to flee immediately after. Nor are the novel's conclusions regarding real prisons and prisoners more hopeful. Removed from their prisons but laboring under the continued necessity of self-division, William and Frederick Dorrit die, as does Merdle—all three, it seems, as a consequence or cost of their self-revelation. Tip dies as well. Mrs. Clennam temporarily gains frenzied physical strength at the novel's end, but the prison-house and its inmate collapse moments later, a hopeless indication that she has been a prisoner too long to have an existence beyond the cell. Prisoners of a Society that cannot tolerate their indelible taint, such characters can never return from the prison.

Indeed, hopeful though it seems in certain ways, even Arthur and Amy's marriage suggests the impossibility of escaping the prison's taint. What seems like a love story that makes the Marshalsea and the novel less bleak comes about, necessarily, only after Arthur falls under the shadow of the prison. Entering the Marshalsea, Arthur soon feels he has entered "into another state of existence," and very soon imprisonment begins "to tell upon him" (*LD* 699; 715). He is William Dorrit remade, living in the same Marshalsea cell, and when Amy comes to tend him, she does so "as lovingly, and GOD knows as innocently, as she had nursed her father in that room when she had been but a baby" (*LD* 736). Arthur's sudden discovery that he loves Amy is thus accompanied by a great fear: that he, "a broken, bankrupt, sick, dishonored, prisoner," can never merit her, free as she is of the prison (*LD* 736). Even as he tells Amy of his love and esteem, therefore, he says also, "The time when you and this prison had anything in common, has long gone by" (*LD* 739). Every detail of the novel suggests otherwise. Amy's letters from Italy have indicated the depth and permanence of her prison taint. Now, at the end of the novel, so does her easy return to the cell: to the lasting realities of her childhood home, to her old station as nurse to a broken debtor, to her old friends and acquaintances at the Marshalsea. Even her fortune has been lost through Merdle's frauds. It is almost as if—like her father, uncle, and brother, like Merdle, like Mrs. Clennam—she cannot have an identity or existence that is separable from the prison.

Manning finds it inconsistent with the novel's satiric program that "Arthur is purged of his economic error and his soul brought to recognize its mate" through his time in the Marshalsea, but really the conclusion fits with what the novel insists all along.[34] Receiving the Marshalsea flavor, Arthur has not been laid too low for Amy; rather, he has been perfectly fitted to the Marshalsea's Child. Indeed, he is more properly suited even than his prison taint suggests, for he differs from William Dorrit in one crucial respect: unlike William, Arthur accepts his separation from Society as a necessary consequence of his financial failure, and he owns up to his imprisonment just as Amy has always done. This does not make the end of the novel any happier or less satiric, for any hope that their marriage offers has little to do with the possibility that they may escape the prison's stain. Instead, the novel provides the consolation that Amy and Arthur may, by willingly eschewing the Society that the novel has condemned, escape at least the devastating self-division that destroys the novel's other prisoners. After their marriage, they "[walk] out of the church alone" and, while the rest of the world makes its "usual uproar," pass "quietly down into the roaring streets" (*LD* 801; 802). "Inseparable" in their union, they are divided from the rest of the world, as the Miltonic echoes of their departure from the prison-Eden suggest (*LD* 802). This division is preferable to the horrors of *Little Dorrit*'s Society—it is the least bleak prospect of a hopelessly bleak novel. Marrying at Saint George's Church just across the street from the Marshalsea, and recording their marriage in the register books of the church, Arthur and Amy enter upon a union which will always rest, quite literally, in the shadow of the prison.

V

It may after all seem curious that Dickens presents in *Little Dorrit* the conclusion that the prison's taint can only be narrated adequately from the first-person perspective of the self in the cell. After all, in his autobiographical fragment and in *David Copperfield*, Dickens had failed to grapple fully with the prison from this perspective. To begin *Little Dorrit* amid a narrative stare only to destroy its authority to speak would, in other words, seem to take Dickens over old—and unsuccessful—ground. But *Little Dorrit* indicates in both its social criticisms and its multiple prisons that for Dickens the prison had become a far more complex place than he had ever made it in *Pickwick Papers* and *American Notes*. No individual character could testify credibly to a vision of the prison as complex as that we find in *Little Dorrit*. Narrating the prison, then, required some measure of omniscient narration, capable of discerning the vast confinement that Society had wrought and of bringing to light the countless hypocrisies that characterize the novel's social world. Yet even as Dickens wrote thus broadly, he recognized still that the private implications of imprisonment constituted a story fundamentally unavailable to the wide omniscient stare. In this way the narrative structure of *Little Dorrit* comes to resemble that of *Bleak House*, and perhaps—since both combine complex social critique with an intensely private story—for many of the same reasons. But in *Little Dorrit* Dickens suggests that every individual mind is a prison, that every private self is varnished over by social necessities, and that every story of self is a story of confinement. Refiguring each mind as a prison unavailable to the stare, Dickens rejects omniscience—not, as Janice Carlisle says, to show what fiction "cannot do," but rather to show the limitations of omniscience in accounting for the private self.[35] In *Little Dorrit*, what omniscience cannot do is see into the cell, so that the novel becomes a powerful statement about narrative form, privacy, and the prison.

Even more important, by making the mind a prison, *Little Dorrit* suggests that the production of psychological narrative actually requires the prison, that self-narrative cannot retreat to a time that precedes psychological boundedness and confinement. When Arthur is first imprisoned, he goes back over his life and finds that, in "his own poor story, [Amy] was its vanishing-point. Everything in its perspective led to her innocent figure" (*LD* 714). Partly, his thoughts indicate his emerging awareness of his love for her. In another way, he is more correct than he knows. Collaborating with Mrs. Clennam to withhold from Arthur the long-hidden story of his birth, Amy really is the vanishing-point of his story. When Arthur stands with Amy in his Marshalsea apartment just before they wed, she asks him as a final favor to burn the paper in her hands. He asks if the paper is a "charm," and she replies, "It is anything you like best, my own . . . if you will only humour me when the fire burns up" (*LD* 798). The fire consumes his life story, the secret of a past he may now never know. Like magic, Amy has made that past disappear in a fashion that suits her function as the Marshalsea's Child: to contain and conceal the ugliness of Arthur's true stain, the illegitimacy of his birth. At the end of *Little Dorrit*, then, we are left with Arthur and Amy, both of whose vanishing-points are the prison and whose stories must always return to the cell to discover origins and meanings. Envisioning the prison as a vanishing-point for their self-accounts, the novel suggests it is in the nature of the prison to create a new self, a new truth, a new psychological identity, and a new self-account as well. This is what *Little Dorrit*'s social critique implies, too, for the novel permits no conception of the self that does not include self-censoring and self-thwarting, the negation of motive and desire. The story of the prison is not just about criminals, punishments, and society, therefore, but about psychological origins—about self-understandings that must return to the cell, and that can take narrative shape only in the first-person account of the Victorian prisoner.

VI

A Tale of Two Cities reaches these same conclusions about privacy, narrative form, and the prison. Critics have rarely considered *A Tale* in light of the novel that preceded it, mostly because *A Tale* is, in many ways, an anomaly in the Dickens canon. Of all Dickens's novels, only *A Tale* and *Barnaby Rudge* are explicitly historical, and it is worth pointing out that both center upon representations of the historical prison: the Bastille, in the case of the former, and the 1788 Gordon Riots at Newgate in the case of the latter. Really, *A Tale* brims with real prisons—La Force, the Abbaye, and the Concièrgerie—even apart from the Bastille, and all of them appear within the context of a French Revolution that Dickens culled from Louis-Sebastien Mercier, Jean-Jacques Rousseau, and Thomas Carlyle.[36] As other scholars have pointed out, Dickens drew from these writers his most vivid images of revolutionary France: the gaunt peasants at Saint Antoine, the cruelties of the *ancien régime*, and the bloody spectacle of the Revolution itself. Indeed, he even asked Carlyle for help in researching the Revolution and was "grateful but staggered when Carlyle sardonically chose two cartloads of books at the London Library and had them all sent to him."[37] This reliance upon formal research is rare in Dickens; so, too, is the extent to which he drew upon the advice of his friend and pupil, Wilkie Collins. Besides mentioning Carlyle, Dickens's "Preface" to the novel credits Collins's play *The Frozen Deep* with having provided "the main idea of [the] story."[38] Thematic parallels between the works suggest that this is true. In 1858 as Dickens planned *A Tale*, he was acting the part of Richard Wardour in Collins's play, and like Sydney Carton, Wardour sacrifices himself to save the rival who has won his beloved's heart. Others have suggested that Collins had an even wider influence upon Dickens's novel, including Walter Clark Phillips who suggested in 1919 that in writing *A Tale* Dickens became Collins's pupil instead of his master.[39] However that may be, Collins surely exerted considerable influence over the novel, so that *A Tale's* particularly un-Dickensian flavor may owe to both historical and artistic sources.

They owe also to the material concerns that pressed upon Dickens's writing in 1859. Dickens had split with his wife and his publishers during the preceding year, so that 1859 found him struggling to succeed afresh with the new magazine *All the Year Round*. To give the periodical a proper send-off, he prepared *A Tale of Two Cities* as its first serial novel. The decision forced him to adopt a weekly twenty-number publication plan, a format he had tried with *Master Humphrey's Clock* in 1840–1841 and *Hard Times* in 1854, and one that he seems genuinely to have disliked. In August of 1859, Dickens complained to Forster of the terrible confinement he felt in these briefer installments, and of the "time and trouble of incessant condensation."[40] Feeling constrained and perhaps eyeing, as in *Little Dorrit*, new artistic aims, Dickens said that he wished to write a "*picturesque* story, rising in every chapter with characters true to nature, but whom the story should express more than they should express themselves by dialogue."[41] This sounds much like Dickens's aim with Miss Wade, and it helps to show how the constraints upon Dickens's time, space, and imagination during the writing of *A Tale* combined to produce a truly curious novel: historical, humorless, short on lively dialogue and vivid characters, and treating a decidedly un-English subject. The novel is, in short, not at all what we expect from Dickens, and buried among 1859's more prominent works—Eliot's *Adam Bede*, Tennyson's first part of the *Idylls of the King*, and Darwin's *The Origin of Species*—it was virtually ignored.[42] Disregarded at first and studied since, mostly, with an eye to its portrayal of the French Revolution, *A Tale* has not been evaluated for its similarities to *Little Dorrit*, though both novels show Dickens's evolving sense of the narrative complexities of the prison.

A Tale unfolds in a world where the only reality is violence. The novel begins in 1775 awash in the blood of riots, robberies, tortures, murders, and executions; it ends in greater violence still, as Carton's death signals the start of a new Reign of Terror more brutal than the *ancien régime*. Between are pages filled with gore and grave-robbing, and bodies maimed and broken in the name of the Revolution. Though the violence stems partly from subversion and revolt, the novel also takes pains to show us the brutality of punishment under the *ancien régime* and England's "Bloody Code." Within this world of authorized violence, the story of Alexandre Manette suggests that no greater injuries can be inflicted than those inflicted by the prison. Manette enters the novel already broken physically and psychologically—so broken, in fact, that he must be "recalled to life" by Jarvis Lorry. Like Alfred Jingle, the Chancery prisoner, William Dorrit, and Arthur Clennam before him, Manette bears the ineradicable scars inscribed upon him by long confinement. These scars owe much in their rendering, as Harry De Puy has shown, to Dickens's lingering memories of the Eastern Penitentiary, which Dickens rewrites in his novel as the very Bastille that England regarded as the epitome of dangerous secrecy and separation.[43] Focusing rather upon the novel's images of penetrated bodies and broken graves than upon the time Manette spends in the Bastille, Catherine Gallagher argues that violence in *A Tale of Two Cities* recreates thematically what is really a narrative "longing for exposure and revelation."[44] As in *Little Dorrit*, however, *A Tale* worries most explicitly about *how* to narrate privacy, especially in the passage that opens "Night Shadows," the novel's third chapter. At bottom, Manette's confinement and self-narrative suggest that the novel's violence does not serve to reveal or expose. Rather, violence in *A Tale* is part of a greater struggle for control: over society, over meanings, and especially over the narration and identity of the private self.

Caught between subversive and authorized acts of brutality, society in the novel is caught as well between competing ideologies that are less concerned to expose truth than to control truth through narrative. Crucial words have multiple meanings in this novel. So do many characters—Carton, Manette, Charles Darnay, and John Barsad—who struggle to retain their power to self-narrate so they can control the narrative construction of their private identities and desires. Amid the violent struggles of *A Tale*, however, authorities rather than individual selves have the power to sift meanings, weigh them against the needs of the social order, and fix the truth. As a mechanism for containing, transforming, and finally producing self-narration—as the vanishing-point, that is, for accounts of the self—the prison is crucial to this ideological aim. Returned to the cell to recover an identity that has long been shadowed by the prison, Manette discovers that the final horror inflicted by the prison is not the considerable physical or psychological taint it inscribes. It is his loss of authority over his own self-account—his powerlessness to resist his narrative construction as an ally of the Defarges, the tribunal, and those who seek Darnay's death. The novel's vision is of a wounding and grotesquely powerful prison, and of narrative authority able to misshape the prisoner and his self-account on the basis of its power over, not its knowledge of, the private identity of the imprisoned subject. What we see in *A Tale of Two Cities*, that is, is an explicit demonstration of how the prison solves the novel's pivotal narrative problem: how to narrate, through the lens of omniscience, private identity and desire.

VII

A Tale of Two Cities begins playfully, with the familiar contradictions that every English schoolchild knows. Then it resolves itself into images of blood. France, the narrator says, has begun to "roll with exceeding smoothness down hill":

> Under the guidance of her Christian pastors, she entertained her-
> self, besides, with such humane achievements as sentencing a
> youth to have his hands cut off, his tongue torn out with pincers,
> and his body burned alive, because he had not kneeled down in
> the rain to do honour to a dirty procession of monks . . . (*TTC* 2)

While France amuses itself with such benign pastimes, "[i]n England,
there was scarcely an amount of order and protection to justify much
national boasting" (*TTC* 3). Burglars and daring highwaymen prowl
London's streets after dark and prey upon the unsuspecting. One robbery,
committed by "the Captain," turns to murder when he "gallantly" shoots
his victim "through the head," and an attempt to rob the Dover mail
leaves three robbers and the mail's guard dead (*TTC* 3). Meantime, in
London, "prisoners . . . [fight] battles with their turnkeys" and the mob
and musketeers shoot each other at St. Giles's (*TTC* 3). Amid the brutal
disorder that characterizes England, the hangman is "ever busy and ever
worse than useless"—and, we are told, "in constant requisition":

> . . now, stringing up long rows of miscellaneous criminals; now,
> hanging a housebreaker on Saturday who had been taken on
> Tuesday; now, burning people in the hand at Newgate by the
> dozen . . . to-day, taking the life of an atrocious murderer, and to-
> morrow of a wretched pilferer who had robbed a farmer's boy of
> sixpence. (*TTC* 3–4)

As these images of torture and execution suggest, the novel is concerned from the beginning—in England and in France—to show the
authorized violence that upholds the social order. Much of this violence
is explicitly legal and punitive, as in the case of the "youth" of the opening pages.[45] This is also true of the torture that is promised for Gaspard
after he murders Monseigneur Evrémonde. As one of the Jacquarie
reports to Defarge, Gaspard has been sentenced as a parricide and will
have "his right hand, armed with the knife . . . burnt off before his face
. . . [and] into wounds which will be made in his arms, his breast, and his
legs, there will be poured boiling oil, melted lead, hot resin, wax, and sul-
phur . . . and he will be torn limb from limb by four strong horses" (*TTC*
205).[46] Darnay faces a similar punishment in England if he is convicted
of treason. As a spectator tells Jerry Cruncher when the latter arrives at
court, Darnay will, if convicted, "be drawn on a hurdle to be half hanged,
and then . . . taken down and sliced before his own face, and then his
inside will be taken out and burnt while he looks on . . . and then his
head . . . chopped off, and [his body] cut into quarters" (*TTC* 70). Besides
these threats of ostentatious brutalities that will be inflicted upon offenders, the authorities in England and France bear also subtler indicators of

the violence that undergirds the social order. The Dover mail, under threat of robbery, carries a guard who bristles with potential violence, and who keeps "an eye and a hand on the arm-chest before him, where a loaded blunderbuss lay at the top of six or eight loaded horse-pistols, deposited on a sub-stratum of cutlass" (*TTC* 6). In France, meanwhile, the peasants at Saint Antoine are subjected to that wearing violence called "Hunger," which gives them the appearance of a "people that had undergone a terrible grinding and re-grinding in the mill" (*TTC* 34). As if the daily horror of misery and neglect is not enough, the poor are also subject to Monseigneur's "fierce patrician custom of hard driving [which] endangered and maimed the mere vulgar in a barbarous manner"—a manner that smashes and kills Gaspard's son (*TTC* 130).

Opposed to these authorized acts of violence, we find ranged the illicit threats of subversion and revolt. In England, besides the robbers, rioters, and inmates, these threats are embodied by Cruncher, whose name and physical appearance promise violence from the moment he enters the novel. His eyes have a "sinister" expression, and his "raggedly bald" head looks "like the top of a strongly spiked wall" (*TTC* 13; 14). As we learn later in the novel, Cruncher threatens the order of things mostly by being a "Resurrection-man"—an illicit trade in which he posits his illegitimate meaning of "resurrection" against the word's Christian sense and against its significance in Manette's being "RECALLED TO LIFE" (*TTC* 10). Indeed, at Darnay's trial Cruncher declares the proposed sentence of torture "Barbarous!" not because he shares Dickens's or the narrator's objections, but because the punishment will "spile" Darnay for the purposes of "resurrectioning" (*TTC* 68). Living by his own codes of meaning and morality, Cruncher even threatens his wife's prayers by calling her "Aggerawayter" and implying violence whenever she seems about to "flop" (*TTC* 65). For Cruncher, any prayer is an affront since it invokes the power that undergirds the standing social and cultural order. In this way he wanders the novel doing violence to accepted norms.

In France the context for subversive violence is much larger, since subversion is a product of—not simply a threat to—the violence enacted on the other side. Writing to Forster in August of 1859 about his research into eighteenth-century France, Dickens declared, "If there be anything certain on earth, I take it that the condition of the French peasant generally was intolerable."[47] Having shown us the brutalities inflicted by the *ancien régime*, the novel shows us their result: the savage mood that grows among the peasants at Saint Antoine. The peasants there who sop up the wine from the broken cask stain what they touch as if with blood, and their mouths "acquire[d] a tigerish smear" (*TTC* 34). A "tall joker" renders the scene thematically explicit by dipping his finger into the wine and scribbling "BLOOD" across a nearby wall (*TTC* 34). The message foreshadows the scenes of horror that will come: Monseigneur driven *"fast to his tomb"* by a knife through his breast; the "seven gory heads on pikes" at the storming of the Bastille; and the three attempts to hang Foulon before the rope finally holds, after which his head is piked and carried "in Wolf-procession through the streets" (*TTC* 154; 269; 275). The culminating image of this subversive violence comes when Manette and Lorry watch the mob at the grindstone recreate the wine spill of hundreds of pages before:

> The eye could not detect one creature in the group free from the smear of blood. . . . [There were] men stripped to the waist, with the stain all over their limbs and bodies; men in all sorts of rags, with the stain upon those rags . . . Hatchets, knives, bayonets, swords, all brought to be sharpened, were all red with it. (*TTC* 321)

Thus the brutality of punishment and neglect breeds the greater horrors of the Revolution.

Despite the images of blood that punctuate *A Tale of Two Cities*, the novel contains no greater violence than that inflicted upon Manette by the prison. The Bastille casts its shadow across the novel, and nearly until the end the cell contains the solution to the novel's great mystery: the relationship between Manette, Darnay, and Madame Defarge that creates the fundamental tension of the plot. At the start, however, Manette illustrates nothing more than the psychological violence done by eighteen years of confinement.[48] Like the remains profaned by Cruncher, Manette has been entombed and must be, as Lorry remarks, "RECALLED TO LIFE." Though "[a] hundred times" Lorry imagines his reunion with Manette, a hundred times, when asked whether he cares to live, the specter responds, "I can't say" (*TTC* 15). Manette's release is therefore an equivocal salvation, caught between the horrors of Cruncher's "resurrectioning" and Carton's spiritual renewal at novel's end. It is also, from the moment Manette enters the novel, a return to *American Notes*. In his travel book Dickens wrote of solitary confinement that he believed "this slow and daily tampering with the mysteries of the brain, to be immeasurably worse than any torture of the body" (*AN* 99). Writing in *A Tale* of Manette's destruction in the Bastille, Dickens returns to the language of *American Notes*, as if he intends to prove his thesis of seventeen years before. Lorry's thought that he is "on his way to dig some one out of a grave" echoes Dickens's remark that the Eastern Penitentiary prisoner is "a man buried alive; to be dug out in the slow round of years" (*TTC* 15; *AN* 101). Also, as Dickens had worried years before, Lucie fears that when she sees her father again it will be like seeing his ghost.[49] Other details also find their way from *Notes* to *A Tale*. While the Eastern Penitentiary prisoner has "a number over his cell-door" that is "the index of his history," Manette responds, when Defarge asks his name, "One Hundred and Five, North Tower" (*AN* 101; *TTC* 49). Manette's shoemaking comes from the Eastern Penitentiary, as does Lorry's and Defarge's fear for Lucie's safety when Manette suddenly reaches for his shoemaker's knife.[50] Of all the novel's details, Manette's mental distraction—his "vacant gaze," his haggardness, his voice's "faintness of solitude and disuse"— especially recalls *American Notes* by attesting to "an anguish so acute and so tremendous, that all imagination of it must fall far short of reality" (*TTC* 45; *AN* 109). Like the Dickensian prisoners before him, Manette has been remade by his confinement, and he exists in *A Tale of Two Cities* as a member of a race apart.

He is also wholly unable to shed the taint left upon him by the prison. Even five years after his release, at Darnay's trial, Manette is "a man of very remarkable appearance in respect of the absolute whiteness of his hair, and a certain indescribable intensity of face: not of an active kind, but pondering and self-communing" (*TTC* 73). These are the lingering effects, it would seem, of long and forced introspection. When called upon to testify, though he remembers nothing of Darnay, Manette suffers "great distress," and even long after the trial the narrator says of Manette that the "pondering or brooding look which made him old, had been upon him, like a heavy cloud, ever since" (*TTC* 88–89). On one hand, the narrator reports, "It would have been difficult . . . to recognise in Doctor Manette, intellectual of face and upright of bearing, the shoemaker of the garret in Paris" (*TTC* 92). But at certain times a gloom falls over him, "as incomprehensible to those unacquainted with his story as if they had seen the shadow of the actual Bastille thrown upon him by a summer sun, when the substance was three hundred miles away" (*TTC* 92). Though he has been recalled to life and returned to the world beyond the cell, Manette cannot escape fully the prison's gloom. He keeps the tools of his shoemaking trade nearby and resorts to them at critical points of mental upset, first briefly when Darnay speaks to him about marrying Lucie, then again for nine nights after their wedding when Manette learns that Darnay is an Evrémonde. When Lorry destroys the tools and the workbench, however, he mistakes physical tokens for psychological cause, and the prison taint proves far more powerful than Lorry reckons. Near the novel's close, having had his old confinement recalled and having failed to free Darnay, the old Manette returns to Lorry's house and begs for his "work." In that moment, Lorry sees Manette "shrink into the exact figure that Defarge had had in keeping" (*TTC* 423). Like the novel it follows, *A Tale of Two Cities* offers us no hope that Manette will escape his taint. Instead, it implies that he is another misshapen self whose vanishing-point is the prison.

Inflicting this psychological wound within the privacy of the cell, the Bastille becomes in *A Tale of Two Cities* the unnarratable prison that *Little Dorrit* contains in so many forms. Except during the storming of the Bastille, when the prison's doors are opened and its power is finally broken, the narrator never shows us Manette's prison cell. Instead, he shows us the Doctor in an imperfect recreation of that cell above the wine-shop of Ernest Defarge. Even our venture into this solitary room, where Defarge keeps Manette under lock and key, suggests an invasion of privacy, and our first glimpse of the Doctor is akin to the scene with the three Jacques who try to peer "through some chinks or holes" into the little room (*TTC* 43). We are eventually permitted to enter the cell with Lucie, Lorry, and Defarge, but we understand Manette's imprisonment no better for that. We know nothing of his crime, he cannot recall his name when asked, and he turns back to his work with "a weary sound that was not a sigh, nor a groan"—the indeterminacy of the act recalling Miss Wade either withdrawing from or being avoided by her fellow travelers (*TTC* 49). Nor can he carry on a conversation or answer the questions his visitors put to him. Instead, the visitors find him "laps[ing] away, even for minutes"; to recall him, we are told, is akin "to stay[ing] the spirit of a fast-dying man" (*TTC* 49). Nor does Lucie's tender outpouring of thoughts and disclosures about Manette's past and her own produce any corresponding intelligence from him. It produces rather a "lethargy," and like so many of *Little Dorrit*'s prisoners, he ends up—when he nestles in Lucie's arms—in obscurity, "curtained . . . from the light" by her tumbled hair (*TTC* 55). The whole scene reinscribes Dickens's metaphor of the hidden prisoner, and, stymied, the narrator finally admits that he is baffled by Manette's secret trials:

> No human intelligence could have read the mysteries of his mind, in the scared blank wonder of his face. Whether he knew what had happened, whether he recollected what they had said to him, whether he knew that he was free, were questions which no sagacity could have solved. (*TTC* 56)

Prisoner of the Bastille, and psychologically transformed by a process unfathomable even to the narrator, Manette has wholly become an inscrutable self. As Dickens had always intended in planning his story of the solitary prison, the period of Manette's confinement figures here not as a story but as a gap, as absence, the unnarratable center of the novel. In this fashion *A Tale of Two Cities* leads Dickens back, through the prison, to the remarkable narrative quandary posed by psychological privacy.

This privacy is, from the opening pages, at the very heart of the novel's narrative concerns. As Lorry rides in the mail with two fellow-passengers on his way to see Manette, the narrator remarks, "Not one of the three could have said, from anything he saw, what either of the other two was like; and each was hidden under almost as many wrappers from the eyes of the mind, as from the eyes of the body" (*TTC* 6). When Cruncher arrives he, too, is obscured by the dark and the mist and the mud, and the mystery of his being is—in this age of violence—a thing much to be feared. But the novel's most important concern with psychological privacy emerges in the narrative intrusion that opens "Night Shadows," the novel's third chapter:

> A wonderful fact to reflect upon, that every human creature is constituted to be that profound secret and mystery to every other. A solemn consideration, when I enter a great city by night, that every one of those darkly clustered houses encloses its own secret; that every room in every one of them encloses its own secret; that every beating heart in the hundreds of thousands of breasts there, is, in some of its imaginings, a secret to the heart nearest it! Something of the awfulness, even of Death itself, is referable to this. . . . My friend is dead, my neighbour is dead, my love, the darling of my soul, is dead; it is the inexorable consolation and perpetuation of the secret that was always in that individuality, and which I shall carry in mine to my life's end. (*TTC* 12)

Occurring so early in the novel, this statement is crucial as a revelation of theme and as an eloquent and self-reflective comment about Dickens's art. The passage attests, like the rest of the novel, to the inviolable privacy of the mind. It attests to the failure of omniscience we find in *Little Dorrit*, and that the split narrative of *Bleak House* implies. But the passage is even more striking within the context of this particular novel, where it comprises *A Tale*'s only use of the narratorial "I" and speaks to the particular problem that Manette poses. Manette has endured this death—has been, that is, recalled to life from the cell—but the narrator implies that Manette still must be summoned back from his narrative death, which is the psychological privacy of the human mind. Imprisonment, death, and privacy are all linked in this narrative vision. More to the point, affirming the unassailable secrecy of human identity within a passage marked by his "I"—by which the narrator identifies himself, too, as a singular human consciousness—the narrator reveals the paradoxical secret that rests in his own act of narration: that omniscience is never really omniscience, and that it can produce narrative but not knowledge when confronted with the inviolable privacy of the self. Even within this historical novel, working from sources and the certainty of the past, the narrator of *A Tale of Two Cities* calls attention to his limitations and reveals his omniscience as a rhetorical sham.

Here as in *Little Dorrit*, the result is the novel's insistence that imprisonment can only be narrated as the first-person account of the self in the cell. The novel is a literal progress toward the unearthing of this story: toward France, the prison, and the recovery of Manette's narrative from his cell at the Bastille. The movement of the plot also parallels Manette's slow recovery of the capacity to fashion a complete narrative of self that includes his identity as a prisoner and his transformation under the power of the cell. First released from prison, unable to recall his name or his story, Manette cannot even explain the puzzling familiarity of Lucie's golden hair. At Darnay's trial, he likewise confesses that his "mind is a blank" regarding the first months after his release (*TTC* 85). But being recalled to life soon permits him to recall life, and to remember the "night when [he] was summoned out" by the Evrémondes (*TTC* 52). Each reference to his long absence conjures a psychological cloud and reminds him of a time that he wants to suppress but that continues to return. Darnay's account of a story he heard in the Tower of London—of the discovery of a secret narrative written by an unknown prisoner—triggers an especially powerful moment of recall, and Manette "suddenly start[s] up, with his hand to his head" in a manner terrifying to behold (*TTC* 119). Manette's discovery of Darnay's real name provides another such moment, so powerful that Manette returns to shoemaking for the next nine nights. Tellingly, Manette first returns to himself narratively just as William Dorrit does: by treating himself as a third-person object rather than as the subject of narrative. Speaking of Manette in the third person, Lorry addresses him on the subject of "an old and a prolonged shock, of great acuteness and severity," and for the first time the doctor can account for the "dread lurking in his mind" (*TTC* 243; 245). The unspeakable has become narratable, but in a form that bespeaks a divided psychological self. That Manette must return to the prison to find the vanishing-point of his story is evidence that, as Chris Vanden Bossche says, "you cannot get out without going back in."[51] Like William Dorrit's gradual collapse, Manette's recovery of self begins in narrative displacement—a creation of self as other—that presages the eventual emergence of privacy into the world of the novel.

This revelation of the private self is, for Gallagher, the novel's great narrative desire. The spectacle of torture and execution, the disinterment of bodies, and the spying of the Jacquarie are for her part of *A Tale*'s "nightmare of transparency, of publicly displaying what is hidden, intimate, secret, in the interests of creating social order and cohesion."[52]

Carol Hanbery MacKay argues this, too, calling the novel a sustained narrative attempt to "transcend the boundaries that separate individual consciousness."[53] Yet to view *A Tale* as revelatory or transcendent in this way is to neglect crucial aspects of the novel—is to make it, in fact, inconsistent with the "Night Shadows" passage and its concern with the privacy of the self. Far from revelatory, as Gallagher and MacKay would make it, *A Tale of Two Cities* shows above all how the psychological self may be constructed, despite its privacy and without regard for its truth, by the perilous narrative power of the prison. Early in the novel, remarking the penal violence inflicted under the authority of the social order, the narrator says that such punishments work according to a simple philosophy: "Whatever is is right" (*TTC* 69). The words carry a more complex meaning than is first clear. For what "is" in *A Tale of Two Cities* always depends upon interpretation, upon controlling truth by inscribing words and people with particular significations. As Andrew Sanders observes in introducing *A Tale*, "How things or persons are called matters a great deal in . . . [this] narrative" (*TTC* x). The novel indicates consistently that the authority to inflict violence and maintain order depends upon the power to control violence's meaning within the social framework. Cruncher's meaning of "resurrection" is less powerful than the meaning endorsed by the Church, just as the tortures and executions of the "youth" and Gaspard are officially sanctioned, though they are more brutal and less just than the murder of Monseigneur, who has carelessly ridden down Gaspard's child.

Ideological and social authority in *A Tale of Two Cities* are thus explicitly linked not to the revelation of essential truths but rather to narrative control over meanings, and particularly the meanings of the private self. In the contested world described by *A Tale*, the key to maintaining order is declaring sides, identifying enemies, and defining the self's loyalty to the social order. This is true at the start of the novel, in the cases of criminals who have offended and thus challenged the rule of the French and English crowns. It is true as well in the emergent French Revolution, where opposition to the social revolt becomes sufficient cause for violent punishment. To identify the enemy authorities must account for the enemy, even including the secrets of the private self. As an instrument of terror and oppression, of both locking away and transforming the self-account, the prison is the authorities' greatest tool for achieving this aim. Returning to the cell to save Darnay through his celebrity as the Bastille prisoner, Manette thus discovers that the greatest horror of the prison is neither physical hardship nor psychological trauma; rather, it is falling under the narrative power of a prison that cares less for truth than for control over truth, and that makes the cell a vanishing-point for not only his story but also his power to tell it. Beneath the novel's terrible violence and its illusion of privacy spoiled, a deeper current runs that is fundamentally allied with the narrative function of the prison. In this portrait—of a prison powerful enough to justify even the narrative construction of the private self—the novel solves the quandary posed by "Night Shadows" and culminates Dickens's vision of the Victorian prison.

VIII

Even amid the violence of its early chapters, *A Tale of Two Cities* links its struggle between subversion and order with the struggle for narrative power over the self. Carrying the threat of physical rending and promising to "discover" his innocence or guilt, Darnay's trial for treason in England at first seems interwoven with the novel's chimerical desire for revelation. More accurately viewed, the trial is but a process of narrative construction, in which representatives of the social order build a "truth" that makes Darnay a traitor and justifies his subjection to penal authority. Even as he stands at the bar, Darnay is "being mentally hanged, beheaded, and quartered, by everybody there" as if he has already been made guilty by narrative upon narrative (*TTC* 72). A mirror stands over him "to throw the light down upon him" and presumably upon his story, too, and the reading of the charges against him makes him into an object of narration: "a false traitor to our serene, illustrious, excellent, and so forth, prince . . . by . . . wickedly, falsely, traitorously and otherwise evil-adverbiously, revealing" English secrets about the war in North America (*TTC* 73; 72). Preempting its own operation in determining justice, the court narrates him a traitor before he has even received due process. The weaver of this guilty narrative is the Attorney-General, who constructs a story of treason that seems to reveal the secrets of Darnay's soul:

> Mr. Attorney General had to inform the jury, that the prisoner before them, though young in years, was old in the treasonable practices which claimed the forfeit of his life. That his correspondence with the public enemy was not a correspondence of to-day, or of yesterday, or even of last year, or of the year before. That, it was certain the prisoner had, for longer than that, been in the habit of passing and repassing between France and England, on secret business of which he could give no honest account. (*TTC* 75)

Accounting, telling, narrating—not *disclosing*—are key to this trial. Constructing this narrative of a treasonous Darnay is the Attorney-General's function, part of a punitive process that draws its legitimacy from pretending to know the "truth," even of the private self. As we have seen in "Night Shadows," however, the pretension cannot possibly *be* "true"; it cannot be more than a fantasy to justify the operation of the social order. Barsad (alias Solomon Pross), a "patriot" "beyond fear and beyond reproach," is called to testify and lies about everything from his name to his family to his occupation (*TTC* 75). Roger Cly, Darnay's "admirable servant" who is really Barsad's brother-spy, does the same (*TTC* 73). Other people testify more honestly: Lorry, to the timing of Darnay's coming on board the packet from Calais; Lucie, to her conversations with Darnay about business and America; Manette, to the mental blank of the days just after his release. No one knows Darnay's true story or business. No one even knows his real name. Yet all of these witnesses—liars and truth-tellers alike—are permitted to narrate a line of Darnay's private truth although he himself is not. Wielding power over both narrative and its meaning, the authorities require not truth but only its appearance, and it is worth noting that Darnay is acquitted because his outer, rather than his inner, identity is called into question by his uncanny resemblance to Carton. In this fashion, the trial contains the fundamental tension of the novel: between the self's power to control its private truth and the greater narrative power of the authorities.

For Darnay the novel hinges upon this struggle. His return to France to visit his uncle reflects it, for the visit is largely Darnay's attempt to forge a new identity and shed the meanings of the past. Recalling the glorious years of unchallenged aristocratic rule, Darnay's uncle tells an old story of the power of the name Evrémonde—of a time when their "ancestors held the right of life and death over the surrounding vulgar" (*TTC* 146). To be an Evrémonde within the *ancien régime* is to rule, and to do so without mercy. But Darnay rejects this self-definition out of hand, choosing instead to forge a new narrative identity for himself and for the name his family bears. Rather than keep a name "more detested than any name in France," he takes a new one and, as he later tells his inquisitors at the Concièrgerie, determines "to live by his own industry in England, rather than on the industry of the overladen people of France" (*TTC* 146; 349). When he requests Lucie's hand, Darnay narrates himself to Manette as a man divided from the rule of the *ancien régime*:

> Like you, a voluntary exile from France; like you, driven from it
> by its distractions, oppressions, and miseries; like you, striving to
> live away from it by my own exertions, and trusting in a happier
> future; I look only to sharing your fortunes, sharing your life and
> home, and being faithful to you to the death. (*TTC* 160)

This struggle to free himself from his old identity is Darnay's life work, and much of the reason he lives in England rather than in France is that in England he can more easily escape the associations of his old name, and the power of the old order. Even when Gaspard murders his uncle, Darnay does not return to France. Instead, he relies upon Gabelle to carry out his orders: to remit all imposts, to cease collecting rents, to seek recourse in no process—in short, to act in favor of the peasants, and thus to begin erasing the old and terrible associations of the Evrémonde name. From afar Darnay invents a new identity and recreates his old one, relying upon his own power to change in the present the narrative meanings of the future and the past.

Darnay is not the only character whose trials hinge upon this struggle to retain narrative power over the self. Cruncher, for instance, maintains a respectable identity during the day as a runner for Tellson's but has another, grotesque one at night as a "Resurrection-man," an identity he must hide to escape the clutches of the law. Barsad, the "Sheep of the prisons," moves from England to France and infiltrates different groups as his profession requires (*TTC* 371). In each place he adopts a new narrative identity that suits the task at hand. Much more even than Cruncher's, Barsad's safety depends upon his power to shape his self-account, as Carton's threat to denounce "Mr. Barsad to the nearest Section Committee" suggests (*TTC* 371). Two others, both centrally related to the novel's concern with narrative and the prison, also underscore the significance of self-narrative power. The first is Manette. Unlike Cruncher and Barsad, the Doctor has no aliases or secret professions, nor does he need to lie in order to escape punishment. Rather, he lives a retiring life as Lucie's father, a respected physician, and a kind friend to men like Lorry, Carton, and Darnay. But for all the serenity of Manette's present life, he is constantly threatened by intimations of a darker, older identity irrevocably linked with the horrors of the cell. Each mention of his old life brings a cloud, and his happiness depends heavily upon keeping that life out of his narrative—upon remaining, psychologically, the Doctor of Beauvais rather than the Bastille prisoner. Indeed, the entire novel tends toward the violent and unwanted intrusion of that old narrative upon the story of the present.

Carton is also linked significantly to this concern with self-narration. Like Miss Wade in *Little Dorrit*, Carton inhabits the novel's fringes, communing frequently with his mirror and making himself hateful to the other characters. As he says after Darnay's trial for treason, "I care for no man on earth, and no man on earth cares for me" (*TTC* 98). Immediately afterwards he insults Darnay to illustrate his point. He drinks too much. He succeeds at nothing. To Stryver he complains of always being "behind" the first rank, of being "nowhere," and of having "had no chance for [his] life but in rust and repose" (*TTC* 105). Self-pitying and self-thwarted, Carton allows all of his acquaintances to see him as the luckless, dissipated, and taciturn wretch that he seems—all, that is, but one. To Lucie alone he reveals a nobler nature, showing her that in his "degradation [he has] not been so degraded but that the sight of [her] . . . has stirred old shadows that [he] thought had died out" (*TTC* 182). His function in the novel—saving Darnay from execution and doing so unsuspected of such a self-sacrificial act—depends upon his ability to control his narrative in this way, and to control his identity in the eyes of those around him. Twice he saves Darnay from death by manipulating his own identity, and as he tells Lucie during his moment of confession, "I shall hold sacred the one good remembrance . . . that my last avowal of myself was made to you, and that my name, and faults, and miseries were gently carried in your heart" (*TTC* 183). For Carton, retaining his self-narrative power is all.

In *A Tale of Two Cities*, however, such narrative power over the self belongs finally only to the authorities, whose privilege it is control the truth. By "Year One of Liberty," revolutionary France is a place of new meanings dictated by a new social order: a "deluge rising from below, not falling from above, and with the windows of Heaven shut, not opened" (*TTC* 335). A new law governs, "[striking] away all security for liberty or life, and deliver[ing] over any good and innocent person to any bad and guilty one" (*TTC* 336). The Carmagnole, not Monseigneur's opulent reception, is the new symbol of French culture; "La Guillotine" supercedes "the Cross" as "the sign of the regeneration of the human race" (*TTC* 336). Everywhere the revolutionaries have created fresh narratives that demystify the old ones and raise a new France from the ruins of the *ancien régime*. In this world of competing ideologies, where the sides that struggle over power must know on which side each person fights, no power to control meaning is more critical or perilous than the one the authorities wield over the private self.

Married to Lucie, living with her and Manette, and a father himself now to little Lucie, Darnay seems to have renarrated his identity successfully and freed himself from both the new France and the old. But under the authority of the new Republic, counter-narratives are already being constructed that will drag him back to the old identity he has always despised. Gabelle's letter, addressed to "Monsieur heretofore the Marquis" unexpectedly renames Darnay according to the exigencies of the old order and draws him into a narrative nightmare (*TTC* 292). Fancying himself an English traveler arrived in France "of [his] own free will," Darnay quickly discovers the impotence of his self-definition (*TTC* 304). He is seized as an "emigrant" and "aristocrat" and informed by the brothers of the Jacquarie that "even his cursed life is not his own" (*TTC*

304). Arrived at Paris Darnay is again renamed, this time as a "prisoner," and is "struck by the disagreeable word" (*TTC* 306). Worse yet, having been proclaimed an enemy of the Revolution and a member of the old aristocracy, Darnay also becomes subject to the novel's most terrible narrative: the knitted register of Madame Defarge. Literally a narrative of life and death and a record that seeks to identify and define others, Madame Defarge's register is the novel's most potent text—one that, written "in her own stitches and her own symbols," only she can read (*TTC* 208). Bearing such authority in *A Tale*, the register reveals the power of narrative not to disclose but to control. It also illustrates the novel's underlying crux, for it is a narrative that—though written over the course of years—cannot speak its "truth" until its author has become an authority, part of the order that owns narrative power. Only then does it replace the old law, naming the enemies to power and ordering them to destruction. Recorded among the names on this death roll, Darnay's story, like his life, is no longer his own.

In this struggle through and over narrative, as Manette's emergent self-account suggests, the authorities have no tool more powerful than the prison. Much as in *Little Dorrit*, the emergence of Manette's prison narrative provides resolution by bringing to light crucial information that has lain hidden. It reveals the connection between Manette and Darnay, demonstrates the terrible depravity of the *ancien régime*, and makes clear, for the first time, the reasons for Manette's confinement. It also testifies to a facet of imprisonment that Dickens well knew, and upon which he had insisted since the days of *Pickwick Papers*: the prison's terrible power to transform and scar the psychological self. Manette's account begins, he explains, only after he has spent a weary decade in solitude, and he records his reasons for choosing suddenly to write:

> I know from terrible warnings I have noted in myself that my reason will not long remain unimpaired, but I solemnly declare that I am at this time in the possession of my right mind . . . and that I write the truth as I shall answer for these my last recorded words, whether they be ever read by men or not, at the Eternal Judgment-seat. (*TTC* 394)

Thus his narrative is, above all, an attempt to record the truth—to write the realities of his old self—before that self is remade irrevocably by the power of the cell. Even so, Manette shows signs throughout his account that imprisonment has already exacted a toll, and that he is not what he was ten years before. At one moment, he writes that he is "weary, weary, weary—worn down by misery" and that he "cannot read what [he has] written with this gaunt hand" (*TTC* 407). Elsewhere he records his creeping sense that he is "growing more and more unequal to the task" he has set for himself, because his "senses are so benumbed, and the gloom upon [him] is so dreadful" (*TTC* 408). He calls his cell a "living grave"— an echo of Lorry's words, and of Dickens's years before—and in the "unbearable agony" to which his captors have subjected him, he "denounce[s] them to Heaven and to earth" (*TTC* 410). Like the Chancery prisoner, the Eastern Penitentiary's inmates, and William Dorrit and Arthur Clennam, Manette has endured the cell and been—as his self-account attests—psychologically misshaped by the grotesque power of the prison.

More important, Manette's self-account intimates that, at bottom, the very purpose of the prison is not only to transform the mind but to arrest, misshape, and seize control over the private narrative of the self. Throughout his self-account Manette records the authority that the prison wields over his narrative. He writes that he can work only "at stolen intervals, under every difficulty," and that he could not begin to write his story until he had "slowly and laboriously made a place of concealment for it . . . in the wall of the chimney" (*TTC* 394). He writes painstakingly, using a "rusty iron point" and "scrapings of soot and charcoal from the chimney, mixed with blood" (*TTC* 394). He uses, too, a system of ellipses to show where he must at times break his narrative and hide it in the wall to avoid being "detected and consigned to an underground cell and total darkness" where he will surely lose his remaining sanity (*TTC* 405). So closely is he watched at times that he writes near the end of his self-account, "These scraps of paper fail me. One was taken from me, with a warning, yesterday. I must finish my record to-day" (*TTC* 409). Part of this account of Manette—perhaps even Manette's first name—must owe to Alexander Dumas and to similar romanticized fictions of the solitary prisoner; indeed, the French subject matter of *A Tale* may have encouraged Dickens in this regard. But confined within a solitary cell and policed by agents of the prison, Manette's difficulty retaining command of his self-account also extends Dickens's own conception of the plight of the imprisoned self. From the start, Manette's imprisonment has been an arrest not of a person—a criminal body and a transgression of the law—but of the story he may tell. It is an arrest of what he has seen and heard, of what he knows and believes of the Evrémondes, and of his power to narrate the truth about events of which he was very much a part. As he confides, he is imprisoned only after he has "writ[ten] privately to the Minister," and he knows that he is a danger to those he loves only because he "possess[es] the knowledge" that he possesses (*TTC* 408). Privacy, knowledge, and the experiences and identity of the hidden self: these are the things that the prison sets out to erase, and that it pretends to erase by overwriting and superceding the prisoner's self-account. When the Evrémondes arrive at Manette's home to spirit him away, they bear his letter as well—and they burn it, as Amy burns Arthur's life story, to destroy the ugliness it contains. Stripped of his narrative of the past and without hope of a narrative for his future, Manette's identity is contained by the cell, dominated by the narrative power of the prison.

First showing that the prison owns this narrative power, the novel's climactic scenes illustrate the terrible consequences of this wresting away of narrative. At first, bearing his celebrity as the Bastille prisoner but hiding his reasons for having once been an inmate, Manette succeeds at helping Darnay. He testifies at Darnay's first trial before the tribunal, weaving his own identity into a careful narrative that makes Darnay a "faithful and devoted" friend to the Doctor and narrating with such "discretion" and "straightforward force of truth and earnestness" that the Jury is persuaded to mercy (*TTC* 351). But even the Bastille prisoner cannot for long assert his narrative power in opposition to the power of those authorities who crave Darnay's blood, for Manette's self-account remains, literally and figuratively, under the shadow of the prison. Ernest Defarge, not Manette, successfully enters the Bastille and drags Manette's long-hidden story to light. Madame Defarge, not Manette, brings the narrative to bear upon Darnay's case at the crucial moment, just as he is about to go free. An agent of the tribunal, not Manette, reads his story aloud and thus enters that story discursively—surrounded, even, by quotation marks—into the greater text of the novel. And the revolutionaries, not Manette, finally determine the meaning of his narrative past in the world of the present, condemning Darnay to death by making the account speak a "truth" that Manette no longer means. Indeed, the President corrupts the narrative entirely by remarking that "the good physician of the Republic . . . would doubtless feel a sacred glow and joy in making his daughter a widow and her child an orphan" (*TTC* 411). Monstrous, cruel, and indicative of the terror with which Dickens regarded the old French upheaval, the tribunal makes Manette wholly subject to the prison's power to construct his identity and private truths. It is fitting that, as Darnay is led away to death, Manette requests his shoemaking tools. In these moments before the tribunal he becomes, wholly and permanently, the figure of the self in the cell.

IX

Murray Baumgarten argues quite credibly that the shifting meaning of Manette's narrative is part of *A Tale of Two Cities'* greater concern with the "inherent difficulties" of the written word.[54] But written meanings are not the only ones that shift in this novel, as the continuous fluctuations of ideology and "truth" suggest. Fashioning Manette's story into the centerpiece of a novel preoccupied with narrative from the cell, *A Tale of Two Cities'* real concern seems to be with the wresting away of self-narrative authority by the prison. This novel makes the prison what it was in *Little Dorrit*: a place of private psychological transformation, a repository for the novel's mysteries and truths, and a place narratable only in the sudden bursting forth of the first-person account of the self in the cell. But Manette's story, vulnerable as it is to narrating others, demonstrates also that one can construct, without knowledge, the private narrative of the psychological self. A place of hopeless solitary confinement, the Bastille is not Reade's ——— Gaol. It does not pretend to produce narrative truth nor to reform gloriously the prisoners it confines. But wielding the same narrative authority as Reade's prison, the Bastille misshapes the prison narrative and reveals the perilous implications of the prison's power over private narration. Characterized by unfeeling savagery against both real and perceived agents of the old *ancien régime*, the Defarges and their Jacquarie are Francis Eden foully remade. They own the same power to make the prisoner's self-account a story-within-a-story in which the meaning lies under their domain. Since neither guilt nor truth matters, all that remains is the narrative power wielded by the authorities and concentrated in the prison: the power to disregard any true self and fix the meaning of private truth without participation from the self-narrator. Darnay's English trial implies this power. So do his final trial in France and the misappropriation of Manette's old story. In this way the novel shows us that even in the world described by the "Night Shadows" passage, filled with inviolable human subjects each a mystery to the other, the private self can always be narrated by the social order.

This subordination of the private self to the narrative power that can construct it underlies, in the end, *A Tale of Two Cities'* most significant conclusions about narrative, the self, and the cell. Thematically, it explains the novel's fascination with reproductions and "echoes," and with doubled characters like the Evrémonde brothers, Darnay and Carton, and the three generations of Lucie Manette all bearing their golden curls. It also explains why Carton can twice substitute himself for Darnay, illustrating the irrelevancy of the true self in the eyes of the law. Extrapolated across the whole of the text, it even explains the novel's fascination with constructed meanings and with the complex interplays of ideology that produce competing social orders, united only in their brutal applications of power. Most important, it explains *A Tale's* conclusion: Carton's final words and actions, and their implications for the world of the novel and the prison. Appearing before Darnay in the Concièrgerie, Carton commands him to take up a pen and write from dictation. We know that the statement is intended for Lucie, though Carton tells Darnay to address it to "no one" (*TTC* 434). The letter begins: "If you remember . . . the words that passed between us, long ago, you will readily comprehend this when you see it. You do remember them, I know. It is not in your nature to forget" (*TTC* 434). Carton means, of course, to direct Lucie to the time when he pledged he "would give his life" to keep a life she loves beside her (*TTC* 184). Mostly, though, it underscores the difficulty of narrating, from outside the self, private identity and desire. The meaning of Carton's final words, addressed to no one, depends upon reaching the correct auditor, upon Darnay's faithful authorship, upon Lucie's reading and interpretation, and upon the ability of Darnay and Lucie to fuse past and present into a complete narrative that will, in the future, yield its retrospective meaning and reveal the nobility of Carton's death. If this sounds confusing, it is because Darnay and Lucie are being asked, according to "Night Shadows," to do the impossible: to account for Carton's inviolable identity, in which lingers, literally in this case, something of "the awfulness, even of Death." It is a tenuous endeavor at best, and even as Darnay writes Carton's drug takes effect, so that the pen—tellingly—begins "trailing off into unintelligible signs" (*TTC* 435). Upon this equivocal document depends the future narration of Carton's self.

In this vision of a private self imperfectly narrated by another, the novel reaches not only the conclusion to its action but also a solution to the quandary posed by "Night Shadows" hundreds of pages before. Gallagher calls the novel's ending a "prophetic vision," and Vanden Bossche says it is a moment of "prophetic closure."[55] Drawing attention to the "long ranks of the new oppressors who [rise] upon the destruction of the old" and will also die at the guillotine, the conclusion does gesture toward prophecy, for the narrator refers to a fictional future that, really, already rests safely in the historical past (*TTC* 465). The novel gains authority by virtue of the truth of this vision. But to whom does this prescience belong? The narrator tells us that this final passage remarks what Carton would have written down "[I]f he had given any utterance to his [thoughts]" (*TTC* 464). As Vanden Bossche asks, however, "Is he telling us what he knows in Carton's words, or is he telling us what Carton *would* have thought; is this the reality or only Carton's fantasy?"[56] The answer, it seems, is that *both* are speaking—the narrator and Carton—in a moment of seamlessly blent public voice and private truth that Dickens had been seeking since *Bleak House*, or perhaps even before. Creating the illusion of authority to speak by invoking a future that is really in the past, the novel speaks, for the first time authoritatively and decisively, about the secrets of the private self. In his sham prescience, the narrator has established a right never possessed by the teller of *Little Dorrit*: the right to construct even interior narrative without fear of contradiction, and without stumblings over the inadequacy of his vision. As Beth

Kemper suggests, this final passage is the instant at which the narrator's resistance to claim his own authority finally dissolves, and at which he becomes "fully conscious of the importance of his role as fiction-builder."[57]

It is a moment made possible by Dickens's vision of the prison. As a central image in his mature fiction, the prison seems to have made first-person narration a surer part of Dickens's powers as an author. *Bleak House, Little Dorrit,* and *A Tale of Two Cities* all express the anxiety of a narrator concerned with the limitations to his omniscience, struggling mightily with the irreconcilability of narrative disclosure and the privacy of the self. Even *Dombey and Son* (1848), which precedes Dickens's mature period, addresses this dilemma, asking for "a good spirit who would take the house-tops off . . . and show a Christian people what dark shapes issue from amidst their homes."[58] The story of Alexandre Manette eliminates the need for this concern by offering a narrated subject who has already lost control over his narrative—whose story of past and present, psychological identity, and private desire already rests under the narrative power of another. The moment is a crucial narrative insight, for it suggests that "true" psychological narratives can always be illusory, can always be constructed under the auspices of a social order determined to control "Whatever is." This does not mean that Dickens rejects the notion of an essential self; rather, "Night Shadows" argues the opposite. But in the prison, a repository for and shaper of private truth, Dickens found a model for how self-narrative authority can be wrested from the self, and how even private identity can be constructed through the socially authorized power to produce narrative.

The author possesses that power. So, through the author, does the narrator. And as long as author and narrator abide by the rules and maintain the pretense and form of first-person disclosure, both may construct narratives of the private self that are more socially legitimate than any genuine self-narration. Indeed, the imprisoned object of narration need not even be formally guilty, for few of Dickens's prisoners ever are. He or she needs only to be an individual, prey to the countless real and metaphorical prisons that crowd upon Dickens's fictional worlds. The social power that authorizes the prison thus justifies any first-person narration undertaken from outside the self, and it is suggestive that among all Dickens's novels only two are written wholly in the first-person. The first, *David Copperfield,* is explicitly autobiographical. But the second, *Great Expectations* (1861), emerged immediately upon the heels of *A Tale of Two Cities,* almost as if Dickens required this idea of a prison that detaches self from self-narrative before he could produce a mostly invented first-person novel. Realizing the narrative possibilities suggested by the prison, Dickens no longer needed to base his first-person accounts upon his own history. He no longer needed the self for whom the self-account was identifiably true. For, after all, the portrait of Alexandre Manette is of a man who has lost his story. As Miss Pross once tells Lorry, "Not knowing how he lost himself, or how he recovered himself, he may never feel certain of not losing himself again" (*TTC* 115). He lost himself, first and for always, in the shadow of the Victorian prison.

Chapter 5

The "Marks System": Australia and Narrative Wounding

> I wonder if my spirit will really grow so humble in the next fifteen or twenty years that I shall whine and whimper before people, branding myself a criminal with every word I utter. Yes, exactly, exactly! That is just why they are deporting me now, that is what they want . . .
> —Fyodor Dostoyevsky, *Crime and Punishment*

A FEW MONTHS BEFORE DICKENS DIED ON JUNE 9, 1870, A YOUNG JOURNALIST half a world away began writing his own account of the prison's shadows. Marcus Clarke was born in 1846 at Kensington, attended school at Highgate with Gerard Manley Hopkins, and grew up reading novels by Dickens and other Victorians. But he is never numbered among Victorian writers, nor is his epic account of the transportation system in Australia ever considered alongside Victorian novels.[1] Instead, most critics regard *His Natural Life* as a distinctly Australian landmark: the first example of a national literature focused upon convicthood, individual suffering, and the collective guilt that shaped the conscience of a nation. Ironically, Clarke believed when he wrote *His Natural Life* that he was mostly following in the footsteps of European authors who had gone before. As he wrote in the "Preface" to the 1874 edition of his novel:

> The convict of fiction has been hitherto shown only at the beginning or at the end of his career. Either his exile has been the mysterious end to his misdeeds, or he has appeared upon the scene to claim interest by reason of an equally unintelligible love of crime acquired during his experience in a penal settlement. Charles Reade has drawn the interior of a house of correction in England,

and Victor Hugo has shown how a French convict fares under the
fulfillment of his sentence. But no writer—so far as I am aware—
has attempted to depict the dismal condition of a felon during his
term of transportation.[2]

This remark suggests that Clarke envisioned his novel as a missing
chapter of the Victorian prison novel and that he wished it—as Reade
and Dickens wished their prison novels—to play a documentary and
even hermeneutic role. Having moved to Australia after his father suffered a breakdown and was institutionalized, Clarke became endlessly
curious about transportation. He attempted unsuccessfully to train himself for sheep farming in the mid-1860s, then settled in Melbourne and
began writing for the *Argus*, a leading colonial newspaper. By 1867 he was
also writing for the weekly *Australasian* and researching transportation in
the Melbourne Public Library. Three years later, his editor at the *Argus*
sent him to Tasmania "to write up the criminal records" for a series of
historical sketches about transportation.[3] There were cultural exigencies
for undertaking this project in 1870, but few political ones. The last
English transportees had arrived in Western Australia on January 10,
1868, so that Clarke's melodramatic exposé of transportation's horrors
was really superfluous, perhaps even anachronistic. At the same time,
though, the gold rush of the early 1850s had attracted so many free settlers to Australia that immigrants for the first time came to outnumber
transportees. As a new arrival to Australia, Clarke may have sensed that
Australians were losing the sense of their distinctive past, or at least the
sense of those characteristics that Clarke believed made Australia distinctive. He also had his own inquisitiveness to satisfy. Beginning to study
transportation in 1867 amid a flurry of popular interest in the dying
penal system, Clarke learned in graphic detail about the miseries endured
by convicts at Norfolk Island and Macquarie Harbor. In Tasmania he even
saw one last relic of the old system: Port Arthur's prison, which still held
a few inmates who were too dangerous to free. Like Dickens's *Sketches by
Boz*, Clarke's historical sketches were eventually collected into a single
volume, *Old Tales of a Young Country*, first published in Melbourne in
1871. The sketches return invariably to violence that makes convicts into
beasts.

His Natural Life began appearing serially in the *Australian Journal* in
March 1870 and drew, in obvious ways, upon these same images of convicts maimed by the cell. According to Clarke's original plan, the novel
should have finished its monthly run in twelve installments. But to the
dismay of *Journal* editor A. H. Massina, it plodded on for twenty-eight
months and an astonishing 370,000 words before reaching its much-
desired end. The novel plunged Richard Devine into the horrors of

Australia only to draw him out again: to prosper during the gold rush, participate in the Ballarat riots, and return wearily but triumphantly to England after three decades of exile. The *Journal's* readers seem to have been unable or unwilling to follow Clarke's hero through this "outrage [of] the probabilities," for the magazine's circulation declined by two-thirds during the novel's run.[4] In fact, had Clarke not produced a shorter, more popular edition of the novel in 1874, Australia's national epic might have been forgotten. On the advice of his friend Charles Gavan Duffy, Clarke strengthened the novel's thematic parallels by making Devine and John Rex half-brothers, and by making their father the victim of the murder for which Devine is wrongfully transported. He also excised nearly half of the original by killing Devine aboard the *Lady Franklin* rather than permitting him to return to life beyond the cell. Thus revised, *His Natural Life* reappeared as a sleek 200,000–word text in 1874, and English and American editions followed in 1875 and 1876. Though some critics reviled Clarke's graphic accounts of penal violence, the revised novel became by any standard an enormous success.[5] Since 1874, it has passed through numerous editions in Australia, England, and the United States, and it has been translated twice into German and once each into Dutch, Swedish, and Russian. The forgotten original, by contrast, was first collected as an unabridged novel in 1970.[6]

For reasons that make perfect sense, most critics have studied the shorter, more available revised edition of the novel. In the cases of the source studies conducted by L. L. Robson, Decie Denholm, and Harold Boehm, the choice matters very little.[7] Devine's miserable experiences as a transportee are virtually the same in the serial and the revised novel, and the details all come from Clarke's single program of historical research. Seizing upon the latent irony of the novel's title, Michael Wilding argues that *His Natural Life* makes Australia into a "natural" prison that, "freed from the restraints of European society," permits prisoners and governors alike to sink into animal brutality.[8] The novel returns repeatedly to images of the convict-beast, most notably in the contest between Gabbett and Jimmy Vetch as they stalk one another hungrily in the bush. For J. F. Burrows these images are the core of the novel, since they reveal the animalizing transformation Australia inflicts upon prisoners. As he concludes from Rex's failed attempt to return to England and Devine's death aboard the *Lady Franklin*, the novel shows that transportation's horrors divide convicts permanently from those outside the cell, for convict-beasts "can no longer live among men who do not share the experience of long years in the penal settlements."[9] This may be—perhaps even ought to be—true of the revised novel, for Australia *is* a violent carceral world and *does* inflict horrifying transformations upon Devine, Rex, and other transportees. It tears convicts permanently from the social order of England and eradicates the reason and compassion that place humans, in the natural order of things, above the lower animals. It also throws convicts into psychological, emotional, moral, and even narrative disarray, so that they become unfamiliar even to themselves. Indeed, in Clarke's novel as in Dickens's and Reade's, the prison's primary function is to wound the prisoner so that he feels his guilty mark—so that he feels, in other words, how completely his identity has been disordered by the miseries inflicted by the cell.

But this reading does not suffice for the original serial, because there Clarke's vision of Australia is different and more complex. By permitting Devine to return from the cell, the original version of *His Natural Life* moves beyond the prison's power to inflict disorder upon the prisoner, insisting finally that the prison forces Devine to turn to self-narration as a way of imposing order upon his private disarray. From the start of the novel Devine's confinement parallels his loss of self-narrative power, and at the end his attempt at narrative self-ordering enables his return from the cell. Between are hundreds of pages in which Devine, wrongly convicted and imprisoned at the outset, sinks to depravity under the rigors of discipline. The novel shows us, in other words, how the prison operates brutally to make Devine what it has insisted he is all along: a guilty self who merits the punishment inflicted upon him. Yet the novel is not finally about even this infliction of private disorder, for the infliction of disorder is not the prison's ultimate aim. Rather, Clarke's Australia aims to make Devine attest to his guilty mark, so that his orderly account of himself must always confess to the disorder inflicted by the prison. Made brutal, desperate, and even murderous by his confinement, Devine can no longer give the innocent self-account he might have given when he was first arrested. Yet he finds that he *must* account for himself, for reclaiming self-narrative power is necessary if he wishes to be free of the cell. He must confess to his old innocence and newer guilt, and to the experiences he has come to own as Devine, Rufus Dawes, and Tom Crosbie. The confession suggests that the prison's entire aim in producing private disorder is to drive the convict to reconceive of his identity, and to force him to account for, and thus order, the disorder the prison has inflicted. Clarke's novel thus reveals something more of the prison than Reade's work or Dickens's. By showing us that Devine's guilty self-narrative is the price of his freedom from the cell, *His Natural Life* implies that the prison's true function is not just to maim or wound, nor just to produce guilt. It is, rather, to make the prisoner forever the author of his own guilty marks.

II

Those marks are etched, in the first place, by the brutality of Devine's prison. Even before Devine reaches Australia, the attempted mutiny aboard the *Malabar* leaves Miles "shot through the breast," the swell of prisoners bursts from below decks with a "guttural snarl" and "horrible roar," and the convicts become a "storm of hideous faces" as they gain the main deck (*HNL* 212; 217). During the melee, one convict is "shot . . . through the head" and leaves the Moocher "spattered with the blood and brains of his unfortunate comrade" (*HNL* 217; 218). Gabbett, in a torn shirt and "bleeding from a cut on his forehead," foams at the mouth as he prepares to fell Maurice Frere (*HNL* 222). If not for *A Tale of Two Cities*, such violence might seem out of place in a Victorian novel. But it is worth noting that here, as with Dickens's France, Clarke is preparing his readers to deal with the realities of a hopelessly violent world. As the narrator introduces us to Macquarie Harbor, we learn of James Williams, who was transported to Australia at age nineteen for picking pockets. Through twenty-six years at the antipodes, we are told, Williams spent "twenty years in irons" and received during his lifetime "more than two thousand lashes" (*HNL* 237). "In 1822," the narrator remarks, "one hundred and sixty-nine men out of one hundred and eighty-two were punished to the extent of two thousand lashes," and escapers routinely commit suicide rather than allow themselves to be retaken (*HNL* 238). Meantime, the prisoners at Phillip's Island are "miserable wretches, deprived of every hope, [and] employed in the most degrading labor" (*HNL* 243). These details presage Devine's new life in Australia and introduce us to the brutalities of his world.

As the novel goes on, its violence grows more awful. The narrator describes child suicide, murder pacts, cannibalism, and torture—a grim parade of prisoners wrecked physically and psychologically by brutal discipline. The scenes are melodramatic, to be sure, compounding upon one another within Clarke's ever-widening condemnation of the already extinct penal system.[10] But as is the case with Reade's novel, the violence is no less compelling—and little less true—for its sensational flavor. Perhaps the worst image is of Kirkland stretched upon the wooden triangle, receiving a flogging for attempting suicide. With Devine acting as unwilling flogger, the first blow from the cat-o'-nine-tails stripes Kirkland's skin "with six crimson bars," and the second makes "blood [bead] on the skin" (*HNL* 464). After another lash "the crimson turn[s] purple" (*HNL* 464). In this way, for the first ten strokes, the narrator follows Kirkland's flogging almost blow by blow, observing finally at the end of these ten that the young man's back is "swollen into a hump" and looks like "a ripe peach which a wilful child has scored with a pin" (*HNL* 465). While Kirkland begs for mercy, Devine draws his fingers through

the strands of the cat', which are "clogged a little," we are told, by
Kirkland's gore (*HNL* 465). Predictably, this scene was one of those to
which contemporary reviewers objected most vehemently, just as reviewers fifteen years earlier had attacked Reade for making the prison a place
of pitiless violence in *It Is Never Too Late to Mend*. Also predictably, despite
melodramatic touches that color the scene, the description of Kirkland's
flogging—like other instances of graphic violence in Clarke's novel—was
drawn from events Clarke had discovered in researching Australia's convict past.

The novel's account of the *Malabar* mutiny is based partly upon the
real convict uprising aboard the *Cyprus* in 1829, which Clarke had
sketched for the *Argus* as one of his *Old Tales of a Young Country*.[11]
Likewise, he probably recorded the story of James Williams's terrible life
and times during his 1870 trip to Tasmania, since details about Williams
appeared in the article "Port Arthur Visited, 1870." Other events—like
the burying of prisoners alive, and the torment of Devine upon the iron
rack—Clarke footnotes, referring readers to the bibliography he append-
ed to the 1874 edition of the novel.[12] Clarke also drew parts of his novel
from the manuscript diary of Thomas Rogers, Norfolk Island's chaplain
under sadistic governor John Price, and from the "murder pacts"
Ullathorne described to Parliament in 1841. Indeed, even the terrible
story of Gabbett's cannibalism is true, based upon the deposition given
by escaper Alexander Pierce before a Select Committee in 1832. In his testimony, Pierce described having eaten fellow-escapers to stay alive in the
bush and said that human flesh tasted "much like a little pork."[13] As for
the excruciating scene of Kirkland's flogging, Robson believes it came
partly from the testimony of E. A. Slade before an 1837 Select Committee
and from Alexander Harris's *Settlers and Convicts* (1847). Clarke was not
as systematic as Reade in conducting his research, nor did he insist so
loudly upon his right to "augment" his historical sources. But it is true
nonetheless that Clarke's research went far to create his certainty that
Australia during transportation was a terribly violent place.

Clarke may have been fascinated by this violence particularly
because he saw its power to transform irrevocably the prisoners subjected to it. Visiting Port Arthur in 1870, he observed of its few remaining
convicts:

> I know that the prisoners seemed all alike in feature, and that I
> could no more distinguish them the one from the other than I
> could swear to a Chinaman or a two-toothed wether. . . . I know
> that I thought to myself that I should go mad were I condemned
> to such a life, and that I caught one of the men looking at me
> with a broad grin as I thought it.[14]

The observations sound Dickensian, as do Clarke's conclusions about the grotesquerie of those convicts vomited forth again into Melbourne's underworld. In the sketch "A Melbourne Alsatia," Clarke introduces readers to the inhabitants of Queen-street, including the "hero of the evening . . . 'Bill the Knifer' . . . an old convict, [who] has undergone numerous sentences. His face was absolutely hideous. He had lost one eye, and his nose and upper lip were eaten away by some loathsome disease, which left a few stumps of teeth and a portion of his jaw and tongue exposed."[15] Elsewhere, in the essay "Port Arthur," Clarke wrote about the real-life Mooney, who appears in the novel and dies as part of a murder pact with Bland and Devine. When Clarke visited Tasmania in 1870, the real Mooney yet survived in the lunatic asylum at Port Arthur, having spent decades in the prison. The old convict seems to have been more pitiable in life than Clarke's novel makes him in death. Peering through a peephole into Mooney's cell, Clarke sees a "grizzled, gaunt, and half-naked old man," a "gibbering animal" with a "peculiar wild-beast smell."[16] Disturbed by his watcher's presence, Mooney rushes to the door and tries to jab his finger into Clarke's eye. He is, the warders tell Clarke, the worst man still imprisoned at Port Arthur, but one must wonder whether his own inclinations or the torments of the prison have made him so. Just as the innumerable convicts at Port Arthur are as indistinguishable as sheep in Clarke's eyes, and just as "the Knifer's" mouth seems twisted into a perpetual wolfish snarl, so Mooney has been made an animal by the horrors of the prison.

These are the images of the convict-beast that L. T. Hergenhan and Michael Wilding have noted, and that Clarke returns to repeatedly in describing Australia's convicts. At the moment Devine is apprehended for Blinzler's murder, his captors look at him "as though he [is] a wild beast"—the first of many hints that the novel's Australia makes convicts into animals (HNL 69). Gabbett is a ravening beast from the first time he appears, and elsewhere convicts are "fed like dogs," treated like "wild beasts," and skulk—when Frere finally subdues them—like "whipped hounds" to their kennel (HNL 264; 426; 596). Small wonder that years after his escape, trying to recall the faces of his prison comrades, Devine remembers only brutes: "All types of the man-beast were reflected in that sinister looking-glass—the fox, the wolf, the tiger, and ape, grinned, snarled, yawned, and mowed by turns" (HNL 869). Even so, in spite of these images of men made into animals, Australia is not the "natural" punishment other critics have called it, for beneath the prison's brutality are complex disciplinary aims. The prison authorities wish to "break the spirit" of the convict rather than simply to wound his body—a complicated disciplinary desire they pursue in several ways. Norfolk Island has a new separate-confinement prison with "eighteen radiating cells," the narrator remarks, "of a pattern approved by some wiseacre in England, who thinks that to prevent a man seeing his fellow-man is *not* the way to send him mad" (*HNL* 581). The outdoor compound at Port Arthur is a "natural" penitentiary surrounded by bush and sea, but it is also guarded by cunning watch-towers that provide inescapable surveillance as well as an "ingenious series of semaphores" by which the authorities can communicate along the length of the peninsula (*HNL* 491; 490). Even at night in his cell Devine cannot escape discipline, for he falls prey to Troke's sly scheme to catch him, half-awake, handing tobacco to Mooney. Such stratagems, as Frere explains to North, are part of a new disciplinary order by which Frere intends to "[set] on every man to spy upon his neighbour" and raise "the worst scoundrels in the place" to be his constables (*HNL* 596). Indeed, Frere exults at knowing:

> [The prisoner-constables] *must* do their duty. If they are indulgent to the prisoners, they know I shall flog 'em. If they do what I tell 'em, they'll make themselves so hated that they'd have their own father up to the triangles to save themselves being sent back to the ranks. (*HNL* 597)

In this way Frere makes his prison a Foucaultian nightmare, determined to make each prisoner predatory, paranoid, and self-disciplining.

The result for Kirkland and Devine is physical, psychological, and even moral disorder. Kirkland enters the prison a pious "son of Methodist parents"—a "white-handed" banking clerk rather than a ruffian—and the narrator suggests that he has been convicted despite lingering doubts about his guilt (*HNL* 451; 450). After his first night in the prison, he emerges from the dormitory stunningly altered: "ghastly pale, bleeding, with his woollen shirt torn, and his blue eyes wide open with terror" (*HNL* 451). In a hint we learn what has happened to Kirkland when a fellow-convict addresses him as "Miss Nancy": he has almost certainly been raped during the night, in violation—as Victorians would have seen it—not only of natural sexuality but also of Kirkland's devout faith (*HNL* 453).[17] A day earlier, reflecting upon the discipline and labor, Kirkland thought that "he had not experienced anything so very terrible after all" and that he might be able to resign himself to the life of a convict (*HNL* 450). The day after his rape, he has been so disordered morally that he attempts suicide, an act of despair that would damn his soul. Devine, too, is maimed irrevocably by his confinement, though like Kirkland his guilt was doubtful before he reached Australia. Eventually Devine becomes the worst rogue at Norfolk Island, but first he passes through several stages of private disarray: obedient acceptance, sullen anger, and furious hatred for his captors. Chained alone to Grummet Rock, "his mind . . . [becomes]

disordered. He [sees] visions, and dream[s] dreams. . . . He [holds] converse with imaginary beings" (*HNL* 266). Like Kirkland, he also despairs and attempts suicide, having come to believe his "pit of torment . . . so deep that one could not even see Heaven" (*HNL* 263). Attempting later to describe his miseries to Frere, he screams, "You are FREE! You can do as you please. You can love, you can work, you can think. I can only *hate*!" (*HNL* 310). The words articulate only dimly the transformation Australia has inflicted upon Devine.

When North meets Devine after the latter has spent seven years at Norfolk Island, he remarks the convict's transformation, writing, "How habitual sin and misery suffice to tantalise 'the human face divine!'" (*HNL* 588). Playing unconsciously upon the spiritual echoes of Devine's name, North suggests that Devine's transformation has been primarily moral—primarily a fall from Edenic grace. But Hergenhan is not entirely correct when he argues, consequently, that violence in the novel serves primarily to conquer "souls."[18] Australia's prisons care nothing for souls, for the prisons are not faith-based and reformative as in Reade's novel, nor do they distinguish between moral and legal crimes. Rather, violence in Australia disorders prisoners morally only as part of a larger program that seeks to disorder them physically, psychologically, and emotionally—a program that seeks, ultimately, to disorder the identity of the confined. Disordering identity, the novel suggests, is part of the prison's greater plan to disorder the private narrative of the self in the cell. Early in the novel, Frere tells Major Vickers that the prison must "treat brutes like brutes" and "[m]ake 'em *feel* what they are" (*HNL* 257). They "are" men declared guilty by the law, and the prison wants to make them feel the guilty identity the courts have inscribed. The prison's authority to brutalize convicts depends upon this guilty narrative, and the tacit function of the Australian prison is to create and produce narratively the guilty self. Asked by Major Vickers to imagine an innocent man transported to Australia, Frere says, "I can't . . . Innocent man, be hanged! They're all innocent if you'd believe their own stories" (*HNL* 258). This, of course, is the novel's point, for prisoners' stories are not to be believed—not, at least, if those stories attest innocence rather than guilt. Instead, tearing the convict away from home, family, and friends, transportation wipes away his narrative past, but for the inescapable fact that he is the guilty object of discipline that the prison requires. "Breaking the spirit" of the convict in *His Natural Life* really means breaking his story, so that the convict's body, mind, and self-account all bear the wounds inscribed by the prison.

III

His Natural Life's account of Devine thus shows that Australia's violence engenders disorder of a distinctly narrative kind. From the moment Devine is entangled mistakenly in Blinzler's murder, his convicthood depends upon the authorities' ability to construct him narratively as the guilty subject they require. Devine is baffled at first by his arrest, so he attends closely to the banter of the constables who have seized him. As he listens to their piecemeal accusations regarding his involvement in Blinzler's murder, he grows aware of the "hideous web of circumstantial evidence, into which he had unwittingly flown" (*HNL* 70). But Devine has not murdered Blinzler, and it seems that a frank account of himself would save him from the danger of the gallows. The narrator remarks, "As a stranger advising another man, he would have said, 'Explain the apparent mystery . . . Tell who your companion was . . . Bring friends to prove your affection for him . . . Shew who you are, and what you have been'" (*HNL* 70–71). Devine does none of these things, choosing instead to suppress the truth. He invents the alias Rufus Dawes and tells the constables he is a sailor. But he leaves the remainder of his private identity to the authorities to construct. Given such license and seeking a murderer, the public and the law invent a guilty account. "No one," the narrator tells us, "doubted his guilt," for all the evidence "was clear against him" (*HNL* 74). To Frere, reading the account in the newspaper, Dawes's guilt is "plain as a pikestaff," and he tells Quaid: "The sailor sees the other one's money, you know, slits his weasand for him in the night, takes the black box and bolts. There's no mystery in *that*, bigod!" (*HNL* 79). The law reaches the same conclusion despite Devine's testimony at his trial, and Rufus Dawes—a narrative fiction—is transported to Australia. By subjugating himself narratively to others who account for him, Devine descends literally and figuratively into the Victorian prison.

In the cell he finds himself renarrated constantly by a prison that insists upon his guilty mark. On the *Malabar*, though he does nothing to antagonize the guards or officers, he is beaten for retrieving Dora's ball, for he steps inadvertently over the line on the deck that divides convict from free. Frere smashes him to the ground, demanding to know "What the devil" he is doing (*HNL* 133). While Devine's first impulse is "to justify himself" with an explanation, he allows his "words to die on his lips. What was the use?" (*HNL* 133). As he recognized when he gave the constables a phony name at the time of his arrest, he has "begun a new life, and he could not reanimate the corpse of the old one and make it speak for him" (*HNL* 71). He is no longer innocent, nor is he to be believed. Rather, Frere calls him a "skulking hound," and Pine judges that Devine's attempt to warn them of the mutiny should be ignored, for the man is "a murderer . . . a most bloodthirsty fellow" (*HNL* 160; 213). Really, the attempt shows how entirely the prison has silenced him. Feverish and delirious, his "parched gullet" permits him to croak only the disordered syllables, "Sarah Purfoy—I heard—to-night—in the prison—MUTINY!" (*HNL* 205). These "desperate efforts to articulate" are misunderstood, and the prison, having already decided on his guilt, makes him the plot's mastermind (*HNL* 205). Appropriately, the disease that has prevented him from speaking is "gaol fever," an affliction that silences every convict sent to Australia. As our narrator tells us, "It was not always necessary to commit crimes in order to be imprisoned at Hell's Gates. The military officers and the Government had unlimited power, and sentences were often passed . . . which . . . gave a false character of desperation to many poor fellows who were more stupid than vicious" (*HNL* 237). Innocent of murder but declared guilty by the law, Devine falls under the narrative power of the prison.

This demonstration of the prison's narrative power shows Clarke's sensitivity to the dynamics that made narrative the key to Australia's carceral society. At Port Arthur, Dora worries to Frere about the prospect of a prisoner uprising, for she feels "how few *we* are in comparison with *them*" (*HNL* 441). During the period in which the novel is set, this was a considerable concern. 53 percent of Tasmania's inhabitants were convicts in 1821, and as many as 68 percent of all Australians were emancipists in 1849.[19] Assigned servants and ticket-of-leave convicts lived among the settlers in a society that depended upon whether one could tell a free story. As Frere remarks to Dora during their time in Sydney, she must "take care" among those in society, for she has "no notion how these people mark the line between 'bond' and 'free'" (*HNL* 504). They do so, the novel suggests, through narrative means. The convict-servant Danny complains to Dora that his wife—a free woman—has twice placed him in the power of the authorities by complaining falsely that he abuses her and is a drunkard. Later in the novel Sarah tries a similar plan, telling Rex that if he does not obey her "he'll find himself in the custody of the police" (*HNL* 819). Since Australia exercises no continuous physical restraint over most of its convicts, the authorities and free settlers collectively ensure proper social stratification by retaining the power to insist at any time upon the convict's guilt, real or feigned. Clarke's Australia is not a simple prison or system of prisons; rather, it is a carceral society upheld by the authorities' power to narrate the convict.

Devine's efforts to help Frere, Mrs. Vickers, and Dora underscore this point after the three are left marooned by the mutiny aboard the *Osprey*. Having survived his leap from Grummet Rock, Devine wanders for several days in the bush before stumbling across the marooned party. Separated wholly from Australian society and the power that authorizes the prison, Devine nearly regains his narrative power and old identity. He helps the party survive in the wild and devises plans for their deliverance. In doing so, he begins to see himself in another light. He can be "of use to somebody" and is no longer "despised" (*HNL* 315). He also replaces Dora's favorite storyteller, Mr. Bates, by telling her about alchemy, dismissing in the process Frere's inaccurate definition of an alchemist as a "man who makes gold" (*HNL* 317). He interprets the significance of the "coracle" that Dora discovers in her book on English history and envisions how he may construct such a boat and save them, even issuing orders to Frere, who is too insipid to understand the plans. Most important, he begins to construct a new self-narrative of his future, in which he is vindicated as an innocent man and "freed from the sordid thraldom which so long had held him" so that he can "take possession of the wealth which was his" back in England (*HNL* 337). As the narrator remarks, "A new life—as he had once pictured it—opened radiant before him, and he felt himself lost, as it were, in the contemplation of his own happiness" (*HNL* 337). Free of the narrative bonds imposed by the prison, the convict Dawes nearly becomes Devine again, in more senses than one. Outside the prison, the narrator tells us, "Maurice Frere's authority of gentility soon succumbed to Rufus Dawes's authority of knowledge" (*HNL* 315). Inside the prison, as the novel shows, knowledge is no prerequisite for narrative power.

But the moment return to Australian society is imminent, Devine reverts, decidedly and involuntarily, to his identity as a guilty self. Admitting Dora to the radiant narrative construction of his future, he asks, "what will you do for me if I bring you and mamma safe home again?" and Dora frankly responds, "Give you a free pardon . . . and Papa shall make you his servant!" (*HNL* 331). Frere guffaws at this unintentional cruelty, and Devine turns away in despair. Dora's comment describes his situation precisely, for as a convict he cannot erase the guilty taint upon his story. No fanciful self-account of future happiness can alter the stain upon his past, nor have his escape from Grummet Rock or the terrors of Macquarie Harbor freed him from the carceral power that owns his story. Returned to civilization, rather, he will reclaim his guilty mark. As if to underscore this point, when the coracle drifts within view of a ship, Frere hits upon the cunning plan of taking credit for the party's survival—since Dora and Mrs. Vickers are too ill to know better—and turning over the "'absconder' . . . to justice" (*HNL* 350). Demanding that Devine hand over the sick child as the ship draws near, Frere ensures that appearances will corroborate this account of his personal heroism and help to renarrate Devine's guilty mark. As we learn later through Mrs. Jellicoe, Frere's official story of the rescue bears little resemblance to the truth:

. . . an escaped prisoner . . . happened to be left behind, and he found them out, and insisted on sharing the provisions—the wretch! Captain Frere was obliged to watch him constantly for fear he should murder them. Even in the boat, he tried to run them out to sea, and escape. He was one of the worst men in the Harbour, they say; but you should hear Captain Frere tell the story. (*HNL* 358)

Assuredly, in Australia's narrative-driven society we will hear no version of the story but Frere's. By forcing Devine to hand over Dora, Frere demonstrates that the prison's power over convict bodies is meant mostly to ensure its power over convict stories.

As Devine endures years in Australia's penal settlements, the novel suggests, the brutality to which he is subjected erodes his power to narrate his identity, and even to command language at all. Called to Sydney to testify at Rex's trial, Devine sees Dora for the first time since he saved her and tries suddenly to tell the whole truth to the court. But his account is heated and ranting. As the narrator says, since Devine's original conviction "[i]t would have been a curious experiment . . . to speculate through what course of brutalisation his intellect must have passed to reduce his eloquence to this level" (*HNL* 389). His angry accusations are, of course, ignored. When Devine escapes his temporary prison in desperation and steals to the Freres' garden for a private word with Dora, the episode recurs. "No words c[o]me" when he tries to speak to Dora, and he is recaptured by Frere (*HNL* 441). Using physically coercive measures to eradicate Devine's natural eloquence, seizing his body to imprison his tale, Clarke's Australia recalls the disordering power of Dickens's Bastille. In both novels, the prison silences all accounts of the convict except the one that the authorities have devised.

But the prison is not content simply to silence Devine's self-account; rather, it wants to force Devine to adopt the guilty self-account that discipline has imposed upon him. The chapter "Breaking a Man's Spirit" demonstrates this premise by drawing a contest of wills between Devine and Frere. As the latter inflicts increasingly vicious punishments, the former grows more defiant. Devine suffers three separate fortnights in solitary confinement and endures repeated floggings, but Frere is not satisfied, for still the convict's "'spirit' [is] not . . . 'broken'" (*HNL* 627). When Frere changes the punishment by sending Devine to grind maize, he tries to guarantee Devine's complicity by chaining his hand to one arm of a two-handled grindstone, then setting a second convict upon the other arm to complete the necessary revolutions. "As the second prisoner turned," our narrator remarks, "the hand of Dawes of course revolved" (*HNL* 627). But Devine is still not broken, and he steels his muscles against the grindstone to prevent it turning at all. Infuriated, Frere flogs him and sends him, with his raw back, to grind cayenne pepper—an excruciating punishment since pepper dust infests Devines's open sores and leaves him "emaciated, blistered, blinded" (*HNL* 627). When, after four days, Devine breaks down and begs for death, Frere rejoices at "this proof of his power" and responds, "No fear . . . You've given in; that's all I wanted" (*HNL* 627). The "proof" of Frere's power is not the labor he demands nor the pain he inflicts nor the discipline he imposes upon Devine. It is, rather, that he forces Devine to attest, in his own words, to his miserable degradation. For the prison this guilty confession is all.

No scene illustrates this aim more thoroughly than that of Devine's flogging at Port Arthur. Devine's flogging culminates the scene that begins with Kirkland being whipped. But Devine refuses to continue beyond the fifty lashes he has been directed to inflict upon Kirkland, and he becomes himself the object of Burgess's wrath. Burgess orders Gabbett to give Devine the other fifty lashes that should have been Kirkland's "and fifty more to the back of 'em" (*HNL* 466). The result is the novel's most disturbing moment. Devine suffers silently through one hundred lashes, though Gabbett "cross[es] the cuts" to make the punishment more agonizing (*HNL* 466). But Burgess is determined to "break the man's spirit" and commands Gabbett to continue beyond one hundred, screaming at Devine, "I'll make you speak, you dog, if I cut your heart out" (*HNL* 467). After twenty more lashes, Burgess receives his wish:

> Having found his tongue, [Devine] gave vent to his boiling passion in a torrent of curses. . . . With a frightful outpouring of obscenity and blasphemy, he called on the earth to gape and swallow his persecutors, for heaven to open and rain fire upon them, for hell to yawn and engulf them quick. It was as though each blow of the cat forced out of him a fresh burst of beast-like rage. He seemed to have abandoned his humanity. (*HNL* 467)

Hergenhan argues that this scene shows "the final horror of an authoritarianism aimed at extinguishing the individual self, [for the body is] the final resort by which it can coerce the strongest of the unyielding."[20] It is not enough that the prison has brutalized Devine, degraded him, and forced him to lead an animal existence in Australia. It is not enough that the prison has silenced him since the start of the novel. The prison requires Devine to confess his degradation with his own voice. He must become in his own telling what the prison has always insisted he is: the bestial, depraved, and guilty self in the cell.

Writing of the Oedipal shades raised by the revised version of the novel, Wilding argues that "guilt becomes a major theme, a major determinant of the book's mood." [21] This is true of both versions of the novel. But because it provides for Devine's return to the world beyond the cell, the original also shows what becomes of that guilt, and how it becomes a permanent feature of Devine's narrative of self. Reflecting upon his flogging and descent into guilty rage, Devine arrives at a revelation:

> He had been flogged before, and had wept in secret at his degradation, but he now for the first time comprehended . . . the full punishment of the 'cat,' as he realised how the agony of the wretched body can force the soul to quit its last poor refuge of unarmed Indifference, *and confess itself conquered.* (*HNL* 482)

Brutality and psychological trial in Australia have achieved the same aim as separate discipline in Reade's fictional reformative penitentiary. They have produced implicitly the same demand for self-reflection, self-ordering, and self-narration. The net effect is to show that in Australia as in England the aim of confinement is to drive prisoners to narrative self-ordering, so that they reconceive of themselves finally as the objects of discipline the prison requires. The guilty self-account is the price that the prison exacts from every self thrust into—or loosed from—the cell. Driven to reveal his identity in the final chapters of the novel, Devine thus finds that he cannot simply sweep away the guilty narrative and identity the prison has thrust upon him. Rather, he must use his self-account to order the disorder of his identity and his past. He must declare that he is the convict Dawes and the free citizen Devine. He must acknowledge his new guilt and reclaim his older innocence. He must fit all into a single, complete, and coherent account of his private identity. By having Devine undertake this process at the end of the novel, Clarke shows us what Reade and Dickens only imply: that the true aim of Victorian confinement was to produce self-narratives that attempt to order the private disorder of the self.

IV

Several characters attempt to escape their guilt without confessing, instead burying their true stories beneath assumed identities that bespeak innocence. Arthur Devine takes the pseudonym Arthur Vern when he immigrates to Australia because he is afraid, as young Quaid puts it, "of disgracing the honourable name of Devine" by becoming a lowly gold-digger (*HNL* 848). Sarah marries John Carr so that she may put her old name—and the rumors that do not "speak too well of Mrs. Purfoy's past history"—to rest (*HNL* 574). And throughout the novel Rex, who Wilding notes is deft at operating "pseudonymously," uses false names to hide his guilty past.[22] He is "Dandy Jack" to associates in England and Leopold

Craven when he first seduces Sarah. Robbing and deceiving his way through England's genteel society, Rex, we are told, ruins a host of "[r]ich spendthrifts," using a new name—Mr. James Crofton, Mr. Anthony Croftonbury, Captain James Crofton—at each stop, lest the guilt attached to his old one presage his wicked designs (*HNL* 195). Likewise, when he escapes Macquarie Harbor with the help of Sarah and Blunt, he masquerades as "a shipwrecked seaman" "attired in garments that [seem] remarkably well-preserved" (*HNL* 551). Once free he becomes John Carr, since the opportune death of the name's real owner allows Sarah to give Rex this identity and make him—again—her husband. Of course, all of these instances are mere preludes to Rex's greatest narrative fraud: his return to England as the long, lost Richard Devine.[23]

Having escaped Norfolk Island, the real Devine attempts a less malicious but equally complete narrative fraud. He has been rescued from the wreck of the *Lady Franklin* by a Sydney-bound vessel, and as a result he knows that his heroism in saving Dora's daughter has resulted—as in saving the mother years ago—in his being carried back to his Australian prison. Indeed, he cannot help but reflect, "these cursed Australias [are] all one vast gaol" (*HNL* 688). For the time being, all that saves him from suspicion are the black clothes and cloak he has taken from North. His freedom in Australia now as before will depend upon his ability to account for himself in a satisfactory way. But when he first boards the *Mosquito*, we are told, "he had not yet formed for himself another history—had not yet forced his bewildered brain to invent a tale which should disarm suspicion," and he spends the hours of the approach to Sydney concocting an appropriate self-account (*HNL* 687). Like Rex he attempts to evade the prison narratively so that he can remain free of it physically. He talks to no one when he lands at Port Phillip, takes the child in his arms, and heads—quite literally—for the hills, not stopping until he reaches a place where he can live quietly. When we next see him, he has found work as a shepherd and is Rufus Dawes no longer. Nor is he Richard Devine. He is Tom Crosbie, and little Dora is his daughter Dorcas. As the narrator says, the new shepherd has a simple tale to tell: "'I married late in life,' said he, 'my wife died in Melbourne a month ago. This is my only one, and I want her love all to myself'" (*HNL* 699). Like Rex, Devine attempts to cover his stain with the self-account of an innocent man.

But neither Rex nor Devine can evade for long their guilty marks, for both men have been remade too entirely by the prison. In part, like the prisoners in Dickens and Reade, their bodies bear the scars of confinement. Sunken into a life of dissipation after his successful return as Richard Devine, Rex becomes "gross," with a heavy paunch, eyes surrounded by "a thicket of crow's feet," and cheeks inflamed because of "frequent application of hot and rebellious liquors" (*HNL* 815). Devine worries that his "scarred back" will give him away in the colonies, and he fears also, when he is arrested during the Ballarat disturbances, that if he is taken to Melbourne for trial "the convict Rufus Dawes" might be "recognised in the bearded Tom Crosbie" (*HNL* 688; 752). Besides these physical scars, both men also bear psychological marks etched upon them by the prison. In England, Rex can no longer feign gentility, for he has been degraded too thoroughly by his years in Australia. During the early stages of his fraud, we are told, the "soothing influence of comfort, respect, and security" nearly refined him, but:

> . . . he gradually became bolder, and by slow degrees suffered his true nature to appear. He was violent to his servants, cruel to dogs and horses, often wantonly coarse in speech, and brutally regardless of the feelings of others. (*HNL* 709)

On one occasion, returning home drunk, Rex crashes about the manor house breaking furniture and bullying servants until he is forced to his room like an "animal, torn, bloody, and blasphemous" (*HNL* 712). Though he does not confess yet the truth of his guilty past, Rex reverts to the beast that the prison has made him.

Devine's psychological scars are, if anything, worse. He does not, once outside the prison, revert like Rex to brutality and dissipation. But he bears constantly the crushing awareness of what he has been and endured. He reveals as much in a conversation with Arthur, when the young man unwittingly says to Devine that even a man innocently convicted "could never come back to society again . . . [for] one could not look upon him as the same. The memory of the frightful scenes through which he had passed would taint him" (*HNL* 754). Shaken, Devine responds:

> You are right, young man . . . The society of the good and pure would justly refuse to be contaminated by the presence of such a man. He is a leper, from whom all healthy beings shrink with disgust. For him remains no love of sister, wife, or child. He is alone in the world—a being apart and accursed . . . (*HNL* 754)

Devine's pained dictum is not entirely true, for Dorcas apparently loves him as a father—indeed, she thinks he *is* her father—and his neighbors do not shrink from him in disgust. But Devine does not refer here to the physical world in which he moves; rather, he attests to his maimed inner life, where he is divided among multiple identities and histories. In his outer being he can appear innocent and good. Privately, though, he has been disordered by the cell.

Of the passages that remark the private disorder engendered by confinement, none is so important as North's diary. North is no saint—he is not, that is, the saintly prison chaplain we find in *It Is Never Too Late to Mend*. In the first place he is "a confirmed drunkard," tormented by the "vulgar and terrible apparition" of the brandy bottle and his "degrading, disgusting, and bestial" inability to conquer his impulse to drink (*HNL* 463). More important, North fails as completely as Eden succeeds when he crusades for humane treatment for the prisoners under his charge. At Macquarie Harbor, North tries to serve as Kirkland's savior, swearing that he will not allow the boy to be flogged. He writes, "I'll shield him with my own body, if necessary. I'll report this to the Government. I'll see Sir John Franklin myself. I'll have the light of day let into this den of horrors" (*HNL* 462). But that evening he is dead drunk, and he arrives the next morning only in time to see Kirkland receive his fifty-first lash. The young man dies, Devine becomes miserable and desperate, and the inquiry that North demands into Kirkland's death comes to nothing, so that North's failure as a spiritual and moral guide is complete. Besides this failure North hides one more sin beneath the cloth of his ministry: he covets his neighbor's wife. It is likely that Clarke derived North's story—written for the most part as journal entries—from the diary of Thomas Rogers, chaplain of Norfolk Island under John Price.[24] But Rogers was no alcoholic, and he neither carried on an illicit liaison with Price's wife nor, that we know, desired to do so. Nor did he commit suicide, finally, because of his ineffectuality and romantic disappointments.[25] That Clarke makes North depart so widely from the source material suggests that the chaplain's diary may be especially important to Clarke's thematic aims.

North writes, in the first entry to his diary, "This journal is my confessor, and I bare my heart to it," and, "Our neighbours of Rome know human nature. A man *must* confess" (*HNL* 560; 561). But the most striking feature of North's diary is that it is *not* a confession—especially not in the Catholic sense, since it is neither entirely honest nor heard by a listener who can absolve North's sins. Rather, for North the diary is an attempt to record and understand the complexities of his guilt so that he can make sense of his disordered inner life. He confesses his alcoholism and calls himself "a wolf in sheep's clothing; a man possessed by a devil, who is ready at any moment to break out and tear him to pieces" (*HNL* 630). He records "[t]he delirium, the fever, the self-loathing, the prostration, the despair" of his compulsion to take liquor, and he proclaims finally that he can "no more help getting drunk, than a lunatic can help screaming and gibbering" (*HNL* 631; 629). He even ponders whether his failure to save Kirkland and Devine at Port Arthur brought Devine to the "horrible state of mind" in which North discovers him at Norfolk Island (*HNL* 590). But North's guiltiest feelings are reserved for Dora, whom we suspect he would seduce if he had the courage. He records his growing desire and feels accused when he reads Balzac's *La Fausse Maîtresse*. In fact, he feels so guilty that he decides *not* to admit everything, even to his diary, for he would "blush to confess all that I have in my heart. –I will *not* confess it, so that shall suffice" (*HNL* 591). Still, his thoughts return to Dora as he considers leaving Norfolk Island. He writes:

> I try to think that the reason of this determination is the frightful condition of misery existing among the prisoners; that because I am daily horrified and sickened by scenes of torture and infamy, I decide to go away . . . But in this journal, in which I bound myself to write nothing but truth, I am forced to confess that these are *not* the reasons. I will write them plainly. '*I covet my neighbour's wife.*' (*HNL* 640)

In this way, North's diary records the sins he sees upon his soul—his psychological sense of his own guilt and unworth. Like Devine, he tries to conceal and reject his hidden guilt, and as a result he exists at Norfolk Island as a prisoner to his alcoholism, ineffectuality, and forbidden desire. His diary is his attempt to grapple narratively with his psychic disorder, and to free himself from the miseries of his prison.

In this, too, North fails, for by the entry of December 9 he has lost his ability to order himself through narrative. His diary erupts into interjections and blasphemies; he is tormented by his vow to see Dora no more and distraught that he has been unable to "save one soul that may plead with [God] for [his]" (*HNL* 642). At one moment he calls God "[c]ruel and implacable," and the next he begs for pity and deliverance (*HNL* 642). Five days later—in his final entry—a calmer, penitent North reads this record of his psychic collapse and asks, "What blasphemies are these that I have uttered in my despair" (*HNL* 643). But his meek contrition does not last. Rather, it deteriorates into the wild entreaty that Dora never know his "rudeness or [his] brutality," and that she not behold him on this verge of madness, a "drivelling spectacle for the curious to point at or to pity" (*HNL* 643). The diary that began as North's confessor thus becomes a place where he begs *not* to confess, and where he attempts to hide rather than reveal his depravity. Failing to grapple successfully with his guilt in his narrative, so that Dora and later Devine must discover and declare his sins, North remains privately and narratively disordered. He fails to retain narrative power over his own disorder and guilt. As a result, like Devine, he descends into the prison. Clarke figures this parallel symbolically by making North's cloak the means of Devine's escape, and by permitting Devine to take North's passage aboard the *Lady Franklin*. Even as Devine moves toward freedom, North succumbs finally to the disorder of the cell.

Gaining and keeping narrative control over guilt is thus an imperative in the novel, the only way to escape finally the horrors of the prison. As a result, like *Little Dorrit*, the novel proliferates in its closing chapters with the confessions of the guilty. Arthur sheds his alias and confesses his real name to Dorcas, partly to pave the way for their marriage but also because, since the Ballarat uprising, "Arthur Vern is a rioter, and a suspected person, without an influential friend. Arthur Devine is, at all events, the cousin of Captain Maurice Frere" (*HNL* 852). On his deathbed, Jerry Mogford confesses his old secret, too, disclosing finally that his brother murdered Blinzler. Mogford thus relieves, at least partly, his guilty conscience, and he frees himself of suspicion for the murder by revealing that his brother was the killer. Rex even confesses his fraud finally, having been caught anyway by the appearance of Dorothea Devine. His confession is an act of revenge rather than guilt, and he torments Dorothea by lingering over her wrenching situation: "*Your husband was a convict, transported for life for killing your father*. Now you know the truth, and I wish you joy of it!" (*HNL* 837). Even Dora, the novel's good angel, finds just before her death a release from the prison that has been her life. She has spent her life miserable, married to Frere, all because a childhood fever kept her from recalling the truth about the marooning and her rescue. That period, the narrator remarks, is a "shadow upon her memory" (*HNL* 427). But aboard the *Lady Franklin*, again confronted by death and in the company of Devine, "she [feels] the cloud that had so long oppressed her brain pass away from it" (*HNL* 684). It is a self-narrative release, an awakening to truths about her past. It is also a recognition of her own guilt, for she sees all at once her long and unwitting complicity in Devine's career of suffering. Finally capable again of shaping the narrative of her past, she returns to the simple phrase she knew as a child: "Good Mr. Dawes" (*HNL* 685).

Uttered on board the sinking *Lady Franklin*, Dora's account of Devine does him no good in the eyes of the prison; rather, the novel suggests that he must narrate himself, in all of his guilt, if he wishes to be free of the cell. Learning that Arthur and Dorcas are in love and that Arthur is his nephew, Devine faces a terrible choice. He recognizes, as Arthur speaks of his profligate uncle Richard returned from adventures around the world, that Rex has usurped his name and inheritance, and that Arthur has been robbed of money he ought rightfully to have. He also realizes that, as the real Richard Devine and Rex's old acquaintance, he has the power to expose the fraud. But between Tom Crosbie and Devine there is a crucial narrative intermediate, as Devine acknowledges in his thoughts:

> The only man who could place Arthur in possession of his fortune was the true Richard Devine. . . . but the true Richard Devine, cannot live again but by means of Rufus Dawes, the convict. . . . The frightful problem admitted but of one solution. To prove that he is Richard Devine, Thomas Crosbie must confess that he is Rufus Dawes! *Now Rufus Dawes is an escaped convict, and the punishment for escaped convicts is hanging.* (HNL 872)

This realization is the novel's most crucial point, for it is the first time that Devine considers weaving into his self-account the realities of his convict past. Throughout the novel he has invented innocent fictions of himself—of his triumphant return to England, of his rescue of Dora, of his quiet identity as Crosbie. But he has not once incorporated into these self-accounts the private meanings of his confinement. The discovery that he must do so, and that doing so requires him to narrate guilt as well as innocence, provides the pivotal psychic crisis of the novel.

The narrator invites our attention to the importance of the scene. Through 350,000 words he has effortlessly painted for us the minds and hearts of those who inhabit Clarke's Australia. But here, as Devine prepares to recall every contour of his private identity, the narrator suddenly and explicitly stumbles, asking:

> How can one set down in cold blood—laboriously drawing characters upon paper—the multitudinous and varied sensations . . . sweeping like storm-birds over that waste and awful ocean whose shores no man hath touched, nor will touch while time rolls. . . . How is it possible to paint the visions which enfolded the soul of Richard Devine. (*HNL* 873)

The narrative musings recall the "Night Shadows" passage of *A Tale of Two Cities* and another omniscient narrator's hesitations over accounting for private identity and desire. As Clarke's narrator attempts to show the process by which Devine assembles his complete identity, his account, too, becomes disordered. He writes confusedly about Devine's thoughts as they range from Amsterdam to Australia, from his early profligacy to his long self-sacrifice, and from recognizable scenes to the ejaculations of a mind in crisis. We find, without coherent explanation, a "fair-haired girl," a "diamond mine," and a "miser-knight" in the narrator's account, while ahead are "the gibbet," the "brutal wrenching out of life," and "the jeers" (*HNL* 873; 874). We discover other things that are more certain: for instance, that Devine's worst fear in confessing his convict past is not the threat of death—"I could die now and happily," he thinks—rather, it is the "awful method of the death" attended by the "shame" of declaring himself guilty (*HNL* 874). Fittingly, he calls upon "North! North! my prison-Christ, who died that I might live" for guidance in his current plight, then slips into a calmer contemplation of the duty that lays before him (*HNL* 875). Unlike North, however—and unlike the narrator, whose account of Devine's thoughts is jumbled and incomplete—Devine apparently grapples successfully in his narrative with the complexities of his guilt and past. He orders them, gives them shape, and learns their meaning. The next morning, Arthur arrives looking for Crosbie and finds him sitting with a "little sealed packet, which from its size would seem to contain a quire of note-paper" (*HNL* 877). The note-paper, we are told, contains Devine's complete life story: the full and true account of his identity, his sacrifice, and his convicthood. Eight hundred pages after becoming Rufus Dawes, Devine reclaims his self-narrative power and tells Arthur, "I am your uncle! I am Richard Devine!" (*HNL* 895).

In recovering his old identity, Devine has become the narrative master of his own guilt, recalled from decades spent as Devine, Dawes, and Crosbie. The younger Quaid appropriately calls Devine's self-account a "confession," for the narrative abounds in attempts to account for his guilty self (*HNL* 901). Indeed, Devine's confession reveals layers of guilt, some older than his miserable experiences in the Australian prison. He admits that he and Blinzler dealt in fake gems, and that he married Dorothea against his father's wishes only to find that he did not love her. Arrested for Blinzler's murder, he suffered himself to be transported without contacting his wife because, he says, he wished to keep her from knowing that her father was a swindler. He has also, as we know and as his self-account must attest, been made guilty many times over by the prison. He has been a killer, an attempted suicide, and an accomplice to brutality and murder. He has howled his rage and depravity at his tormenters. The life story he provides cannot attest to innocence, at least not honestly; instead, it can only control the disclosure and meaning of his guilty past. Devine narrates that disclosure, and he forbids Arthur and Dorcas to read it until they reach Blinzler's lab in Amsterdam. As if to underscore the point, Devine even arrives in the middle of their reading and snatches the document away, insisting that the remainder—the account of his imprisonment—is only "a record of [his] despair" (*HNL* 910). Every detail of the scene suggests that Devine has reclaimed his power over his self-narrative. He has done so not by erasing his guilt, but by ordering in his self-account the disorder inflicted by the prison.

V

In 1898 Arthur Patchett Martin wrote that he felt, like many Australians who wished to forget the national convict stain, "a kind of patriotic regret—that a man so gifted as Clarke should have devoted such an immense amount of labor to . . . have this national stigma recorded in indelible ink."[26] The sentiment is understandable but ungenerous, the more so because Clarke's novel expands our conception of the relation between narrative, the self, and the cell. Concluding as it does, *His Natural Life* signals its kinship to Reade's work and to Dickens's, filling in—as Clarke intended—a chapter missing from the greater context of the Victorian prison novel. In Reade, the prison demands self-narrative explicitly as part of the reformative process, seizes interpretive and narrative control over it, and justifies as a result the process by which the "other" can narrate the private self. In Dickens, though he implies that the prison destroys the self's power over its self-account, the prison's more explicit function is to wound the prisoner, physically and psychologically, so that body *and* identity remain always under the shadow of the cell. *His Natural Life* is crucial because it unites these visions of Victorian confinement, permitting Reade's and Dickens's critiques of the cell to converge into a coherent picture of the prison's aim. Clarke's Australia demands narrative *and* wounds the self, so that the self in the cell must finally, as Devine shrewdly notes, "*confess itself conquered.*" This is what Troke wants when he orders Gabbett to flog Devine, and what Frere wants when he forces Devine to grind pepper until his raw wounds blister. In this way, the novel suggests that the prison's final disciplinary and narrative aim is to inscribe guilt not just to wound the self, but to wound the self's story. It is to inflict trauma in order to catalyze the self-narrative production of guilty identity, private disorder, and illicit desire. The strategy is a tacit acknowledgement of the function of autobiography: to use narrative to explore and make sense of the discontinuities of the private self. But it also demonstrates that the prison deliberately produces guilt so that it can require guilty self-narration—so that the imprisoned self must finally author the story that makes it a proper object of punishment.

In spite of its narrative power, the prison needs this complicity to justify its operation, authority, and existence. Rather than simply account for the self through its power as a privileged external narrator, the prison needs the self to produce its own account of identity and desire so that the guilty narrative that emerges takes the form of a confession of private truth. Clarke's novel illustrates this point by making the omniscient narrator stumble suddenly in accounting for Devine, just at the moment when Devine is attempting to order his private disorder in the confession that declares his identity. The narrator's sudden incapacity implies that

Devine rather than the narrator must finally control his guilty narrative. It implies that the narrator, in spite of his omniscience, or perhaps the author must conjure the illusion that Devine's private narrative finally proceeds from Devine himself. After all, the prison's inscription of wounds and scars upon Devine is vindicated more entirely if he gives a guilty account of himself than if the prison constructs guilty accounts of him. Likewise, the prison novel mimics this narrative form, since the novel seems most honest in accounting for the psychological traumas inflicted by confinement if its account of the prison seems to come, finally, in the form of first-person narration. First-person narration—or at least the appearance of it—thus becomes the token by which the prison and the novel justify and perpetuate their power to narrate the private self. Private disorder—real or suspected—becomes the invariable justification for the "other" to produce private narratives of guilt, psychological trauma, and illicit desire. It is no accident that Devine rather than another character says at the novel's end that the sullied diamond is a "black and useless atom, fit emblem of [his] dark and wasted life" (*HNL* 911). The prison *and* the novel both require him to narrate, in his own words, the disorder inflicted by the cell.

Chapter 6

The Self in the Cell: *Villette, Armadale,* and Victorian Self-Narration

> I now for the first time contemplate my course as a whole; it is a first
> essay, but it will contain, I trust, no serious or substantial mistake, and
> so far will answer the purpose for which I write it. I purpose to set noth-
> ing down in it as certain, of which I have not a clear memory. . .
> —John Newman, *Apologia Pro Vita Sua*

THOUGH RICHARD DEVINE SEEMS NOT TO KNOW IT IN *HIS NATURAL LIFE*, HIS decision to write an account of himself at the end of the novel places him in excellent Victorian company. During the second half of the nineteenth century, almost everyone who was anyone wrote an autobiography, with the result that the period marked a golden age of sorts in the narrative production of the self. John Stuart Mill published his *Autobiography* in 1873, and Charles Darwin's appeared in 1887. Besides these eminent Victorians, Leigh Hunt, Harriet Martineau, and Anthony Trollope wrote autobiographies during the century, John Henry Newman published *Apologia Pro Vita Sua* (1864), and Robert Southey wrote the "Recollections" that prefaced his *Life and Correspondence* (1850). As Janice Carlisle points out, 1850 was an especially important year for autobiography if we consider also authors' creative attempts to account for their lives.[1] *David Copperfield* finished its serial run in October of that year, and William Wordsworth's *The Prelude* and Alfred Tennyson's *In Memoriam* also appeared. Meantime, three years before and three years after mid-century, Charlotte Brontë published *Jane Eyre* and *Villette*, both of which—besides masquerading as autobiographies—draw from events in Brontë's life. None of this is meant to suggest that first-person narrative was a sudden Victorian innovation. But it is true that

Victorians turned self-narrative into a major literary mode. In a period remembered mostly for George Eliot's pastoral sprawls, Thackeray's vast histories, and Dickens's massive social critiques, Victorian autobiographies and first-person novels stand distinct: scattered but powerful brushes with the private self.

The ostensible purpose of most of these self-narratives is the chronological ordering of the events that constitute a "life." Brooks argues in *Reading for the Plot* that Victorian narratives reflect generally a "confidence in narrative explanation . . . [as] a tracing of origins. We know what we are because we can say where we are, and we know this because we can say where we came from."[2] One result of this confidence is that Victorian autobiographies often read like factual chronicles of a perfectly remembered and comprehensible life marching steadily toward the grave. Samuel Butler's *The Way of All Flesh* implies this earthly progression in its title, just as *Jane Eyre* begins with Jane's childhood and *Copperfield* with a birth that David cannot possibly remember. As for real autobiographies, Darwin, too, reminds readers of the temporality of human existence, for he remarks at the start, "I have attempted to write [my self-account] as if I were a dead man in another world looking back at my own life. Nor have I found this difficult, for life is nearly over with me."[3] Mill strives for this same impersonal summing up, at least in the sense that he tries to show how events in his past helped to shape his character as an adult. As he claims in his *Autobiography*, his aim in writing is mostly to account for "an education which was unusual and remarkable" and the development of opinions in a "mind which was always pressing forward."[4] Even Newman, whose *Apologia* may be the most personal Victorian self-narrative, says that he has no desire to provide a deeply reflective treatise; rather, he wants "simply to state facts" regarding his reasons for leaving the Anglican church—reasons he explains, fittingly, by showing the progress of his religious thought through time.[5] Fact, order, and progress are the explicit watchwords of Victorian first-person writing, even in novels like Collins's *The Woman in White* (1860) and *The Moonstone* (1868) in which the narrators do not pretend to account fully for their lives. For Walter Hartright, Franklin Blake, and the indefatigable Miss Clack, the invariable purpose of self-accounting is still to deliver the facts—in their cases so that a fictional detective or real-life reader can make sense of past events.

These obsessive returns to chronological and factual beginnings imply another kind of return, too—a psychological one into the origins of identity and desire. Mill belies this wish by saying that he wants to describe his education mainly to explain the evolution of his character, and Darwin and Trollope imply it by narrating specially selected childhood scenes that seem to foreshadow their adult lives.[6] Similarly, though

Newman says in *Apologia* that he wants only to "state facts," his 1865 "Preface" to the book claims a more ambitious aim: making his readers "understand . . . [his] most private thoughts and feelings."[7] This is the motive that impels Miss Wade to share her "History of a Self-Tormentor," and it is the motive that drives Mrs. Clennam to confess before Blandois can reveal her secrets. It is also the wish that drives so many first-person narrators in Victorian fiction to account for moments of psychological trauma and origin that they scarcely understand. Jane recounts the vague terrors of the red room, and Esther Summerson describes her unnerving dreams. Pip, though he seems not to remark the symbolic implications of the scene, begins in *Great Expectations* by describing the origins of his name even as he places himself, tellingly, among the graves of parents he has never known. Each of these moments hints at a part of identity that rests beyond the power of facts to describe. Each reminds us that facts, chronology, and even narrative are methods of *inventing* rather than *discovering* a coherence for the self. Over and over, Victorian first-person novels show us narrators in the act of constructing their identity, treating themselves as narrative "others" whom language will express and define. Not for nothing does David Copperfield begin his story by saying, "Whether I shall turn out to be the hero of my own life, or whether that station will be held by anybody else, these pages must show."[8] For Victorian self-narrators as for Victorian prisoners, he reminds us, the motive for autobiography is the desire to impose order upon a disordered self.

Perhaps this explains why so many Victorian first-person novels return to images of the prison. *Copperfield* shows us the King's Bench and Pentonville, and *The Way of All Flesh* thrusts Ernest Pontifex into Coldbath-fields. On other occasions, because they require private disorder as a pretext for offering sustained self-narration, Victorian novelists force their autobiographers to endure the private traumas engendered by solitary confinement. Jane's time in the red room is one example, and young David's five-day sentence to his bedroom is another. Esther, Lucy Snowe, and Ernest find that the solitary cell is a place of illness and psychological crisis. Taken together, these moments imply what characters like Bertha Mason, Magwitch, and Mademoiselle Hortense make explicit: that confinement is the necessary consequence of guilt and mental aberration, both of which must be thrust into the prison. To remain free of the cell, Jane, Pip, and Esther must repress the transgressive impulses that these alter egos embody, and they must live consciously as divided selves. It ought really to be no wonder that these self-narrators often sound like Victorian prisoners, for—like Thomas Robinson, Alexandre Manette, Richard Devine, and other inmates—they are impelled by private disorder to use self-narration to invent coherence and meaning for their divid-

ed selves. Thus even Victorian novels that have nothing to do with literal prisons show us self-narrators whose stories emanate from the solitude
of the cell. That they do suggests a tantalizing possibility about Victorian
fiction: that Victorian novelists, whether or not they were writing of the
cell, drew their power to invent the private self—imaginatively and ideologically—from the narrative power reposed in the prison.

No novels suggest this possibility more strongly than Brontë's *Villette*
or Wilkie Collins's *Armadale* (1866). At first, these novels may seem sadly
out of place in this study, for neither even contains a prison. Nor, in fact,
do the novels seem to have much in common with one another. But
despite their differences these works coincide at a crucial structural and
thematic point: both depend upon self-narratives composed in the solitude of the cell. The novels give us women—Lucy Snowe and Lydia
Gwilt—who labor in prisons from the start, subject incessantly to social
constraints and the pressures of the stare. Imprisoned in this way, both
women live consciously divided between public and private selves, suppressing their guilty desires behind veneers of rationality and *sang-froid*.
Both become perfectly respectable governesses, and both manage almost
entirely to escape detection by the social stare. But each novel insists that
the private self must finally be exposed, for the culmination of each plot
depends upon accounting for the disordered self. In *Villette*'s case this
dependence is clear, for the novel *is* Lucy's great attempt to narrate herself entirely—to invent from her fragmented identity an account of a
substantial and coherent self. In *Armadale*, though the reliance is subtler,
it is no less complete. Despite its broad concerns with fate, crime, and
detection, Collins's novel depends ultimately upon discovering the guilty
desires that motivate Lydia's action—desires that are accounted for only
in her private writing. Only in solitude can Lucy and Lydia own up to
their desiring selves. Only solitude forces them to turn their narrative
stares inward, upon the frightening reality of their private disarray.
Guilty, desiring, and self-divided, Lucy and Lydia retreat into the solitude
of the prison, and they use self-narration to impose order upon their disordered identities. In doing so, they reveal something crucial about
Villette and *Armadale* and about the broad narrative implications of nineteenth-century confinement: even in Victorian novels that have nothing
to do with prisons, authors' attempts to narrate the self begin and end in
the cell.

II

In *Sexual Politics* in 1969, Kate Millett wrote of *Villette*, "Escape is all over
the book; *Villette* reads like one long meditation on a prison break."[9]
Considering the subject and timing of *Sexual Politics*, we might expect
that the ideas in it were fresh and new, perhaps even radical and revolu-

tionary. In many ways, they were. But Millett was not saying something new about Brontë's novel when she pointed out Lucy's captivity. In the hundred and fifty years since *Villette* was published, probably no critic has doubted that Lucy is a prisoner. But neither has one ever suggested that her captivity or self-account has anything to do with the Victorian prison. For the first century after *Villette* appeared in 1853, readers assumed mostly that Lucy's confinement reflects Brontë's own—during her dismally lonely time in Brussels in 1842–1843, for example, and her decades of isolation at Haworth. Though Brontë took pains to conceal these personal details from her readers, her death in 1855 prompted her father to ask Elizabeth Gaskell to memorialize Charlotte in a biography. Two years later, Gaskell published *The Life of Charlotte Brontë* (1857) and revealed to every reader in Victorian England the private miseries of Brontë's life. Drawn mostly from Gaskell's recollections, interviews with friends and family, and Brontë's letters to Emily, Ellen Nussey, Mary Taylor, and other confidantes, the biography disclosed crucial details about Brontë's time in Brussels, even hinting that she may have suffered a romantic disappointment there at the hands of her schoolmaster, Constantin Heger. As Tom Winnifreth points out, Gaskell's book exposed so many parallels between Brontë and Lucy that, "even though the Heger story could only be guessed at . . . the biographical school of criticism more or less took over the novel."[10] The results were a century of critical attention devoted to Brontë rather than her heroine and benign neglect of certain implications of Lucy's prisons.

That changed late in the 1970s when feminist scholars especially began to reconsider the novel. In *The Madwoman in the Attic* (1979), Sandra Gilbert and Susan Gubar laid much of the foundation for feminist readings of the novel, arguing that Lucy is confined mostly by her lack of alternatives, the pressures she faces to conform to gender expectations, and the crushing psychological consequences of her repression. As they argue, it is Lucy's mind that becomes "a dark and narrow cell . . . a chamber of terrible visions, not the least of which is that of being buried alive."[11] Since Gilbert and Gubar, other critics have made feminist, psychoanalytic, and even Foucaultian approaches to the novel, mostly discovering new ways to argue that Lucy's prisons are the result of social constraints, and that she and her self-account are scarred by her efforts to repress desire. Kate Lawson reads Lucy as an example of the idea that "the human subject is a divided one," and Christina Crosby argues that the novel is really about Lucy's "synthesis of her divided self."[12] For Sally Shuttleworth and Patricia Johnson, Lucy's prisons depend partly anyway upon the disciplinary power of the social stare.[13] During the last quarter-century, scholars have produced endless readings of Lucy as desiring, repressed, neurotic, and divided, and of her self-account as elusive, "devious, duplicitous," and—as Lucy calls it—"heretic."[14] Almost invariably, these readings conclude that Lucy's arrival at Fauborg Clotilde is a victory, for Lucy's room of her own delivers her from her social prisons and allows her, in the form of her self-account, to assert her power of self-definition in defiance of her captors. "Had Brontë's heroine 'adjusted' herself to society, compromised, and gone under," Millett wrote, "we should never have heard from her."[15] In other words, despite its deliberate concealments and evasions—the scars it bears, one might say, from Lucy's confinement—Lucy's autobiography shows that she has emerged finally from the shadow of her many prisons.

These are persuasive arguments about *Villette*, and not just because they have been repeated so often. Lucy labors under social and economic constraints from the beginning of the novel, and her life consists of a series of moves from one confining situation to another. From Bretton she goes to Miss Marchmont's service, and from there to Madame Beck's surveillant pensionnat. But these are not Lucy's only prisons, nor are they the ones that matter most to her self-account. Rather, *Villette* hinges finally upon Lucy's solitary cells and their power to drive her to disorder, self-reflection, and the narration of her private self. During the weeks of the long vacation at the pensionnat, Lucy struggles against the apparitions raised by hypochondria and hysteria. When she seeks out privacy in the garden and the grenier, she is terrified by the ghostly nun. In other words, though Lucy ought to find these escapes from the stare liberating, she does not—or at least not always. Instead, like so many real Victorian prisoners before her, she finds that her escapes into solitude are moments of private terror in which she encounters the most terrifying parts of her divided self. They are also the moments that enable Lucy to write a complete account of her disordered identity. Partly, Lucy requires solitude so that she can act upon her desire and permit her hidden self to enter the visible world that her narrative describes. Partly, she requires it so that she has a safe space from which to write, where she can commit to paper the guilty secrets of her transgressive desire. But Lucy needs solitude mostly for the same reason that, in theory, Victorian prisoners did: because she is guilty and disordered, and she must be impelled to introspection and psychological crisis if she is to confess her transgressive desires. Of all the events that comprise Lucy's story, her moments of solitary trauma reveal the most about her inner world, for in solitude she must turn her narrative stare inward and look upon the full scope of her psychic disarray. Her self-narrative is her attempt to impose order upon that disorder, so that she can emerge a complete and coherent self through her self-narration. Written from the solitude of Fauborg Clotilde, Lucy's self-account is not a celebration of her freedom from the prison. It is proof, rather, that she is another Victorian prisoner, driven to disorder and self-narration by the cell.

III

When *Villette* begins Lucy is not literally a prisoner, but she is imprisoned—as critics have pointed out—by the constraints of her gender and class. Lucy paints Bretton as a childhood Eden that she visits twice each year. But her account of her last stay there mentions that her godmother has "come in person to claim [her]" from events "whose very shadow . . . sufficed to impart unsettled sadness" (*V* 6). Though Lucy never says so, these "events" seem to imply the disintegration of her family and home, so that Lucy may come to Bretton on this last occasion, as Chiara Briganti suggests, as an exile rather than a visitor.[16] Whether or not this is so, Lucy describes her early life in images of the prison. As we see from the metaphor of storm and shipwreck that opens chapter four, Lucy describes herself as a prisoner of fate, tossed about by forces she cannot master. At times this is really the case, as when Polly Home first comes to Bretton during a storm, and when storms threaten Paul Emanuel's crossing from the West Indies. Indeed, Lucy makes storms her narrative refrain in the novel, using them always to mark her moments of emotional and psychological trial. Elsewhere, she recalls more concrete prisons that hint at her scanty alternatives. As Miss Marchmont's nurse Lucy confines herself to "[t]wo hot, close rooms," and later she enters the oppressive discipline of Mme. Beck's pensionnat (*V* 50). Both places require Lucy to repress desire and steel herself to the "self-reliance and exertion . . . forced upon [her] by circumstances" (*V* 47). In Miss Marchmont's service, Lucy writes, "her pain, [was] my suffering—her relief, my hope—her anger, my punishment—her regard, my reward" (*V* 50). The Rue Fossette bristles with a similar disciplinary demand: "a surveillance that left . . . no moment and no corner for retirement," and that forces Lucy to remain always the perfect *sang-froid* (*V* 100). Gilbert and Gubar conclude on these grounds that Mme. Beck is the very "symbol of repression," and Shuttleworth observes that the pensionnat operates like a Panopticon.[17] Really the pensionnat is no more imprisoning than Lucy's other early homes. It only exemplifies the constraints to which she is always subject.

Driven into these prisons by economic need and a dearth of alternatives, Lucy chooses consciously to live as a divided self. Outwardly, she is dutiful and meek, playing masterfully her role as a *sang-froid*. Inwardly, she seethes, waging constant war against her imagination and passion. Even at Bretton—though she once remarks of Polly, "I wished *she* would utter some hysterical cry, so that *I* might get relief" [emphasis mine]—she constantly contrasts Polly's obvious passions with her own outward calm (*V* 18). While Polly thrills visibly to see her father approach the Bretton house, Lucy watches "calmly from the window"; when Mr. Home leaves and Polly cries out, Lucy writes, "I, Lucy Snowe, was calm" (*V* 16; 28). From her earliest days Lucy makes impassivity her ideal for outer conduct, and she even describes emotional upset at Bretton only when it is Polly's rather than her own. Dividing herself in this way between her public and private selves, Lucy remarks that as governess to Mme. Beck's children she must lead "two lives—the life of thought, and that of reality" (*V* 105). On her first day as teacher of the second division, Lucy's repressed self even takes corporal form. While Mme. Beck spies through a peephole in the wall, Lucy must take physical hold of Dolores—whose name means upset and disorder—subdue her, and thrust her into a closet. She also carries on private dialogues in which reason, "vindictive as a devil," vanquishes "Imagination" and "divine Hope" (*V* 328). Consciously maintaining this private split, Lucy even writes two versions of her letters to Graham: one that she withholds, shaped by "Feeling" and expressing a "closely clinging and deeply honouring attachment"; and one that she sends, dictated by the "dry, stinting check of Reason" (*V* 363–364). Leading an inner life so different from her outer one, Lucy cannot on the night of the concert even recognize her image in the mirror. Instead, she receives "the 'giftie'" of seeing herself "as others see [her]" (*V* 298). The result, she tells us, is a "jar of discord, a pang of regret"—a sudden apprehension of the gap between her public and private selves (*V* 298).

Post-modern critiques of *Villette* have routinely gotten this far: to discussions of Lucy's socially determined prisons and analyses of the repression and self-division they inflict upon her. But critiques that address the novel's prisons in this broad way tend to forget that *Villette* also contains other prisons, physical ones, with walls and doors that lock Lucy away in solitude. Lucy is shut in the grenier to learn her part for Mme. Beck's fête and finds herself in "solitary confinement" during the long vacation at the pensionnat (*V* 264). At other times, often, Lucy seeks solitude and escapes into a cell of her own. She is happy to find herself alone while viewing the Cleopatra, and she retreats to the grenier to read Graham's letters in secret. She also moves gradually toward her private space at Fauborg Clotilde, where she finally writes her self-account. These places are not jails or penitentiaries, and Gilbert and Gubar regard them mostly as metaphors for the "dark and narrow cell" of Lucy's mind. They also distinguish—unadvisedly perhaps—between Lucy's lonely room at Fauborg Clotilde and her other solitary cells. While Miss Marchmont's rooms, the grenier, and other private spaces reflect Lucy's cell-like mind, in their estimation, Fauborg Clotilde is a "comfortable space" that Lucy "wins" through her growing awareness of the uses of narrative and self-definition.[18] They neglect to point out, though, that Lucy's other solitary cells also play crucial narrative roles. As Athena Vrettos observes, private spaces in *Villette* serve typically to contain Lucy's passion and desire, and Lucy seeks them out in order to "express her conflicting sense of restriction and release."[19] To the extent that this is so, the novel's physical cells reinforce the idea that Lucy is self-divided, for they suggest that she needs a physical space in which she can become disordered—or at least disorderly—and indulge her other, desiring self. But they also imply throughout the novel what Fauborg Clotilde makes explicit: that Lucy requires solitary cells if she is to self-narrate, since these cells permit her and even impel her to explore and express the transgressive passions she must usually hide.

Brontë's biographers have often pointed out, quite correctly, that Lucy's isolation in *Villette* mostly mirrors Brontë's own, not only during the time she wrote the novel but also during the early 1840s, when she experienced Belgium in the same lonely way as Lucy.[20] Charlotte and Emily went together to Brussels in February 1842 to study at the Pensionnat Heger, but by the end of the year Emily had returned to England. The following April, Charlotte wrote to Ellen Nussey that she felt deeply her "solitude in the midst of numbers," and she became increasingly estranged from Heger and his wife (*Life* 254). She wrote to Emily in May 1843 that Heger had apparently "taken to considering [her] as a person to be left alone . . . and consequently he has in a great measure withdrawn . . . I get on from day to day in a Robinson-Crusoe-like condition—very lonely."[21] Gilbert and Gubar point out that Charlotte had grown to admire and perhaps even love Heger, and that her transgressive passion "ended first in a kind of solitary confinement imposed upon Brontë by his wife, and finally in his refusal to respond to Brontë's letters from England."[22] By June 1843 Charlotte was indescribably lonely, and she lamented to Nussey that she felt it most "on the holidays— when all the girls and teachers go out to visit . . . [and] the silence of all the house weighs one's spirits like lead."[23] Like Lucy, Charlotte also had to endure the pensionnat's long vacation, the threat of which rendered her "downcast" and made her "days and nights of a weary length" (*Life* 260). By Christmas 1843, Charlotte had had enough of her dismal existence. She packed her things and returned to Haworth and the company of her sisters.

As she prepared to write *Villette* a decade later, these old sorrows returned with greater force. Long supported at Haworth by the company of Emily and Anne and the occasional presence of her brother Branwell, Charlotte endured the rapid, successive deaths of all three during eight months of 1848 and 1849. Branwell died in September 1848, and Emily slipped into a torpor and followed him to the grave before Christmas. Anne, always the most frail, lasted until May of the following year. She died on the way to Scarborough, where she and Charlotte had hoped that she might regain her strength. Bereft suddenly of her siblings and life-long companions, Charlotte sat alone in the dining room at Haworth where she and her sisters had engaged in lively literary discussions. Now, as Gaskell points out, the characters Charlotte created were her only companions "in the quiet hours, which she spent utterly alone" (*Life* 470). Two months after Anne's death, Charlotte wrote to Nussey that "the house was . . . all silent—the rooms . . . all empty . . . So the sense of desolation and bitterness took possession of me. The agony that *was to be undergone* and *was not* to be avoided, came on" (*Life* 376). Nussey visited Haworth occasionally, doing what she could to cheer Charlotte's dreary world. Even so, in August 1852, just two months before finishing *Villette*, Charlotte's grief seems to have reached its apex. She wrote to Nussey, "The evils that now and then wring a groan from my heart—lie in position—not that I am a *single* woman and likely to remain a *single* woman—but because I am a *lonely* woman and likely to be *lonely*."[24] She was partly wrong, for she married Arthur Nicholls in 1854. Still, Charlotte's words demonstrate the hold that loneliness had upon her, and how firmly, at the time she wrote *Villette*, she believed that solitude was part of her identity. Writing during 1851 and 1852 the final pages of Lucy's self-account, Charlotte had to confront, as Helene Moglen puts it, "the one irreducible fact of her life: her loneliness."[25]

Moglen is correct, but it is worth noting that Charlotte's loneliness filled her with more than grief. For Charlotte knew from childhood that solitude could inflict trauma upon the private self. As a girl she had a habit of "making out" imaginary scenes, and her school-fellow Mary Taylor even recalled an instance when Charlotte:

> . . . sat in the dressing-room until it was quite dark, and then observing it all at once [took] sudden fright.
>
> From that time her imaginations became gloomy or frightful; she could not help it, nor help thinking. She could not forget the gloom, could not sleep at night, nor attend in the day.[26]

The moment hints at a deeply felt psychological crisis—at a brush, perhaps, with the psychic death that springs from the sudden apprehension that the self is disorderly and endangered, capable at any moment of dissolving entirely. For Charlotte, this sense of psychic disintegration produced a lifelong terror of solitude. In 1838 she suffered through a period when she "would turn sick and trembling at any sudden noise, and could hardly repress her screams when startled" (*Life* 182). Five years later, the long vacation at the Pensionnat Heger left Charlotte sleepless in the "deserted dormitory," prey to a terrible "fear respecting those whom she loved, and who were so far off . . . oppressing her and choking up the very lifeblood in her heart" (*Life* 260). After that fear had been realized in the deaths of her brother and sisters, Charlotte wrote to Nussey from the solitude at Haworth to complain that she had "presentiment[s]" of evil and was sometimes "haunted with a sense of sickening distress."[27] By 1846 she looked back on the long vacation as a period during which she was nearer to hysteria than natural worry, and she blamed her psychic discomfort on "Hypochondria—A most dreadful doom . . . the concentrated anguish of certain insufferable moments and the heavy gloom of many long hours—besides the preternatural horror which seemed to cloth existence and Nature—and which made Life a continual waking nightmare."[28] In 1851 she visited phrenologist J. P. Brown in an effort to penetrate the source of her perpetual anxieties.[29] These efforts to name her malady show Charlotte struggling to use language—especially the language of science and psychology—to impose order upon the disorder engendered by solitude.

Lucy makes this same attempt in *Villette*, calling attention repeatedly to the upset engendered by her solitary cells. Early on, Lucy's lonely room in the London inn forces her to tears, and then to a "dark interval of most bitter thought" (*V* 62). Later, when she is locked in the grenier by M. Paul, Lucy's thoughts turn morbid again. She says that each winter cloak hangs from its peg "like a malefactor from his gibbet," and when she returns to the spot later to read her letter from Graham, she is disturbed for the first time by the ghostly nun (*V* 188). These lesser terrors are mere preludes to Lucy's distress during the long vacation. Haunted at first by a real monster, "the cretin," with her "warped" body and inexplicable "propensity . . . to evil," Lucy continues to see monsters even after the cretin departs (*V* 220). They are the horrifying products of her diseased imagination. The last two weeks of the vacation are "tempestuous and wet," wracked by the storms that always signal her inner turmoil (*V* 219). Appropriately, amid the tempest, Lucy experiences the long vacation as a waking nightmare, crowded with the apparitions of her sick fancy. She finds that the "ghostly white beds" turn into specters with "wide gaping eye-holes" that look upon the "dead dreams of an elder world" (*V* 224). She also finds "unendurable" the "pitiless and haughty voice in which Death challenge[s] [her] to engage his unknown terrors" (*V* 223). Later, looking back on the miseries of her solitude, Lucy writes:

> The world can understand well enough the process of perishing for want of food: perhaps few persons can enter into or follow out that of going mad from solitary confinement. They see the long-buried prisoner disinterred, a maniac or an idiot!—how his senses left him—how his nerves first inflamed, underwent nameless agony, and then sunk to palsy—is a subject too intricate for examination, too abstract for popular comprehension. (*V* 392)

Like Dickens in *American Notes*, Lucy imagines solitary prisoners as people "buried alive," and like Dickens, she insists that madness is the grotesque and inevitable result of solitary confinement. More to the point, and also like Dickens, Lucy implies that her writing will serve the hermeneutic aim of accounting for—in the interest of popular comprehension—the psychological disruptions and disorder that the solitary prison inflicts upon the confined.

Lucy's borrowed eloquence on solitude and madness thus suggests that her self-account is meant to order the private disorder engendered by her prisons. Driven to conscious self-division, she will use narrative to create coherence; driven repeatedly to private terror, she will use narrative to sort out the complexities of her transgressive desire. But Lucy's remarks tend nevertheless to obscure what she undergoes in the cell, for the truth of the matter is that solitude does *not* drive Lucy mad, at least not in the sense of making her a maniac or an idiot. Nor does she wish her readers to perceive her in this way. Rather, Lucy's moments of solitude are descents into *disorder*, which she can acknowledge and explore only in the privacy of the cell. Freed in solitude from the pressures of surveillant stares and gender constraints, Lucy finds sometimes that her solitary cells are escapes that enable her to indulge passion and imagination. More often, she finds that these places are dens of terror, marred by her need to abdicate to the uncontrollable power of her desire. In solitude, "calm" Lucy entertains hopes about Graham and her unfulfilled sexual yearning. In solitude, she trembles at specters and phantoms that her rational self would never acknowledge. Locked alone repeatedly in *Villette*'s solitary cells, Lucy finds that to indulge desire is to surrender to it, and to succumb to its intrinsic irrationality and disorder. Thus Lucy's moments of solitude force her to reflect upon the full complexities of her private self.

Because they do so, they also make it possible for her to impose order upon that self in narrative. *Villette* begins at Bretton with Lucy in the position of voyeur. She hovers over Polly and Graham, and later over Mme. Beck and M. Paul. All the while, she orients her self-account around what she sees rather than what she thinks or feels. She reports on carelessly flung *billets-doux* and the frightening appearances of the ghostly nun, and the events that she describes in *Villette* are mostly the spectacles she sees: the concert, the Cleopatra, Vashti, and the festival. But encircled by surveillant prisons where Lucy is watcher and watched, she can never—the novel suggests—narrate herself entirely. To narrate herself to completion, rather, Lucy must have private spaces in which she can permit her desiring self to enter the visible world of the novel. Only in solitude can she acknowledge and act upon the transgressive promptings of her desire. Only by showing herself in private spaces can the narrating

Lucy render the hidden part of her divided self. Thus *Villette* makes images of Lucy's solitude a crucial symbolic pattern, implying repeatedly that she needs privacy if she is to explore herself, contemplate her desire, and undertake an act of self-narration that allows her to invent a complete and coherent identity. Lucy's autobiography from Fauborg Clotilde is this act of self-narration—her great effort to become more than a nobody or shadow in her fictional world. Arrived at Fauborg Clotilde at the end of her story, Lucy has not finally escaped her prisons and "won" a comfortable space from which to write. She has exchanged her social prisons for a solitary one that enables self-narration and requires it—one that makes her, that is, into the very image of the Victorian self in the cell.

IV

Lucy's narrative suggests from the first that she needs solitude if she is to account completely for her divided self. When she is surrounded by others, Lucy watches, so that from the time she is a child she plays the narrative role of a voyeur. She watches Mrs. Bretton as she reads the letter Lucy fears is from home, and she stares as a "small crib" and "tiny rosewood chest" appear suddenly in her bedroom (*V* 7). She also watches as Warren returns to Bretton bearing the mysterious bundle—Polly—that casts Lucy out of Eden. Considering Lucy's penchant for staring, it is fitting that her first impulse is to unwrap the bundle so that she can "get a peep at the face" (*V* 9). Though her godmother tells Lucy to "[t]ake no notice at present," she reports, "I did take notice: I watched Polly rest her small elbow on her small knee, her head on her hand; I observed her draw a square-inch or two of pocket-handkerchief from the doll-pocket of her doll-skirt, and then I heard her weep" (*V* 10–11). This first description of Polly presages the self-narrative that will come, for it rivets our attention on Polly rather than on Lucy—a displacement of attention that characterizes almost the entire novel. Especially when Lucy shows us emotional turmoil in *Villette*, the turmoil almost always belongs to others. In the novel's early chapters, Polly's pleasures and pains are the center of Lucy's attention. Lucy spies while Polly weeps "under restraint, quietly and cautiously," and she tries to catch the words of Polly's whispered prayers (*V* 12). She also notes that Polly is "a little busy-body" as the child waits upon her father (*V* 19). For Lucy, Polly is always most riveting when she interacts with the novel's men. If Polly is quietly engaged with needlework at Mrs. Bretton's side, Lucy ignores her, for "under such circumstances: she [is] not interesting" (*V* 30). But the instant that Graham arrives in the evening, Lucy resumes her vigilance, hinting in her preoccupation with the pair the stirrings of her unstated desire. Only when Lucy looks at such passions in these early chapters does she include them in her story. Thus her self-narrative treats desire as the province of the narrated "other."

As the novel proceeds, Lucy derives most of her story from this outward stare, ignoring her private self and treating externalities as the events that constitute her "life." Certainly this is true at the pensionnat, where Lucy watches secretly the transactions between Graham and Rosine, pries into the contents of *billets-doux*, and sees spectral nuns leap suddenly from shadows. This propensity for staring also allows Lucy to describe other characters meticulously, though she rarely remarks her own appearance. She writes of "dark" and "austere" M. Paul and describes Graham's "perfect" Grecian chin (*V* 179; 132). She also lingers over descriptions of her godmother, Mme. Beck, Ginevra, and her fellow-teachers at the pensionnat. Indeed, Lucy becomes so adept at spying in the Rue Fossette that she even spies on Mme. Beck—a program of counter-surveillance that shows us Lucy is aware that she can control others by staring at them. Lucy is aware of this even early in the novel, for, on Polly's first morning at Bretton, just as the girl is about to bare her grief to her nurse, Lucy rises from a feigned sleep in order "to check this scene while it [is] yet within bounds" (*V* 13). At the pensionnat, besides spying on her employer, Lucy stares at "Dr. John," transgressing (as she well knows) the bounds of her gender and station. As she does so, she thrills at "an idea new, sudden, and startling" that "rivet[s] [her] attention with an overmastering strength and power of attraction" (*V* 136).[30] That new idea might be the stirrings of her sexual yearning, or it might be the sudden apprehension that Dr. John is Graham Bretton. Or it might be the sense of power she enjoys from employing her transgressive stare.[31] Early in the novel, at least, watching seems to provide Lucy with the power to know and account for the world in which she moves. A full decade after her days at Bretton, when she, Polly, and Graham reunite at La Terrasse, Lucy again slips easily into the role of voyeur.

But situated within a world in which she is watcher and watched, Lucy can never, the novel suggests, account entirely for her private self. Basing her self-narrative upon what she sees, Lucy has no opportunity to narrate the desiring self that she withholds deliberately from view. She slips occasionally—when, for instance, she trembles to help Graham set Fifine's arm, and when she shouts finally, "Vive l'Angleterre, l'Histoire et les Héros!" in response to M. Paul's goading (*V* 493). For the most part, though, she plays the *sang-froid*, concealing parts of her identity from those around her. As Lucy's self-narrative progresses, she grows to resent increasingly her self-willed insubstantiality. She refuses to accept a position as a companion to Polly, saying, "I was no bright lady's shadow," and she stings under Ginevra's taunt that she may be more than the "nobody" Ginevra has thought her (427; 440). When Ginevra asks,

"Who *are* you, Miss Snowe?" Lucy retorts: "I am a rising character: once an old lady's companion, then a nursery-governess, now a school-teacher" (*V* 440; 442). Lucy's response is straightforward, in one sense, for it is a typical Victorian account of the events that have made up her life. But her words also indicate her growing awareness that she must become psychically and narratively complete if she is to avoid the pain of disregard. When Graham tells Lucy that she is "inoffensive as a shadow," she recoils mentally in a way that shows she is pained by his failure to see her equally—in selfhood if not in beauty—with his beloved Polly:

> Oh!—I wished he would just let me alone—cease allusion to me. These epithets—these attributes I put from me. His "quiet Lucy Snowe," his "inoffensive shadow," I gave him back . . . With a now welcome force, I realized his entire misapprehension of my character and nature. He wanted always to give me a rôle not mine. Nature and I opposed him. He did not at all guess what I felt: he did not read my eyes, or face, or gestures; though, I doubt not, all spoke. (*V* 454–455)

To become capable of speaking clearly with her voice and her narrative, Lucy must gain social and economic independence so that she can escape the imprisoning power of the stare. More important, she must engage in self-discovery and self-invention if she wishes finally to become whole. Having withheld desire for so long from the visible world of the novel, she must turn her narrative stare inward upon the terrors of her disordered self.

She can only do so, her narrative suggests, in the solitude of the prison. Even her moments of imperfect solitude—"solitude in the midst of numbers"—show us a Lucy who, free from the stare, observes the external world as a way of exploring and ordering her private feelings. She confesses that she prefers to visit Villette's picture-galleries by herself, for, as she says, "[i]n company, a wretched idiosyncrasy forbade me to see much or to feel anything" (*V* 283). But alone, she can stare unmolested at the Cleopatra and use her staring as a means of encountering her own desire—of beginning to arrange, as she puts it, the "wretched untidiness" of her disordered private world (*V* 285). The concert is another opportunity, amid the spectacle of performance, to contemplate her identity away from the social stare. On one hand, given over explicitly to thinking about the King of Labassecour, Lucy claims a sort of prescience regarding his private identity, for she writes, "if I did not *know*, at least I *felt*" the nature of the King's upset (*V* 303). What she feels so acutely, however, is the misery of her own position. It is Lucy who bends her brows "to that peculiar and painful fold" because of her foreignness to

Villette; Lucy whose sorrows stem from "the effects of early bereave-
ment"; and Lucy who is "embittered by that darkest foe of humanity—
constitutional melancholy" (*V* 304). She may surmise correctly that the
King suffers from that "strangest spectre, Hypochondria" (*V* 303). But her
words also echo Graham's diagnosis of her, and Brontë's diagnosis of her
own anxieties during the long vacation at the pensionnat. Having just
come upon her own image in the mirror and mistaken it for the image
of another, Lucy has discovered the narrative split between subject and
object. Through the King, she begins to explore the function of that split
in her own self-account, writing about her private disquiet without abandoning her narrative stance as a voyeur.

The scene in which Lucy watches Vashti underscores Lucy's discovery that she is the subject and object of her self-narration. The interest of
the scene rests mostly in Lucy's conscious embrace of Vashti as a
repressed, tormented, and desiring version of her own private self. Like
Vashti, Lucy refuses to become a spectacle, for she rejects a role as the
object of the male gaze and sexual desire. Like Vashti, too, Lucy must
endure the inner torments engendered by that rejection, suffering the
private upheavals produced by repression and self-division. Because Lucy
sees in Vashti these traits that correspond with her own divided and disordered self, Vashti becomes a point of psychic reference around which
Lucy can arrange her understanding of her private world. Even the timing of the performance—just after Lucy has received Graham's first letter
and after her first encounter with the ghostly nun—indicates its relation
to the growing presence of Lucy's desire. Throughout the performance,
Lucy is preoccupied not only with Vashti but also with the effect the
scene has upon Graham. For Lucy the performance "disclose[s] power
like a deep, swollen, winter river, thundering in cataract, and bearing the
soul, like a leaf, on the steep and steely sweep of its descent" (*V* 371). But
Graham is "revolted" by the apparition, and Lucy sees in his revulsion
the difference between her passionate being and his: he is "*impressionable
. . .* as dimpling water, but, almost as water, *unimpressible*: the breeze, the
sun, moved him—metal could not grave, nor fire brand" (*V* 372). No
Vashti—and by association no Lucy—can rouse Graham from dumb
serenity to passion. Lucy's realization that this is so depends upon her
ability to recognize herself in Vashti's tragic presence, and it leads her to
mark that night in her "book of life, not with white, but with a deep-red
cross" (*V* 373). Graham, Ginevra, the Cleopatra, and Vashti all crowd
upon Lucy's thoughts this night, for Lucy reads in Vashti—and narrates
through her—the disappointments and prospects of her own desire. So
powerful is Lucy's psychological identification with the scene that, at her
moment of greatest emotional intensity, the theater catches fire and the
performance stops. Besides hinting at the intensity of Lucy's desiring self,

the interruption suggests that there are limitations to Lucy's ability to self-narrate. Though "imperfect solitude" frees her to treat herself as a narrative other, Lucy can go only so far in public toward discovering and describing her desiring self.

To complete her self-exploration, Lucy must have solitude, for she must turn her stare wholly inward upon the disorder engendered by her desire. She does so first in the grenier, when M. Paul locks her away in solitude so that she may learn her lines for the fête. She imagines herself an inmate, "fasting and in prison," but she also hints that being "[p]erfectly secure from human audience" allows her to indulge passion and imagination (*V* 189). She enters fully into the "emptiness, frivolity, and falsehood" of the piece as long as she is alone, so much so that M. Paul, listening at the door, enters with a resounding "Brava!" (*V* 189; 190). When she must act the scene again under the pressure of the stare, Lucy discovers that playing a role—dressed half as a man and half as a woman—allows her to speak her desire for the first time without fear of discovery.[32] Her success in the part stems partly from her ability to ignore the audience, and to think "of nothing but the personage [she] represent[s]" (*V* 195). But it stems, too, from her partial escape from the constraints imposed upon her by gender expectations—constraints that normally prohibit her from attesting to the stirrings of her desire. Wooing Ginevra in the role of the fop and thus competing, in a fashion, with Graham, Lucy is overwhelmed by an impulse "to eclipse the 'Ours'" that is her dramatic rival (*V* 196). She wishes to desire and be desired, to serve simultaneously as a possessor and object of the gaze. Publicly she enacts a scene that displays her own private longing, living for a few moments the inner life of passion that she cannot express in her own character. The solitude afforded by the grenier is the originary moment for this impulse, as Lucy knows well. When she receives Graham's first letter and is "bent . . . on finding solitude *somewhere*" in which to read it, she returns to the privacy that the grenier affords (*V* 349).

Retreating into the grenier a second time to escape the necessity of self-division, Lucy expects her solitude to be a psychological indulgence: an opportunity to act upon the promptings of her desire. She anticipates that reading Graham's letter in private will be a feast to her famine of emotional need, "a bubble," as she says, "but a sweet bubble—of real honey-dew" (*V* 350). Even in retrospect it seems a feast to the Lucy who narrates, for in thinking of the letter she absolves Graham at once for any pain that he caused her, all "for the sake of that one dear remembered good!" (*V* 350). Yet even as Lucy recalls and relives this ecstatic approach to her desire, she suggests that her desire was and is a matter for private terror. In the solitude of the grenier, Lucy finds the ghostly nun, a spectral embodiment of her repression that will haunt her throughout the novel. For a woman in Lucy's economic and social position, to confess and enact her desire would lead, at least figuratively, to imprisonment, alienation, and (metaphorically) being buried alive. But the nun represents a psychological as well as a social danger, for she gives substance to Lucy's greatest fear: that her identity might be irremediably split, between her conscious, rational self and a self mastered by uncontrollable desire. Even the older, narrating Lucy approaches the scene in the grenier with trepidation, lapsing suddenly into present-tense questions that seem driven by fear. She asks, "Are there wicked things, not human, which envy human bliss? Are there evil influences haunting the air, and poisoning it for man? What was near me?" (*V* 351). Desire is the simple answer to Lucy's last question, for this scene is as "near" as Lucy gets to confessing and fulfilling her sexual longing for Graham. But the complicated answer is disorder, for her narrative approach to desire is an approach to the unruliness and self-division that inhere in her desiring self. The narrating Lucy breaks off after her final question, turning instead to the spectacle of the ghostly nun, and at the end of the chapter—within the scene, so to speak—she refuses to mention the nun to Mme. Beck. Lucy the character and Lucy the narrator find that solitude afflicts them, as it had afflicted Brontë, with intense private terror. As a character and as a narrator, Lucy imposes order upon that disorder by composing and controlling her self-account.

Lucy encounters a similar terror in the solitude of the long vacation. Much like the nun, the pensionnat's cretin embodies Lucy's psychological turmoil. As Briganti observes, "Attendance on the cretin implies daily intercourse with a mind estranged from itself, living in perennial exile."[33] Mental alienation—from others and from her maimed inner life—is Lucy's difficulty during the vacation, and she is acutely conscious throughout of the growing signs of her psychic disturbance. Forced by solitude to stare at nothing but her disintegrating private self, she thrills at the morbid certainty that she is a "permanent foe" to Fate—one of the accursed who "must deeply suffer while they live" (*V* 220). She also makes Ginevra into "a sort of heroine," bathed in the light of "True Love" (*V* 222). Given over to these imaginings, Lucy realizes that in solitude "a malady is growing" upon her mind, but that malady leads her gradually toward a burgeoning self-discovery—a growing desire to identify her narrative position relative to Ginevra, Fate, and her own psychic disintegration (*V* 222). Looking deeply into herself and aware of the signs of her disorder, Lucy has a horrifying dream in which:

> . . a cup was forced to my lips, black, strong, strange, drawn from
> no well, but filled up seething from a bottomless and boundless
> sea. . . . Amidst the horrors of that dream I think the worst lay

here. Methought the well-loved dead, who had loved *me* well in
life, met me elsewhere, alienated: galled was my inmost spirit
with an unutterable sense of despair about the future. (*V* 223)

She dreams here of the difference between her apparent and true selves,
the first of which is loved in her earthly life while the other is hated and
even abandoned when it is finally revealed. She also dreams of death and
psychic dissolution: the unknowable, unnarratable terror that culminates
human experience, the mingled longing for and horror of which rest at
the center of the human unconscious.

For Lucy the result of these psychological disruptions is her first
explicit attempt to use narrative to order her disordered self. Unable to
endure solitude any longer, Lucy flees from the pensionnat to the
Catholic confessional, where she attempts, "as well as [she can]," to
describe "the mere outline of [her] experience" (*V* 226). Her story is fal-
tering, fragmented, and incomplete. Indeed, it reads like a conversion
narrative—an autobiography of spiritual death and rebirth, from which
Lucy seems to awaken to the familiar objects of her childhood Eden. As
Lucy convalesces at Bretton *cum* La Terrasse, Graham even asks, "what
[her] religion now is? Are you a Catholic?" (*V* 262). Lucy rejects this idea,
just as she has rejected it already by mocking Père Silas's suggestion that
they ought to speak at his home. Had she kept her appointment with the
priest, Lucy writes, "the probabilities are that . . . I might just now,
instead of writing this heretic narrative, be counting my beads in the cell
of a certain Carmelite convent on the Boulevard of Crécy in Villette" (*V*
228). These words contain the crux of Lucy's meaning in traveling to the
church at all, for Lucy's rebirth at Bretton is not so much religious or spiritual as it is narrative—a rebirth into memory, experience, and desire.
Driven by solitude to terror and self-reflection, Lucy does not confess to
Père Silas to win spiritual salvation; rather, she does so as a way of ordering her disordered mind and staving off psychological collapse by making sense of her private traumas. For the first time in the novel she confesses the terror of her desire. In the process, she fashions a "heretic" self-
account that defies the social demand that she remain always the *sang-
froid*. Awakening at La Terrasse in the company of Mrs. Bretton and
Graham, Lucy returns to her psychic origins. Fittingly, the awakening is
the start of a chain of events—the episodes with the nun, the Cleopatra,
the concert, and Vashti—that permit Lucy to recover and account for her
desiring self. By desiring, Lucy has transgressed. By bursting from solitude into confession and narrative self-ordering, she recreates the reformative mechanism of the solitary Victorian prison.

In this process of solitary self-ordering and self-narration, Lucy's
opium-induced walk through Villette comprises the final stage. Lucy is

not really by herself during her walk, for she is surrounded at the festival by revelers. But the episode begins and ends in her solitary room at the pensionnat, and during the walk Lucy is very much alone. She is withdrawn, shunning and silencing even Graham when he seems about to discover her. More than this, having been dispossessed of Graham and forsaken apparently by M. Paul, Lucy has never felt so thoroughly estranged from the people around her. Indeed, the influence of the drug seems even to estrange Lucy from her rational, dispassionate self. Showing us in this way that Lucy is irremediably isolated, this episode in particular reads like Millett's prison break. Lucy imagines the classrooms as "great dreary jails" and flees the vicinity of the Rue Fossette where, she says, "I cannot stay; I am still too near the old haunts; so close under the dungeon, I can hear the prisoners moan" (*V* 652; 653). A physical escape, her walk is a psychological unshackling, too, for the opiate rouses her "Imagination . . . impetuous and venturous" and, for the first time, permits her fancy to supplant reason as the master of her body (*V* 651). Released from the necessity of *sang-froid* and repression, she takes a journey through Villette that reads like a journey through her private self. Her path through the festival takes her through her conscious and unconscious past, for she enters the park through "a gap in the paling" that she noticed once unconsciously but recalls now vividly and with force (*V* 651). She also seems to meet at the festival everyone she has ever known: Mrs. Bretton, Graham, Polly, Mme. Beck and Desirée, Père Silas, Madame Walravens, M. Paul, and—though she does not know it until later—Ginevra and de Hamal. This is Lucy's odyssey through the history of her identity and desire: a return in the first place to her longing for Graham, which she professes to have folded up within herself like a "tent of Peri-Banou," but also a contemplation of her new desire for M. Paul (*V* 662). For Lucy the exploration of her desire centers again upon the terrifying image of the nun, animated this time in the form of Justine Marie.

The arrival of the nun this final time creates for Lucy a "crisis and . . . revelation" that permit her, at last, to invent an orderly account of her desire (*V* 672). She perceives suddenly that the people around her—particularly Mme. Beck, Père Silas, and Madame Walravens—are part of a conspiracy, a "secret junta," intent upon robbing her of M. Paul and thwarting her secret longing (*V* 666). She believes that she can see finally that their machinations lie behind the pattern of her life, and behind the mystery M. Paul's sudden disappearance. Having spent the entire novel accounting for the desires, motives, and actions of others, Lucy thus fashions an account of herself in which *her* desire for M. Paul is the force that impels the story. She makes her desire orderly, in other words, by ordering her narrative around it. She also identifies Justine Marie as the substance behind her psychological shadow and thus puts a name to the terror that has haunted her inner life. Driven by solitude to reflect upon the morbid terrors of her private identity, Lucy succeeds at using narrative to impose order upon her disordered identity—a task that is, from the beginning, her purpose in writing her autobiography at all. Mary Jacobus observes that "[t]he wardrobe mockingly bequeathed to Lucy by the eloped Ginevra and de Hamal labels her as the nun of the Rue Fossette—at once accusing her of animating the spectre from within herself, and forcing her to recognize its true identity."[34] Having won the power to name the nun, in other words, Lucy wins the power to name herself. Returning to the pensionnat after her midnight walk through the festival, Lucy destroys another of the nun's physical manifestations, demystifying its presence and proving able, once and for all, to account for it within the greater narrative of her identity and desire.

V

That she does so from the solitude of Clotilde should give us pause to consider whether Lucy has escaped from or rather entered the Victorian prison. Retired into the solitude and economic liberty afforded by M. Paul's generosity—but not hindered by his presence or will—Lucy tells us that she spends "the three happiest years of [her] life" committed to the daily function of her pensionnat and the preparations for M. Paul's eventual return (*V* 711). She has enacted if not consummated her desire by expressing it to him, and in that act she has found a fulfillment that was never before possible. But to suggest that the culmination and creation of Lucy's story resides in her new freedom from constraint is to ignore the consequences of her other descents into solitude. It is also to ignore the process by which she confronts, orders, and narrates her private disarray. Like the Victorian prisoner, Lucy encounters her private truths because she is driven to do so, left in solitude with nothing to contemplate but her own repressions and self-division. She must account for her private disorder or go mad, forced to acknowledge the hopeless fragmentation of a self she can neither narrate nor comprehend. Suggesting that Lucy is split between reason and passion, Vashti and Cleopatra, duty and desire, Patricia Johnson argues that "Lucy oscillates between the two sides; and in this movement, the gap between the two sides, she finds her own voice."[35] But Lucy's self-narrative is not meant to mediate her identity or exist in the gap between her public and private selves. Indeed, if Lucy has learned anything from her dealings with Graham and Ginevra, it is the danger of mediation—the danger of remaining insubstantial by omitting parts of her divided self. Lucy's aim is to incorporate the full range of her psychological being into her self-narrative, and to use that narrative to invent a coherent—if complex—private self. The scientific languages of hypochondria and phrenology that creep into the novel indicate this desire to order and name psychological phenomena. So, too, does the repeated metaphor of storm and shipwreck that obscures Lucy's psychological trials. Offering a self-narrative that at one moment offers a poetic account of "the continent of Europe, like a wide dream-land" and the next demands, "Cancel the whole of that, if you please, reader," Lucy controls and arranges her text to ensure that it contains both poles of her identity, both halves of a self divided and in need of narrative integration (*V* 76).

And yet, despite Lucy's efforts to present a controlled and orderly self-account, we know that her narrative is not complete—that her character has not risen fully into linguistic being. There are too many things she never tells us, and that she takes narrative delight in withholding, as if she is calling attention willfully to the information she omits. She never reveals the tragedy that follows her time at Bretton, nor the "short, strong answer" she receives when she asks M. Paul, "Do I displease your eyes *much*?" (*V* 699). We are also left with Lucy's maddening refusal to disclose his fate at the end of the novel. On one hand, as Nancy Sorkin Rabinowitz argues, Lucy's narrative games make us "more conscious of the medium of the tale, and consequently of the authority of the teller."[36] But they should also alert us to the role that readers play finally in inventing Lucy's private self. Certainly Lucy *could* tell us the events and outcomes of these crucial situations. But there are places in her private self where she will not or perhaps cannot go—back into the anguish of her young womanhood, for instance, or into the greater grief of M. Paul's death. Just as Lucy misunderstands the meaning of Justine Marie's fleshly presence, so she may be unable to articulate fully the terror that the ghostly nun represents. Borislav Knezevic reads *Villette* in this fashion, suggesting that the novel is about the impossibility of self-knowledge, the impossibility of knowing the Lacanian real that rests at the heart of desire.[37] Lucy can give us order, pattern, form, and language. But psychologically unfinished and perhaps unarticulable, she can never narrate herself to completion. Instead, she can offer us only a reading of her old self by her new one, an autobiographical process of self-division and interpretation. The duty of deciphering Lucy's story thus falls to the reader, just as it falls to the narrating Lucy who must read her past in a search for meaning. Brontë suggested this truth, unconsciously perhaps, with her mocking answers to readers' demands that she reveal M. Paul's fate.[38] The question that Lucy seems most to want to answer—"Who *are* you, Miss Snowe?"—is the very one that she cannot answer through her self-narration. Partly, what *Villette* shows, then, is the role of reading and interpretation—particularly reading and interpretation by the other—in the invention of the private self.

It is hardly a new achievement to conclude that the novel is about the failure of self-representation and the need for interpretation if we are to understand Lucy's self-account. Twenty years ago Gilbert and Gubar observed that *Villette* contains the "mature recognition of the necessity and inadequacy of self-definition," and a number of other critics have since concluded much the same.[39] But it is telling that Brontë situates this novel and this message within the solitude of so many metaphorical prisons. Attesting to the guilty desire of a divided and disordered self, Lucy's story belongs in the cell, for it is the confession—and Lucy the transgressor—that the Victorian prison is meant to confine. More to the point, if Brontë really means *Villette* to demonstrate that narrating identity is a matter of reading and interpretation, then she shows above all that narrating the self is always a matter of acquiring narrative power, so that the self can be made into an object of invention by the "other." Brontë thrusts Lucy into the cell, in other words, because she requires the narrative power reposed in the prison. *Villette*'s solitary cells impel Lucy's confession and contain its peril, just as Brontë's writing of the novel seems to have depended upon the same solitude, the same mental agony, and the same necessity of self-reflection. We cannot know for certain whether Brontë *could* have produced *Villette* situated comfortably among her sisters at Haworth. But it may be enough to know that she *did* not— that for Brontë as for Lucy solitude seems to have created not only private disorder but also the possibility that it might be expressed. Uttered from the cell, Lucy's self-account must always remain there, for it is an act of narrative invention made possible by the Victorian prison.

VI

Armadale, too, depends upon the prison's narrative power, especially in its portrayal of Lydia Gwilt. Written along with *No Name* (1862) in the years between *The Woman in White* and *The Moonstone*, *Armadale* has never been considered a great novel. T. S. Eliot—who proclaimed *The Moonstone* "the first and greatest of English detective novels"—lamented early last century that *Armadale* had "no merit beyond melodrama," and Collins's biographer Kenneth Robinson called the novel "a failure."[40] In 1956, Nuel Pharr Davis observed that the novel "did not catch on with English readers," for it sold only slightly more than 1,000 copies from its English printing.[41] But *Armadale* is not so far afield from *The Woman in White* and *The Moonstone* as these complaints imply—at least not structurally or thematically. Like Collins's more famous works, *Armadale* is essentially a sensation novel about crime, guilty secrets, and the dangerous disorders of the private self. The novel hinges upon guilt and its detection: the discovery of past events and their place in a narrative chain that will explain crime. Set mostly in 1851, the novel is so obsessed with discovering and ordering events that it starts with a "Prologue" set twenty years earlier, in which Allan Wrentmore confesses to the murder that sets the narrative chain in motion.[42] But unlike conventional detective stories, *Armadale* is not concerned only with discovering the past. It wants also to see into a future that the past might determine or predict. As Robert Ashley writes, "[f]atality and foreboding brood over *Armadale* as over no other Collins novel," so much so that the novel treats fate as a sort of thematic prison.[43] To look forward even as it looks back, the novel employs surveillance, staring obsessively at the past and present to find clues that will reveal the future.

But amid the surveillance that characterizes the novel, *Armadale* arrives finally at the conclusion that seeing into the future requires seeing into the private self. The key to *Armadale*'s future action is Lydia, for she dictates ultimately each twist and turn of the action. The criminal intrigues are hers, as are the guilty motives. As Jenny Bourne Taylor remarks, this is so much the case that the chapters of *Armadale* that are narrated from Lydia's diary make her twice over the "author of the plot."[44] Discerning the shape of the novel's future thus requires accounting for Lydia's guilty desire and criminal impulses. As a study of erotic beauty, criminal cunning, and murderous desire, *Armadale*'s *femme fatale* is stunning—more fascinating than Marian Halcombe among Collins's heroines, and more formidable by far than Mary Braddon's Lady Audley. Lydia's crimes begin when she is twelve with the forgery that connects her to *Armadale*'s plot, and during the next two decades, she commits theft, bigamy, and murder—first when she poisons Waldron, and nearly again when she poisons Midwinter. In the six months of *Armadale*'s action, she also makes romantic conquests of Allan Armadale, Midwinter, and old Bashwood, and we learn that her past includes not only her marriage to Waldron but also liaisons with Manuel and the unfortunate music teacher who—in desperate desire for adolescent Lydia—blows out his brains and ends up in an asylum. Small wonder that Lydia requires a nightly dose of laudanum to get to sleep. As John Sutherland points out in introducing Collins's novel, several Victorian murderesses were tried, convicted, and executed in the fifteen years prior to *Armadale*'s composition. Likely Collins drew upon all of them in creating Lydia, just as he based Maria Oldershaw on the infamous Victorian procuress Rachel Leverson. Writing roughly one-fifth of the novel as Lydia's private diary, Collins hints even structurally that *Armadale* is a deliberate portrait of criminal intent, designed to see into and account for the thoughts and motives of a Victorian murderess.

Naturally, Lydia outraged almost every contemporary critic of the novel. One reviewer from the *Reader* did laud Collins for the "extraordinary ability with which he dissects evil minds."[45] But most critics received the novel badly and blasted Collins for giving readers such an objectionable heroine. H. F. Chorley denounced Collins's decision to portray "one of the most hardened female villains whose devices and desires have ever blackened fiction," complaining that her "practices belong to the police-cells, but not the pages over which honest people should employ and enjoy their leisure."[46] A reader from the *Westminster Review* likened her to the fascinating-but-grotesque "big black baboon" of Richardson's traveling menagerie, and one from the *London Quarterly Review* called her a character "from which every rightly constituted mind turns with loathing."[47] Of course, Collins invited such criticism by giving *Armadale* a preemptive "Foreword" in which he dismissed readers who would judge the book according to "Clap-trap morality" and claimed that his novel was simply "daring enough to speak the truth" (*A* "Foreword). In an especially withering response, the *Spectator*'s reviewer asked:

> Is it, then, the whole truth about the world in which we live that it is peopled by a set of scoundrels qualified by a set of fools, and watched in retributive providence in the shape of attornies [sic] and spies? Is it the object of half the world to cheat the other half, and the object of the other half to put itself in the way of being cheated? Is it true that all women are idiots till they are twenty, intriguers and murderesses until they are forty, and customers of hags who restore decayed beauty until they are eighty? . . . the fact that there are such characters as he has drawn, and actions such as he has described, does not warrant his overstepping the limits of decency, and revolting every human sentiment.[48]

Reviewers who hated Lydia so intensely had little patience for her diary. The *Spectator* went on to ask whether "murderesses keep journals of . . . literary merit and equal power of mental anatomy," and Eliot complained decades later that the diary is "tedious and even unplausible [sic] (for . . . Miss Gwilt, commits herself to paper far too often and far too frankly)."[49] Both criticisms may be correct from artistic points of view. But Lydia's diary is the immortal part of a work much less fine. It is also the part that reveals the novel's reliance upon the narrative power reposed in the prison.

Composed in solitary moments when Lydia escapes from the novel's staring, her diary is—like Lucy's autobiography—an attempt to use narrative to impose order upon her disordered self. Explicitly, of course, Lydia uses her diary like the omniscient narrator uses the novel: to keep track of events future and past and to place them in the order that will make sense finally of the novel's narrative chain. In her diary, Lydia records events exactly as they occur so that she can remember them, and she also uses the diary to keep track of the complex machinations that will shape the future of *Armadale*'s plot. But as the diary's pages show, Lydia's greatest obstacle to sorting out her designs is making sense of the conflicting impulses of her disorderly desire. Lydia is haunted by her old guilt and harassed by her addiction; she is torn between her desire to love Midwinter and her impulse to murder his half-brother. Guilty, cruel, repressed, self-loathing, and self-divided, Lydia endures private trials each time she is forced by solitude to consider her complicated motives and desires. For Lydia as for Lucy, narrating the self is a way of enduring and mastering these trials. It is a way of inventing the coherence and meaning of a self driven to profound disorder by the cell. Thus *Armadale*'s search for its narrative order constricts into a search for the narrative order of a single identity. That search occurs in solitude, into which Collins thrusts Lydia so that he may subject her to the narrative power of the Victorian prison.

VII

Armadale begins, like most sensation novels, determined to establish a complete and orderly account of the events that will explain the plot. Most of the novel is set in 1851 amid Lydia's intrigues against Midwinter and Allan. But *Armadale* opens with a "Prologue" that begins before the beginning, so to speak: in 1832, when a dying Allan Wrentmore reaches Wildbad just in time to confess to his cousin's murder. Even before Wrentmore arrives on the scene, the "Prologue" is preoccupied with what will happen, and when. The doctor, mayor, and landlord wait into the dark hours of evening for the sick man to come, part of a scene that bristles with anticipation. Wrentmore's appearance when he is carried into the hotel shows that he has reached the baths too late, so that the only question to answer is when, not if, he will die. As the doctor reports after examining his new patient, "If I give him a week more to live, I give him what I honestly believe to be the utmost length of his span" (*A* 15). In an episode that foreshadows the novel's dramatic and thematic concerns, Wrentmore spends his last hours closeted with Neal, trying desperately to account for his guilty past. As Wrentmore speaks, Neal, the doctor, and even Mrs. Wrentmore are drawn irresistibly to listen to his confession. They are transfixed by the story of murder and deceit—so much so that Mrs. Wrentmore, when her husband sends her away, eavesdrops just outside the door. Determined to hear all of Wrentmore's guilty story, the three auditors belie what is really the novel's wish: to discover past events, so that they become part of a complete narrative chain that explains the intrigue at the heart of the novel.

If *Armadale* were a typical detective story, this discovery of an old crime might rest at the center of its plot. But appearing so early,

Wrentmore's confession suggests that some other concern occupies the novel. That concern is with the shape of the future and the crimes that may yet come. Though Wrentmore's confession looks backward to a crime far in the past, it closes with a frightening admonition to his son:

> . . . I, going down into my grave, with my crime unpunished and unatoned, see what no guiltless minds can discern. I see danger in the future, begotten of danger in the past—treachery that is the offspring of *his* treachery, and crime that is the child of *my* crime. . . . I see My Crime, ripening again for the future . . . and descending, in inherited contamination of Evil, from me to my son. (*A* 47)

This is the obsession with fatality that impels *Armadale*'s search for narrative order. Looking for clues that will discover the shape of the future, the novel turns upon the question of "whether we are, or are not, the masters of our own destinies" (*A* 48). That search for clues unfolds as a series of attempts to see the future by looking obsessively at the present and past. The doctor makes such an attempt at Wildbad when he examines Wrentmore and predicts how long he will live. Midwinter, after reading the confession, looks everywhere for signs that he is bound to his father's fatal predictions.[50] Decimus Brock, at the start of "Book the First," takes a mental "journey through the past years of his own life," reflecting upon how "the events of [the] years" he has spent in service with Mrs. Armadale seem all to be "connected with the same little group of characters" (*A* 53). Though Brock's ruminations look backward explicitly, he, too, arrives at the question that consumes the novel: "What was to happen next?" (*A* 77). It is the attempt to answer this question that turns the novel, eventually, into the narrative of the self in the cell.

First, though, it makes the novel eminently surveillant, as if the narrator hopes to make sense of the future by detecting the present and past. Surveillance is everywhere in *Armadale*, from London to Thorpe-Ambrose to the structure of the novel. Writing of *The Woman in White*, Sutherland points out that Collins's narrative technique is typically "forensic," for it mimics the processes by which the police assemble evidence that completes the story of crime.[51] This is also true of *Armadale*, which includes omniscient narration and an array of private texts in its effort to discover and arrange the events of its plot. The "Prologue" reports Wrentmore's confession, and "Book the Second" begins with private letters between Lydia and Oldershaw. In subsequent books, too, the novel relies upon omniscience and epistolary prying, but it also turns to Lydia's diary, composed during the moments when she can escape from sight. Eminently able to invade these private texts, the narrator seems to be a model of

Foucaultian omniscience, for even when he is not narrating he arranges and "disciplines" the various narratives that comprise the novel. When he is narrating, he shows us mostly an array of amateur and professional detectives, so that the novel depends thematically as structurally upon the power of the stare. Though Wrentmore wants Neal to compose a new part of his confession in the "Prologue," Neal insists upon reading over what is already written, so that the old writing is also exposed to view. Brock, though he is a man of the cloth, commands his servant to watch night and day for the woman with the red Paisley shawl. At other points in the novel and for various reasons, Allan watches for Neelie Milroy, Lydia and Midwinter watch for Allan, and—in one remarkable instance—Bashwood watches for Allan while Midwinter spies on Bashwood. Amid such intrusiveness even private letters are in peril, and not just from the narrator, as Mrs. Milroy and her nurse show by opening, reading, and re-sealing one of Lydia's. Detectives lurk everywhere in Collins's novel, waiting always for the chance to seize the power that surveillance seems to afford. As Catherine Peters remarks, the result is that *Armadale* shows us "a nightmare world, in which even thoughts cease to be private, a picture of English society as a claustrophobic prison."[52]

Most of the staring is, of course, directed at Lydia. This is true even for the narrator, who divulges repeatedly the contents of her private letters and diary. But it is also true within the plot, where Lydia is perhaps the most watched woman in English literature. She is watched by Brock and his man in London when she is known only as the woman in the red Paisley shawl, and she is watched, too, by Mrs. Milroy when the Major hires her as a governess. As Lydia writes to Oldershaw, Mrs. Milroy studies her face and figure in every "attractive light" and sets her nurse to barge in upon Lydia and the Major each time the pair is alone (*A* 286). Nor is Lydia free from surveillance about the grounds at Thorpe-Ambrose, for Midwinter and Allan both make her the object of their gaze. Midwinter, we are told, fixes his eyes so "steadily . . . on her" when he meets her that he is quite nearly entranced by the "breathless astonishment which . . . [holds] him spell-bound" (*A* 278). Bashwood watches her in this way, too, deluding himself eventually into believing that she will become his wife. Lydia also endures the staring of other spies with less interest in her alluring qualities but a great deal of interest in her identity and past. Brock and his man spy first but give way to Pedgift's man, and he gives way in turn to the novel's only professional detective, Jemmy Bashwood. Having hired his son to spy upon Lydia, the elder Bashwood tells Jemmy, "I want to know all about her. . . . The worst, and the best—the worst, particularly" (*A* 520). His desire is also the desire of the novel. For Lydia is the center of the novel's past and future crimes, and she is also—fittingly—the center of its attention. Thus *Armadale* implies throughout that Lydia's detection rests at the heart of the novel's plot.

But detecting Lydia is much harder than it sounds. Certain moments in the novel suggest that Collins despised surveillance, and that he meant his novel to attack it rather than sing its praises. When we first meet Jemmy and discover his occupation, for instance, the narrator calls him "the vile creature whom the viler need of Society has fashioned for its own use" (A 516). Likewise, the Major criticizes Allan for investigating Lydia without explaining his reasons. Sutherland conjectures that these moments reveal Collins's scorn for the species of private investigator produced by the 1857 Matrimonial Causes Act, which "mobilized a whole new army of amateur and unofficial detectives; namely, the suspicious spouse and his or her agent."[53] He also points out that, considering their sexual escapades during the 1850s, Collins and his friend Dickens had plenty to fear from "gimlet-hole" peepers like Jemmy (A 517). Even so, *Armadale* suggests that society has much more to fear from Victorian criminals. The villains who shape the novel's plot are guarded, ingenious, and acutely conscious of their need to defeat the stare. Oldershaw earns a living by "making up battered old faces and worn-out old figures to look like new"—a shabby echo of Mrs. General in *Little Dorrit*—and Dr. Downward is:

> . . . one of those carefully constructed physicians, in whom the public—especially the female public—implicitly trust. He had the necessary bald head, the necessary double eyeglass, the necessary black clothes, and the necessary blandness of manner, all complete. (A 160; 341)

Both characters are proof against the merely casual glance. As Sutherland argues, by the 1850s Victorians were abandoning the notion that crime would "out" simply because criminals were brutal, stupid, or grotesque. Instead, they were coming to regard crime as "an intellectual problem to be 'solved'"—a changing attitude that produced the 1856 Police Act, meant to pit "detective intelligence against this criminal cunning."[54] Hinting at this need for a new strategy against Victorian crime, Pedgift tells his son at the end of the novel, "We live, Augustus, in an age eminently favourable to the growth of all roguery which is careful enough to keep up appearances" (A 673).

No rogue in *Armadale* keeps up appearances nearly so well as Lydia. Even her last name, Gwilt, implies not only her guilt but also the gilt exterior that hides her vicious impulses and moral decay. As her name promises, she proves eminently able to elude the surveillance upon which the novel depends. She does so partly by evading her pursuers when she knows she is being watched: changing cabs, changing apartments, and wearing a veil that allows her to slip anonymously into the London crowds. She also does so by choosing, like Lucy, to live consciously as a divided self. Like Lucy, Lydia enters the novel as a governess, filling a post that implies by its nature the need for repression and self-denial. Like Lucy, she is perpetually watched and divides her identity between public and private, *sang-froid* and passion, the concealment and expression of her desiring self. Of course, for Lydia this must be the case, for her secrets are much more dangerous than Lucy's: forgery, theft, bigamy, addiction, murder in the past, and a plan to murder again. Determined like Lucy to maintain perfect self-control, she also maintains her outward calm even under the novel's incessant watching and the deliberate provocations of those who spy. Nearer the mark than he even suspects, Pedgift tells Allan that Lydia reminds him of the most wicked women he has seen in the prisons, all of whom "had a secret self-possession that nothing could shake" (*A* 368). For Lydia as for Lucy, self-possession is her protection against the power of the stare—a way of hiding guilt and disorder from the public world of the novel.

Lydia also recognizes, like her Brontëian counterpart, the power that surveillance affords over narrative meaning, and she seizes and manipulates that power when she can. Letting Oldershaw's maid be seen wearing her clothes but not her veil, Lydia leads Brock to err entirely in describing "Miss Gwilt" to Midwinter. Hiding behind the trees in Major Milroy's garden so that she hears without difficulty "every word" that Allan and Neelie say, Lydia foils the pair's plan to elope (*A* 431). Finding herself followed by Pedgift's spy, she turns upon the man rather than avoid him, flinging his hat into a ditch and complaining to Midwinter that she is being harassed. Detecting the detective, she subjects him to the surveillant power that seems to control meaning in the novel. Perhaps her most important contrivance in this regard is her success in leaving London on the same train as Allan, since their departure together produces the very rumor her intrigues require: that she and Allan have planned a clandestine marriage somewhere away from the stare. Lydia proves repeatedly that she knows the uses and limitations of surveillance, and she manages often, as a result, to turn visible events into a narrative that hardly resembles her true designs. Indeed, it is fitting that she receives her greatest setback when she sends Allan away with Manuel and cannot know whether Allan has died at sea or whether he might return. By losing sight of Allan, she loses her power over him—her power to control his place in the narrative she weaves. For Lydia as for the novel, surveillance seems to be a means of creating narrative order in a complex and secretive world.

Even so, as Lydia's manipulations only begin to suggest, *Armadale* is finally—like *Little Dorrit*—a story beyond the power of surveillance to tell. But the problem in *Armadale* is not an inability to see into the prison; rather, it is an inability to see into the motives and desires that will shape the future action of the novel. The novel abounds in detections of the past, from Wrentmore's confession in the "Prologue" to Jemmy's dazzling work in laying Lydia's history bare. Having completed his investigation, he describes to his father her entire criminal career: her vagabond childhood with the Oldershaws, her forgery at Wrentmore's behest, and her subsequent adventures as a bigamist, murderess, and convict. In a novel obsessed with detecting the order of things, Jemmy has conquered a considerable difficulty, for he has accounted for Lydia from past to present in an unbroken narrative chain. Having done so, he tries to predict her future course, too, hinting to his father that she just might poison another husband. Jemmy closes his tale by adding, "For the present, all you need know, you do know" (*A* 532). But the truth is that neither Jemmy nor the novel has discovered all that must be known about Lydia, for Jemmy does not predict correctly the future action of the novel. Though Lydia plans and even attempts to poison Allan at novel's end, she finally kills herself instead in a tortured act of self-loathing. What Jemmy's account of Lydia misses is knowledge of her private self—knowledge of the motives that drive her to commit suicide rather than repeat the past. Thus Jemmy's account of Lydia sees effect but not cause, pattern but not meaning, and guilt but not desire. Like the Major's malfunctioning clock, it is not an "expression of order" but an "expression of the desire for order."[55] In a novel in which the future will be shaped by desire's promptings, the wish for narrative order cannot finally be satisfied through surveillance.

Rather, as certain clues show all along, discovering narrative order in *Armadale* means discovering the order of the private self. Private disorder leers from every corner of the novel, from Mrs. Milroy's obsessive jealousy to Bashwood's eventual collapse. Almost from the start the novel hints that making sense out of such disorder is the key to seeing into the future. Thus Midwinter tries to discern the truth of his father's raving predictions, and Midwinter and Hawbury attempt to interpret Allan's ominous dream. Partly, the novel's fascination with psychological disorder reflects Collins's interest in the life of the nerves—his fascination with mesmerism and clairvoyance, for example, and his bouts with his own mysterious nervous complaints.[56] Mostly, it comes from Collins's desire to see into and account for a Victorian murderess. As a sensation author Collins was prone to use current events to fashion his stories, and Sutherland and Richard Altick both point out that Collins may have based Lydia on any of several women who were convicted at mid-century of poisoning their husbands.[57] Sarah Chesham committed at least three murders before she was convicted and executed in 1851, the year in which *Armadale* is set, and Constance Wilson, another "career poisoner," was hanged in 1862 at Newgate before a crowd of 20,000 (*A* xvi). Madeleine Smith was tried for poisoning her lover when he threatened to expose the affair, but she was acquitted on the Scottish verdict of "not proven" amid loud cheers of approval from the gallery—cheers that become cries of dismay in *Armadale* when Lydia is found guilty of murdering Waldron.[58] Such cases inspired shock, horror, debate, and above all profound curiosity about the nature of women who kill, so much so that hundreds of respectable middle-class Victorian women "flocked to the courtrooms and vied for seats" during Smith's trial.[59] Wanting to capitalize on this curiosity by narrating his murderess "from the inside," Collins makes his novel depend upon discovering the order of the events that Lydia's motives will shape (*A* xvi). The result is a novel that finds narrative completion only in Lydia's attempts to order her divided, guilty, desiring self.

She makes those attempts by accounting for herself in the solitude of the prison. Forced into solitude by the pressure of the stare, Lydia writes her diary so that she can record her designs, explore her guilt and addiction, and—most important—sort out the complex and contradictory impulses of her divided self. She is torn between her hatred of Allan and love of Midwinter, and between her impulse to return to her old guilt and her wish to mend her ways. The diary is not, like Lucy's autobiography, a deliberate attempt to invent for public eyes a narrative of a complete and coherent identity. But it is an attempt to impose order upon disorder, so that Lydia can decide what course she will take amid the conflicting promptings of her desire. Because it is the narrative space in which Lydia contemplates the future contours of her crimes, her diary is also the only text that can predict the novel's future even as it records the events of the present and past. Thus Lydia's process of narrative self-ordering replaces the efforts to detect her as the central movement of the plot, and the diary, watched over by the novel, comes to stand *for* the novel—an expression of its wish to see into the future by accounting for the self. But Lydia cannot explore her disordered self or compose her diary before the intrusive eyes of the novel; rather, she can do so only by locking herself away in the solitude of the prison. Having made Lydia and her self-exposition the pivot upon which *Armadale* turns, Collins thrusts her into solitude and forces her to undertake the self-reflection, self-ordering and self-narration that are always the task of the self in the cell. That he does so suggests that his novel, like *Villette*, derives its authority to invent the private self from the narrative power reposed in the prison.

VIII

Armadale's narrative desire to impose order upon the private self appears first in the attempts to interpret Allan's dream. By uniting past and future into a single psychological crisis, the dream reinscribes the prediction of Wrentmore's confession and reaffirms the novel's desire to discover its narrative chain. The dream looks forward and back, or so it seems, since it incorporates the father whom Allan has never known into a series of scenes that may yet be played out: the Shadow of a Woman standing beside a pool; the Shadow of a Man breaking a statuette; the Woman-Shadow and Man-Shadow together handing Allan a drink that renders him unconscious. Like Lucy's dream at the deserted pensionnat, Allan's dream hints at death and the possibility of psychological dissolution. For Midwinter, the dream is a thing that must be interpreted so that it can help to make sense of the events that may come. He watches aboard *La Grace de Dieu* as Allan's countenance changes from an image of "perfect repose" to "the distorted face of a suffering man," and the minute they are saved Midwinter makes Allan relate every detail of the dream so that he may commit it to paper (*A* 135). Midwinter's desire to record the dream is the novel's first hint that narrative production will be its method of imposing order upon psychological phenomena and private disarray. As Downward's "System" treats the symptoms of the body in its attempt to normalize the mind, so Midwinter invents the dream as a tangible narrative—made truly concrete finally by its inclusion in the space of the novel. Thus Midwinter, Downward, and *Armadale* all imply that deciphering psychological meaning requires turning the private self into a physical text.

The morning after the dream finds Midwinter and Hawbury quarreling over the dream's meaning, with battle-lines drawn sharply between superstition and reason. Too aware of the past, Midwinter regards the dream as fatal: "a warning to [Allan] to avoid certain people," most of all Midwinter himself (*A* 140). But Hawbury argues that "a reasonable man is [not] justified in attaching a supernatural interpretation to any phenomenon which comes within the range of his senses, until he has certainly ascertained that there is no such thing as a natural explanation" (*A* 143). Accordingly, he forces Allan to exercise his memory in an effort to account for every detail of the dream, recreating in the process the novel's method of seeking meaning in the narrative order of the past. For the next several chapters, the dream stands poised between the superstitious and scientific views. Worse, rather than solve the conundrum, the novel offers a third interpretation that issues from Brock as he lays dying: God, in his infinite wisdom, has given Allan this vision of past and future not to doom him but rather to show Midwinter that only he may save Allan and thus atone for his father's sin. Refusing to resolve this three-sided interpretive contest, Collins and his narrator have left most critics to assume that the dream is related fundamentally to the novel's question of whether fate or free will governs the order—or disorder—of human existence. Robinson calls "the idea of fatality" the center of the novel, since in *Armadale* "Wilkie's obsession with Doom is given full rein," and Ashley concludes much the same.[60] Writing of Collins's use of the Major's Strasbourg Clock, Lisa Zeitz and Peter Thoms argue that *Armadale* is "deeply concerned with the working out of lives in time and with the issues of determinism, free will, providence, and chance that the pattern of those lives invites us to consider."[61]

Certainly the novel invites us to consider these issues from the moment of Wrentmore's confession, for it offers itself as an inquiry into metaphysical cause and narrative pattern, and the uncertain relation between the future and the past. Suggesting that Allan's dream is mostly a problem of psychological interpretation, though, Collins point to a difficulty that is more practical than metaphysical: how to account for, from an external perspective, the complex meanings of the private self. From the time that Allan begins to dream, Midwinter realizes that the psychological event belongs to Allan rather than himself. Yet as Midwinter, Hawbury, and Brock set to work upon interpreting the dream, it becomes clear that their efforts to unravel Allan's psyche reveal no private truths but their own. Midwinter's fear that the dream is a premonition of evil reflects the suppressed secrets and fears of his own past, and Hawbury's interpretation signals no more than the rationality that makes him a man of science. Brock's interpretation, rooted in Christian faith, reveals an orthodox view of spiritual salvation that Allan never reflects in any other way. Indeed, of all the interpretations offered for Allan's dream, the one that most reveals Allan is his own: that the dream is a result of "indigestion" and ought to be forgotten altogether (*A* 140). In *Armadale* the quest to decipher another's psychological meaning is always only self-revelatory, symptomatic of a failure to see from outside the mysteries of the private self.

For Midwinter, especially, this proves to be the case, for besides Lydia he is the novel's most interesting psychological study. He enters the first book feverish and in "a disordered state of mind" (*A* 59). Afterward, though his fever subsides, he retains the symptoms of continued anxiety and agitation. He nearly becomes hysterical when he watches the "catastrophe of the puppets" in the Major's clock, almost falls into catalepsy when he first sees Lydia, and finds himself unable to write in Naples because of his nerves (*A* 225). Taylor suggests that "[b]y giving Allan the dream which reproduces Midwinter's anxieties, the novel directly makes use of Collins's interests in mesmerism, clairvoyance, and the possibility of psychological transmission"—an argument that resonates more fully when we consider that Allan and Midwinter are doubled characters, separate halves of the same disintegrated self.[62] But treating the dream as an originary moment of Midwinter's motive and desire, Collins also looks ahead to Freud and the concept of the primal scene. Added to what Midwinter already knows of his past, Allan's dream becomes a point of psychological fixity for Midwinter, for it is a moment that both reinforces his distrust of himself and permits him to order his future action and intent. He avoids Allan repeatedly and cites the dream as his reason. He also compares his external world constantly with the scenes of the dream, seeking resemblances between inner and outer events that will help him to order his disordered self. Determined to impose narrative order upon physical events and private desire, Midwinter makes Allan's dream into the essential moment of his own narrative, permitting the dream to shape the desires and motives that will determine his actions throughout the novel. From the dream Midwinter derives not Allan's place in *Armadale*'s narrative but his own. In the process he demonstrates that the secrets of the novel's future have nothing to do with fate; rather, they inhere in the private meanings of the psychological self.

For Midwinter, investigating those meanings requires the solitude of the prison. He runs off alone at the novel's start to consider his course after Brock demands that he "give a proper account of himself" (*A* 67). When Lydia completes the dream's Second Vision at Hurle Mere, he vanishes again and considers leaving for good in order to stave off the dream's predictions. Alone in his room trying to write a letter that will explain his actions to Allan, Midwinter manages only a note that is "barely intelligible—sentences were left unfinished; words were misplaced one for the other" (*A* 271). Seeking to order himself through narrative, Midwinter degenerates into linguistic chaos. Even his marriage to Lydia consists of, to her sorrow, a series of retreats into his solitary room, where he may think and write and also consider the riddle of future and past. These solitary moments comprise Midwinter's great personal and psychological crises, and they ought to help the reader penetrate his motives and desires. Yet the novel rarely shows us the moments in which Midwinter's self-reflection and self-ordering actually occur. We see him try to write his farewell to Allan, and he confesses his fears sporadically to two other characters—to Brock early in the novel, and to Lydia much later. But we do not see his private struggle to conquer his feelings for Lydia. Instead, he marries her and retreats into solitary confinement, separating us from the mystery of his thoughts and intentions. Even his attempt to write to Allan is observed but not disclosed, since it remarks Midwinter's failure to express himself but withholds the unintelligible letter from view. At the very threshold of psychological disclosure, our staring narrator pauses, so that Midwinter remains like Pickwick in the

Fleet: filled with psychological meanings that the novel never discloses. The novel's great investigator of the narrative order of the private self, Midwinter moves us no closer to answering the question the novel really asks: not what *has* happened, but what *will* happen in a future shaped by the intent, motive, and desire of *Armadale*'s *femme fatale*.

Only Lydia's private self-narration can answer that question. She is the center of the action, and her letters and diary—besides recording her criminal designs—penetrate to the core of the novel's concern with narrative order and the disordered self. Taken together, her private texts are a culmination conceived in the solitude of the prison. For most of the novel Lydia seems haunted not by solitude but by staring, the system of power and restraint that seems to undergird the novel. But like Lucy, Lydia avoids the stare by retreating into the solitude of the cell. Even the first time we see her in the red Paisley shawl, she wears a veil in order to isolate herself. As she corresponds with Oldershaw regarding her scheme to become governess at Thorpe-Ambrose, Lydia finds herself hounded by spies and becomes—because of her attempts to evade the stare—"to all intents and purposes a prisoner" (A 215). Withdrawn mentally from those around her because of her criminal designs, Lydia becomes isolated physically as well, until even Oldershaw disappears from her schemes and correspondence. At Thorpe-Ambrose, she is glad of Neelie's hatred because it enables her to "get rid of [Neelie] out of lesson-time and walking-time," and she chooses a telling method of defying Allan's and Pedgift's suspicions: she quits her employment with the Milroys and takes a "cheap lodging on the outskirts of town" where she can escape the novel's staring but still do some spying of her own (A 284; 355). When Lydia's marriage to Midwinter fails, she is left alone but for her laudanum and her diary—the "secret friend," as she calls it, "of [her] wretchedest and wickedest hours" and the narrative of her solitary prison (A 545).

As Jonathan Craig Tutor observes, the diary's explicit purpose is to record the "minutiae" of Lydia's designs.[63] But the novel suggests, too, that the diary is a sort of narrative culmination: a repository of the secrets Lydia keeps even from Oldershaw and thus from the staring of the novel. As Lydia tells Oldershaw of the diary, "I have written [in it] the story of my days (and sometimes the story of my nights) much more regularly than usual for the last week," and she consults the diary in order to recall events that her "head is too weary to calculate without help" (A 423). As a record of Lydia's actions and thoughts during the weary months of her intrigues, her diary will tell us much more than Jemmy can about her motives and desires. Explicitly, Lydia declares that she keeps her diary in order to prevent herself from "forgetting anything important" as her intrigues widen: "[I]n my situation," she writes, "I dare not trust anything to memory" (*A* 424; 485). Accordingly, its record of events is at least as complete as the remainder of the novel, for it even includes the same characters and mimics—in Bashwood's and Lydia's spying—the surveillant and detective practices we find elsewhere. She records in it Midwinter's confession, for instance, though she withholds that narrative from Oldershaw, and she records also what she sees of Neelie and Allan and their plans to elope. Midwinter, Bashwood, Pedgift, the Milroys, Allan, Neelie, and Oldershaw all move through Lydia's self-narrative world. In this fashion, replacing the omniscient narrator through most of books three and four, Lydia seems to know and account for everything, and her meticulously kept diary echoes the novel's own obsession with creating narrative order from the events of the present and past.

But Lydia's diary is more than a factual and chronological ordering of *Armadale*'s events; it is an investigation of her disordered self, and an attempt to impose order upon her divided identity and guilty desire. Though Lydia plays the *sang-froid* in the novel's public spaces, her letters to Oldershaw—also written from solitude—belie her dangerous nature from the start. Long before we are privy to the diary, Lydia's letters reveal her addiction to laudanum and her inclinations to violence, anger, and spite. Thinking of Neelie's horrible piano-playing she writes to Oldershaw that "[h]alf the musical girls in England ought to have their fingers chopped off . . . and . . . Miss Milroy's fingers should be executed first" (*A* 285). She also uses her letters to announce her scorn for Allan and her designs to steal his money and estate. The diary is a narrative enlargement of these matters, and it is a more complex and complete self-revelation than anything she writes to Oldershaw. While she asks Oldershaw by letter to replenish her supply of drops, for example, her diary alone contains her private benediction upon laudanum's inventor:

> I thank him from the bottom of my heart, whoever he was. If all the miserable wretches in pain of body and mind, whose comforter he has been, could meet together to sing his praises, what a chorus it would be! . . . "Drops", you are a darling! If I love nothing else, I love you. (A 427)

She also uses her diary to expand upon her loathing for Neelie—a "dowdy, awkward, freckled creature, who ought to be perched on a form at school, and strapped to a back-board to straighten her crooked shoulders"—her scorn for Allan's stupidity and ineloquence, and her disdain for Bashwood, whom she has made into her spy (*A* 428). Though we learn from Lydia's letters that she is unsavory and designing, to be sure, her diary reveals a fuller measure of her arrogance and malice.

It also reveals a secret at which her letters barely hint: that she is, inexplicably, fond of Midwinter. In her first letter to Oldershaw from Thorpe-Ambrose, Lydia writes, "I hate him," but she changes her mind immediately and declares, "No, I don't; I only want to find out about him" (*A* 286). As the novel wears on, she does find out about him—his real name, his connection with Allan, and his father's crime—and in doing so she finds solace in the company of this other person as deeply troubled as she. At first, her diary calls Midwinter one "whom—well, whom I *might* have loved once, before I was the woman I am now" (*A* 425). But Lydia is not so dead emotionally as she seems to believe. As she and Midwinter correspond, she writes, "[s]omething flutters in the place where my heart used to be" (*A* 489). Ten days after Midwinter lays his secrets bare to her, Lydia confides to her diary, "it is impossible to deceive myself any longer. Come what may of it, I love him" (*A* 501). This self-discovery makes Lydia's identity more complex than it first seems, for it shows that she is divided not only between public and private but also between hate and love, calculation and desire, and the conscious embrace and conscious rejection of her guilty self. For Midwinter's sake Lydia even considers giving up her designs on Allan, so that she remains torn between her criminal impulses and her desire to love Midwinter and attempt to reform.

Her diary is her attempt to order this disorder, and to mend in narrative the discontinuities of her private self. Even its first entry, which Lydia plans as a record of Midwinter's confession, is really self-investigative, for she writes, "I wonder whether I should have loved my children if I had ever had any?"—a hint at her unacknowledged sexual desire (*A* 426). As the diary progresses, it becomes clear that Lydia can solve any riddle except the one posed by her hopelessly divided self. She cannot understand why the story of Midwinter's confession weighs upon her mind, nor why she cannot turn her thoughts from that confession to her schemes. "What *can* be the secret of [Midwinter's] hold on me?" she wonders; "Why don't I take my sleeping drops and go to bed?" (*A* 490; 440). Revolving in her mind the possibility of poisoning Allan as she poisoned Waldron long ago, she cannot even decide whether the second murder ought to be less terrible to think about than the first. Frustrated by her inability to understand her disordered thoughts, she asks, "Am I mad? Yes; all people who are as miserable as I am, are mad. I must go to the window and get some air. Shall I jump out? No; it disfigures one so, and the coroner's inquest lets so many people see it" (*A* 434). Despising Neelie, loathing Allan, and determined nonetheless to become mistress of Thorpe-Ambrose, Lydia finds herself entirely unable to act upon her conscious desire. Her diary becomes less an elaboration of her plan than an unsatisfactory interrogation of her private self:

Why do I keep a diary at all? Why did the clever thief the other day (in the English newspapers) keep the very thing to convict him, in the shape of a record of every thing he stole? Why are we not perfectly reasonable in all that we do? Why am I not always on my guard and never inconsistent with myself, like a wicked character in a novel? Why? why? why? (*A* 559)

She writes, she says, "*because* I must," and she "must" because self-narration is the only way in which she can get to the bottom of her disordered self (*A* 559).

That self-narration holds the key to *Armadale*'s desire for narrative order, since it reveals the motives and impulses that shape the culmination of the novel. Torn between her love for Midwinter and her impulse to carry out her plan, Lydia wants above all to decide upon her future course. She blames her insomnia on her "trying, for the hundredth time, to see [her] way clearly into the future," and the questions she asks in her diary revolve around what will happen next (*A* 440). Each step of Lydia's plan requires that she weigh the actions and reactions of those around her: Allan, Pedgift, Major Milroy, Neelie, and especially Midwinter. Despite her calculations Lydia cannot see her proper course:

What *is* the way? I can't see it. I could tear my own hair off my head! I could burn the house down! If there was a train of gunpowder under the whole world, I could light it, and blow the whole world to destruction—I am in such a rage, such a frenzy with myself for not seeing it! (*A* 434).

She sees her way only when she finds—unintentionally, she says—the letter from Manuel that prodded her to murder years before. The moment is critical, for like Wrentmore in the "Prologue," Lydia introduces into the novel a text that looks simultaneously forward and back. On one hand, the letter drove Lydia to commit murder long ago, but it seems here as if it will also impel her to murder again. Fate, providence, design—Lydia might blame the discovery of the letter on all three. She tells us repeatedly, "I never sought it," and she marries Midwinter to remove the temptation of pursuing her plan (*A* 444). But the letter does not prompt Lydia to attempt murder simply because of providence or fate; rather, it prompts her to murder because the attempt is, in the end, a manifestation of her secret desire: to kill Allan because she despises him, and to become once again her guilty self. Looking at her old identity and merging it with her new desire, Lydia makes her diary into an account of her future and the novel's—a future in which she will murder Allan.

Thus Lydia's diary promises to complete *Armadale*'s narrative chain by showing us the motives that impel her to act. The diary reveals the private meanings that Jemmy and the narrator cannot, and it solves the problem that hinders Midwinter's efforts to interpret Allan's dream. Yet Lydia's diary is no more correct in the end than Jemmy's prediction, so that the novel seems at the last to betray its structural and thematic reliance upon her private narration. Though "Book the Third" and "Book the Fourth" are told almost entirely through Lydia's diary, the novel's final book returns to omniscience to account for Allan's return and the manner of Lydia's attempt on his life. Moreover, while we watch Lydia's plans unfold with Dr. Downward's help, she vanishes through most of the climactic action. In this sense, the novel abandons Lydia's self-narrative at the precise moment of its denouement and hints that it will find its culmination beyond the diary's margins. Of all the predictions made for the novel's future, in fact, only Brock's approaches the truth, for Midwinter does turn out to be the instrument of Allan's salvation. In this way, the novel retreats from Lydia thematically as it does structurally, for it seems to offer a providential Christian view that Collins might have hoped would mollify the novel's critics. Immersed thoroughly in the consciousness of its murderess for the previous two books, *Armadale* seems suddenly in its final book to abandon its attempt to account for the motives and desires of its Victorian murderess.

But the denouement does depend ultimately upon Lydia's self-narration, undertaken—fittingly—in the imprisoning solitude of Downward's asylum. Retreating narratively from its murderess and seeming to abandon private narration, *Armadale* permits Lydia in the end to author her death: not only in her suicide but also in the note she leaves behind. Partly, the note may have been Collins's olive branch to his critics, for it concludes tritely that crime does not pay. As Lydia observes, "Even my wickedness has one merit—it has not prospered. I have never been a happy woman"—a quote that Collins chose eventually as the epigram for the novel (*A* 666). But more important, the note is Lydia's confession, expressing the guilt she can never erase, in spite of her love for Midwinter, from her conception or narrative of her private self. Her diary records this self-horror, and the insuperable difference it places between them. She asks:

> Is there an unutterable Something left by the horror of my past life, which clings invisibly to me still? . . . Oh me! is there no purifying power in such love as mine? Are there plague-spots of past wickedness on my heart which no after-repentance can wash out? (*A* 546)

This is Lydia's great fear—that she bears an ineradicable psychic and moral taint—and the first line of her suicide note confesses that she is "worse than the worst" Midwinter can think of her (*A* 665). Writing that conclusion upon the same paper that bears Brock's prediction of *Armadale*'s future, Lydia demonstrates that the novel's sweeping questions about fate, doom, and providence are overwritten, literally and finally, by the power of private, guilty desire. Thus the narrative world of *Armadale*, once so enormous and complex, shrinks to the dimensions of a single identity conceived narratively in the solitude of the prison.

IX

For all the measured steps taken to complete *Armadale*'s narrative chain, the book remains—like *Villette*—one of those rare Victorian novels that resist resolution. Even at the end Allan has not learned the secret of Midwinter's past, nor why his friend married Lydia under the name Allan Armadale. Nor does Collins finally offer anywhere in the novel a single meaning for Allan's dream. Mocking his readers gently instead, Collins composed an "Appendix" to the novel in which he gives readers the right "to interpret it by the natural or the supernatural theory, as the bent of their own minds may incline them" (*A* 678). In this manner, Collins permits the dream to remain insubstantial, related uncertainly to the greater text, and he signals that the resolution to the novel is willfully, not accidentally, elusive. Above all, Lydia fails herself to come to narrative completion, for her diary closes prematurely, as a function of the space it fills rather than because it finishes accounting for the self it means to express. As Lydia writes in her last entry:

> I might be in a humour to sit here for some time longer, thinking thoughts like these, and letting them find their way into words at their own will and pleasure—if my Diary would only let me. But my idle pen has been busy enough to make its way to the end of the volume. I have reached the last morsel of space left on the last page; and whether I like it or not, I must close the book this time for good and all . . . (*A* 611–612)

Three times in "Book the Fifth" Lydia promises Bashwood that he shall "know all" if he waits till morning, but the story never comes (*A* 654). Instead we get only her confession: hastily written, incomplete, and suppressed at last by Midwinter and Allan at the close of the novel. The end of *Armadale*—and the end of Lydia—is less a completion of the story than a withdrawal of narrative and a deferral of the wholeness the novel has promised.

But if *Armadale* offers, like *Villette*, a maddeningly incomplete self-portrait from the cell, at least it indicates why. Forced to end her diary because of the constraints of the physical page, Lydia implies the inescapable truth of all self-narration: that to write the self at all is to confine it to the narrative space of the prison. This is so partly because the process of rendering private identity into language is confining, for it limits what the self "is" to what can be conveyed and expressed. Like Lucy's autobiography, Lydia's diary can include only so much, and it can never include all that she contains. On the contrary, writing the self, ordering it, and confining it to a single expression of its shape is a means of imprisoning it precisely because the self becomes—at least in the eyes of the reader—no more than the total of what is said about it. Self-narration thus produces *a* truth of the self rather than *the* truth of the self, and self-narrative becomes something like Freud's primal scene: an archetypal moment or vision to which the self returns in its quest to discover origins, coherence, and meaning. Restricting the possible ways in which the self might be defined or expressed, self-narration is a way of placing the self where it may be controlled and contained—of placing it, that is, in the prison. This is especially true in *Villette* and *Armadale*, since both novels contain the self-accounts of women who are privately guilty, privately disordered, and privately prey to desiring impulses that are transgressive, and even criminal. In both instances, self-narrative confines these guilty and desiring selves, after the fashion of a real prison.

Collins's and Brontë's novels turn to images of the prison, then, partly because the self-accounts they offer are inherently imprisoning—inherently part of the narrative investigation and restraint of the private self. But this does not explain entirely why these authors, so different in other ways, return to and depend upon images of the solitary cell. During the Victorian period, critics often complained of the extent to which sensation novels relied upon real events and argued that Victorian sensation fiction marked a creative low—a loss of confidence in the inventive power of the literary imagination.[64] This may be partly true. Writing for rational and empirical Victorian readers, Victorian novelists contrived a rational and empirical fictional mode, especially in sensation novels, where authors had to make hopelessly improbable plots seem plausible. More so than Dickens but less so than Reade, Collins certainly discovered ideas for his novels in events of the day. But one could charge Brontë with something similar, since she depends so much upon her own life—the events of her days, so to speak—in *Villette* and her other novels. More to the point, as *Armadale* and *Villette* both show, the very novels that seem to rely upon "facts" sometimes take extraordinary license in their attempts to narrate the private self. No authorial sagacity can see into the mind of a Victorian murderess like Lydia or see fully her motives and desires. Likewise, there are moments in *Villette* when Brontë tries to account for Lucy's deepest desires—the parts of her private self that she most fears, and that she least understands. Such psychological phenomena are always only matters for speculation, for they are inaccessible as "knowledge" or "facts." But *Armadale* and *Villette* do not pursue their heroines less eagerly because they have no facts to go on. On the contrary, *Armadale*'s enthusiastic invasion of Lydia's diary suggests that Collins was especially aggressive in attempting to narrate the private self.

This desire to narrate the private self is the fundamental similarity between the Victorian novel and the Victorian prison, for both ultimately satisfied that desire by claiming the same narrative power—the power to invent an account of private identity and desire when the self to be narrated is guilty and aberrant, incapable apparently of providing a complete or honest account of its own private truth. Lucy and Lydia both seem in their self-narratives to be elusive, transgressive, desiring, and disordered. They *must* seem this way, *Villette* and *Armadale* suggest, if the novel is to account for their private selves. Collins and Brontë make their heroines into prisoners—psychologically and metaphorically—because the pretext of private aberration and guilt justifies the prison's and the novel's power to invent an account of private identity and desire. In the Victorian novel, in other words, the narration of the private self is always a power play, premised upon the right of the normal, narrating "other" to narrate the eminently guilty self. In this sense, it is more than coincidence that both novels—in leaving the explicit confines of the prison— offer self-narratives by women, for in the Victorian age women were less able than men (though perhaps more able than convicts) to retain power over their self-accounts. Thus Lucy adopts the language of medicine and phrenology to validate her self-narration, and Collins conceives of Lydia as a character whom he can invent with impunity. Neither woman becomes an object of private invention until she is thrust into the solitude of the cell. Drawing upon the narrative power reposed in the Victorian prison, *Villette* and *Armadale* show us that the influence of that power was not confined to prison novels. Rather, the Victorian prison enabled a much broader literary and even cultural effort to use narrative to invent and imprison the guilty, desiring self.

Conclusion
Narrative Power and Private Truth: Freud, Foucault, and *The Mystery of Edwin Drood*

How few men should I choose to entrust with the drawing up a narrative of some delicate and interesting transaction of my life? How few, though, corporally speaking, they were witnesses of what was done, would justly describe my motives, and properly report and interpret my words?

—William Godwin, *Enquiry Concerning Political Justice*

THROUGH MORE THAN THIRTY YEARS, THEN, AND IN AUTHORS FROM DICKENS TO Brontë, Victorian novels suggest that the relation between the prison and private narrative has much more to do with Freudian psychoanalysis than with Foucault's discussions of surveillance. This is a difficult distinction to make, for Foucault's writing about the prison has a great deal to do with modern psychoanalysis, at least in the sense that he regards both as participating in the same mechanisms of social power. Both wield the power to define the human subject as guilty or aberrant, and both can, as a result, insist that the guilty subject be made into an object of discipline and punishment. But the exercise of power in the Victorian prison had very little to do with surveillance. Rather, it had to do with locking the self in solitude, inscribing guilt upon it, forcing it to account for its own disordered identity and guilty desire, and seizing the power to subject that self-account to the inventive power of the authorial other. In this post-Foucauldian age, scholars have been prone to consider the prison *only* in its social, surveillant dimensions, arguing that the prison confines, watches, disciplines, and participates in a fantasy of omniscience regarding private identity and desire. Taking Foucault as their starting point, they also argue that the prison's clearest relation to

219

narrative form is that the novel participates in its own fantasy, using omniscient narration to account for even the most private parts of the self. Prison chaplains like John Clay and John Field pretended to know prisoners' private thoughts. But many other Victorians recognized that the prison's apparent ability to discover the inmate's secrets had nothing to do with their power to *know* the private self. It had to do with the prison's power to *invent* the self, in a first-person account of crime and punishment that the prison demanded and controlled.

Thus Victorian prison novels do not pretend finally to know the private self, nor does narrative omniscience constitute the real relation between the Victorian prison and narrative form. Instead, Victorian prison novels call attention repeatedly to the narrative power reposed in the prison and show that the prison tended inevitably to permit the narrative invention of the self. From *Pickwick Papers* to *Armadale*, Victorian prison novels show that the prison's purpose is to produce and control the self-account. Reade's novel shows explicitly how the prison forces Thomas Robinson to self-narration, and *Little Dorrit* has several characters—William and Amy, Miss Wade, Mrs. Clennam, and Arthur—whose confessions bear the ineradicable scars of their confinement. *A Tale of Two Cities* and *His Natural Life* suggest that even the prison's mental and physical violence is meant to scar the narrative, not the body, of the Victorian self in the cell. Mired in discussions of the Victorian prison that begin and end with Foucault, scholars have failed to see that first-person narration, more than surveillance, is the means by which the novel reflects the prison's power. The effect of this power, as *Villette* and *Armadale* show, is to open any self to the possibility that it might be invented by the authorial "other," for any self might be presumed to contain the repressions and self-divisions that make it guilty. Drawing consciously and deliberately from the prison's power to invent the private self, Victorian novelists turned to the prison in order to justify increasingly interior fictions. In doing so, they prefigured Freud's psychoanalytic techniques and enabled the inward migration of the modern novel.

Since early last century literature scholars have recognized the significance of Freud's work to discussions of fiction's thematic concerns. But only more recently have they begun to consider how his writing might shed light on narrative form. In 1984 Brooks contributed his study of the novel as Freudian masterplot, arguing that the novel functions— like the unconscious—according to metaphor, metonymy, repetition, and the death wish. More recently, Ronald Thomas provided a provocative discussion of how the dreams that appear in Victorian novels narrativize and politicize the unconscious self.[1] Despite important differences between their work, Brooks and Thomas both remark the similarity between Freud's psychoanalytic methods and Victorian detective novels.

As Brooks points out, Freud's earliest case histories place him in a "Holmesian posture, pressing his patients for the symptomatic clues, reaching back to uncover a moment of trauma, a scene of crime that makes sense of all subsequent events."[2] Steven Marcus agrees, writing that:

> ... human life is, ideally, a connected and coherent story, with all the details in explanatory place, and with everything ... accounted for, in its proper causal or other sequence. Inversely, illness amounts at least in part to suffering from an incoherent story or an inadequate narrative account of oneself.[3]

This is especially true of Victorian self-accounting, which treated the production of order as the final aim of self-narration. Freud's psychoanalytic method, described in his case histories, meant to complete the story of the self by reading it, mending its ruptures, filling its gaps—by supplying, that is, the narrative connections that unite the seemingly dissolute conscious self. For Freud, psychoanalysis was a simple equation: narrative completion equals psychological cure. Thus, as Toril Moi writes of Freud's case history of Dora, "[he] seems positively obsessed with the incomplete status of his text" and seeks "nothing less than the *complete elucidation* of Dora, despite his insistence on the fragmentary nature of his material."[4]

Freud mimics Victorian detectives partly, then, because his project is discovery, but he also echoes them because his method of cure requires the invention of narrative order: a comprehensible and complete account of the disclosures *and* omissions of the self. In *The Interpretation of Dreams* (1900), Freud says that his particular innovation in dream analysis is the treatment of the whole dream—its successful and inadequate conveyances—as the "Holy Writ" of the unconscious.[5] This means reading every part of the dream, the said and unsaid, for clues to neurosis and repression. The body, with its complex of somatic compliances, comprises one part of this text. Freud writes:

> When I set myself the task of bringing to light what human beings keep hidden within them, not by the compelling power of hypnosis, but by observing what they say and what they show, I thought the task was a harder one than it really is. . . . [but] no mortal can keep a secret. If his lips are silent, he chatters with his finger-tips; betrayal oozes out of him at every pore. And thus the task of making conscious the most hidden recesses of the mind is one which it is quite possible to accomplish.[6]

The comment about hypnosis suggests a supremely confident Freud, who prefers his inductive methods to any coaxing or any cajoled expression

on the part of his patients. As Marcus writes, "The patient does not merely provide the text; he also *is* the text, the writing to be read, the language
to be interpreted."[7] That is, Freud treats the dream and body as "Holy
Writ" in the sense that he considers them signs that require interpretation so that he can reveal the unspoken of repression, motive, and desire.
Thus Lacan writes of Freud's psychoanalytic method, "Impediment, failure, split. In a spoken or written sentence something stumbles. Freud is
attracted by these phenomena, and it is there that he seeks the unconscious."[8] Treating the disordered self as a narrative to be recovered, Freud
presumes that the self cannot speak fully. He also underscores implicitly
that his *inventive* power—to translate and interpret—rather than his *detective* power will form the basis of his attempt to narrate and cure.

In other words, Freud's completion of the psychological text hinges
upon the simultaneous participation and diminution of the narrating
self, an act of self-accounting in which the self-account's content and
meaning are subsumed by the greater narrative authority of the analyst.
Freud confesses that Dora resists stubbornly sometimes his interpretations of her disorder, and that she is often opposed to the psychological
reality he describes for her. But as Marcus observes, Freud "adopts no
methods for dealing with it. The demon of interpretation has taken hold
of him, and it is this power that presides over the case of Dora."[9] Lacan
compares Freud's method to the work of an editor who collates, deci-
phers, and incorporates the languages of mind and body into a coherent
narrative that he "punctuates," fixing with that punctuation the meaning of the text.[10] But if Freud fixes the meaning, then he also controls the
story—a story that must *seem* still to come from Dora so that it is accepted as an account of her self rather than of his own. After all, she, not
Freud, suffers from psychic and narrative incoherence; her story, not his,
must be completed by psychoanalysis. In a narrative that he claims is
Dora's self-expression—the sum of what she says and cannot say—Freud
invents the "truth" about her private identity. He identifies her repressions and the unconscious contours behind them. He establishes the primal scene that has shaped, in an unremembered time, the essence of her
unconscious. Indeed, having (re)constructed the primal scene in his psychoanalytic sessions, Freud frequently placed that scene at the center of
treatment and self-understanding in an attempt "to reverse the conventional wisdom that valued the recollected event over the constructed
event."[11] In his analysis of the "Wolf Man," where he created his most
memorable primal scene, Freud wrote that the "profound conviction of
the reality of these primal scenes, [is] a conviction which is in no respect
inferior to one based upon recollection."[12]

The narrative of the private self that emerges from this (re)construc-
tive process is fact and fiction, truth and invention—a text written ulti-

mately by analyst and analysand. It is a narrative dialectic that records the narrative struggle of a disordered self against a normalizing, authorial other, whose power to account for the self always wins out since it always derives from the social desire to control difference by professing to "discover" it. Thus Moi concludes that "[Freud] is left, then, master of the *writing* of Dora. And even though his text bears the scars of the struggle between him and his victim, it is a victorious Freud who publishes it."[13] Moi reads Freud's treatment of Dora unkindly, to be sure, but her prose suggests a crucial point about the narrative act. Framing Freud's contest with Dora as a contest between oppressor and oppressed—the master and victim, so to speak, of narrative language and form—Moi describes Freud as an authorial jailer, using his narrative power over an abnormal self to invent an account of the unknowable of the human unconscious.

The Victorian prison novel thus resembles Freud's case histories mostly because it precedes them—because it presages, that is, the techniques Freud used to narrate the disordered, unknown, and ultimately *unknowable* mysteries of private desire. Partly, the resemblance derives from history, for it indicates Freud's intellectual connection to a fundamentally positivist faith in the ability to know, measure, and categorize the mind. Like advocates of the reformative Victorian prison, Freud believes in a penetrable and malleable human psyche. Indeed, Freud confesses that the primary difference between him and the hypnotists, mesmerists, and other psychologists that he identifies in *The Interpretation of Dreams* rests in the method of rather than the desire for achieving psychological discovery. Instead of coaxing the private self to speak during a state of altered consciousness, Freud circumvented the need for the repressed parts of the self to participate at all. He did so by assuming the presence of a guilty self rendered mute by its deliberate and unconscious repressions, reading that self in the signs of spoken language and the physical body, and recreating—however subtly—the reformative mechanism of the Victorian separate-system prison. A real-life Francis Eden, Freud demanded and doubted the narrative of the guilty self, and he insisted that psychological cure depends finally upon disclosures that rest beyond the power of the self-narrator. Confronted with difference, aberration, and a guilty subject who cannot be trusted to account for himself, Freud claimed—like Eden—the narrative power reposed in the prison.

Conducting complex psychological explorations within the confines of fictional prisons, Victorian novelists assume this same power and invoke this same right to invent the self. They bridge the gap between social desire and narrative form, adopting and adapting the prison's rules for the narrative invention of identity and desire. Like Freud, they treat the physical body as text, marking it with signs of psychological upset and implying the need to read the body in order to understand private trauma. Like Freud, they begin the process of psychological construction by forcing the prisoner to self-narration, using the self-narrative as the essential account of guilt and difference. Perhaps most important, like Freud again, they presume that self-accounting will fail, for they make their self-narrators into disordered selves who are incapable of narrating fully their identity or desire. Maimed psychologically, physically, and narratively by the cell, the prisoners of Victorian fiction are invariably divided, and their disorder makes it not only possible but desirable that their private selves be invented by an authorial other. Thus it is disorder—or at least the presumption of disorder—that lays prisoner and analysand open to narrative power, and the prison always "discovers" a narrative of guilt just as Freud always "discovers" a narrative of psychological rupture. Enabled by the prison, narrative inventions of the private self must always find the prison, by accounting for a self who suffers from the guilt and aberration that the prison is meant to punish. The result is the inevitable inscription of the prison—the self-division it produces, the disorder it inflicts, and the guilt it requires—upon the narrated "I" as the primal scene, so that the prison becomes the moment of repetition and the essence of psychological identity and desire.

II

Had Dickens only lived to complete *The Mystery of Edwin Drood*, perhaps he would finally have expressed fully this relation between Freud and the prison novel. This is easy to say, of course, as Droodians have demonstrated for years. One may speculate with relative impunity, after all, about the end of an unfinished novel. But shaped from dreams, steeped in addiction, and mired in the mysteries of unconscious desire, *Drood* has the makings of Dickens's most powerful psychological novel, and one that would have tended inexorably to the cell. When he died in 1870, Dickens had written only six of the twelve numbers he planned for *Drood*, and for the unfinished parts he did not leave even the chapter outlines he had used since *Dombey and Son*. The solutions to the novel, like Edwin himself, vanished without a trace. "[I]nevitably a tantalizing, unsatisfying thing," Angus Wilson writes, the novel is the most maddening of incompletions: a murder mystery with no murder, and a detective novel with no detection.[14] Some critics believe that Edwin has been strangled; some, that he has been tossed from the top of the cathedral tower or pushed down its stairs.[15] Still others insist that Edwin is not dead at all—that he has survived an attempt on his life and returned disguised as Dick Datchery, in which guise he will investigate his own apparent murder.[16] All agree that Edwin has been the target of foul play, and that the culprit is his uncle, John Jasper. By 1911, no fewer than 82 pieces had appeared on *Drood*, many of them whole books devoted to solving the plot, and 53 more were published by 1929.[17] While Wilson guessed a quarter-century ago that Felix Aylmer's *The Drood Case* (1964) might be the "last magnificent rocket in this long firework display of detective ingenuity," time has proven him far wrong.[18] New books on the subject appeared in 1980 and 1992, and an Italian novel of 1989 made the Drood mystery the center of a plot that assembles great fictional detectives at an international conference on unfinished literature.[19] Like Jasper to his nightmarish dream, critics seem drawn irresistibly and repeatedly to the horror of Edwin's demise.

Nothing short of Dickens's return from the grave would end these debates. But it is worth noting that, amid the wrangling over plot, one point has been lost: that *Drood* is not about events so much as the method of their exposition—how they may emerge into narrative from the gap of the human unconscious. Dickens likely would have harrumphed at the uncertainty over *Drood*'s plot, for to him (if to no one else) the fate of Edwin was clear. He was to die at the hands of his uncle. No single piece of evidence is enough to carry this point, or the debate over plot would have ended long ago. But in the months before his death Dickens reportedly told at least three men—Forster, Charley Dickens, and Luke Fildes (*Drood*'s illustrator)—that Edwin was dead, even confiding to the last that Jasper's neck-tie must be larger in one illustration "for Jasper strangles Edwin Drood with it."[20] To his son Dickens worried that *Drood*'s opening numbers revealed too much of the mystery rather than too little. In the "Preface" to an 1895 edition of *Drood*, Charley recalled having asked his father, during their last walk together at Gad's Hill, if Edwin were dead, "Whereupon he turned upon me with an expression of astonishment at my having asked such an unnecessary question, and said: 'Of course; what else do you suppose?'" (*ED* xxvii). Without a finished novel, any conclusions about *Drood* are, as Philip Collins observes, "tentative."[21] But *Drood* has surely become more mysterious in Dickens's death than he ever could have made it had he lived, and most of the mystery has been devised by the critics. Four years before beginning *Drood*, Dickens prophesied this outcome for *Our Mutual Friend* (1865), writing in its "Postscript":

> When I devised this story, I foresaw the likelihood that a class of readers and commentators would suppose that I was at great pains to conceal exactly what I was at great pains to suggest: namely, that Mr. John Harmon was not slain, and that Mr. John Rokesmith was he. . . . thinking it worth while, in the interests of art, to hint to an audience that an artist (of whatever denomina-

tion) may perhaps be trusted to know what he is about . . . I was
not alarmed by the anticipation.[22]

Surely Dickens never expected his son to belong to this "class of readers,"
and in 1865 he probably had no idea what sort of novel he might begin
next. But unlike lesser sensation writers—Braddon, for instance, or
Reade—Dickens never relied on plot alone to generate the interest for his
fictions. It is unlikely that he should suddenly have done so in *Drood*.

Rather, as evidence within and beyond the novel suggests, Dickens
meant his novel to center upon exposition of the guilty secret buried in
Jasper's unconscious. *Drood* is fascinated throughout with closed spaces,
and also with the process by which they may be sounded, penetrated,
and revealed. Among the novel's concealments, the most important one
is the means of Edwin's disappearance, and the real mystery is how the
story of his demise may finally be gotten from Jasper. Even critics who
insist that Edwin is alive do not deny Jasper's guilt, or the centrality of
his guilt to the working up of the denouement. If Jasper has not murdered Edwin, they reason, he has at least meant to do so (and may believe
he has done so). Some speculative versions of the denouement suggest
that Jasper is to be made guilty of killing Neville Landless, if no one else,
as the younger man pursues Jasper to the top of the tower. In the six finished parts of the novel, the "good" characters have already stopped
looking for Edwin and begun weaving suspicions about Jasper, suggesting that he alone knows for sure what has become of the missing man.
But the novel suggests that Jasper "knows" the crime only in the depths
of his unconscious: in his moments of addiction, and in the repeated violent dream that is his primal scene. Like *Armadale*, though *Drood* wants
to discover a crime, it implies that the revelation of the plot is bound up
inextricably with accounting for Jasper's identity and desire.[23] Thomas
argues that "the real mystery of *Edwin Drood* is not 'Who did it?' but
'What is the nature of the person driven to this crime?'"[24] The question
fits with what Dickens reportedly told Forster about his new book.
According to Forster:

> . . . the originality of [*Drood*] was to consist in the review of the
> murderer's career by himself at the close, when its temptations
> were to be dwelt upon as if, not he the culprit, but some other
> man, were the tempted. The last chapters were to be written in
> the condemned cell, to which his wickedness, all elaborately
> elicited from him as if told by another, had brought him.[25]

Droodians who prefer a more elaborate mystery have frequently
challenged the merit of Forster's recollections. But if they are true, as I

believe, they shed enormous light upon what Dickens felt were his greatest challenges in writing the novel. Before relating even this much of his plan to Forster, Dickens remarked that his "idea for the new story" was "a very strong one, though difficult to work."[26] The problem that he confronted, Forster's account suggests, was finding an adequate means by which readers could see, know, and understand Jasper's guilty unconscious and the crime it contains. On one hand a loving uncle, Jasper is also a consummate liar and murderer and engages in deliberate concealments intended to deflect suspicion. He also maintains a conscious division between his life at Cloisterham and his life of addiction. But as Dickens takes great pains to show, Jasper's self-division reaches finally beyond conscious thought, instead marking a genuine decentering of his conscious self within the greater matrix of unconscious desire. His addiction, which he consciously conceals, is a way to subvert consciousness and annihilate the will—a way, as Jasper senses, to free himself from conscience and repression. His repeated opium-induced dream of murder suggests that it is through Jasper's unconscious rather than conscious self that his violent desire will enter the novel. This is not to suggest that Jasper is a clinical split personality—a sort of Cybil in choirmaster's clothing—for this is clearly not the case. Rather, through Jasper Dickens explores the part of private identity that rests beyond self-understanding, self-narration, and conscious thought. Addict, dreamer, and murderer: Jasper constitutes Dickens's deepest investigation of the human unconscious. The crime of *Drood* lives only there, and Dickens believed it could emerge into narrative meaning only—as Forster's remembrances suggest—as a story told as if by another.

For Dickens such a story required the presence of the Victorian prison. Thirty years earlier, he had shown in "A Visit to Newgate" and "Fagin's Last Night Alive" that he recognized the power of condemnation and solitude to impel the self to introspection and narrative self-ordering. Just before beginning *Drood*, Dickens had *Oliver Twist* in mind, for it was during his reading tour in 1868–1869 that he conceived the idea for the *Sikes and Nancy* reading that became his obsession and probably hastened his end.[27] The idea of centering his new novel upon a murder might have come from this preoccupation with *Twist*, and so might the idea of confining Jasper to a condemned cell where he could review his criminal career. But Dickens's return to the prison in *Drood* is decidedly more complex, for it bears the marks of his long-evolving sense of the relation between narrative and the prison. For thirty years Dickens had traced the prison's power to shape the self and self-account. From *Pickwick Papers* to *A Tale of Two Cities* he had recorded the prison's power to demand, control, and invent even the most private story of the self in the cell. In *Drood* Dickens required that power, for the novel depends upon narrating a self that is not only divided but decentered, alienated irremediably from an identity and desire that reside in the unconscious. In one sense, Thomas precedes me in this argument, having written a decade ago that in *Drood* the "psyche is a field of knowledge . . .which . . . can be fully known only in a cultural context—in this case, a prison cell."[28] But he is interested ultimately in dreams, not cells, and he fails to recognize that *Drood* is not really about acquiring *knowledge* of Jasper, however much the quest for knowledge fits with the novel's program of detection. It is rather—as ingenious Droodians have shown so often without meaning to—about *inventing* Jasper: about reading, interpreting, and constructing his crime from the fragments and gaps of his imperfect self-narrative. Jasper's unconscious story of transgression and desire is the great absence of Dickens's last novel. All indications are that Dickens meant to transform that absence into presence by turning, one last time, to the narrative power reposed in the prison.

III

However *Drood* might finally have ended, it begins immersed in the attempt to narrate the unconscious. It opens unlike any other Dickens novel. There is no omniscient flourish, nor a candid self-introduction. Instead, we find the stream of a very curious consciousness perplexed amid the visions of a dream:

> An ancient English Cathedral town? How can the ancient English Cathedral town be here! The well-known massive grey square tower of its old Cathedral? How can that be here! There is no spike of rusty iron in the air, between the eye and it, from any point of the real prospect. What IS the spike that intervenes, and who has set it up? Maybe, it is set up by the Sultan's orders for the impaling of a horde of Turkish robbers, one by one. . . . Some vague period of drowsy laughter must be devoted to the consideration of this possibility. (*ED* 1)

To the extent that the dream contains information that is basic to the theme and plot, *Drood*'s unusual introduction performs, however uncertainly, the functions of a more traditional Dickensian beginning. As the novel draws on, we will learn more about the relation between the dream and the mystery of Edwin's disappearance. We will discover that the dreamer is Jasper, and that the dream is one manifestation of a vision he has seen "millions and billions of times"—a primal scene that contains the essence of the criminal and the crime (*ED* 207). In the pages to come we will also find that the ancient cathedral town is Cloisterham, and we will see that the dream presages two crucial features of the novel's plot:

the intrusion of a perilous East upon the quiet cathedral town, and the crime and violence that ensue from its arrival.

By situating these clues to the plot within Jasper's dream, Dickens underscores from the start that discovering the mystery of the crime in *Drood* means deciphering the mystery of the unconscious self. The opening lines of the novel are indeterminate and uncertain, for they do not belong to an identifiable speaker nor make a deliberate attempt to tell a story. As the narrator observes, we have stumbled into the mystery through the medium of a "scattered consciousness," the piecing together of which into identity and criminal intent comprises the central movement of the novel (*ED* 1). Collecting that scattered consciousness, the novel implies, will be extraordinarily hard. The dream we enter upon is shaped by opium, "incoherent" and "to no purpose" the dreamer supposes after listening to the "chattering and clattering" of his dazed companions (*ED* 3). Three times our unnamed dreamer declares that these mutterings—and hence the visions that inspire them—are "unintelligible!" but presumably they will not remain so (*ED* 3). On the contrary, their hints and clues will be infused repeatedly into the novel, worked out through time, and assembled gradually into coherence and meaning. As Thomas writes, "[t]he intelligibility of the crime in *Drood* apparently depends upon the intelligibility of a dream."[29] More than this, the intelligibility of crime and dream are intertwined with the mystery of the dreamer's identity, all three of which must be explained if the novel is to complete the narrative it has begun. Naming the crime in *Drood* will mean naming the decentered self and making intelligible the disordered meanings of his unconscious.

This is the novel's thematic fascination: to penetrate private spaces, expose them, and name what they contain and conceal. Mrs. Crisparkle keeps a "wonderful closet" at Minor Canon Corner, its mysteries "to be disclosed by degrees" as the doors slide apart; tellingly, when the doors open they reveal that "[e]very benevolent inhabitant of this retreat [has] his name inscribed upon his stomach" (*ED* 79). Datchery, meant clearly as *Drood*'s primary detective, makes it part of his business to name Deputy, calling him "Winks" near the end of part six as Deputy conjoins him not to make that name "public" (*ED* 213). Datchery also tracks his progress by keeping score on the inside of the door of his corner cupboard, and he does so in "the old tavern way . . . Illegible, except to the scorer" (*ED* 214). When detection is complete, presumably, the scoring and the narrative of the crime will be complete as well, so that these mysteries will become simultaneously intelligible in the world of the novel. Of course, no character in *Drood* is more concerned with discovery and revelation than Durdles, who spends his life in a constant search for "old 'uns" buried beneath the cathedral (*ED* 30). He links himself to Jasper implicitly by comparing his method of "sound[ing] for" the buried dead to Jasper's ability to "pitch [his] note," and it is Durdles who notes that Jasper tries to "make a pitch-pipe" of the keys—which Jasper does, as many critics suppose, so that he may identify by sound the key to Mrs. Sapsea's tomb, where he plans to hide Edwin's body (*ED* 35; 31). In his unceasing search for the dead, Durdles reflects the desire of the novel, for he attempts to see what cannot be seen and know what is hidden. As he explains to Jasper, "Durdles comes by *his* knowledge through grubbing deep for it, and having it up by the roots when it don't want to come" (*ED* 36). Knowledge of the crime certainly "don't want to come" in *Drood*, so likely it will be Durdles who sounds Mrs. Sapsea's tomb, discovers Edwin's body, and reveals the fact of the crime. Pitting Durdles against Mayor Sapsea in the first six parts, Dickens contrasts Durdles's grubbing with the Mayor's superficial "reputation . . . for knowledge," so that Durdles's discovery of the body in the precise place where Sapsea's inscription admonishes onlookers to "WITH A BLUSH RETIRE" will provide a telling conclusion (*ED* 25; 28). In *Drood* as in *Little Dorrit*, grubbing for roots—not looking at surfaces—is the key to producing an account of the crime.

But as *Drood*'s opening sequence suggests, solving the mystery has far less to do with finding Edwin than with piecing together Jasper's fragmented identity and narrating his private self. Of all the characters in the novel, only Jasper contains knowledge of Edwin's disappearance, for the crime exists as a motive and as an event only in his guilty desire. In this sense, *Drood* resembles *Armadale*, and Jasper resembles Lydia insofar as he seeks concealment by leading consciously the life of a divided self.[30] Respectable choirmaster by day, he is an addict and murderer by night, a division that he maintains partly by pursuing his addiction in London, where he conceals his real name from the Princess Puffer. In Cloisterham he hides his darker self, satisfying his addiction—when he must—in the privacy of his rooms. As the narrator remarks of Jasper's position as a choirmaster, "Constantly exercising an Art which brought him into mechanical harmony with others . . . it is curious to consider that the spirit of the man was in moral accordance or interchange with nothing around him" (*ED* 203). Jasper tells Edwin this much at the start of the novel, but even his confession is a concealment, not only of his addiction—which he brushes aside by calling it "a pain—an agony—that sometimes overcomes me"—but also of his murderous designs and passion for Rosa (*ED* 10). Nor does he tell Rosa about his passion, though she knows of it, for she confides to Helena, "He has made a slave of me with his looks. He has forced me to understand him, without his saying a word; and he has forced me to keep silence, without his uttering a threat" (*ED* 53). Some critics suggest that Jasper's power over Rosa is mesmeric, an intangible manipulation that she can sense but not define. Outwardly, though, Jasper is "self-repressed," and far from being suspected in Edwin's disappearance he is feared to have his heart "too much set upon his nephew" (*ED* 173; 6). Jasper's is a history of conscious self-conceal-ment, and ringed about increasingly by detectives—Datchery, Grewgious, and the Princess, among others—he grows "[i]mpassive, moody, solitary, resolute, concentrated on one idea . . . liv[ing] apart from human life" (*ED* 203). The novel's business, like Durdles's, is to drag up by the roots this private identity that "don't want to come" and make narrative sense of the criminal and the crime.

The trope of the consciously divided self that we find in *Drood* was not new to Dickens, nor yet to the genres of prison and detective novels to which *Drood* generally belongs. William Dorrit is also divided between the public fiction of his social existence and the private truth of his prison taint, and so, in a more complex fashion, is Alexandre Manette. More, as in modern detective novels, *Drood* requires like *Armadale* that an obstacle to discovering the crime be the criminal's skill at evasion and concealment—at maintaining the untroubled veneer of the normal social self. Jasper like Lydia must prevent his guilty narrative from emerg-ing into the public space of the novel. But Jasper is just one example of *Drood*'s fascination with the divided self. Datchery, if he is disguised, pres-ents a case in which self-division will aid rather than hinder detection. Neville and Helena Landless are twins, one self divided into two, and they share a psychic bond that indicates their permanent inseparability. As Neville tells Crisparkle, "You don't know, sir, yet, what a complete understanding can exist between my sister and me, though no spoken word—perhaps hardly as much as a look—may have passed between us" (*ED* 50). Such clairvoyance, coupled with Helena's boldness in Jasper's presence—she should not be afraid of him "under any circumstances"— has suggested to some critics that she, too, possesses mesmeric powers, a certain control over the unconscious self (*ED* 51). Whether or not this is true, she clearly plays conscience and reason to Neville's violence and passion, illustrating and mending simultaneously their division by mak-ing him psychically whole.[31] Even Miss Twinkleton, who does not par-ticipate in the novel's crime or detection, has "two distinct and separate phases of being" (*ED* 15). Jasper's division is more purposeful, and more purposefully concealed, than any of these, and of all the novel's charac-ters he escapes most consistently the narrative invasion of his thoughts. Collectively, *Drood*'s divided selves remind us of the difficulty of detect-ing, exposing, and completing from "outside" the private narrative that would account for Jasper's crime.

Like *Armadale*, *Drood* seems at first as if it will complete this narration in the criminal's own hand: in Jasper's private diary, a record of his actions and desire. We see the diary first in chapter ten, appropriately titled "Smoothing the Way," and even here—long before Edwin disappears—the diary hints of blood. On the night of Neville's and Edwin's first argument, Jasper records his "morbid dread" of "horrible consequences resulting to [his] dear boy," and also that he has "dark intangible presentiments of evil" concerning the outcome of the strife (*ED* 86; 87). Far from exposing his crime or himself, Jasper's diary is a conscious narrative performance, a symptom of rather than antidote to his deliberate self-concealment. The chapter title implies as much by hinting that the diary is preliminary to a growing plan. But Dickens gives other clues, too, that Jasper's diary does not resemble Lydia's in the honesty of its self-exploration. Jasper tells Mr. Crisparkle that his private journal is—curiously—"A Diary of Ned's life too," and the fact that he shows it to Crisparkle at all marks it as a designedly public rather than private text (*ED* 86). He offers it to Crisparkle as a sort of testimony, calling upon the minor canon to "witness . . . what my state of mind honestly was, that night" (*ED* 87). Later, after Edwin disappears, Jasper uses the diary to show Crisparkle that he means to be the detective and avenger of the crime rather than its perpetrator, promising, "That I never will relax in my secresy [sic] or in my search. That I will fasten the crime of the murder of my dear dead boy, upon the murderer. And That I devote myself to his destruction" (*ED* 146). Already concealed by the myriad stratagems that separate his private identity from his public character, Jasper invokes the diary as an account of his private truth and fashions it all the while into a tool for fastening blame upon Neville. This is the operation of the criminal mind, "a horrible wonder apart" that the narrator says is unfathomable even to "its own professed students" (*ED* 175). Closing himself to the possibility of honest self-reflection or self-narration, Jasper closes as well the possibility that he will reveal, in his own words, the narrative of Edwin's disappearance.

If Jasper's deliberate self-division were the only obstacle to the narration of the crime, *Drood* might promise a simpler ending, or at least an ending more in keeping with the modern detective novel. After all, Jasper might be compelled by his guilt to confess, or he might be found out by one of the novel's detectives. Even by the end of *Drood*'s six finished numbers, several detectives have attached themselves to Jasper, threatening to discover not only his guilty secrets but also the fact of the crime. Grewgious has tracked Jasper about London, perhaps even to the opium den, and the Princess has followed him to Cloisterham and met Datchery and Deputy, bearing all the while a confidence that she "may have learned the secret of how to make [Jasper] talk" (*ED* 209). When Datchery asks if she knows Jasper, she replies, "Know him! Better far, than all the Reverend Parsons put together know him"—after which Datchery, in the novel's final line, "adds one thick line to the score, extending from the top of the cupboard door to the bottom" (*ED* 216). These detectives aside, the ubiquitous Deputy may have seen something of the murder, or Durdles may yet find the body. Apart from what Rosa, Crisparkle, and the Landlesses may come to suspect by the end of the novel, Jasper's public and private selves have begun already to converge before the eyes of *Drood*'s detectives. His error in pressing his suit upon Rosa even gives them a clue to the motive that could drive him to kill. In other words, Jasper's deliberately hidden self has emerged already far enough into the light that, if Durdles finds Edwin's body and the trial of a murderer must begin, Jasper may replace Neville as the primary suspect in the investigation.

But as Dickens takes pains to show from the start, narrating the crime in *Drood* is no simple matter of discovery and detection. Rather, imbuing the novel with coherence and meaning requires accounting for not only Jasper's conscious self-division but also a deeper fragmentation that rests beyond his control: the decentered nature of his conscious self. Just before noting Miss Twinkleton's two spheres of being, *Drood*'s narrator says:

> . . . in some cases of drunkenness, and in others of animal magnetism, there are two states of consciousness which never clash, but each of which pursues its separate course as though it were continuous instead of broken (thus if I hide my watch when I am drunk, I must be drunk again before I can remember where) . . . (*ED* 15)

Yet the description seems more apt to Jasper or Durdles than to Miss Twinkleton. *Drood* rarely accounts for Durdles's drunken thoughts, but it catches Jasper constantly in the state of altered consciousness produced by opium. Jasper lives situated precariously between his life of conscious thought and the ceaseless repetition of his unintelligible dream, and the dream's failure to emerge entirely into meaning poses the most difficult mystery of the novel. On one hand, the fact of Jasper's addiction is conscious, an act of will, and part of the darker self that he deliberately conceals. But his addiction is also his attempt to abdicate the will, so that he can conquer repression and—like Lucy during her opium walk at the end of *Villette*—subjugate his conscious self to the uninhibited play of desire. Jasper's forbidden desire for Edwin's death lives for him only beyond repression and conscious thought, and it belongs, consequently, to a part of himself that he cannot utter. As Jasper explains to the Princess in *Drood*'s last finished chapter, he has come to her over and over again "on purpose," for he had something in his mind that he "[m]ight or might not do" (*ED* 208; 206). At her opium den, unshackled psychologically by the power of the drug, he committed the murder "hundreds of thousands" and "millions and billions of times," and in his own quarters, looking in upon the sleeping Edwin, he "lights his pipe, and delivers himself to the Spectres it invokes at midnight" (*ED* 207; 38). The "Specters" are almost certainly visions of the death that Jasper intends for Edwin, for his moments of addiction are descents into the repetition of the primal scene that is shaped by his unconscious desire. Likely, Jasper also attacks Edwin while under the influence of the drug, since he can only indulge his guilty desire when he is freed from repression and will. Murder is the language in which Jasper makes articulate the inexpressible kernel of his unconscious self.

The crime in *Drood* threatens to go unnarrated, then, because it is unknowable, part of the narrative gap comprised by the human unconscious. Certain moments suggest that Jasper may be dimly *aware* of his guilt. His efforts to frame Neville seem deliberate, for example, and so do the implications of his collapse before Grewgious, when Rosa's guardian tells him that she and Edwin had already broken their engagement. If we are to believe Forster, Dickens intended that "[d]iscovery by the murderer of the utter needlessness of the murder for its object, was to follow hard upon commission of the deed."[32] But for Jasper the story of the crime is the story of the dream, and both remain part of the scattered consciousness struggling toward coherence across the course of the novel. Even after the crime, Jasper's narration of the dream remains encoded, for it is an incomplete account that must be interpreted to decipher its relation to the events of the novel. He speaks of the "journey" and the "fellow-traveller," and when he conjures the vision a final time in "The Dawn Again," he notes a new feature in the dream by saying cryptically, "and yet I never saw *that* before" (*ED* 208). Thomas suggests that Jasper's words reflect his determination to preserve, not mend, his scattered consciousness—that he is "a man who is intent on *not* saying what is on his mind."[33] This is obviously true. Yet there is a sense, too, in which Jasper *cannot* speak the dream just as he cannot speak the crime—in which he cannot, as in the opening scene, account for the moments in which his conscious self suffers the intrusion of unconscious desire. As he tells the Princess, "I did it so often, and through such vast expanses of time, that when it was really done, it seemed not worth the doing," and he calls his final vision—the only one, if he has killed Edwin, driven by recollection rather than invention—"the poorest of all" (*ED* 207; 208). The murder exists more completely in his unconscious than in his conscious self, even after it has been committed. Thus, as Stephen Connor argues, Jasper's return to the opium den to see the vision one last time is an attempt "to recapture the condition of non-fulfillment"—to continue, that is, to commit the crime.[34] As a matter of law, Jasper's guilt may inhere in the moment when he takes Edwin's life. As a matter of psychology, his guilt is as ancient as Cloisterham's cathedral and requires a great deal of grubbing and delving into remembrance and unconscious desire.

The question upon which *Drood* rests is not, then, what is the story of the crime, but rather, how can the story of the crime be told—how can it emerge from Jasper's unconscious self into the fullness of narrative completion. As Doris Alexander observes, "[e]veryone knows 'who done it,' for it was certainly done by the villain of the book John Jasper."[35] But Jasper of all people may not quite know "who done it," at least not in the sense of being able to account for it, completely and coherently, as part of his private self. He cannot confess to the crime because confession implies self-revelation, fixing not only the meaning of the crime but also the meaning of his decentered self, and his diary shows us that he wields only an imperfect power to narrate his identity and desire. Even when he attempts to conceal his connection to the crime, he records in the diary the very meanings that he wishes to hide. His evil presentiments about Edwin's fate are evil presentiments about himself. His wish to detect the killer is a wish to detect the secret of his desire. His devotion to the discovery and destruction of the murderer is a devotion to self-discovery and self-destruction—the events toward which the whole of the novel tends. Several critics have remarked the justice and irony of Jasper leading the search for a murderer who turns out to be himself. But the real significance of his diary is the lesson it affords in reading and interpretation, for it shows us his self-narrative failure and insists that his decentered self must be interpreted and invented rather than revealed. In *Drood*, narrating desire and identity—fixing the meaning of the primal scene—is beyond the power of the narrating self. For Jasper to tell the story of crime that is also the account of his private identity and desire, his self-account must be read, interpreted, and completed through the narrative power of another.

Thus Jasper must be thrust finally into the Victorian prison. No one can say for sure how *Drood* would have ended—how Dickens would have accounted ultimately for Edwin's disappearance, Datchery's identity, or the innumerable lesser mysteries that will exist always for readers of the novel. Nor have I any need or desire to involve myself in the debates. But amid the maddening fact of the novel's incompleteness, one thing at least seems certain: that *The Mystery of Edwin Drood* is headed inexorably for the prison. This claim might be plausible for any number of reasons— because Jasper is a villain, or because the novel is about crime, or perhaps even just because Forster said so. But *Drood* seems headed for the prison because its resolution requires the prison, for only there can the divided and disordered Jasper be brought to narrative completion. He cannot account for himself completely or coherently, nor—if he killed Edwin while under the influence of opium—is the crime even part of his conscious identity. During more than thirty years of writing, Dickens turned repeatedly to the prison when he wished to narrate the private self, and in *A Tale of Two Cities* he invoked explicitly the prison's power to wrest control of the self-account away from the Victorian prisoner. Completing an account of Jasper requires, then, that the prison become part of the novel's denouement, for the novel's detectives must not only elicit Jasper's imperfect self-narrative but also claim the power to make it into a complete and coherent account of the crime.

In this sense, perhaps the most likely ending anyone has proposed for *Drood* is one in which Jasper ends up in the condemned cell for killing not Edwin but Neville, whom Jasper pushes from the cathedral tower (in something of a Bill Sikesian moment) when the younger man divines Jasper's guilt, accuses him, and pursues him up the cathedral stairs. Hoping to clear her brother's name of suspicion, Helena visits Jasper in prison and uses her mesmeric powers—and perhaps a good dose of opium—to elicit his confession to Edwin's murder. Listening to an incoherent self-narrative that reads like Jasper's dream at the start of the novel, Helena will play psychoanalyst to Jasper's uncertain attempt to account for Edwin's murder. She will interpret his repressions and confessions and complete the narration of the crime. She will separate the primal scene of his dream from the reality of the event. She will fix the meaning of his story and invent a coherent account of his guilt. In the end, she will become—and the reader along with her—arbiter of the meaning of Jasper's private identity and desire. As we were at the novel's beginning, so we will be at its end: psychoanalysts seeking to mend Jasper's ruptures by making sense of his self-account. George Wing suggests that maybe "some part of Dickens's personality, sensitive to his imminent death, was aware that Jasper's story could never be fully told."[36] If this was so, it is all the more reason for *Drood* to approach the cell, where the narrative invention of Jasper can be undertaken by another. In *The Mystery of Edwin Drood* Dickens would have shown us the deliberate narrative invention of Jasper's self by the normalizing power of the authorial other. Thus Dickens's final return to the prison—his own ineradicable primal scene—delivers a proto-Freudian text: more case history than mystery, and tending inevitably to permit the formal narrative invention of the unconscious.

IV

Selves have been narrated over and over through centuries of English literature, from Shakespearian soliloquies to Joyceian streams-of-consciousness and in varying shades between. But Victorian prison novels signify especially, for they are the first subgenre to engage explicitly the mechanisms of power that permit this literary invention of the self. Prison novels identify the psychological inviolability that makes the private self impossible to know, and they express profound unease in their attempts to narrate subjectivity with any degree of precision. They also call our attention to the prison's power to inflict psychological trauma, and to use that trauma as a pretext for divorcing the truth about the self from the narrative that professes to describe him. In novel after novel, Victorian authors turn to the prison to provide us with a self who must fail inevitably at self-narration, and whose invention the novel thus simultaneously justifies and undertakes. This is true in Dickens, Reade, and Clarke, and in Charlotte Brontë and Wilkie Collins. It is also true of the authors who followed them, who continued to use the self in the cell as an image of psychological trauma and self-narrative failure. *The Way of All Flesh* gives us near its conclusion Ernest thrust into Coldbath-fields, where he wakes after a long illness to discover that his old opinions on Christianity are overthrown and that he wishes to abandon his clerical life. Thus he finds "that imprisonment ha[s] cut his life into two parts, the one of which could bear no resemblance to the other."[37] Even so, during his convalescence, Ernest makes no headway in his attempts to descibe his new self to the prison chaplain, who "brushe[s] Ernest to one side as if he [is] a fly."[38] Only once he has left the prison can Ernest embark upon a new career and claim his new identity. Joseph Conrad's *The Secret Agent* (1907) shows us a similar self-narrative failure in Michaelis, "the ticket-of-leave apostle," who is broken physically by confinement, left "virtually a cripple," compared with the "young and slim" locksmith he had been fifteen years before.[39] Intent upon writing his "Autobiography of a Prisoner," Michaelis retreats to the "confined space" of a cottage in the country, since the "seclusion, and solitude in a small four-roomed cottage [are] favourable to his inspiration."[40] But his attempt to "liberat[e] his inner life" has already been silenced, for he has "lost the habit of consecutive thinking"—the power to order and arrange the details of his identity and desire—during his time in prison.[41]

In the end, it may be no accident that Stephen Dedalus begins to come to linguistic awareness in the solitude of the infirmary. However revolutionary Joyce's techniques for narrating the private self, the power that undergirds them belongs to the Victorian prison. Writing in an age when the novel became the dominant literary form, Victorian novelists seem to have recognized not only their commercial power but also their social responsibility. They sought to justify upon socially acceptable grounds their authority to invent the private self. Their frightening accounts of the prison suggest that this authority did not come without pain—that they sensed, however fearfully, the growing power of narrative discourse to shape what Victorians believed about their world. But the truth of the matter is that prison novelists did not participate in fantasies of omniscience about the private self. Nor did they reject, as Foucault does, the possibility of autonomous and genuine human subjectivity. They only rejected the idea that subjectivity can ever be narrated fully, since the self can never account for its disruptions, divisions, and desires. Ironically, this view of Victorian prison novels moves them much nearer to Foucault's work than any discussion of surveillance probably can, since prison novels thus become part of a long trajectory of thought that has provided us with techniques for inventing and controlling the private self. As Foucault remarked in an interview in 1977, preserving the social order has always been "the true role of psychiatry. This is its climate, and this is the horizon of its birth."[42] The birth of the penitentiary merely prefigures and enables, in other words, the birth of psychoanalysis. It does so, at least partly, through the mode of the Victorian prison novel. Calling attention to the array of power relations implicit in the prison's narration of the self, prison novels illustrate that self-narrative—not the subject—is invariably a matter of invention. In doing so, they set the stage for what Freud and Foucault came finally to suppose: that every self is a prisoner laboring in the shadow of the cell.

Notes

NOTES TO THE INTRODUCTION

[1] Jeremy Bentham, *Panopticon, or the Inspection-house: Postscript; Containing Further Particulars and Alterations Relative to the Plan of Construction Originally Proposed; Principally Adapted to the Purpose of a Panopticon Penitentiary House* (Dublin: Thomas Byrne, 1791), p. 5.

[2] Bentham, p. 3.

[3] Bentham, p. 122.

[4] Michael Ignatieff, *A Just Measure of Pain: The Penitentiary in the Industrial Revolution, 1750–1850* (New York: Pantheon, 1978), p. 87.

[5] In truth, Bentham's *Panopticon* was not written, at least initially, as a proposal to the Crown for a national penitentiary, nor was the idea behind the building really his. Rather, living in Russia during 1786, Bentham saw in a copy of the *St. James Chronicle* sent to him from England that the County of Middlesex was considering plans for a new county workhouse. As he wrote to his father in a letter that, amended, served as the opening letter of *Panopticon*:

> It occurred to me that the Plan of a Building, lately contrived by my Brother [Samuel] for purpose in some respects similar and wch. under the name of Inspection House or The Elaboratory He is about erecting here might afford some Hints for the above Establishment . . .

This fragment is preserved in Volume 3 of *The Correspondence of Jeremy Bentham* (ed. Ian R. Christie. 11 vols. London: Univ. of London, The Athlone Press, 1971), p. 509.

Bentham's proposal did not succeed with the Middlesex magistrates, who received it in March 1787, about the time that Bentham began working on a draft of a letter to Pitt. He never sent the letter. In 1790 he peddled his idea for the Panopticon to authorities in Ireland, then finally wrote to Pitt on January 26, 1791, before also recommending his plan to friends in Scotland and France. By the end of 1791, Bentham had not received a single offer to construct the penitentiary. For a synopsis of Bentham's attempts to advance his Panopticon proposal during 1790–1792, see *Correspondence*, v. 4, pp. xxiv-xxvii.

[6] Walter Lowe Clay, *The Prison Chaplain: A Memoir of the Reverend John Clay, B.D., Late Chaplain of Preston Gaol* (Montclair: Patterson Smith, 1969), p. 74; Henry Mayhew and John Binny, *The Criminal Prisons of London, and Scenes from Prison Life* (London: Frank Cass and Co., 1968), p. 235.

[7] Clay, p. 74.

[8] Seán McConville, *A History of English Prison Administration* (London: Routledge and Kegan Paul, 1981), p. 112, fn. 32.

[9] Mayhew and Binny give the most complete account of Millbank's architecture, including floor plans and architectural drawings. See especially pp. 232–266.

[10] D. A. Miller, *The Novel and the Police* (Berkeley: Univ. of California Press, 1988), p. x; p. ix.

[11] I have in mind here Miller's *The Novel and the Police*; Mark Seltzer's *Henry James and the Art of Power* (Ithaca; London: Cornell Univ. Press, 1984); and Audrey Jaffe's *Vanishing Points: Dickens, Narrative, and the Subject of Omniscience* (Berkeley; Los Angeles: Univ. of California Press, 1991).

[12] Miller, p. 162.

[13] Seltzer, p. 16.

[14] Jeremy Tambling (*Dickens, Violence and the Modern State: Dreams of the Scaffold* [New York: St. Martin's, 1995]) actually devotes chapters 4 and 5 to *Little Dorrit* and *A Tale of Two Cities*, respectively, though his first chapter—titled "Prison Bound: Dickens, Foucault, and *Great Expectations*"—makes his critical bias clear.

[15] John Bender, *Imagining the Penitentiary* (Chicago; London: Univ. of Chicago Press, 1987), p. 11.

[16] W. H. Auden, "In Memory of W. B. Yeats," *The English Auden: Poems, Essays and Dramatic Writings 1927–1939* (ed. Edward Mendelson. London: Faber and Faber, 1977), p. 242.

[17] Michel Foucault, *Discipline and Punish: The Birth of the Prison* (trans. Alan Sheridan. New York: Pantheon, 1977), p. 237.

[18] Foucault, p. 170.

NOTES TO CHAPTER 1

[1] Quoted in J. M. Beattie, *Crime and the Courts in England 1660–1800* (Princeton: Princeton Univ. Press, 1986), p. 468. This entire account of Middleton's case comes from Beattie, pp. 467–468.

[2] Beattie, p. 468.

[3] Beattie, p. 464.

[4] Beattie discusses both cases in *Crime and the Courts*. Like Middleton, Waller

was convicted of delivering false evidence in an attempt to earn rewards. The victim at Smithfield Market, whom Beattie does not name, was convicted of perhaps an even more vicious crime. Hoping to win rewards by helping to prosecute highwaymen and robbers, the man had lured young men into committing such crimes. Then he would turn them over to the local authorities. For Beattie's excellent discussion of how the pillory was used in Surrey during the eighteenth century, see especially pp. 464–468.

[5] Daniel Defoe, *Moll Flanders* (ed. James Sutherland. Boston: Houghton Mifflin, 1959), pp. 238–239.

[6] Bender, p. 13.

[7] Paul Rock in *Making People Pay* (London; Boston: Routledge and Kegan Paul, 1973) identifies at least nine debtors prisons that operated in London around 1800. These included the Marshalsea, the Fleet, the Queen's Bench; Poultry, Giltspur Street, and Borough Compters; Newgate, Ludgate, and Whitecross Prisons. Many of these prisons were "attached" to the courts which fed them prisoners. As Rock points out, "the Fleet was, in its later life, the prison of the Courts of Chancery; and the Marshalsea and Queen's Bench belonged to the courts of the same names" (p. 308). For a succinct discussion of debtors' prisons in England during the eighteenth and early nineteenth centuries, see Rock, pp. 307–314.

[8] Rock, p. 309.

[9] Quoted in McConville, p. 73. McConville's second chapter provides a detailed discussion of just how riotous and foul eighteenth-century prisons could be, and how dismally they were managed.

[10] Roger Lee Brown, *A History of the Fleet Prison, London: The Anatomy of the Fleet* (Lewiston: Edwin Mellen Press, 1996), p. 101.

[11] Quoted in Ignatieff, p. 34.

[12] Bender, p. 14.

[13] Bender, p. 14, and McConville, p. 71, both recount these stories of England's most infamous eighteenth-century prisoners.

[14] Rock, p. 309.

[15] McConville, p. 51.

[16] McConville, p. 51. The principle by which prisons were permitted to become such pestilent, noisome places was called "*squalor carceris*" and served, as McConville shows, a very particular ideological and deterrent aim. If prisoners found the prisons disagreeable, the theory ran, they ought to have taken a great deal more care to keep out of them.

[17] McConville, p. 341.

[18] McConville, p. 58.

[19] Robert Hughes discusses the ritual of English public executions in the second chapter of *The Fatal Shore* (New York: Alfred A. Knopf, 1987). See pp. 31–36.

[20] Quoted in Beattie, p. 529.

[21] Quoted in Beattie, p. 490.

[22] Actually, Ignatieff contends that this percentage may have been much higher, for during the 1760s, at least, 70 percent of all sentences handed down at the Old Bailey were to transportation, and even more convicts like-

ly went to America as a condition of their royal pardons. See Ignatieff, p. 20.

²³ Beattie, p. 546. As Beattie points out, more than 63 percent of noncapital sentences in Surrey from 1763–1771 were to transportation, but that number declined to 37 percent during the four years before the War.

²⁴ Beattie, p. 552.

²⁵ See William Hay's *Remarks on the Laws relating to the Poor with Proposals for their Better Relief and Employment* (1751) and Joseph Massie's *A Plan for the Establishment of Charity Houses for exposed or deserted Women and Girls . . .* (1758).

²⁶ Ignatieff, p. 46; Beattie, p. 538, fn. 33. The increase in prosecutions and convictions can be regarded, of course, as reflective of a new bourgeois desire to protect well-to-do persons and their property from the ravening masses of the urban poor—an argument that fits perfectly with Foucault's analysis of the rise of the penitentiary. Had this been the only pressure England faced during the 1760s and 1770s, however, the Crown might well have simply expanded the existing programs of criminal administration. That is, increased convictions could have meant more transportees and more executions rather than a shift toward a new sentencing pattern that favored imprisonment.

²⁷ Beattie, p. 546.

²⁸ Herman Mannheim provides in *Pioneers in Criminology* (2nd ed. Montclair: Patterson Smith, 1972) an excellent introduction to and discussion of Cesare Beccaria, his penological philosophy, and his influence upon prison reform during the late eighteenth century. See especially pp. 44–45.

²⁹ Making the situation even more complicated, victims of crime during the 1700s were expected to pay prosecution costs out of their own pockets. Late in the eighteenth century, fed up with the alarming rates of unprosecuted petty crimes, some communities even initiated private associations for the prosecution of felons to pay for and otherwise encourage victims to press their suits in court. For an excellent discussion of prosecution and conviction in England, see Adrian Shubert, "Private Initiative in Law Enforcement: Associations for the Prosecution of Felons, 1744–1856" in *Policing and Punishment in Nineteenth Century Britain* (ed. Victor Bailey. London: Croom Helm, 1981): 25–41.

³⁰ McConville, p. 83.

³¹ Ignatieff, p. 52.

³² Quoted in McConville, p. 109.

³³ Hughes, p. 64.

³⁴ McConville, p. 112, fn. 32.

³⁵ The *Times*, September 12, 1838, p. 6 col. a. Future references to the *Times* appear parenthetically in the text. Director of Irish Prisons Sir Walter Crofton made a similar complaint in the 1857 essay, "Can Intermediate Prisons Materially Aid in Solving the Difficulties of the Convict Question?" (*Transactions of the National Association for the Promotion of Social Science* [ed. G. W. Hastings. London: John W. Parker and Son, 1859]: 376–383) by writing:

When it was in our power to remove our convicts in these large masses to our colonies, we had cared but little for their reformation. Expatriation was our panacea. Our sole reformatory agent was the employment placed at our disposal in a new country, in which the antecedents of the criminal in the old did not appear against him. (p. 377)

[36] David Philips, *Crime and Authority in Victorian England: The Black Country, 1835–1860* (London: Croom Helm, 1977), p. 15. In addition to initiatives like Private Associations for the Prosecution of Felons, the Parliamentary Reward System also made prosecution more likely beginning in 1818. Previously, this system had provided a restitution of prosecution expenses of up to £40 for those who helped to convict criminals of certain rewardable offenses. In 1818 the system was amended in recognition that constables and sheriffs sometimes resisted interfering with criminals until they committed such a rewardable offense—until, in the cant phrase, they "weighed forty pounds." See J. J. Tobias, *Crime and Industrial Society in the 19th Century* (New York: Schocken Books, 1967), p. 223.

[37] Quoted in Clay, p. 67.

[38] Quoted in William Forsythe, *The Reform of Prisoners, 1830–1900* (London: Croom Helm, 1987), p. 20.

[39] Bentham, pp. 142–143. Late in the eighteenth century, "silent association" became the term for disciplinary regimens in which prisoners were permitted to work and take exercise in groups, but only under unbroken surveillance and condition of absolute silence. Through the first half of the nineteenth century, silent association continued as the primary alternative to the separate confinement advocated by G. O. Paul early in the century and England's national Prison Inspectorate after 1835.

[40] During Millbank's first three years of operation, 10 prisoners died at the penitentiary. Three times that many died—mostly of scurvy—during the first half of 1823. An article that appeared in the *Times* early in July 1823 ("Increasing Mortality at the Penitentiary," 7/4/23, 3a) listed the number of deaths annually at Millbank, 1817–1823, as follows: "1817, three; 1818, four; 1819, three; 1820, eleven; 1821, twenty; 1822, twenty-one; 1823 up to the 1st of July, thirty-one.—Total, 93."

[41] Playfair takes a particularly cynical—but useful and persuasive—view of nineteenth-century English prison administration in *The Punitive Obsession: An Unvarnished History of the English Prison System* (London: Gollancz, 1971). According to Playfair, prison reform in England has always been unable to escape its desire to punish offenders, even when penologists have expressed most powerfully their intention to make the penitentiary into an explicitly reformative institution.

[42] McConville, p. 163.

[43] These punishments, because they involved various kinds of rotating machinery, were called collectively "the wheel." Normally, prisoners were expected to complete a certain number of hours or revolutions each day. Especially on the tread-wheel, the prisoner who could not keep up risked

bodily injury, since larger prisons like Coldbath-fields had enormous tread-wheels on which several prisoners walked at once. Falling upon or under the wheel because of fatigue could mean being crushed, unless your fellow-labor-ers were attentive enough to stop. Occasionally, both hand-cranks and tread-wheels were arranged so that they performed productive labor like grinding flour or corn. More frequently, they were simply used to punish, and to ensure that prisoners grew accustomed to working for their bread.

44 U. Henriques, "The Rise and Decline of the Separate System of Prison Discipline," *Past and Present* 54 (1972), p. 74.

45 Hughes, p. 282.

46 Hughes, p. 283.

47 Hughes, p. 231.

48 Hughes, p. 301.

49 John Barry, *Alexander Maconochie of Norfolk Island, a Study of a Pioneer in Penal Reform* (London; New York: Oxford Univ. Press, 1958), p. 42. A. W. Baker also remarks that "[c]onsiderably fewer" than 10% of transportees spent time in the penal stations. See Baker, *Death is a Good Solution: The Convict Experience in Early Australia* (St. Lucia: Univ. of Queensland Press, 1984), p. 3.

50 Quoted in Hughes, p. 301.

51 Hughes, p. 377.

52 Hughes, p. 480.

53 Quoted in Hughes, p. 478.

54 The best account of Alexander Maconochie and his tenure at Norfolk Island is given by Barry in *Alexander Maconochie of Norfolk Island.*

55 Quoted in McConville, p. 164.

56 McConville, p. 164.

57 McConville, p. 170.

58 Quoted in Forsythe, p. 27.

59 John Field, *Prison Discipline: And the Advantages of the Separate System of Imprisonment, with a Detailed Account of the Discipline Now Pursued in the New County Gaol at Reading* (2 vols. London: Longman, Brown, Green, and Longmans, 1848), v. 1, p. 347.

60 The Fifth Report of Pentonville's governor, quoted in Forsythe, p. 63.

61 Quoted in McConville, p. 353.

62 Playfair, p. 40.

63 Terence Morris and Pauline Morris, *Pentonville: A Sociological Study of an English Prison* (London: Routledge and Kegan Paul, 1963), p. 12.

64 Mayhew and Binny include a "bird's-eye view" drawing of Pentonville in *Criminal Prisons of London.* See p. 116.

65 Mayhew, p. 120; p. 168.

66 Ignatieff, p. 7.

67 Quoted in Mayhew, p. 114.

68 The *Times* ran four prominent articles on Pentonville in the weeks lead-ing up to its opening. See for instance articles on 11/21/42, 3d; 11/26/42, 6b; 11/28/42, 5c; and 12/13/42, 5c.

69 John Silby, *A Letter on the Superior Advantages of Separate Confinement Over*

the System of Prison Discipline, at Present Adopted in Gaols and Houses of Correction (London: John Hatchard and Son, 1838), p. 1; quoted in Clay, p. 142.

[70] Quoted in Clay, p. 144.

[71] Quoted in Clay, p. 287.

[72] Field, v. 1, p. 352.

[73] Field, v. 1, p. viii.

[74] H. S. Joseph, *Memoirs of Convicted Prisoners: Accompanied by Remarks on the Causes and Prevention of Crime* (London: Wertheim and Co., 1853), p. viii.

[75] Joseph, p. 113.

[76] William Andrews, *To Tell a Free Story: The First Century of Afro-American Autobiography, 1750–1865* (Urbana; Chicago: Univ. of Illinois Press, 1986), p. 20.

[77] Gipps, quoted in Hughes, p. 308.

[78] Hughes, p. 308.

[79] Hughes, p. 310.

[80] According to Forsythe, by 1856 forty of England's 121 prisons had implemented separate discipline, and 43 more claimed to have adopted substantial portions of the separate program. See p. 102.

[81] Mayhew, pp. 91–92; p. 199.

[82] Mayhew gives these numbers as 166,942 total prisoners and 9,669 debtors in 1849. See p. 84.

[83] Playfair, p. 80.

[84] Ignatieff, p. 105.

[85] Playfair, p. 40. Before the House of Lords, Lyndhurst delivered this address:

> He understood that two young men, one of the age of 17, the other above 20, were sentenced to solitary confinement in the Penitentiary for the period of a year. And what had been the result! One, a young man possessing great acuteness of intellect when he went in, came out an idiot! and was now confined as an idiot in Marylebone workhouse, not capable of being employed even to break stones. (Hear, hear.) The other . . . also came out an idiot. (Hear, hear.) . . . It was the more important that he should now make this statement in the face of the public and of Her Majesty's Ministers, because he now understood that there was an intention existing to extend this system of prison government throughout the country. (*Times* 2/27/38, 3a)

[86] Hughes, p. 493.

[87] Hughes, p. 493.

[88] Quoted in Hughes, p. 494.

[89] Quoted in Hughes, p. 495.

[90] Quoted in Hughes, p. 494.

[91] The *Times* reprinted extensive portions of the Molesworth Report on September 12, 14, and 27, 1838. See 9/12/38, 6a; 9/14/38, 6e; and 9/27/38,

7a.

[92] In the decade after the Molesworth Report, the *Times*, at least, paid much more attention to England's prisons. Between 1828 and 1837, the *Times* printed only six articles each year on England's various prisons. That number tripled during the decade that followed. To be sure, some of the increase in 1841 and 1842 stemmed from intense curiosity regarding arrangements at the new Model Prison just before it opened. Much more of it, though, owed to growing fears that England's prisons were inflicting dismal consequences upon the inmates they confined.

[93] See Mayhew and Binny, p. 103; p. 115. According to these writers the rate of "criminal lunacy" in all of England's prisons between 1842 and 1849 was only 5.8 prisoners in 10,000. Pentonville's insanity rate was 27 per 10,000.

[94] Mayhew and Binny, p. 115.

[95] Quoted in Field, v. 2, p. 266.

[96] Quoted in Field, v. 2, p. 266.

[97] Ignatieff, p. 11.

[98] Mayhew and Binny, p. 168.

[99] Ironically, both men died in prison. Russell took his own life while working at Millbank Penitentiary, likely because of enormous financial disappointments when his speculations in the railroads failed. Crawford died suddenly at Pentonville during a meeting of the commissioners. McConville gives somewhat fuller accounts of both deaths in *A History of English Prison Administration*. See pp. 216–217, fn. 166.

[100] See Mayhew and Binny, pp. 114–115.

[101] The hand-crank's manufacturer, J. G. Underhey, testified during the inquiry that the discrepancy between the crank's nominal and actual weights was caused by a flaw in its design, and that he had urged Austin to purchase a newer model. Perhaps relishing the idea of setting his prisoners more difficult labor than the records would suggest, Austin ignored the suggestion. See Joseph Allday's edited version of the Royal Commission's inquiry into Birmingham Gaol, called *"Truth is Stranger than Fiction": True Account of the Proceedings Leading to, and a Full and Authentic Report of, the Searching Inquiry, by Her Majesty's Commissioners, into the Horrible System of Discipline Practised at the Borough Gaol of Birmingham* (ed. Joseph Allday. Birmingham: J. Tonks, 1853). Future references to *Truth* appear parenthetically in the text.

[102] The "punishment jacket" employed at Birmingham Gaol was half straitjacket, half torture device. It was made of stiff canvas and mounted to the wall a few inches above the floor. In front, the collar was fitted with a harsher piece of material so as to rasp the prisoner at the throat and hinder his breathing in case he grew tired and allowed his head to fall forward toward his chest. Once in the jacket, the prisoner could attempt to keep his body rigid and head erect in order to take the pressure off his neck and shoulders, but no prisoner could hold that position for long. When he relaxed and his head rolled forward, he choked. The result of the jacket was most frequently severe cramping of the limbs, coupled sometimes with unconsciousness from respiratory obstruction.

[103] The *Times* carried excerpts of the report on September 8, 1853 (7f) and

September 12, 1853 (9f).

[104] W. Bayne Ranken, "The Origin and Progress of the Discharged Prisoners' Aid Society," *Transactions of the National Association for the Promotion of Social Science* (ed. G.W. Hastings. London: John W. Parker and Son, 1859), p. 369; Mary Carpenter, *Our Convicts* (2 vols. Montclair: Patterson Smith: 1969), v. 1, p. 11.

[105] Matthew Davenport Hill, *Suggestions for the Repression of Crime, Contained in Charges Delivered to the Grand Juries of Birmingham* (London: John W. Parker and Son, 1857), p. 15.

[106] Consider for instance Bulwer-Lytton's *Pelham* (1828), *Paul Clifford* (1830), and *Eugene Aram* (1832); Ainsworth's *Jack Sheppard* (1839); and Dickens's *Oliver Twist* (1839) and *Barnaby Rudge* (1841).

[107] Dickens, quoted in Hughes, p. 584.

[108] Jaffe, p. 7; p. 6.

NOTES TO CHAPTER 2

[1] Edgar Johnson, *Charles Dickens: His Tragedy and Triumph* (2 vols. New York: Simon and Schuster, 1952), v. 1, p. 17.

[2] Peter Brooks, *Reading for the Plot* (Cambridge; London: Harvard Univ. Press, 1984), p. 155.

[3] Natalie McKnight, *Idiots, Madmen, and Other Prisoners in Dickens* (New York: St. Martin's, 1993), p. 6.

[4] E. Johnson, v. 1, p. 88. For more thorough accounts of Dickens's career as a journalist, see E. Johnson, pp. 47–104; and Kathryn Chittick, *Dickens and the 1830s* (Cambridge: Cambridge Univ. Press, 1990), ch. 1.

[5] Scholars working to recover Dickens's journalism from these early days have met with limited success, for his contributions to the newspapers were generally unsigned. The editors of Dickens's *Collected Papers* (2 vols. eds. Arthur Waugh, Hugh Walpole, Walter Dexter, and Thomas Hatton. Bloomsbury: Nonesuch, 1937) were able to identify only one example of his early reporting—his now-famous account of Lord Grey's reception at Edinburgh which appeared in the *Morning Chronicle* and was "probably the first newspaper report by Dickens that was ever printed," v. 1, p. 3.

[6] This according to a letter from Dickens to Ainsworth on June 21, 1837 in *The Letters of Charles Dickens* (12 vols. eds. Madeline House, Graham Storey, and Kathleen Tillotson. Oxford: Clarendon Press, 1974–2002), v. 1, p. 275. Future references to Dickens's letters are to this edition and appear parenthetically by volume and page number in the text. I am also indebted to Philip Collins's *Dickens and Crime* (3rd ed. New York: St Martin's, 1994), especially pp. 52–67, for its account of Dickens's visits to and familiarity with London's prisons. One can also see in Dickens's letters from the mid-1830s other references to appointments he made and letters of introduction for his planned visits. See for instance in *Letters*, v. 1, his letters to: John Macrone, 10/27/35, p. 83; Macrone, 10/29/35, p. 84; Catherine Hogarth, 11/5/35, p. 88; George Cruikshank, 12/8/35, p. 102; and Macrone, 12/9/35, p. 103.

[7] John Forster, *The Life of Charles Dickens* (2 vols. London: Chapman and Hall; New York: Oxford Univ. Press, n. d.), v. 1, p. 166; v. 1, p. 106.

[8] Collins, *Dickens and Crime*, p. 167.

[9] See for example Forster, v. 1, pp. 19–33; E. Johnson, v. 1, pp. 27–46; Peter Ackroyd, *Dickens* (New York: Harper Collins, 1990), pp. 56–105; and Michael Allen, *Charles Dickens's Childhood* (Basingstoke; Hampshire: Macmillan, 1988). I have fashioned this brief sketch from these longer accounts. Of all these biographies, Allen's—because of its focus upon Dickens's youth—details most thoroughly the time before, during, and just after John Dickens's incarceration.

[10] For a detailed discussion of the dates and circumstances surrounding John Dickens's imprisonment and release, see Allen, pp. 79–95.

[11] Dickens, quoted in Forster, v. 1, p. 25.

[12] E. Johnson, v. 1, p. 42.

[13] Dickens, quoted in Allen, p. 91.

[14] E. Johnson, v. 1, p. 35.

[15] Allen argues persuasively—in contrast with earlier biographers—that Dickens's time at Warren's lasted only from just before his twelfth birthday until March or April of 1825. See pp. 101–103.

[16] Dickens, quoted in Forster, v. 1, p. 10.

[17] Forster, v. 1, p. 34. See Johnson, v. 1, p. 48, for an account of Dickens's return to school.

[18] McKnight, p. 10.

[19] Forster, v. 1, p. 70.

[20] For fuller discussions of the linguistic aspect of Dickens's comedy in this novel, see Garrett Stewart, *Dickens and the Trials of Imagination* (Cambridge: Harvard Univ. Press, 1974); Robert L. Patten, "'I Thought of Mr. Pickwick and Wrote the First Number': Dickens and the Evolution of Character," *Dickens Quarterly* 3 (1986): 18–25; and Steven Marcus, "Language into Structure: Pickwick Revisited," *Daedalus* 101.1 (1972): 183–202.

[21] Many critics, including this one, consider Pickwick's journey from innocence to awareness the fundamental theme of the novel. See for instance Stewart; Eliot Engel, "The Maturing of a Comic Artist: Dickens' Leap from *Sketches by Boz* to *Pickwick Papers*," *Victorians Institute Journal* 9 (1980): 39–47; and Anny Sadrin, "Fragmentation in *The Pickwick Papers*," *Dickens Studies Annual* 22 (1993): 21–34.

[22] Collins makes very little of *Pickwick Papers* and the Fleet, mentioning only a handful of times a particular episode or character from the novel. While his silence is understandable considering his focus on crime and criminal prisons, it is worth noting that he dwells much longer upon William Dorrit's confinement in the Marshalsea—and upon *Little Dorrit* as a whole—than upon *Pickwick Papers*. It seems almost as if the latter novel merits less attention either because it is part of Dickens's immature artistic conception of the prison or because it is not, like the Marshalsea, part of Dickens's own experience of the cell.

[23] Angus Easson, "Imprisonment for Debt in *Pickwick Papers*," *Dickensian* 64 (1968): 105–112. In *Dickens, from Pickwick to Dombey* (New York: Basic Books,

1965), Steven Marcus argues that the novel is completely situated in the present tense—an argument that echoes, in certain ways, Easson's contention that *Pickwick's* portrayal of the Fleet is mostly concerned with the contemporary conditions in the prison.

[24] Charles Dickens, *Pickwick Papers* (ed. James Kinsley. Oxford: Clarendon Press, 1986), p. 632. Further references to the novel are to this edition and appear parenthetically in the text.

[25] Throughout the eighteenth century, Parliament passed a number of successive though erratically timed Insolvency Acts meant to alleviate debtors' prisons from the burden of confining those with no hope of paying. By an act of 1813, however, the Insolvency Court became a permanent feature of debtor law, allowing all prisoners of three months or more standing to apply to the court for their discharge. Aside from his desire to achieve a realistic portrayal of the life of the imprisoned debtor, Dickens seems to have no reason for introducing George or his suit into the account of the Fleet. For fuller accounts of the Insolvency Court and the various acts that preceded it, see Brown, especially pp. 144–148; or Rock, pp. 310–315.

[26] Marcus, "Language into Structure," p. 184.

[27] Sadrin, p. 24.

[28] Stan S. Rubin, "Spectator and Spectacle: Narrative Evasion and Narrative Voice in *Pickwick Papers*," *Journal of Narrative Technique* 6 (1976), p. 195.

[29] Stewart, p. 35.

[30] The editors of Volume 3 of Dickens's *Letters* suggest that Dickens had read Martineau's *Society in America* (1837) and *Retrospect of Western Travel* (1838), as well as Marryat's *A Diary in America* (1839) and Buckingham's *America . . . the Northern and Free States* (1841) to prepare himself for his visit to America, and that he later referred admiringly to Trollope's *Domestic Manners of the Americans* (1832), though only after his return to England.

[31] Sidney P. Moss, *Charles Dickens' Quarrel with America* (Troy: Whitston, 1984), p. 81.

[32] For discussions of these issues and how they tainted Dickens's visit to the United States, see Moss; Jerome Meckier, "Dickens Discovers America, Dickens Discovers Dickens: The First Visit Reconsidered," *Modern Language Review* 79 (1984): 266–277; Myron Magnet, *Dickens and the Social Order* (Philadelphia: Univ. of Pennsylvania Press, 1985), especially pp. 175–182; and David Parker, "Dickens and America: The Unflattering Glass," *Dickens Studies Annual* 15 (1986): 55–63.

[33] William Sharpe, "A Pig Upon the Town: Charles Dickens in New York," *Nineteenth-Century Prose* 23.2 (1996): 12–24; E. Johnson, v. 1, p. 443.

[34] In the edition of *American Notes* used for this study, over seventeen pages are devoted to accounts of the prisons in Boston, New York, and Philadelphia (the longest by far). Conversely, the entire chapter on slavery occupies only fourteen pages, and much of this material is merely quoted and reproduced wholesale from newspaper advertisements for runaway slaves and accounts of brutality in Southern and frontier states. Despite Dickens's animosity toward the American press, the "Concluding Remarks" chapter containing his condemnation of "this frightful engine in America" runs only nine total

pages, not all of which are devoted solely to the press. See Charles Dickens, *American Notes* (London: Oxford Univ. Press, 1957), p. 248. Future references to *American Notes* are to this edition and appear parenthetically in the text.

[35] Collins, *Dickens and Crime*, p. 13.

[36] Collins, *Dickens and Crime*, p. 123.

[37] Dickens, quoted in Forster, v. 1, p. 264.

[38] Patrick J. McCarthy, "Claiming Truth: Dickens and *American Notes*," *Nineteenth-Century Prose* 23.2 (1996), p. 3.

[39] Charles Dickens, "A Visit to Newgate," *Sketches by Boz* (London: Oxford Univ. Press, 1957), p. 202.

[40] The editors of Dickens's *Letters* suggest in a footnote that Dickens refers here to his sitting that morning for artist Francis Alexander, where he was forced to meet several of Alexander's friends and was watched by crowds as he walked to and from the studio. See v. 3, p. 20.

[41] Jerome Meckier, *Innocent Abroad, Charles Dickens's American Engagements* (Lexington: Univ. of Kentucky Press, 1990), p. 6.

[42] Meckier, "Dickens Discovers America," p. 268. See also Meckier, *Innocent Abroad*, p. 6.

[43] The use of such hoods at the Eastern Penitentiary was not discontinued until 1904. For a complete consideration of the origins and disciplinary regimen of the Eastern Penitentiary, see Negley K. Teeters and John D. Shearer, *The Prison at Philadelphia, Cherry Hill* (New York: Columbia Univ. Press, 1957).

[44] In *American Notes* Dickens expands upon the phrase, saying of the prisoner: "He is a man buried alive; to be dug out in the slow round of years; and in the meantime dead to everything but torturing anxieties and horrible despair" (*AN* 101). This phrase also provides the basis for the memorable message of the opening chapter of *A Tale of Two Cities*, "Recalled to Life."

[45] D. A. Miller, p. 25.

[46] Teeters and Shearer, p. 115.

[47] Teeters and Shearer, p. 130; p. 122.

[48] Collins, *Dickens and Crime*, p. 129.

[49] Collins, *Dickens and Crime*, p. 51.

[50] In *Idiots, Madmen, and Other Prisoners*, McKnight argues—incorrectly—that all of Dickens's prison accounts use sunbeams and other shafts of light to represent the hope that the prisoner is "not completely isolated, that some escape is possible." In *American Notes*, and in *Little Dorrit* as I shall later show, this is not at all the case. See McKnight, p. 113.

[51] Dickens, quoted in Collins, *Dickens and Crime*, pp. 147–148.

[52] Magnet, p. 176.

[53] Foucault, p. 277.

NOTES TO CHAPTER 3

[1] See Walter Clarke Phillips, *Dickens, Reade and Collins: Sensation Novelists* (New York: Columbia Univ. Press, 1919).

² George Orwell, "Charles Reade," *The Collected Essays, Journalism, and Letters of George Orwell* (4 vols. eds. Sonia Orwell and Ian Angus. New York: Harcourt, Brace, and World, 1968), v. 2, p. 34.

³ Reade, quoted in Charles L. Reade and the Reverend Compton Reade, *Charles Reade, D. C. L., Dramatist, Novelist, Journalist: A Memoir Compiled Chiefly from His Literary Remains* (New York: Harper, 1887), pp. 198–199. Future references to this text appear as *Memoir* in the notes.

⁴ Charles Reade, *Hard Cash* (London: Chatto and Windus, 1927), p. i.

⁵ E. G. Sutcliffe, "Charles Reade's Notebooks," *Studies in Philology* 27 (1930), p. 64. Sutcliffe and Wayne Burns ("More Charles Reade Notebooks," *Studies in Philology* 42 [1945]: 824–842) have studied between them all thirty-six of Reade's notebooks. Sutcliffe's research covers the thirty-two volumes that were donated to the London Library in 1916 by Reade's grand-nephew Herbert Reade. Burns writes about the other four, which are housed in the Morris Parrish Collection at Princeton University.

⁶ See *Memoir*, especially p. 195 and p. 243, for comparisons of Reade's popularity with Stowe's.

⁷ James Fitzjames Stephen, "The License of Modern Novelists," *Edinburgh Review* 106 (July 1857): 64–81.

⁸ Quoted in letters between Hill and Brougham, in Rosamond Davenport Hill and Florence Davenport Hill, *The Recorder of Birmingham: A Memoir of Matthew Davenport Hill, with Selections from His Correspondence* (London: Macmillan and Co., 1878), p. 332.

⁹ Clay, p. 262.

¹⁰ Sheila Smith, "Propaganda and Hard Facts in Charles Reade's Didactic Novels," *Renaissance and Modern Studies* 4 (1960): 135–149.

¹¹ Charles Reade, "Facts Must be Faced," *Readiana, Comments on Current Events* (London: Chatto and Windus, 1883), p. 323.

¹² Walter Frewen Lord, *The Mirror of the Century* (London: John Lane, 1906), p. 253.

¹³ For a complete account of Reade's early dramatic career, see Elton Smith, *Charles Reade* (Boston: Twayne, 1976), pp. 15–28.

¹⁴ Reade, quoted in Wayne Burns, *Charles Reade, a Study in Victorian Authorship* (New York: Bookman, 1961), p. 101.

¹⁵ *Memoir*, p. 195.

¹⁶ E. Smith, p. 32.

¹⁷ *Memoir*, p. 198.

¹⁸ Sutcliffe, "Notebooks," p. 82.

¹⁹ See especially pp. 256–276 of *It Is Never Too Late to Mend* (London: Chatto and Windus, 1925) for an illustration of the way Reade makes use of the Rules he obtained from Reading Gaol. Future references to the novel are to this edition and appear parenthetically in the text.

²⁰ Burns, *Charles Reade*, p. 158. The books in Reade's repertoire, according to Burns, included Field's *Field on Prison Discipline* (1848), Kingsmill's *Chapters on Prisons and Prisoners* (2nd ed., 1852), and Hepworth Dixon's *The London Prisons* (1850).

²¹ Field, v. 1, p. 146. For a full discussion of Reade and his mother's Evangelicalism, see Burns, *Charles Reade*, pp. 21–29.

²² Reade, quoted in Burns, *Charles Reade*, p. 155.

²³ Charles Reade, *The Autobiography of a Thief, and Other Stories* (London: Chatto and Windus, 1924), p. 19. Future references to *Autobiography* are to this edition and appear parenthetically in the text.

²⁴ M. D. Hill, *Suggestions*, p. 103.

²⁵ Mary Carpenter provides a full description of Crofton's system in *Reformatory Prison Discipline, as Developed by the Right Honorable Sir Walter Crofton in the Irish Convict Prisons* (London: Longman, Green, Reader and Dyer, 1872). During the 1850s, Crofton's system was so successful that English Director of Prisons Joshua Jebb faced constant pressure to abandon the existing ticket-of-leave system in favor of Crofton's, which incorporated closer surveillance over prisoners working outside the prison walls.

²⁶ See for instance Mary Carpenter's *Our Convicts* (Montclair: Patterson Smith, 1969); Frederic Hill's *Crime: Its Amount, Causes and Remedies* (London: Murray, 1853); and Charles Dickens's articles "Chips: Small Beginnings" (v. 1, pp. 239–240), "Boys to Mend" (v. 2, pp. 421–432), and "In and Out of Jail" (v. 2, pp. 477–488) in *Charles Dickens' Uncollected Writings from* Household Words, *1850–1859* (2 vols. ed. Harry Stone. Bloomington; London: Indiana Univ. Press, 1968).

²⁷ Reade draws this scene at greater length and with deeper melodramatic shades, but pp. 99–100 of the novel echo faithfully the account Dodson gave during the Birmingham inquiry. See *Truth*, p. 16.

²⁸ Maconochie's testimony during the Birmingham inquiry showed that the magistrates dismissed him, ostensibly, for mismanaging the prison's funds. Really the "mismanagement" was an authorized but misrecorded advance of his salary. Dissatisfied with Maconochie's humane treatment of the convicts, the magistrates used the incident to justify firing him. The novel's "O'Connor"—who has "written very intelligent books on crime and punishment, which are supposed to have done their share in opening the nation's eyes to the necessity of regenerating its prisons"—is dismissed for the same reasons (*NTL* 88). For an account of Maconochie's career at Birmingham Gaol, see Barry, *Alexander Maconochie*, pp. 196–206. *Truth*, meanwhile, includes much of the testimony regarding Maconochie's dismissal. See pp. 139–143.

²⁹ Charles Reade, "A Terrible Temptation," *Readiana*, p. 287.

³⁰ Reade, quoted in Burns, *Charles Reade*, p. 155.

³¹ Phillips, p. 207.

³² E. G. Sutcliffe, "Psychological Presentation in Reade's Novels," *Studies in Philology* 38 (1941), p. 521.

³³ Sutcliffe, "Psychological Presentation," p. 530.

NOTES TO CHAPTER 4

¹ Charles Dickens, "Pet Prisoners," *Miscellaneous Papers* (London: Chapman and Hall; New York: Charles Scribner's Sons, 1914), p. 222. The essay first

appeared in *Household Words* on April 27, 1850, just as Dickens was working on the early chapters of *David Copperfield*.

2 Dickens, "In and Out of Jail," v. 2, p. 488.

3 Dickens, "In and Out of Jail," v. 2, p. 488.

4 Charles Dickens, "The Ruffian," *The Uncommercial Traveller and Reprinted Pieces, Etc.* (London: Oxford Univ. Press, 1958), p. 302.

5 In his letter to Forster, Dickens referred to the much publicized case of Thomas Smedley. See *The Letters of Charles Dickens* (3 vols., ed. Walter Dexter. Bloomsbury: Nonesuch, 1938), v. 3, p. 118.

6 See Charles Dickens, "Capital Punishment," *Miscellaneous Papers*, p. 41.

7 Dickens, "The Ruffian," p. 303.

8 Collins, *Dickens and Crime*, p. 17.

9 Ackroyd, p. 72; E. Johnson, v. 2, p. 884.

10 Dickens, quoted in Ackroyd, p. 860.

11 Dickens, quoted in Ackroyd, p. 860.

12 Brian Rosenberg, Little Dorrit's *Shadows: Character and Contradiction in Dickens* (Columbia; London: Univ. of Missouri Press, 1996), p. 47.

13 Philip Collins argues in *"Little Dorrit: The Prison and the Critics"* (*London Times Literary Supplement* [April 18, 1980]: 445–446) that Hepworth Dixon's review was only a lucky hit, and that no other critic paid attention to *Little Dorrit's* prisons until Edmund Wilson wrote *The Wound and the Bow* (1941). This is not entirely true. In his *Life of Charles Dickens* (London: Walter Scott; New York: Charles Scribner's Sons, 1887), Frank Marzials discusses the prison taint that falls upon the Marshalsea's prisoners, and T. A. Jackson wrote in *Charles Dickens: The Progress of a Radical* (London: Lawrence and Wishart, 1937)—a work that Wilson credits—of the symbolic parallels between *Little Dorrit's* prisons and its indictment of vapid, hypocritical society. Wilson's analysis *is* a landmark, though more because it explores the psychological consequences of confinement than because it calls attention to *Little Dorrit's* prisons. See Marzials, p. 130; and Jackson, pp. 165–170.

14 J. Hillis Miller, *Charles Dickens: The World of His Novels* (Cambridge: Harvard Univ. Press, 1958), p. 229. See also Edmund Wilson, *The Wound and the Bow* (Boston: Houghton Mifflin, 1941), pp. 51-57. Of the critical studies on *Little Dorrit*, Miller's is perhaps the most thorough, for it discusses not only the psychological implications of confinement but also Dickens's use of different forms of imprisonment and reliance upon images of light and shadow. Miller does not take up, however, the relationship between the prison and the novel's narrative form. See Miller, pp. 227–247.

15 Lionel Trilling, *The Opposing Self* (New York: Viking Press, 1955), p. 51.

16 See for example Trey Philpotts, "The Real Marshalsea," *Dickensian* 87 (1991): 133–145; and McKnight's discussion of *Little Dorrit* in *Idiots, Madmen, and Other Prisoners in Dickens*.

17 Charles Dickens, *Little Dorrit* (ed. Harvey Peter Sucksmith. Oxford: Clarendon, 1979), p. 1. Future references to the novel are to this edition and appear parenthetically in the text.

18 Tambling argues in *Dickens, Violence and the Modern State* that *Little Dorrit*, in its rendering of this joyless London Sabbath and Mrs. Clennam, is

Dickens's fiercest attack on religious asceticism—a form of Christianity that he found imprisoning. See Tambling, p. 119.

[19] Dickens's notes for a later chapter of the novel indicate that he deliberately drew Mrs. Clennam in a state of *"Parallel imprisonment"* with the Father of the Marshalsea. For the notes, see *Little Dorrit*, p. 808. In 1966, Paul D. Herring published an edition of Dickens's notes for the novel. See "Dickens' Monthly Number Plans for *Little Dorrit*," *Modern Philology* 64 (1966): 22–63.

[20] Philpotts, p. 133. Indeed, Philpotts suggests that the only possible—not certain—discrepancy he could discover between Dickens's account and the real architectural plan for the Marshalsea is in the location of the chandler's shop. See Philpotts, p. 143.

[21] The Marshalsea closed in 1849, which could explain why that same year Dickens suddenly took an interest in producing autobiography and autobiographical fiction. The prison's closing may have awakened old wounds he wished to salve with his writing.

[22] Philpotts, p. 138.

[23] McKnight, p. 111. Tambling disagrees with McKnight on this same point. See Tambling, p. 100.

[24] Rosenberg, p. 24.

[25] Edwin Pugh, quoted in *Dickens:* Dombey and Son *and* Little Dorrit, *a Casebook* (ed. Alan Shelston. London: Macmillan, 1985), p. 132.

[26] Trilling, p. 55.

[27] William G. Wall, "Mrs. Affery Flintwinch's Dreams: Reading and Remembering in *Little Dorrit*," *Dickens Quarterly* 4 (1993), p. 205.

[28] In her article *"Little Dorrit*: Necessary Fictions" (*Studies in the Novel* 7 [1975]: 195–214), Janice Carlisle suggests that Amy's participation in the family's fictions is so complete that, in the novel's first half, she is not the positive character that she seems by the end of the book. See especially pp. 199–200.

[29] Sylvia Manning, "Social Criticism and Textual Subversion in *Little Dorrit*," *Dickens Studies Annual* 20 (1991), p. 146.

[30] Steven Marcus has discussed the images of separate confinement that recur throughout *David Copperfield*. See Marcus, "Dickens and the Representation of Punishment," *Perspectives on Punishment, an Interdisciplinary Exploration* (ed. Richard Mowery Andrews. New York: Peter Lang, 1997): 87–111.

[31] Amy's longing for the Marshalsea is another example of what Philip Collins calls Dickens's awareness "that prisoners too had mixed feelings about their 'home'." As Collins argues regarding the Eastern Penitentiary, though, Dickens would not have viewed this longing "as a vindication of the prison's regime." Rather, here as in the cases of William Dorrit, Alexandre Manette, and Wilkins Micawber, this longing indicates the permanent scars left by the prison's terrible psychological operation, unfitting its inmates for life beyond the walls of the cell. See Collins, *Dickens and Crime*, p. 51.

[32] Collins, *Dickens and Crime*, p. 138.

[33] For a summary of critical perspectives on Miss Wade and a discussion of Miss Wade's sexual implications, see Anna Wilson, "On History, Case History,

and Deviance: Miss Wade's Symptoms and Their Interpretation," *Dickens Studies Annual* 26 (1998): 187–201. See also Edward Heatley, "The Redeemed Feminine of *Little Dorrit*," *Dickens Studies Annual* 4 (1975): 153–164; and Dianne F. Sadoff, "Storytelling and the Figure of the Father in *Little Dorrit*," *Charles Dickens: New Perspectives* (ed. Wendell Stacy Johnson. Englewood Cliffs: Prentice Hall, 1982): 121-141.

34 Manning, p. 130.

35 Carlisle, *"Little Dorrit,"* p. 211.

36 Dickens identified these sources in a letter to John Forster in August of 1859. See *Letters* (Nonesuch, 1938), v. 3, p. 117. Several studies have taken pains to examine Dickens's use of Carlyle's *The French Revolution* (1837), to which Dickens paid homage in the "Preface" to the novel. For analyses of Dickens's use of Carlyle's work, see Murray Baumgarten, "Writing the Revolution," *Dickens Studies Annual* 12 (1983): 161-176; Michael Timko, "Splendid Impressions and Picturesque Means: Dickens, Carlyle, and *The French Revolution*," *Dickens Studies Annual* 12 (1983): 177–195; and Michael Goldberg, *Carlyle and Dickens* (Athens: University of Georgia Press, 1972), chapter 7.

37 E. Johnson, v. 2, pp. 947–948.

38 Charles Dickens, "Preface," *A Tale of Two Cities* (ed. Andrew Sanders. Oxford: Oxford Univ. Press, 1988). Future references to the novel are to this edition and appear parenthetically in the text.

39 Phillips, p. 186. For discussions of Wilkie Collins and *A Tale of Two Cities*, see also Philip Collins, "A Tale of Two Novels: *A Tale of Two Cities* and *Great Expectations* in Dickens' Career," *Dickens Studies Annual* 2 (1972): 336–351; and H. J. W. Milley, "Wilkie Collins and *A Tale of Two Cities*," *Modern Language Review* 34 (1939): 525–534.

40 Dickens, from a letter to Forster, August 25, 1859, *Letters* (Nonesuch, 1938), v. 3, p. 118.

41 Dickens, from a letter to Forster, August 25, 1859, *Letters* (Nonesuch, 1938), v. 3, p. 118.

42 Other books published during the fertile year of 1859 include John Stuart Mill's *On Liberty* and Stuart Smiles's *Self-Help*. For a discussion of the contemporary reception of *A Tale of Two Cities*, see Collins, "A Tale of Two Novels," p. 336.

43 Harry De Puy, "American Prisons and *A Tale of Two Cities*," *Cahiers Victoriens et Édouardiens: Revue de Centre d'Etudes et de Recherches Victoriennes et Edouardiennes de l'Université Paul Valéry* (April 25, 1987): 39–48.

44 Catherine Gallagher, "The Duplicity of Doubling in *A Tale of Two Cities*," *Dickens Studies Annual* 12 (1983), p. 126.

45 Andrew Sanders points out in his "Notes" to *A Tale of Two Cities* that Dickens likely took the details of the youth's punishment from the 1766 case of Chevalier de la Barre, of whom he probably read in Voltaire. See the novel, pp. 476–477.

46 Again, Dickens likely modeled this punishment after a real case, in this instance the punishment against Robert Francois Damiens, who was executed in this manner in 1757 after he—as Dickens points out—"made an

attempt on the life of the late King, Louis Fifteen" (*TTC* 205). Readers of Foucault will recognize the case of Damiens from the opening chapter of *Discipline and Punish*, which uses it to illustrate the *ancien régime*'s inscription of penal power upon the body. See Foucault, pp. 3–6.

⁴⁷ Dickens, from a letter to Forster, August 25, 1859, *Letters* (Nonesuch, 1938), v. 3, p. 117.

⁴⁸ It is perhaps not chance that the period of Manette's confinement— almost eighteen years—marks as well the interval between *American Notes* and *A Tale of Two Cities*, as if Dickens figures Manette's imprisonment according to the length of time he has been confined in Dickens's memory and imagination.

⁴⁹ Dickens wrote of no ghosts in *American Notes*, but he did so in letters to Forster, where Dickens worried that dreadful apparitions nightly visited the solitary prisoners of Pittsburgh's Western Penitentiary. See *Letters* (Clarendon, 1974), v. 3, p. 181.

⁵⁰ Dickens had this fear while touring the Eastern Penitentiary. As he wrote in *American Notes*, one cell held a "villainous, low-browed, thin-lipped" inmate "who, but for the additional penalty, would have gladly stabbed me with his shoemaker's knife" (*AN* 103).

⁵¹ Chris R. Vanden Bossche, "Prophetic Closure and Disclosing Narrative: *The French Revolution* and *A Tale of Two Cities*," *Dickens Studies Annual* 12 (1983), p. 214.

⁵² Gallagher, p. 128.

⁵³ Carol Hanbery MacKay, "The Rhetoric of Soliloquy in *The French Revolution* and *A Tale of Two Cities*," *Dickens Studies Annual* 12 (1983), p. 197.

⁵⁴ Baumgarten, p. 161.

⁵⁵ Gallagher, p. 132; Vanden Bossche, p. 209.

⁵⁶ Vanden Bossche, p. 211.

⁵⁷ Beth Kemper, "The 'Night Shadows' Passage in *A Tale of Two Cities*: Narrative Anxiety and Conscious Fiction-Building," *Kentucky Philological Review* 10 (1995), p. 25.

⁵⁸ Charles Dickens, *Dombey and Son* (ed. Alan Horsman. Oxford: Clarendon, 1974), p. 620.

NOTES TO CHAPTER 5

¹ Clarke's novel has also gone by the longer title *For the Term of His Natural Life*. Clarke originally named the serial version *His Natural Life* in 1870 and also used this short title for the first book edition in 1874, published by George Robertson in Melbourne. The following year, Richard Bentley published the first English edition under the same name. But when Bentley reissued the novel in 1884 and 1885, he offered it under the longer title, though on whose authority (other than his own) remains a mystery. The novel is now known by the shorter and longer titles, and it may be that the longer title has become the more common of the two. In this study I use the title *His Natural Life*, since it is the only name under which the unabridged serial novel—the subject of this study—has appeared.

² Marcus Clarke, "Preface," *For the Term of His Natural Life* (Victoria: Lloyd O' Neil, 1970), p. 19. In the article "Charles Reade, Wilkie Collins, and Marcus Clarke" (*Australian Literary Studies* 11 [1984]: 400–404), P. D. Edwards makes the point that Clarke based his documentary style in *His Natural Life* upon Reade's in *It Is Never Too Late to Mend*. See Edwards, p. 401.

³ Clarke, quoted in Brian Elliott, *Marcus Clarke* (Oxford: Clarendon Press, 1958), p. 153.

⁴ Henry Gyles Turner and Alexander Sutherland, *The Development of Australian Literature* (London; New York: Longmans, Green, and Co., 1898), p. 331. According to Michael Wilding (*Marcus Clarke* [Melbourne; London; New York: Oxford Univ. Press, 1977), Massina claimed that the *Australian Journal*'s readership dwindled from 12,000 to 4000 during the twenty-eight-month run of *His Natural Life*. Whether the decline was all Clarke's fault is a matter of conjecture. See Wilding, p. 17.

⁵ The *Athenaeum* and the *Saturday Review* criticized Clarke's graphic accounts of the atrocities committed under penal discipline in Australia. On the whole, however, English critics admired the novel's force and epic scope. For a complete discussion of the critical reaction to the novel's first English edition, see L. T. Hergenhan, "The Contemporary Reception of *His Natural Life*," *Southerly* 31 (1971): 50–63.

⁶ After the revised edition of *His Natural Life* became popular, the *Australian Journal* reserialized the novel in 1886. Later, in 1929 and 1939, the serial was collected into book editions that claimed to be unabridged but condensed or omitted the serial's lengthy Melvillian chapter on hurricanes. For an account of *His Natural Life*'s complex publishing and textual history, see Stephen Murray-Smith's "Introduction" to *His Natural Life* (ed. Stephen Murray-Smith. London; New York; Victoria: Penguin, 1970), especially pp. 12–14. Future references to the novel are to this edition and appear parenthetically in the text.

⁷ All three studies are mostly concerned with the sources of Clarke's accounts of brutality in the transportation system. See L. L. Robson, "The Historical Basis of *For the Term of His Natural Life*," *Australian Literary Studies* 1 (1963): 104–121; Decie Denholm, "The Sources of *His Natural Life*," *Australian Literary Studies* 4 (1969): 174–178; and Harold J. Boehm, "*His Natural Life* and Its Sources," *Australian Literary Studies* 5 (1971): 42–64. Of these articles, Robson's is the most comprehensive, since it covers a wide array of sources that Clarke almost certainly used in writing his novel. Denholm focuses upon sources Clarke discovered during his trip to Tasmania in 1870. Boehm's essay discusses the bases for specific characters in the novel.

⁸ Michael Wilding, "Marcus Clarke: His Natural Life," *The Australian Experience* (ed. W. S. Ramson. Canberra: Australian National Univ. Press, 1974), p. 21. L. T. Hergenhan also makes this argument in *Unnatural Lives: Studies in Australian Fiction about the Convicts, from James Tucker to Patrick White* (St. Lucia; London; New York: Univ. of Queensland Press, 1983), p. 54.

⁹ J. F. Burrows, "*His Natural Life* and the Capacities of Melodrama," *Southerly* 34 (1974), p. 300.

¹⁰ See Burrows on Clarke's use of melodrama in the novel.

[11] See Marcus Clarke, "The Seizure of the 'Cyprus'," *Old Tales of a Young Country* (Sydney: Sydney Univ. Press, 1972), pp. 133–140.

[12] In "Marcus Clarke," Wilding observes that many contemporary readers complained that Clarke had exaggerated, and he includes the following notice, excerpted from the *Australian Journal* in June 1872 near the end of *His Natural Life*'s serial run:

> Mr. Clarke has prepared an appendix, which will be published when *His Natural Life* is issued in a volume from the press. This appendix will give incontestable authorities for all statements made in the work concerning convict discipline.

See Wilding, p. 21.

[13] Pierce, quoted in Robson, p. 111.

[14] Marcus Clarke, "Port Arthur," *Marcus Clarke: For the Term of His Natural Life, Short Stories, Critical Essays and Journalism* (ed. Michael Wilding. St. Lucia; London; New York: Univ. of Queensland Press, 1976), p. 521.

[15] Marcus Clarke, "A Melbourne Alsatia," *A Colonial City, High and Low Life, Selected Journalism of Marcus Clarke* (ed. L. T. Hergenhan. St. Lucia: Univ. of Queensland Press, 1972), p. 130.

[16] Clarke, "Port Arthur," p. 524.

[17] As in modern prisons, Australia's penal settlements contained countless instances of consensual and non-consensual homosexual encounters. Hughes writes in *The Fatal Shore* that "homosexuality . . . flourished . . . especially on the chain gangs and in the outer penal settlements," and that Norfolk Island in particular was reputed to be a "citadel of sodomy." See Hughes, p. 264; p. 271.

[18] Hergenhan, *Unnatural Lives*, p. 49.

[19] Hughes, p. 231; p. 591.

[20] L. T. Hergenhan, "The Corruption of Rufus Dawes," *Southerly* 29 (1969), p. 218.

[21] Wilding, *Marcus Clarke*, p. 29.

[22] Wilding, "Marcus Clarke," p. 32.

[23] Clarke probably took his idea for Rex's masquerade from the contemporary case of Arthur Orton—the "Tichborne claimant"—who attempted a similar fraud during the early 1870s. For a more thorough discussion of the Orton case, see Boehm, "Sources," p. 52.

[24] Arthur Patchett Martin, *The Beginnings of an Australian Literature* (London: Henry Sotheran and Co., 1898), p. 19.

[25] In fact, Thomas Rogers lived to be ninety-nine years old. For a comparison of the real-life Rogers with Clarke's fictional James North, see Boehm, "Sources," especially pp. 45–50. Barry's *The Life and Death of John Price* also provides information about Rogers, and in *The Fatal Shore* Hughes discusses Rogers's involvement in the administration of John Price. See especially Hughes, pp. 535–548.

[26] Martin, p. 20.

NOTES TO CHAPTER 6

¹ For a good brief discussion of autobiographical production during the middle of the nineteenth century, see Janice Carlisle, "The Face in the Mirror: *Villette* and the Conventions of Autobiography," *The Brontës: Modern Critical Views* (ed. Harold Bloom. New York: Chelsea House, 1987), especially pp. 131–134.

² Brooks, pp. 275–276.

³ Charles Darwin, *The Autobiography of Charles Darwin 1809–1882* (ed. Nora Barlow. New York; London: W. W. Norton, 1976), p. 21.

⁴ John Stuart Mill, *Autobiography* (ed. Jack Stillinger. Boston: Houghton Mifflin, 1969), p. 3.

⁵ John Henry Newman, *Apologia Pro Vita Sua* (ed. Ian Ker. London; New York: Penguin, 1994), p. 17.

⁶ Darwin, for example, describes an occasion on which he "beat a puppy . . . simply from enjoying the sense of power," and he suggests that his guilt regarding his cruelty explains the fact that his "love of dogs . . . [became] for a long time afterwards, a passion." Trollope, as a way of characterizing the early poverty that determined him to work hard to earn a respectable living, writes of an occasion on which his schoolmaster stopped him in the street to ask him "whether it was possible that Harrow School was disgraced by so disreputably dirty a little boy." Neither event is particularly important except insofar as it seems to constitute a formative moment for private identity. See Darwin, p. 27; and Anthony Trollope, *An Autobiography* (eds. Michael Sadleir and Frederick Page. Oxford: Oxford Univ. Press, 1950), p. 4.

⁷ Newman, p. 3.

⁸ Charles Dickens, *David Copperfield* (ed. Nina Burgis. Oxford: Clarendon, 1981), p. 1.

⁹ Kate Millett, *Sexual Politics* (Garden City: Doubleday, 1969), p. 146.

¹⁰ Tom Winnifreth, *The Brontës* (New York: Macmillan, 1977), p. 137.

¹¹ Sandra Gilbert and Susan Gubar, *The Madwoman in the Attic: The Woman Writer and the Nineteenth-Century Literary Imagination* (New Haven; London: Yale Univ. Press, 1979), p. 401. This fear of being "buried alive" is also familiar from Dickens's writing on the Eastern Penitentiary in *American Notes* and the opening chapters of *A Tale of Two Cities*.

¹² Kate Lawson, "Reading Desire: *Villette* as 'Heretic Narrative'," *English Studies in Canada* 17 (1991), p. 53; Christina Crosby, *The Ends of History: Victorians and "The Woman Question"* (New York; London: Routledge, 1991), p. 126.

¹³ See Sally Shuttleworth, "'The Surveillance of a Sleepless Eye': The Constitution of Neurosis in *Villette*," *One Culture: Essays in Science and Literature* (ed. George Levine. Madison: Univ. of Wisconsin Press, 1987), especially pp. 314–317; and Patricia Johnson, "'This Heretic Narrative': The Strategy of the Split Narrative in Charlotte Brontë's *Villette*," *Studies in English Literature* 30 (1990), especially p. 625.

¹⁴ Mary Jacobus, "The Buried Letter: Feminism and Romanticism in *Villette*," *Women Writing and Writing About Women* (ed. Mary Jacobus. New York: Barnes

and Noble; London: Croom Helm, 1979), p. 43; Charlotte Brontë, *Villette* (eds. Herbert Rosengarten and Margaret Smith. Oxford: Clarendon, 1984), p. 228. Future references to the novel are to this edition and appear parenthetically in the text.

Despite widespread critical agreement about Lucy and the dimensions of her confinement, *Villette* has received an astonishing amount of scholarly attention during the last twenty-five years. For other readings of Lucy as a victim of desire, division, and neurosis, see Chiara Briganti, "Charlotte Brontë's *Villette*: The History of Desire," *West Virginia University Philological Papers* 35 (1989): 8–20; Borislav Knezevic, "The Impossible Things: Quest for Knowledge in Charlotte Brontë's *Villette*," *Literature and Psychology* 42 (1996): 65–99; and Athena Vrettos, "From Neurosis to Narrative: The Private Life of the Nerves in *Villette* and *Daniel Deronda*," *Victorian Studies* 33 (1990): 551–579. Other critics have extended this argument by addressing the relation between Lucy's desire and neurosis and her role as both possessor and object of the gaze. See Janet Freeman, "Looking on at Life: Objectivity and Intimacy in *Villette*," *Philological Quarterly* 67 (1988): 481–511; and Jill Matus, "Looking at Cleopatra: The Expression and Exhibition of Desire in *Villette*," *Victorian Literature and Culture* (eds. John Maynard and Adrienne Auslander Munich. New York: AMS, 1993): 345–367. For analyses of *Villette* based upon the techniques of Lucy's elusive self-narration, see Karen Chase, *Eros and Psyche: The Representation of Personality in Charlotte Brontë, Charles Dickens, and George Eliot* (London; New York: Methuen, 1984), especially pp. 66–91; LuAnn McCracken Fletcher, "Manufactured Marvels, Heretic Narratives, and the Process of Interpretation in *Villette*," *Studies in English Literature* 32 (1992): 723–746; and Nancy Sorkin Rabinowitz, "'Faithful Narrator' or 'Partial Eulogist': First-person Narration in Brontë's *Villette*," *Journal of Narrative Technique* 15 (1985): 244–255.

[15] Millett, p. 147.

[16] Briganti, p. 11.

[17] Gilbert and Gubar, p. 408; Shuttleworth, p. 319.

[18] Gilbert and Gubar, p. 437.

[19] Vrettos, p. 563.

[20] For discussions of Lucy's isolation and misery during this period, see Juliet Barker, *The Brontës* (New York: St. Martin's, 1994), pp. 412–435; and Winifred Gérin, *Charlotte Brontë, the Evolution of a Genius* (Oxford: Clarendon, 1967), pp. 216–255. See also Elizabeth Gaskell, *The Life of Charlotte Brontë* (ed. Alan Shelston. London; New York: Penguin, 1975), pp. 224–268. Future references to Gaskell's *Life* are to this edition and appear parenthetically in the text.

[21] Charlotte Brontë, from a letter to Emily Brontë, May 29, 1843, *The Letters of Charlotte Brontë* (2 vols. ed. Margaret Smith. Oxford: Clarendon, 1995–), v. 1, p. 320.

[22] Gilbert and Gubar, p. 400.

[23] Charlotte Brontë, from a letter to Ellen Nussey, (late?) June 1843, *Letters*, v. 1, p. 325.

[24] Charlotte Brontë, from a letter to Ellen Nussey, August 25, 1852, in *The Shakespeare Head Brontë: The Life and Letters* (4 vols. eds. Thomas James Wise,

M. A. Oxon, and John Alexander Symington. Oxford: Shakespeare Head, 1932), v. 4, p. 6.

25 Helene Moglen, *Charlotte Brontë, the Self Conceived* (New York: W. W. Norton, 1976), p. 190.

26 Mary Taylor, quoted in Clement Shorter, *The Brontës, Life and Letters* (2 vols. London: Hodder and Stoughton, 1908), v. 1, p. 118.

27 Charlotte Brontë, from two letters to Ellen Nussey, February 16, 1850 and October 23, 1850, *The Shakespeare Head Brontë*, v. 3, p. 77; v. 3, p. 173.

28 Charlotte Brontë, from a letter to Margaret Wooler, November/December 1846, *Letters*, v. 1, p. 505.

29 For discussions of Brontë's formal investigations into human psychology, see Vrettos, and Nicholas Dames, "The Clinical Novel: Phrenology and *Villette*," *Novel: A Forum on Fiction* 29 (1996): 367–390.

30 As Lucy remarks in the paragraphs leading up to her sudden recognition that Dr. John is Graham Bretton, "It was not perhaps my business to observe the mystery of his bearing, or search out its origin or aim; but, placed as I was, I could hardly help it. He laid himself open to my observation . . . " (*V* 135).

31 Freeman argues this point, too. See especially p. 486.

32 A famous anecdote from Gaskell's *Life* comes from Charlotte's father, Patrick Brontë, who recalled:

> When my children were very young, when, as far as I can remember, the oldest was about ten years of age, and the youngest about four, thinking that they knew more than I had yet discovered, in order to make them speak with less timidity, I deemed that if they were put under a sort of cover I might gain my end; and happening to have a mask in the house, I told them all to stand and speak boldly from under the cover of the mask. (*Life* 94)

It is impossible to know whether Charlotte had this event in mind as she composed her account of the fête. But the idea of speaking private truth from behind a mask resonates throughout the scene of Lucy's acting.

33 Briganti, p. 14.

34 Jacobus, p. 54.

35 P. Johnson, p. 622.

36 Rabinowitz, p. 248.

37 See Knezevic, p. 67.

38 Several readers wrote to Brontë's publishers requesting "exact and authentic information respecting the fate of M. Paul Emanuel." Brontë's letter to W. S. Williams in March 1853 may indicate the typical tenor of her response to such queries: "I have sent Lady Harriet an answer so worded as to leave the matter pretty much where it was. Since the little puzzle amuses the ladies, it would be a pity to spoil their sport by giving them the key." See *The Shakespeare Head Brontë*, v. 4, p. 54.

39 Gilbert and Gubar, p. 437. See also Crosby, pp. 138–142; Dames, p. 388; Fletcher, p. 741; Freeman, pp. 507–508; and Knezevic, pp. 93–95.

[40] T. S. Eliot, "Wilkie Collins and Dickens," *Selected Essays* (New York: Harcourt, Brace, 1950), p. 413; p. 416; Kenneth Robinson, *Wilkie Collins, a Biography* (New York: Macmillan, 1952), p. 191.

[41] Nuel Pharr Davis, *The Life of Wilkie Collins* (Urbana: Univ. of Illinois Press, 1956), p. 244. Davis says, though, that *Armadale*'s sluggish sales may not owe entirely to lack of interest in the novel. As he points out, England was in the midst of a severe financial slump at the time of the novel's publication, and it is also the case that Mudie was forced to purchase more copies than he first intended. In the United States, the novel was even popular enough to save *Harper's Weekly*, which had been considering halting publication because of the low sales that followed the Civil War. Besides Davis, see John Sutherland's "Note on the Text" in *Armadale* (ed. John Sutherland. London; New York: Penguin, 1995), p. xxxii. Future references to the novel are to this edition and appear parenthetically in the text.

[42] Though Sutherland follows the original serialization plan for the novel as it appeared in *The Cornhill*, I have chosen here to refer to the Penguin edition's "Book the First" as the "Prologue," in keeping with the changes Collins made when he prepared the novel for book publication. Removed some twenty years from the action of the novel proper, the first section of the novel seems much more like a "Prologue" than a first book. Perhaps this is what Collins sensed as he went back over his manuscript in late spring, 1866. My references to the "Prologue," then, are to the Penguin edition's "Book the First," and my references to subsequent books are one behind those in the Penguin edition. That is, my "Book the First" is Penguin's "Book the Second," and so forth.

Also, to avoid confusion with the several Allan Armadales, I refer to the murderer by his birth name, Wrentmore, and to his son by the name he takes, Ozias Midwinter. Through the remaining discussion, I only refer to the Allan Armadale of the second generation as "Allan."

[43] Robert Ashley, *Wilkie Collins* (New York: Roy Publishers, 1952), p. 85.

[44] Jenny Bourne Taylor, *In the Secret Theatre of the Home: Wilkie Collins, Sensation Narrative, and Nineteenth-Century Psychology* (New York: Routledge, 1988), p. 163.

[45] Quoted in Catherine Peters, *The King of Inventors: A Life of Wilkie Collins* (Princeton: Princeton Univ. Press, 1991), pp. 272–273.

[46] Chorley's review appeared in the *Athenaeum* on June 2, 1866. Quoted in *Wilkie Collins: The Critical Heritage* (ed. Norman Page. London: Routledge and Kegan Paul, 1974), p. 147.

[47] Quoted in Page, p. 158; p. 156.

[48] Quoted in Page, pp. 149–150.

[49] Quoted in Page, p. 149; Eliot, pp. 413–414.

[50] As Sutherland notes in his introduction to *Armadale*, it is no accident that the books in Midwinter's possession when he first appears are the plays of Sophocles and Goethe's *Faust*. Throughout the novel Midwinter stands counterpoised between a fear of Oedipal doom and the possibility of free will. See *Armadale*, p. xxiv.

[51] John Sutherland, "Wilkie Collins and the Origins of the Sensation Novel," *Wilkie Collins to the Forefront: Some Reassessments* (eds. Nelson Smith and R. C. Terry. New York: AMS, 1995), p. 80.

[52] Peters, p. 275.

[53] Sutherland, "Wilkie Collins," p. 76. The Act made divorce easier to obtain if the filing spouse—the complainant—could offer proof of spousal misconduct, especially proof of adultery.

[54] Sutherland, "Wilkie Collins," p. 75.

[55] Lisa M. Zeitz and Peter Thoms, "Collins's Use of the Strasbourg Clock in *Armadale*," *Nineteenth-Century Literature* 45 (1991), p. 501.

[56] Much like Charlotte Brontë, Collins suffered through periods of severe depression and a mysterious affliction he called "rheumatic gout." Always drawn to fashionable psychological theories, he also became a friend and patient of John Elliotson, the pioneer of medical hypnosis—a relationship that resonates in the resolution of *The Moonstone*. For discussions of Collins's well-documented nervous complaints and subsequent addiction to the opium he took as a palliative, see Peters, pp. 249–257 and 312–337; and William M. Clarke, *The Secret Life of Wilkie Collins* (London: W. H. Allen and Co., 1989), p. 103 and pp. 163–166.

[57] See Sutherland's "Introduction" to *Armadale*, p. xvi; and Richard Altick, *The Presence of the Present: Topics of the Day in the Victorian Novel* (Columbus: Ohio State Univ. Press, 1991), pp. 525–526.

[58] For a complete account of Madeleine Smith's case (and several other fascinating murders), see Mary S. Hartman, *Victorian Murderesses: A True History of Thirteen Respectable French and English Women Accused of Unspeakable Crimes* (New York: Schocken Books, 1977), pp. 51–84.

[59] Hartman, p. 84.

[60] Robinson, p. 191; Ashley, p. 85.

[61] Zeitz, p. 498.

[62] Taylor, p. 159.

[63] Jonathan Craig Tutor, "Lydia Gwilt: Wilkie Collins's Satanic, Sirenic Psychotic," *University of Mississippi Studies in English* 10 (1992), p. 38.

[64] See Winifred Hughes, *The Maniac in the Cellar: Sensation Novels of the 1860s* (Princeton: Princeton Univ. Press, 1980).

NOTES TO THE CONCLUSION

[1] I have in mind Brooks's *Reading for the Plot* and Ronald R. Thomas's *Dreams of Authority: Freud and the Fictions of the Unconscious* (Ithaca; London: Cornell Univ. Press, 1990).

[2] Brooks, p. 270.

[3] Steven Marcus, "Freud and Dora: Story, History, Case History," *In Dora's Case: Freud—Hysteria—Feminism* (eds. Charles Bernheimer and Claire Kahane. New York: Columbia Univ. Press, 1985), p. 71.

[4] Toril Moi, "Representations of Patriarchy: Sexuality and Epistemology in Freud's Dora," *In Dora's Case: Freud—Hysteria—Feminism* (eds. Charles

Bernheimer and Claire Kahane. New York: Columbia Univ. Press, 1985), p. 185; p. 185; p. 194.

[5] Sigmund Freud, *The Interpretation of Dreams* (trans. James Strachey. New York: Avon, 1965), p. 552.

[6] Sigmund Freud, *Dora: An Analysis of a Case of Hysteria* (ed. Philip Rieff. New York: Macmillan, 1963), p. 69.

[7] Marcus, "Freud and Dora," p. 81.

[8] Jacques Lacan, *The Four Fundamental Concepts of Psychoanalysis* (trans. Alan Sheridan. ed. Jacques-Alain Miller. New York: W. W. Norton, 1977), p. 25.

[9] Marcus, "Freud and Dora," p. 85.

[10] Jacques Lacan, "The Function and Field of Speech and Language in Psychoanalysis," *Écrits: A Selection* (trans. Alan Sheridan. New York: W. W. Norton, 1977), p. 99.

[11] Ned Lukacher, *Primal Scenes: Literature, Philosophy, Psychoanalysis* (Ithaca; London: Cornell Univ. Press, 1986), p. 21.

[12] Sigmund Freud, "From the History of an Infantile Neurosis," *Three Case Histories* (ed. Philip Rieff. New York: Macmillan, 1963), p. 209.

[13] Moi, p. 197.

[14] Angus Wilson, "Introduction," *The Mystery of Edwin Drood* (ed. Arthur J. Cox. London; New York: Penguin, 1974), p. 11.

[15] Richard M. Baker (*The Drood Murder Case: Five Studies in Dickens's* Edwin Drood [Berkeley; Los Angeles: Univ. of California Press, 1951]) argues that Edwin has been strangled, as does Ray Dubberke (*Dickens, Drood, and the Detectives* [New York: Vantage, 1992]). Charles Forsyte, in *The Decoding of Edwin Drood* (New York: Charles Scribner's Sons, 1980) suggests rather, in a conclusion he has written himself, that Edwin has been pushed or thrown from the top of the tower—a dramatic and unlikely possibility, it seems to me.

[16] See for instance Richard A. Proctor, *Watched by the Dead: A Loving Study of Dickens' Half-Told Tale* (London: W. H. Allen, 1887); and Andrew Lang, *The Puzzle of Dickens's Last Plot* (London: Chapman and Hall, 1905).

[17] Angus Wilson, p. 13.

[18] Angus Wilson, p. 13.

[19] Forsyte's book appeared in 1980 and Dubberke's appeared in 1992. The Italian novel, written by Carlo Fruttero and Franco Lucentini, is called *The D. Case: The Truth about* The Mystery of Edwin Drood (trans. Gregory Dowling. New York: Harcourt Brace Jovanovich, 1989) and is described briefly by Gerhard Joseph in, "Who Cares Who Killed Edwin Drood? Or, On the Whole, I'd Rather Be in Philadelphia," *Nineteenth-Century Literature* 51 (1996): 161–175. Recent articles have continued to offer solutions to the mystery. See for instance Doris Alexander, "Solving the Mysteries of the Mind in *Edwin Drood*," *Dickens Quarterly* 3 (1992): 125–131; and Elsie Karbacz and Robert Raven, "The Many Mysteries of *Edwin Drood*," *Dickensian* 90 (1994): 5–18. The last study provides the most innovative consideration of *Drood* to appear in many years.

[20] Fildes took over as illustrator when it became clear that Dickens's original choice, Wilkie Collins's son Charles, was too ill to undertake the task. Fildes

reported his special information regarding Edwin's fate in a letter that appeared in the *Times Literary Supplement* on November 3, 1905, but the fact that he suppressed this detail for more than thirty years makes his testimony somewhat suspect. The letter is quoted in *The Mystery of Edwin Drood* (ed. Margaret Cardwell. Oxford: Clarendon, 1972), p. xxvi. Future references to the novel are to this edition and appear parenthetically in the text.

[21] Collins, *Dickens and Crime*, p. 296.

[22] Charles Dickens, "Postscript," *Our Mutual Friend* (London: The Folio Society, 1982), p. 779.

[23] Though there is no space to develop the idea here, *Drood* seems drawn heavily—in Neville's resemblance to Midwinter, Jasper's opium addiction, and the importance of crime and confession—from *Armadale*, and perhaps from *The Moonstone* as well. Having watched Collins's rapid rise to literary prominence, Dickens may have written *Drood* so that he could "out-Collins" Collins with a stunning crime novel of his own.

[24] Thomas, p. 221.

[25] Forster, v. 2, p. 891.

[26] Dickens, quoted in Forster, v. 2, p. 891.

[27] As Forster reported in his biography, and as later writers of Dickens's life have repeated, "the *Sikes and Nancy* scene, everywhere his prominent subject, exacted the most terrible physical exertion from him." In fact, Dickens's doctor Carr Beard and several close acquaintances discouraged the continued performance of the scene, but to no avail. Almost until he was forced to halt the reading tour, Dickens continued to perform the scene, despite the discomfort that it caused him. See Forster, v. 2, p. 883.

[28] Thomas, p. 222.

[29] Thomas, p. 220.

[30] Perhaps the most thorough analysis of Jasper's self-division was supplied more than three decades ago by Charles Mitchell, "*The Mystery of Edwin Drood*: The Interior and Exterior of the Self," *ELH* 33 (1966): 228–246. I agree, however, with Ronald Thomas, who argues that viewing Jasper as a man divided neatly between interior and exterior does not account for the collapse of his unconscious into his conscious self.

[31] As Neville tells Crisparkle, Helena even "dressed as a boy, and showed the daring of a man" when the two ran away as children (*ED* 49). Several critics have argued that this experience with cross-dressing may be important for Helena later in the novel if she is to play a part in Jasper's unmasking.

[32] Forster, v. 2, p. 891.

[33] Thomas, p. 224.

[34] Steven Connor, "Dead? Or Alive? *Edwin Drood* and the Work of Mourning," *Dickensian* 89 (1993), p. 99.

[35] Alexander, p. 125.

[36] George Wing, "*Edwin Drood* and *Desperate Remedies*: Prototypes of Detective Fiction in 1870," *Studies in English Literature* 13 (1973), p. 685.

[37] Samuel Butler, *The Way of All Flesh* (New York: Modern Library, 1998), p. 324.

[38] Butler, p. 303.

[39] Joseph Conrad, *The Secret Agent* (ed. Roger Tennant. Oxford: Oxford Univ. Press, 1983), p. 110; p. 106.

[40] Conrad, p. 120.

[41] Conrad, p. 120; p. 77.

[42] Michel Foucault, "Enfermemente, Psychiatrie, Prison: Dialogue avec Michel Foucault et David Cooper," *Change* 32/33 (1977), p. 78. The translation of this passage is my own, taken from the original quotation: ". . . la société recontre partout une masse de problèmes . . . et nous autres, psychiatres, nous sommes *les* fonctionnaires de l'ordre social. C'est à nous à réparer ces désordres. Nous sommes une fonction d'hygiène publique. C'est la vraie vocation de la psychiatrie. Et c'est son climat, et c'est son horizon de naissance."

Works Cited

Ackroyd, Peter. *Dickens*. New York: Harper Collins, 1990.

Alexander, Doris. "Solving the Mysteries of the Mind in *Edwin Drood*." *Dickens Quarterly* 3 (1992): 125–131.

Allday, Joseph, ed. *"Truth is Stranger than Fiction": True Account of the Proceedings Leading to, and a Full and Authentic Report of, the Searching Inquiry, by Her Majesty's Commissioners, into the Horrible System of Discipline Practised at the Borough Gaol of Birmingham*. Birmingham: J. Tonks, 1853.

Allen, Michael. *Charles Dickens' Childhood*. Basingstoke; Hampshire: Macmillan, 1988.

Altick, Richard. *The Presence of the Present: Topics of the Day in the Victorian Novel*. Columbus: Ohio State Univ. Press, 1991.

Andrews, William. *To Tell a Free Story: The First Century of Afro-American Autobiography, 1750–1865*. Urbana; Chicago: Univ. of Illinois Press, 1986.

Ashley, Robert. *Wilkie Collins*. New York: Roy Publishers, 1952.

Auden, W. H. "In Memory of W. B. Yeats." *The English Auden: Poems, Essays and Dramatic Writings 1927–1939*. Ed. Edward Mendelson. London; Boston: Faber and Faber, 1977. 241–243.

Bailey, Victor, ed. *Policing and Punishment in Nineteenth-Century Britain*. London: Croom Helm, 1981.

Baker, A. W. *Death is a Good Solution: The Convict Experience in Early Australia*. St. Lucia: Univ. of Queensland Press, 1984.

Baker, Richard M. *The Drood Murder Case: Five Studies in Dickens's Edwin Drood*. Berkeley; Los Angeles: University of California Press, 1951.

Barker, Juliet. *The Brontës*. New York: St. Martin's, 1994.

Barry, John Vincent. *Alexander Maconochie of Norfolk Island, a Study of a Pioneer in Penal Reform*. London; New York: Oxford Univ. Press, 1958.

————. *The Life and Death of John Price, a Study of the Exercise of Naked Power.* Melbourne; Cambridge; New York: Cambridge Univ. Press, 1964.

Baumgarten, Murray. "Writing the Revolution." *Dickens Studies Annual* 12 (1983): 161–176.

Beattie, J. M. *Crime and the Courts in England 1660–1800.* Princeton: Princeton Univ. Press, 1986.

Bender, John. *Imagining the Penitentiary.* Chicago; London: Univ. of Chicago Press, 1987.

Bentham, Jeremy. *The Correspondence of Jeremy Bentham.* Ed. Ian R. Christie. 11 vols. London: Athlone Press, 1971.

————. *Panopticon, or the Inspection-house: Postscript; Containing Further Particulars and Alterations Relative to the Plan of Construction Originally Proposed; Principally Adapted to the Purpose of a Panopticon Penitentiary House.* Dublin: Thomas Byrne, 1791.

Boehm, Harold J. "*His Natural Life* and Its Sources." *Australian Literary Studies* 5 (1971): 42–64.

Briganti, Chiara. "Charlotte Brontë's *Villette*: The History of Desire." *West Virginia University Philological Papers* 35 (1989): 8–20.

Brontë, Charlotte. *Villette.* Eds. Herbert Rosengarten and Margaret Smith. Oxford: Clarendon, 1984.

————. *The Letters of Charlotte Brontë.* 2 Vols. Ed. Margaret Smith. Oxford: Clarendon, 1995–.

Brooks, Peter. *Reading for the Plot.* Cambridge; London: Harvard Univ. Press, 1984.

Brown, Roger Lee. *A History of the Fleet Prison, London: The Anatomy of the Fleet.* Lewiston: Edwin Mellen, 1996.

Burns, Wayne. *Charles Reade, a Study in Victorian Authorship.* New York: Bookman, 1961.

————. "More Reade Notebooks." *Studies in Philology* 42 (1945): 824–842.

Burrows, J. F. "*His Natural Life* and the Capacities of Melodrama." *Southerly* 34 (1974): 280–301.

Butler, Samuel. *The Way of All Flesh.* New York: Modern Library, 1998.

Carlisle, Janice. "The Face in the Mirror: *Villette* and the Conventions of Autobiography." *The Brontës: Modern Critical Views.* Ed. Harold Bloom. New York: Chelsea House, 1987. 131–153.

————. "*Little Dorrit*: Necessary Fictions." *Studies in the Novel* 7 (1975): 195–214.

Carpenter, Mary. *Our Convicts.* 2 Vols. Montclair: Patterson Smith, 1969.

————. *Reformatory Prison Discipline, as Developed by the Right Honorable Sir Walter Crofton in the Irish Convict Prisons.* London: Longman, Green, Reader, and Dyer, 1872.

Chase, Karen. *Eros and Psyche: The Representation of Personality in Charlotte Brontë, Charles Dickens, and George Eliot.* London; New York: Methuen, 1984.

Chittick, Kathryn. *Dickens and the 1830s.* Cambridge: Cambridge Univ. Press, 1990.

Clarke, Marcus. *For the Term of His Natural Life.* Victoria: Lloyd O' Neil, 1970.

———. *His Natural Life.* Ed. Stephen Murray-Smith. London; New York; Victoria: Penguin, 1970.

———. *Marcus Clarke:* For the Term of His Natural Life, *Short Stories, Critical Essays and Journalism.* Ed. Michael Wilding. St. Lucia; London; New York: Univ. of Queensland Press, 1976.

———. *Old Tales of a Young Country.* Sydney: Sydney Univ. Press, 1972.

Clarke, William M. *The Secret Life of Wilkie Collins.* London: W.H. Allen and Co., 1989.

Clay, Walter Lowe. *The Prison Chaplain: A Memoir of the Reverend John Clay, B.D., Late Chaplain of the Preston Gaol.* Montclair: Patterson Smith, 1969.

Collins, Philip. *Dickens and Crime.* 3rd ed. New York: St. Martin's, 1994.

———. "*Little Dorrit*: The Prison and the Critics." *London Times Literary Supplement* (April 18, 1980): 445–446.

———. "A Tale of Two Novels: *A Tale of Two Cities* and *Great Expectations* in Dickens' Career." *Dickens Studies Annual* 2 (1972): 336–351.

Collins, Wilkie. *Armadale.* Ed. John Sutherland. London; New York: Penguin, 1995.

Connor, Steven. "Dead? Or Alive? *Edwin Drood* and the Work of Mourning." *Dickensian* 89 (1993): 85–102.

Conrad. Joseph. *The Secret Agent.* Ed. Roger Tennant. Oxford: Oxford Univ. Press, 1983.

Crofton, Walter. "Can Intermediate Prisons Materially Aid in Solving the Difficulties of the Convict Question?" *Transactions of the National Association for the Promotion of Social Science.* Ed. G. W. Hastings. London: John W. Parker and Son, 1859. 376–383.

Crosby, Christina. *The Ends of History: Victorians and "The Woman Question".* New York; London: Routledge, 1991.

Daleski, H.M. "Large Loose Baggy Monsters and *Little Dorrit*." *Dickens Studies Annual* 21 (1992): 131–142.

Dames, Nicholas. "The Clinical Novel: Phrenology and *Villette*." *Novel: A Forum on Fiction* 29 (1996): 367–390.

Darwin, Charles. *The Autobiography of Charles Darwin 1809–1882.* Ed. Nora Barlow. New York; London: W. W. Norton, 1958.

Davis, Nuel Pharr. *The Life of Wilkie Collins.* Urbana: Univ. of Illinois Press, 1956.

Defoe, Daniel. *Moll Flanders.* Ed. James Sutherland. Boston: Houghton Mifflin, 1959.

Denholm, Decie. "The Sources of *His Natural Life*." *Australian Literary Studies* 4 (1969): 174–178.

De Puy, Harry. "American Prisons and *A Tale of Two Cities.*" *Cahiers Victoriens et Édouardiens: Revue du Centre d'Etudes et de Recherches Victoriennes et Édouardiennes de l'Université Paul Valéry.* (April 1987): 39–48.

Dickens, Charles. *American Notes and Pictures from Italy*. Oxford: Oxford Univ. Press, 1957.

———. *Charles Dickens' Uncollected Writings from* Household Words, *1850–1859*. 2 Vols. Ed. Harry Stone. Bloomington; London: Indiana Univ. Press, 1968.

———. *Collected Papers*. 2 Vols. Eds. Arthur Waugh, Hugh Walpole, Walter Dexter, and Thomas Hatton. Bloomsbury: Nonesuch, 1937.

———. *David Copperfield*. Ed. Nina Burgis. Oxford: Clarendon, 1981.

———. *Dombey and Son*. Ed. Alan Horsman. Oxford: Clarendon, 1974.

———. *The Letters of Charles Dickens*. 12 Vols. Eds. Madeline House, Graham Storey, and Kathleen Tillotson. Oxford: Clarendon, 1974–2002.

———. *The Letters of Charles Dickens*. 3 Vols. Ed. Walter Dexter. Bloomsbury: Nonesuch, 1938.

———. *Little Dorrit*. Ed. Harvey Peter Sucksmith. Oxford: Clarendon, 1979.

———. *Miscellaneous Papers*. London: Chapman and Hall; New York: Charles Scribner's Sons, 1914.

———. *The Mystery of Sir Edwin Drood*. Ed. Margaret Cardwell. Oxford: Clarendon, 1972.

———. *Our Mutual Friend*. London: The Folio Society, 1982.

———. *Pickwick Papers*. Ed. James Kinsley. Oxford: Clarendon, 1986.

———. *Sketches by Boz*. London: Oxford Univ. Press, 1957.

———. *A Tale of Two Cities*. Ed. Andrew Sanders. Oxford: Oxford Univ. Press, 1988.

———. *The Uncommercial Traveller and Reprinted Pieces, Etc.* London: Oxford Univ. Press, 1958.

Dostoyevsky, Fyodor. *Crime and Punishment*. Ed. George Gibian. New York; London: W. W. Norton, 1964.

Dubberke, Ray. *Dickens, Drood, and the Detectives*. New York: Vantage, 1992.

Easson, Angus. "Imprisonment for Debt in *Pickwick Papers*." *Dickensian* 64 (1968): 105–112.

Edwards, P. D. "Charles Reade, Wilkie Collins, and Marcus Clarke." *Australian Literary Studies* 11 (1984): 400–404.

Eliot, T. S. "Wilkie Collins and Dickens." *Selected Essays*. New York: Harcourt Brace, 1950. 409–418.

Elliot, Brian. *Marcus Clarke*. Oxford: Clarendon, 1958.

Engel, Eliot. "The Maturing of a Comic Artist: Dickens' Leap from *Sketches by Boz* to *Pickwick Papers*." *Victorians Institute Journal* 9 (1980): 39–47.

Field, John. *Prison Discipline: And the Advantages of the Separate System of Imprisonment, with a Detailed Account of the Discipline Now Pursued in the New County Gaol at Reading*. 2 Vols. London: Longman, Brown, Green, and Longmans, 1848.

Fletcher, LuAnn McCracken. "Manufactured Marvels, Heretic Narratives, and the Process of Interpretation in *Villette*." *Studies in English Literature* 32 (1992): 723–746.

Forster, E. M. *Aspects of the Novel*. New York; London: Harcourt, Inc., 1927.

Forster, John. *The Life of Charles Dickens*. 2 Vols. London: Chapman and Hall; New York: Oxford Univ. Press, n.d.

Forsyte, Charles. *The Decoding of Edwin Drood*. New York: Charles Scribner's Sons, 1980.

Forsythe, William. *The Reform of Prisoners, 1830–1900*. London: Croom Helm, 1987.

Foucault, Michel. *Discipline and Punish, the Birth of the Prison*. Trans. Alan Sheridan. New York: Pantheon, 1977.

———. "Enfermement, Psychiatrie, Prison: Dialogue avec Michel Foucault et David Cooper." *Change* 32/33 (1977): 76–110.

Freeman, Janet. "Looking on at Life: Objectivity and Intimacy in *Villette*." *Philological Quarterly* 67 (1988): 481–511.

Freud, Sigmund. *Dora: An Analysis of a Case of Hysteria*. Ed. Philip Rieff. New York: Macmillan, 1963.

———. *The Interpretation of Dreams*. Trans. James Strachey. New York: Avon, 1965.

———. *Three Case Histories*. Ed. Philip Rieff. New York: Macmillan, 1963.

Fruttero, Carlo, and Franco Lucentini. *The D. Case: The Truth About The Mystery of Edwin Drood*. Trans. Gregory Dowling. New York: Harcourt Brace Jovanovich, 1989.

Gallagher, Catherine. "The Duplicity of Doubling in *A Tale of Two Cities*." *Dickens Studies Annual* 12 (1983): 125–145.

Gaskell, Elizabeth. *The Life of Charlotte Brontë*. Ed. Alan Shelston. London; New York: Penguin, 1975.

Gérin, Winifred. *Charlotte Brontë, the Evolution of Genius*. Oxford: Clarendon, 1967.

Gilbert, Sandra, and Susan Gubar. *The Madwoman in the Attic: The Woman Writer and the Nineteenth-Century Literary Imagination*. New Haven; London: Yale Univ. Press, 1979.

Godwin, William. *Enquiry Concerning Political Justice*. Ed. Isaac Kramnick. London; New York: Penguin, 1976.

Goldberg, Michael. *Carlyle and Dickens*. Athens: Univ. of Georgia Press, 1972.

Hartman, Mary S. *Victorian Murderesses: A True History of Thirteen Respectable French and English Women Accused of Unspeakable Crimes*. New York: Schocken Books, 1977.

Heatley, Edward. "The Redeemed Feminine of *Little Dorrit*," *Dickens Studies Annual* 4 (1975): 153–164.

Henriques, U. "The Rise and Decline of the Separate System of Prison Discipline." *Past and Present* 54 (1972): 61–93.

Hergenhan, L. T., ed. *A Colonial City, High and Low Life, Selected Journalism of Marcus Clarke*. St. Lucia: Univ. of Queensland Press, 1972.

———. "The Contemporary Reception of *His Natural Life*." *Southerly* 31 (1971): 50–63.

———. "The Corruption of Rufus Dawes." *Southerly* 29 (1969): 211–221.

———. *Unnatural Lives: Studies in Australian Fiction about the Convicts, from James Tucker to Patrick White.* St. Lucia; London; New York: Univ. of Queensland Press, 1983.

Herring, Paul D. "Dickens' Monthly Number Plans for *Little Dorrit.*" *Modern Philology* 64 (1966): 22–63.

Hill, Frederic. *Crime: Its Amount, Causes and Remedies.* London: Murray, 1853.

Hill, Matthew Davenport. *A Charge Delivered to the Grand Jury of the Borough of Birmingham, Michaelmas Quarter Sessions for 1848.* London: Charles Knight, 1848.

———. *Suggestions for the Repression of Crime, Contained in Charges Delivered to the Grand Juries of Birmingham.* London: John W. Parker and Son, 1857.

Hill, Rosamond Davenport, and Florence Davenport Hill. *The Recorder of Birmingham: A Memoir of Matthew Davenport Hill, with Selections from His Correspondence.* London: Macmillan and Co., 1878.

Hughes, Robert. *The Fatal Shore.* New York: Alfred A. Knopf, 1987.

Hughes, Winifred. *The Maniac in the Cellar: Sensation Novels of the 1860s.* Princeton: Princeton Univ. Press, 1980.

Ignatieff, Michael. *A Just Measure of Pain: The Penitentiary in the Industrial Revolution, 1750–1850.* New York: Pantheon, 1978.

Jackson, T. A. *Charles Dickens: The Progress of a Radical.* London: Lawrence and Wishart, 1937.

Jacobus, Mary. "The Buried Letter: Feminism and Romanticism in *Villette.*" *Women Writing and Writing About Women.* Ed. Mary Jacobus. New York: Barnes and Noble; London: Croom Helm, 1979. 42–60.

Jaffe, Audrey. *Vanishing Points: Dickens, Narrative, and the Subject of Omniscience.* Berkeley; Los Angeles: Univ. of California Press, 1991.

James, Henry. *The Art of the Novel.* New York; London: Charles Scribner's Sons, 1934.

Johnson, Edgar. *Charles Dickens: His Tragedy and Triumph.* 2 Vols. New York: Simon and Schuster, 1952.

Johnson, Patricia E. "'This Heretic Narrative': The Strategy of the Split Narrative in Charlotte Brontë's *Villette.*" *Studies in English Literature* 30 (1990): 617–631.

Joseph, Gerhard. "Who Cares Who Killed Edwin Drood? Or, On the Whole, I'd Rather Be in Philadelphia." *Nineteenth-Century Literature* 51 (1996): 161–175.

Joseph, H. S. *Memoirs of Convicted Prisoners: Accompanied by Remarks on the Causes and Prevention of Crime.* London: Wertheim and Co., 1853.

Karbacz, Elsie, and Robert Raven. "The Many Mysteries of *Edwin Drood.*" *Dickensian* 90 (1994): 5–18.

Kemper, Beth. "The 'Night Shadows' Passage in *A Tale of Two Cities*: Narrative Anxiety and Conscious Fiction-Building." *Kentucky Philological Review* 10 (1995): 22–26.

Knezevic, Borislav. "The Impossible Things: Quest for Knowledge in Charlotte Brontë's *Villette.*" *Literature and Psychology* 42 (1996): 65–99.

Lacan, Jacques. *Écrits: A Selection.* Trans. Alan Sheridan. New York: W. W. Norton, 1977.

———. *The Four Fundamental Concepts of Psychoanalysis.* Trans. Alan Sheridan. Ed. Jacques-Alain Miller. New York: W. W. Norton, 1977.

Lang, Andrew. *The Puzzle of Dickens's Last Plot.* London: Chapman and Hall, 1905.

Lawson, Kate. "Reading Desire: *Villette* as 'Heretic Narrative'." *English Studies in Canada* 17 (1991): 53–71.

Lord, Walter Frewan. *The Mirror of the Century.* London: John Lane, 1906.

Lukacher, Ned. *Primal Scenes: Literature, Philosophy, Psychoanalysis.* Ithaca; London: Cornell Univ. Press, 1986.

MacKay, Carol Hanbery. "The Rhetoric of Soliloquy in *The French Revolution* and *A Tale of Two Cities.*" *Dickens Studies Annual* 12 (1983): 197–207.

Magnet, Myron. *Dickens and the Social Order.* Philadelphia: Univ. of Pennsylvania Press, 1985.

Mannheim, Hermann. *Pioneers in Criminology.* 2nd ed. Montclair: Patterson Smith, 1972.

Manning, Sylvia. "Social Criticism and Textual Subversion in *Little Dorrit.*" *Dickens Studies Annual* 20 (1991): 127–147.

Marcus, Steven. *Dickens, from Pickwick to Dombey.* New York: Basic Books, 1965.

———. "Dickens and the Representation of Punishment." *Perspectives on Punishment, an Interdisciplinary Exploration.* Ed. Richard Mowery Andrews. New York: Peter Lang, 1997. 87–111.

———. "Freud and Dora: Story, History, Case History." *In Dora's Case: Freud—Hysteria—Feminism.* Eds. Charles Bernheimer and Claire Kahane. New York: Columbia Univ. Press, 1985. 56–91.

———. "Language Into Structure: Pickwick Revisited." *Daedalus* 101.1 (1972): 183–202.

Martin, Arthur Patchett. *The Beginnings of an Australian Literature.* London: Henry Sotheran and Co., 1898.

Marzials, Frank T. *Life of Charles Dickens.* London: Walter Scott; New York: Charles Scribner's Sons, 1887.

Matus, Jill L. "Looking at Cleopatra: The Expression and Exhibition of Desire in *Villette.*" *Victorian Literature and Culture.* Eds. John Maynard and Adrienne Auslander Munich. New York: AMS, 1993. 345–367.

Mayhew, Henry, and John Binny. *The Criminal Prisons of London, and Scenes from Prison Life.* London: Frank Cass and Co., 1968.

McCarthy, Patrick J. "Claiming Truth: Dickens and *American Notes.*" *Nineteenth-Century Prose* 23.2 (1996): 1–11.

McConville, Seán. *A History of English Prison Administration.* London; Boston: Routledge and Kegan Paul, 1981.

McKnight, Natalie. *Idiots, Madmen, and Other Prisoners in Dickens.* New York: St. Martin's, 1993.

Meckier, Jerome. "Dickens Discovers America, Dickens Discovers Dickens: The First Visit Reconsidered." *The Modern Language Review* 79 (1984): 266–277.

———. *Innocent Abroad, Charles Dickens's American Engagements.* Lexington: Univ. Press of Kentucky, 1990.

Mill, John Stuart. *Autobiography.* Ed. Jack Stillinger. Boston: Houghton Mifflin, 1969.

Miller, D. A. *The Novel and the Police.* Berkeley; Los Angeles; London: Univ. of California Press, 1988.

Miller, J. Hillis. *Charles Dickens: The World of His Novels.* Cambridge: Harvard Univ. Press, 1958.

Millett, Kate. *Sexual Politics.* Garden City: Doubleday, 1969.

Milley, H. J. W. "Wilkie Collins and *A Tale of Two Cities.*" *Modern Language Review* 34 (1939): 525–534.

Mitchell, Charles. "*The Mystery of Edwin Drood*: The Interior and Exterior of Self." *ELH* 33 (1966): 228–246.

Moglen, Helene. *Charlotte Brontë, the Self Conceived.* New York: W. W. Norton, 1976.

Moi, Toril. "Representations of Patriarchy: Sexuality and Epistemology in Freud's Dora." *In Dora's Case: Freud—Hysteria—Feminism.* Eds. Charles Bernheimer and Claire Kahane. New York: Columbia Univ. Press, 1985. 181–199.

Morris, Terence, and Pauline Morris. *Pentonville: A Sociological Study of an English Prison.* London: Routledge and Kegan Paul, 1963.

Moss, Sidney P. *Charles Dickens' Quarrel with America.* Troy: Whitston, 1984.

Newman, John Henry. *Apologia Pro Vita Sua.* Ed. Ian Ker. London; New York: Penguin, 1994.

Orwell, George. "Charles Reade." *The Collected Essays, Journalism and Letters of George Orwell.* 4 Vols. Eds. Sonia Orwell and Ian Angus. New York: Harcourt, Brace, and World, 1968. 34–37.

Page, Norman, ed. *Wilkie Collins: The Critical Heritage.* London: Routledge and Kegan Paul, 1974.

Parker, David. "Dickens and America: The Unflattering Glass." *Dickens Studies Annual* 15 (1986): 55–63.

Patten, Robert L. "'I Thought of Mr. Pickwick, and Wrote the First Number': Dickens and the Evolution of Character." *Dickens Quarterly* 3 (1986): 18–25.

Peters, Catherine. *The King of Inventors: A Life of Wilkie Collins.* Princeton: Princeton Univ. Press, 1991.

Philips, David. *Crime and Authority in Victorian England: The Black Country, 1835–1860.* London: Croom Helm, 1977.

Phillips, Walter Clarke. *Dickens, Reade and Collins: Sensation Novelists.* New York: Columbia Univ. Press, 1919.

Philpotts, Trey. "The Real Marshalsea." *Dickensian* 87 (1991): 133–145.

Playfair, Giles William. *The Punitive Obsession: An Unvarnished History of the English Prison System.* London: Gollancz, 1971.

Proctor, Richard A. *Watched by the Dead: A Loving Study of Dickens' Half-Told Tale.* London: W. H. Allen, 1887.

Rabinowitz, Nancy Sorkin. "'Faithful Narrator' or 'Partial Eulogist': First-person Narration in Brontë's *Villette.*" *Journal of Narrative Technique* 15 (1985): 244–255.

Ranken, W. Bayne. "The Origin and Progress of the Discharged Prisoners' Aid Society." *Transactions of the National Association for the Promotion of Social Science.* Ed. G. W. Hastings. London: John W. Parker and Son, 1859. 368–371.

Reade, Charles. *The Autobiography of a Thief, and Other Stories.* London: Chatto and Windus, 1924.

———. *Hard Cash.* London: Chatto and Windus, 1927.

———. *It Is Never Too Late to Mend.* London: Chatto and Windus, 1925.

———. *Put Yourself in His Place.* London: Chatto and Windus, 1929.

———. *Readiana, Comments on Current Events.* London: Chatto and Windus, 1883.

Reade, Charles L., and the Reverend Compton Reade. *Charles Reade, D. C. L., Dramatist, Novelist, Journalist: A Memoir Compiled Chiefly from His Literary Remains.* New York: Harper, 1887.

Robinson, Kenneth. *Wilkie Collins, a Biography.* New York: Macmillan, 1952.

Robson, L. L. "The Historical Basis of *For the Term of His Natural Life.*" *Australian Literary Studies* 1 (1963): 104–121.

Rock, Paul. *Making People Pay.* London; Boston: Routledge and Kegan Paul, 1973.

Rosenberg, Brian. Little Dorrit*'s Shadows: Character and Contradiction in Dickens.* Columbia; London: Univ. of Missouri Press, 1996.

Rubin, Stan S. "Spectator and Spectacle: Narrative Evasion and Narrative Voice in *Pickwick Papers.*" *Journal of Narrative Technique* 6 (1976): 188–203.

Sadoff, Dianne F. "Storytelling and the Figure of the Father in *Little Dorrit.*" *Charles Dickens: New Perspectives.* Ed. Wendell Stacy Johnson. Englewood Cliffs: Prentice Hall, 1982. 121–141.

Sadrin, Anny. "Fragmentation in *The Pickwick Papers.*" *Dickens Studies Annual* 22 (1993): 21– 34.

Seltzer, Mark. *Henry James and the Art of Power.* Ithaca; London: Cornell Univ. Press, 1984.

Sharpe, William. "A Pig Upon the Town: Charles Dickens in New York." *Nineteenth-Century Prose* 23.2 (1996): 12–24.

Shelston, Alan, ed. *Dickens:* Dombey and Son *and* Little Dorrit, *a Casebook.* London: Macmillan, 1985.

Shorter, Clement. *The Brontës, Life and Letters.* 2 Vols. London: Hodder and Stoughton, 1908.

Shuttleworth, Sally. "'The Surveillance of a Sleepless Eye': The Constitution of Neurosis in *Villette*." *One Culture: Essays in Science and Literature*. Ed. George Levine. Madison: Univ. of Wisconsin Press, 1987. 313–335.

Silby, John. *A Letter on the Superior Advantages of Separate Confinement Over the System of Prison Discipline, at Present Adopted in Gaols and Houses of Correction*. London: John Hatchard and Son, 1838.

Smith, Elton. *Charles Reade*. Boston: Twayne, 1976.

Smith, Sheila. "Propaganda and Hard Facts in Charles Reade's Didactic Novels." *Renaissance and Modern Studies* 4 (1960): 135–149.

Stephen, James Fitzjames. "The License of Modern Novelists." *Edinburgh Review* 106 (July 1857): 64–81.

Stewart, Garrett. *Dickens and the Trials of Imagination*. Cambridge: Harvard Univ. Press, 1974.

Sutcliffe, E. G. "Charles Reade's Notebooks." *Studies in Philology* 27 (1930): 64–109.

———. "Psychological Presentation in Reade's Novels." *Studies in Philology* 38 (1941): 521–542.

Sutherland, John. "Wilkie Collins and the Origins of the Sensation Novel." *Wilkie Collins to the Forefront: Some Reassessments*. Eds. Nelson Smith and R. C. Terry. New York: AMS, 1995. 75–90.

Tambling, Jeremy. *Dickens, Violence and the Modern State: Dreams of the Scaffold*. New York: St. Martin's, 1995.

Taylor, Jenny Bourne. *In the Secret Theatre of the Home: Wilkie Collins, Sensation Narrative, and Nineteenth-Century Psychology*. New York: Routledge, 1988.

Teeters, Negley K., and John D. Shearer. *The Prison at Philadelphia, Cherry Hill*. New York: Columbia Univ. Press, 1957.

Thomas, Ronald R. *Dreams of Authority: Freud and the Fictions of the Unconscious*. Ithaca; London: Cornell Univ. Press, 1990.

Timko, Michael. "Splendid Impressions and Picturesque Means: Dickens, Carlyle, and *The French Revolution*." *Dickens Studies Annual* 12 (1983): 177–195.

Tobias, J. J. *Crime and Industrial Society in the 19th Century*. New York: Schocken Books, 1967.

Trilling, Lionel. *The Opposing Self*. New York: Viking, 1955.

Trollope, Anthony. *An Autobiography*. Eds. Michael Sadleir and Frederick Page. Oxford: Oxford Univ. Press, 1950.

Turner, Henry Gyles, and Alexander Sutherland. *The Development of Australian Literature*. London; New York: Longmans, Green, and Co., 1898.

Tutor, Jonathan Craig. "Lydia Gwilt: Wilkie Collins's Satanic, Sirenic Psychotic." *University of Mississippi Studies in English* 10 (1992): 37–55.

Vanden Bossche, Chris R. "Prophetic Closure and Disclosing Narrative: *The French Revolution* and *A Tale of Two Cities*." *Dickens Studies Annual* 12 (1983): 209–221.

Vrettos, Athena. "From Neurosis to Narrative: The Private Life of the Nerves in *Villette* and *Daniel Deronda.*" *Victorian Studies* 33 (1990): 551–579.

Wall, William G. "Mrs. Affery Flintwinch's Dreams: Reading and Remembering in *Little Dorrit.*" *Dickens Quarterly* 4 (1993): 202–206.

Wilding, Michael. *Marcus Clarke.* Melbourne; London; New York: Oxford Univ. Press, 1977.

———. "Marcus Clarke: His Natural Life." *The Australian Experience.* Ed. W. S. Ramson. Canberra: Australian National Univ. Press, 1974: 19–37.

Wilson, Angus. "Introduction." *The Mystery of Edwin Drood.* By Charles Dickens. Ed. Arthur J. Cox. London; New York: Penguin, 1974.

Wilson, Anna. "On History, Case History, and Deviance: Miss Wade's Symptoms and Their Interpretation." *Dickens Studies Annual* 26 (1998): 187–201.

Wilson, Edmund. *The Wound and the Bow.* Boston: Houghton Mifflin, 1941.

Wing, George. "*Edwin Drood* and *Desperate Remedies*: Prototypes of Detective Fiction in 1870." *Studies in English Literature* 13 (1973): 677–687.

Winnifreth, Tom. *The Brontës.* New York: Macmillan, 1977.

Wise, Thomas James, M. A. Oxon, and John Alexander Symington, eds. *The Brontës: Their Lives, Friendships, and Correspondence.* 4 Vols. Oxford: Shakespeare Head, 1932.

Zeitz, Lisa M., and Peter Thoms. "Collins's Use of the Strasbourg Clock in *Armadale.*" *Nineteenth-Century Literature* 45 (1991): 495–503.

Index

Abbaye prison, the, 129
Ackroyd, Peter, 105
Adam Bede (Evans), 130
Ainsworth, William Harrison, 46, 50
Alexander, Doris, 235
Allday, Joseph, 89
All the Year Round. See Dickens, Charles: and *All the Year Round*
Altick, Richard, 205
Ambrose, Rev. Sherwin, 44, 89
America (United States): in *American Notes*, 30, 53–54, 65–78, 106, 134–135; Dickens's visit to, 51, 65–66, 70–71, 103; mentioned, 22, 29; prisons in, 30, 42, 66–78; slave autobiographies in, 34–35; transportation to, 4–5, 8, 19–21, 23
American Notes. See Dickens, Charles: Works
Andrews, Edward, 44–46, 82, 86, 89–90, 98
Apologia Pro Vita Sua (Newman), 175–177
Argus, 152, 156
Armadale. See Collins, Wilkie: Works
Art of the Novel, The (James), 103
Ashley, Robert, 198, 208
Aspects of the Novel (Forster), 49
Athenaeum, 108
Auden, W. H., 7–8
Austin, William, 44–45, 82, 86, 89–90, 101
Australasian, 152
Australia: assignment system in, 27–28, 36–37, 39–40, 161; Botany Bay, 23, 27; brutality in, 28, 36–37, 39–41, 152, 156–157; cannibalism at, 156; as carceral society, 8–9, 27, 36, 161; chosen for transportation, 23; con-

ditions investigated by Parliament, 39–40; convict discipline in, 27–29, 36–37, 39–41, 156–157; end of transportation to, 40–41; the First Fleet to, 23; gold rush in, 84–85, 152–153; in *His Natural Life*, 47, 151–174; homosexuality in, 40; in *It Is Never Too Late to Mend*, 92, 97; Launceston, 27; Macquarie Harbor, 28, 36, 40, 152, 155, 162, 166, 168; Melbourne, 152, 157, 166–167; Molesworth Report on, 39–40; Moreton Bay, 40; and narrative power, 8, 36–37, 161; New South Wales, 23, 27–28, 36, 40–41; Norfolk Island, 28, 36, 40, 44–47, 51, 152, 156–159, 166, 168–169; Parramatta, 27; and Pentonville, 33, 42–43; population figures of, 27, 161; Port Arthur, 28, 152, 156–158, 161, 164, 169; Sydney, 27, 39, 161, 163, 166; transportation to, 5–8, 23, 27–29, 38–41, 44–47, 151–152, 156–157, 161; Van Diemen's Land, 27–28, 36, 41, 152, 156–157, 161
Australian Journal, 152–153
autobiography: Dickens's attempt at, 52–53, 105, 127; in *His Natural Life*, 173–174; by inmates, 31–32, 34–36; in *It Is Never Too Late to Mend*, 83–87, 95–97, 101; in *The Secret Agent*, 237; and separate discipline, 8–9, 11, 31–32, 34–36, 83–86; by slaves, 34–35; Victorian, 175–177; in *Villette*, 180, 187, 193–196, 199, 206, 216.